The Mind and Heart
of the Negotiator

Leigh Thompson

J.L. Kellogg Graduate School of Management
Northwestern University

 Prentice Hall, Upper Saddle River, New Jersey 07458

Acquisitions Editor: Stephanie Johnson
Assistant Editor: Lisamarie Brassini
Editorial Assistant: Dawn Marie Reisner
Editor-in-Chief: Natalie Anderson
Production Editor: Cynthia Regan
Managing Editor: Dee Josephson
Manufacturing Buyer: Kenneth J. Clinton
Senior Designer: Ann France
Cover Design: Jill Little
Illustrator (Interior):   Rainbow Graphics, Inc.
Composition: Rainbow Graphics, Inc.
Cover Illustration: Robert Weeks

Copyright © 1998 by Prentice-Hall, Inc.
A Simon & Schuster Company
Upper Saddle River, New Jersey 07458

The research in this manuscript was supported by grants from the National Science Foundation (#SBR92-10298 and #PYI91-57447). This manuscript was written while the author was a fellow at the Center for Advanced Study in the Behavioral Sciences, with support from NSF grant #SBR90-22192.

Library of Congress Cataloging-in-Publication Data

Thompson, Leigh.
   The mind and heart of the negotiator / Leigh Thompson.
      p.   cm.
   Includes bibliographical references and index.
   ISBN 0-13-270950-3
   1. Negotiation in business.   I. Title.
   HD58.6.T478   1998   97-25122
   658.1′052—dc21   CIP

Prentice-Hall International (UK) Limited, London
Prentice-Hall of Australia Pty. Limited, Sydney
Prentice-Hall Canada, Inc., Toronto
Prentice-Hall Hispanoamericana, S.A., Mexico
Prentice-Hall of India Private Limited, New Delhi
Prentice-Hall of Japan, Inc., Tokyo
Simon & Schuster Asia Pte. Ltd., Singapore
Editora Prentice-Hall do Brasil, Ltda., Rio de Janeiro

Printed in the United States of America

10 9 8 7 6 5 4 3 2

To Bob, Sam, and Ray with eternal love

Brief Contents

Contents

Preface

Negotiation is a topic of great interest to executives, master of business students, undergraduates, lawyers, doctors, social workers, realtors, engineers, nurses, administrators, and people in the public sector. I have taught negotiations to all of these groups. One of the most frustrating experiences for a student of negotiation occurs when reading material is unconnected, redundant, and lacking integration. I wrote this book so that negotiators could have a "big picture" view of negotiation with readily accessible insights, strategies, and practices. Key concepts presented alongside deep "spikes" of theory, data, and concrete examples create a powerful learning experience. The book has three unique structural features:

- *Progressive complexity*: The introductory chapters are the most simple and provide the foundation upon which more complex ideas are built. Each chapter subsumes principles from the earlier chapters. Two chapters (5 and 6) are somewhat technical. I advise the graduate student to carefully read these "tooling up" chapters. In some undergraduate courses, chapters 5 and 6 might be used as appendices.

- *Internal depth*: Each chapter is constructed like a deep-sea dive—the reader is equipped with the proper analytical tools and encouraged to submerge deeply into the topic; at the end of the chapter, the reader resurfaces slowly, so as not to get the "bends," and key take-away points are summarized.

- *Interdisciplinary focus*: The ideas in the book represent a large body of descriptive and prescriptive research in the areas of social psychology, judgment and decision making, and group behavior. At a very broad level, this book represents a marriage of several disciplines: economics, psychology, sociology, communication, and organization behavior. No single discipline lays claim to negotiation; its richness lies in the fact that scholars from different disciplines have contributed to descriptive and prescriptive insights.

The book is organized into 14 chapters. The first chapter ("Negotiation: The Big Picture") lays out the framework for the book and introduces the basic building blocks for analyzing negotiations. Chapters 2 through 4 take the negotiator to the bargaining table. Chapter 2 ("Preparation: What to Do Before Negotiation") provides the key steps and strategies to take before commencing negotiations. The focus in this chapter is on claiming resources, dividing the pie, power analysis, and knowing when to walk away from the bargaining table. Chapter 3 ("The Conduct of Negotiation: What to Do at the Bargaining Table") walks the naïve negotiator and seasoned professional through the critical steps of the negotiation dance and also provides a "Dear Abby" checklist on the most common questions and tricky moves. The focus is on what information to assess, whether to make the first offer, and how to respond to common bargaining ploys and tactics. In Chapter 4 ("Integrative Negotiation: How to Be Strategically Creative"), we introduce the integrative bargaining model that underlies our main approach to all types of negotiation situations. Integrative bargaining is presented in an analytical fashion and supplemented with several examples.

Chapters 5 ("Rational Behavior: A Prescriptive Approach") and 6 ("Judgment and Decision Making: Deciding Among Sure Things and Risky Prospects") are the most technical in the book, and, as noted above, could be skipped without endangering learning, but are included for those who want a complete understanding of where joint gains come from and the anatomy of decision making. In chapter 5, we discuss principles of normative models as they apply to decision making. This chapter is important for clarifying how to make rational decisions. As we'll see, individual decision making is the basis for mutual decision making, or negotiation. In chapter 6, we explore how negotiators reason and make judgments in negotiation.

Chapters 7 ("Social Cognition: A Look into the Mind of the Negotiator") and 8 ("Biases and Illusions: Stumbling Blocks on the Road to Successful Negotiation") point to the most common, but deadly, mistakes in negotiation and how to correct them. In chapter 7, we examine how negotiators think about other people. Chapter 8 presents a compendium of the most common pitfalls that plague negotiators and concludes with a checklist of negotiation hazards.

Chapters 9 ("Groups and Teams: Multiple Parties at the Bargaining Table") and 10 ("Relationships and Emotion: Building Rapport") deal with the complexity of multiple partners, long-term relationships, positive and negative emotion, and how to build rapport in negotiations. The dynamics of negotiation change dramatically when another player joins the bargaining table and coalitions can form; in chapter 9, we enlarge the primary bargaining table to include three or more negotiating principals. In chapter 10, we explore relationships among negotiators and the role of emotion at the bargaining table.

Chapter 11 ("Social Justice, Fairness, and Social Utility: All's Fair") deals with the important concept of "fairness" but cautions that multiple ideas of fairness exist that may be incompatible with one another. In chapter 12 ("Social Dilemmas and Other Noncooperative Games: We're All in This Together") we approach negotiations as games of moves and discuss the issue of developing and maintaining trust. The classic prisoner's dilemma game is analyzed and its multiparty equivalent, the social dilemma, is treated as well, with applications to real-world industries.

In chapter 13 ("Experience, Expertise, and Learning: Best Practices for Peak Performance"), methods for learning and practicing negotiation skills are introduced. Finally, we come full circle in chapter 14 ("Environmental, Technological, and Cultural Clashes: When the Going Gets Tough") and wrestle with the challenges of negotiating natural resources, negotiating via information technology, and negotiating across cultural boundaries.

The writing of this book would not have been possible were it not for the opportunity to spend my sabbatical year at the Center for Advanced Study in the Behavioral Sciences. The inspirational support of Bob Scott and Neil Smelser, the wonderful mix of scholars from several different disciplines, and a grant to the center from the National Science Foundation made the writing of this book a joy. My research studies cited in the book were all supported by grants from the Decision, Risk, and Management program in the National Science Foundation.

Virtually all of the ideas in this book are a product of collaborations with my students, mentors, and colleagues over the past 10 years: Linda Babcock, Max Bazerman, Susan Brodt, Terri DeHarpport, Craig Fox, Bill Fulton, Dedre Gentner, Bob Gibbons, Kevin Gibson, Rich Gonzalez, Reid Hastie, Dennis Hrebec, Dacher Keltner, Peter Kim, Rod Kramer, Laura Kray, Terri Kurtzberg, John Levine, Allan Lind, George Loewenstein, Jeff Loewenstein, Beta Mannix, Terry Mitchell, Don Moore, Michael Morris, Keith Murnighan, Janice

Nadler, Linda Palmer, Erika Peterson, Harris Sondak, Tom Tyler, Kathleen Valley, Leaf Van Boven, and Laurie Weingart. I owe a special thanks to the students of my negotiations courses at Kellogg who "pilot-tested" the book, particularly Ingrid Morris. The writing of this book would not have been possible without the skilled editorial hands of Claire Buisseret and Kathleen Much. Finally, Katie Shonk is the person who led the book through its long journey. I am indebted to her guidance and editorial skills.

CHAPTER 1

Negotiation:
The Big Picture

Tory was ecstatic: Two weeks ago, she had landed a highly competitive job at a major food products company. For the past two weeks, Tory had been enjoying her new position as assistant head of one of the company's most profitable divisions. Most of her time had been spent in meetings with her senior manager, Dana, concerning the division's plans for renegotiating their contract with one of their major suppliers. The plan was for the two of them to fly to New York next week for negotiation talks with the supplier. Tory was excited about her role and all that she would learn.

Today, Dana called Tory from home and explained that she had a medical emergency and that Tory would have to take sole responsibility for negotiating with the supplier.

"You can't go to New York?" Tory asked, trying not to show her agitation. "What about a conference call?" Dana explained, "No, I am having immediate back surgery and I can't travel. You'll have to go, and you'll have to work on those important issues we've been struggling with here." Tory suggested that the meeting time could be changed. Dana explained that the meeting had been pushed back far too many times already and that it was either next Wednesday or six months from now and that delay was unattractive in both parties' eyes.

Tory nervously tried to review the key points of the contract that needed revision. "So, the big issues are the on-time guarantee and the variable costs?" Dana explained that the suppliers were not going to like the proposed changes. "So, what should my approach be?" asked Tory. "Should I be tough and insist upon those terms or should I be open to compromise?" Dana responded, "Tory, you're in charge now; that's your decision."

1

H ow should Tory negotiate in this situation? What is the most effective way to achieve her goals with the supplier? This is the type of fundamental question that every negotiator asks him- or herself. Consider what it takes to negotiate successfully in the following situations:

- a manager pulling together a multimillion-dollar contract with another firm
- a graduate accepting her first full-time job with an employer
- two roommates allocating household chores and living expenses
- spouses making decisions about child-care arrangements
- a group of friends deciding how to spend an evening in the city
- a group of financial analysts negotiating foreign policy

As these examples suggest, negotiation does not occur only in Mexican bazaars, corporate boardrooms, and international diplomatic meetings. Rather, we negotiate with others almost every day of our lives. Our most important negotiations take place in our own homes and workplaces. With our rapidly changing workplace and increased career mobility, negotiation skills are more and more essential for successful navigation through life and career (Neale and Bazerman, 1991). It is difficult to imagine how we could get through a week or even a day without negotiating.

This book focuses on the skills necessary for effective negotiation. The good news is that these skills are effective across a wide range of situations, ranging from multiparty, high finance deals to one-on-one casual exchanges. The bad news is that the skills are not immediately obvious and a lot of preparation is necessary. The rest of this chapter will introduce the fundamental components and characteristics of negotiation, beginning with a definition of negotiation.

BEDROCK PRINCIPLES

Negotiation is a decision-making process by which two or more people agree how to allocate scarce resources. There are three main elements in this definition of negotiation: judgment, interdependence, and cooperation.

Negotiation is not a contest of wills or a match of strength, but rather, involves logic and reasoning. This book examines the key judgments that negotiators must make (chapters 2, 3, and 5) and then explores what often goes wrong that impedes negotiator effectiveness (chapters 6, 7, and 8).

The presence of two or more people implies that the decision-making process is inherently interdependent—that is, what one person does affects the other party. It is not sufficient for us to focus only on our own judgment skills to be an effective negotiator; we must understand how to interact, persuade, and communicate with others. The effective negotiator knows how to work with others to achieve his or her objectives. In chapters 9, 10, 11, and 12, we discuss groups, relationships, fairness, and social dilemmas, respectively.

The desire to reach mutual agreement reveals the **cooperative** aspect of negotiation. Many people regard negotiation to be combative, and that there can be only one winner and someone must lose. This is a gross misunderstanding that we address in chapter 4.

DEBUNKING NEGOTIATION MYTHS

Everyone would like to be a good negotiator. The truth, however, is that most people are not effective negotiators—at least, not as effective as they would like to be. Many people have theories about what it takes to be an effective negotiator. Usually, these ideas are incorrect and not supported by facts. Hanging on to such erroneous beliefs is particularly problematic because it hinders our ability to learn to be effective negotiators. We expose four myths about negotiation behavior.

Myth #1: "Good Negotiators Are Born"

A pervasive belief is that to be a good negotiator a person has to have the right genes. This is inaccurate; there are very few "natural" negotiators. Good negotiators are not born; they are self-made. Effective negotiation, like other skills, requires practice and study. The problem is that most of us don't get an opportunity to develop effective negotiation skills in a disciplined fashion. Rather, we learn by doing. Although experience is helpful, it is not sufficient.

Myth #2: "Experience Is a Great Teacher"

We've all met that person at the cocktail party or on the airplane who proudly claims to have 20 years in the business and therefore "must be doing something right." Many young managers have been intimidated at the bargaining table when the person they face is substantially older and more "experienced."

It is only partly true that experience improves negotiation skills. There are three strikes going against experience as an effective teacher. First, most people who claim to have "extensive experience" are referring to unaided experience. Unaided experience is a poor teacher. Can you imagine trying to learn math without ever turning in homework, taking tests, memorizing tables, and getting graded? Without diagnostic feedback, it is very difficult to effectively learn from experience. Second, our memory tends to be selective. We remember our successes and forget our failures. This is comforting to our ego, but does not improve our skills. Third, experience tends to improve our confidence, but not our accuracy. Unwarranted confidence can be dangerous because it leads people to take unwise risks.

Myth #3: "Good Negotiators Take Risks"

We've all seen the movie or read the book wherein the protagonist gambles on what appear to be incredibly small odds and manages to come out ahead. The message is that good negotiators take risks, defy the odds, and step out on a limb. Whereas this works in the movies, it does not lead to success in real negotiations. Effective negotiators do not take risks—they know how to evaluate a decision situation and make an optimal choice given the information that is available to them. In some instances, it may be wise to choose a risky course of action; but in other instances, sticking with the status quo or a less risky alternative is wiser. The key is to know how to evaluate different courses of action and to choose wisely among them so as to maximize one's outcomes. Risky decision making is discussed in chapter 5.

Myth #4: "Good Negotiators Rely on Intuition"

An interesting exercise is to ask people to describe their approach to negotiation. Many seasoned negotiators explain their strategy to be one of "gut feeling" or "intuition." Another way of summing up such a strategy is that one "flies by the seat of his or her pants." These people lack a proactive, prescriptive strategy for approaching negotiation situations. People are reluctant to admit this, however, so they construct a theory after the fact to justify their actions. This is not effective negotiation.

In contrast, effective negotiators are self-aware. Their strategies are proactive, not posthoc. They can articulate the methods and strategies they use. Moreover, they can apply these principles to different situations. They are not victims of arbitrary features of the situation. Most of the important "work" of negotiation takes place before the negotiator is seated at the bargaining table. It takes place in the days, hours, and minutes ahead. It is called **preparation,** and is discussed in chapter 2.

BASIC ARCHITECTURE OF NEGOTIATION

We present a basic architecture for studying negotiation. This architecture serves three interrelated functions: analytic, diagnostic, and strategic. As an analytical tool, it provides a means to conceptualize negotiation and to predict behavior of ourselves and others. As a diagnostic tool, it allows us to evaluate negotiations retrospectively—in a sense, perform a postmortem on negotiated interactions with an eye toward learning, insight, and improvement. Finally, as a strategic tool, it provides knowledge about how to construct negotiation situations to best serve our objectives.

Conflict

Conflict and negotiation are not the same thing. **Conflict** is the perception of differences of interests among people. Negotiation is a decision-making process in which two or more people make joint decisions about the allocation of scarce resources. Negotiation is one of many methods that may be used to resolve perceived conflict of interest. The "Conflict Tree" model (shown in Figure 1–1) illustrates the relationship between conflict and negotiation.

Unfortunately, conflict has a bad reputation; people assume that differences in interest are undesirable and should be immediately reduced—ideally, they should never be permitted to emerge in the first place. But conflict, in and of itself, is not good or bad; it merely reveals perceived differences of interest. Furthermore, the negotiation of differences of interest is not necessarily unpleasant or unproductive. In fact, differences of interest can often improve the welfare of the parties involved, their relationship, and the well-being of related persons and organizations (Pruitt and Rubin, 1986).

Intrapersonal, Interpersonal, and Intergroup Conflict

Conflict may occur at the intrapersonal, interpersonal, or intergroup level. The focus in this book is on the interpersonal level. We briefly define all three types for clarity. **Intrapersonal conflict** is conflict that occurs within one person. Freud and other psychoanalysts spoke of this kind of conflict in describing the battle of drives or wills within a single individual. There are three types of intrapersonal conflict that most of us have experienced at some time in our lives (Lewin, 1935; Coombs and Avrunin, 1988; Miller, 1944). In **approach–**

FIGURE 1–1. Conflict Tree Model

approach conflicts, we are attracted to two (or more) options but may choose only one (e.g., the student choosing whether to go to Stanford or Harvard). In **avoidance–avoidance conflicts,** we avoid two (or more) undesirable options but must choose one (e.g., the medical patient must choose among different painful treatments for an illness). Finally, in **approach–avoidance conflicts,** we consider a single option that has both attractive and unpleasant aspects (e.g., a move to a new city promises delightful weather but exorbitant living expenses).

Interpersonal conflict is conflict between two or more people. Conflict between two persons is **dyadic conflict;** conflict among three or more persons is **multiparty conflict.**

Intergroup conflict occurs between members of different groups representing personally relevant social, cultural, or political categories. For example, conflict between racial groups, political factions, union and management, or divisions within a company are all instances of intergroup conflict.

There is an intimate relationship between intrapersonal, interpersonal, and intergroup conflict. The dynamics at one level are often similar to the dynamics at other levels. Consider Fran, a middle-level manager at a large consulting company. Fran is concerned about her future in the company and is toying with the idea of leaving to form a small, specialized consulting company with two of her associates. Staying at the large company offers more stability, but less potential. Forming a new company promises great challenge but possible failure. Fran is torn; at the intrapersonal level, this is clearly an approach–approach conflict.

Fran's business associates, Michael and Frank, are pressuring Fran to leave the company and join with them in forming their own consulting group. However, Fran has some conflict concerning management style and practice with Michael and fears that Frank and Michael might form a voting coalition against her when making policy. This is interpersonal conflict.

The consulting business is fiercely competitive. Fran has thought about her potential competitors—other small consulting firms as well as the large multinational companies. Fran is concerned about this level of intergroup competition.

Fran's situation is a common one, involving all three levels of conflict.

Consensus Conflict and Scarce Resource Competition

There are two major types of interpersonal conflict: consensus conflict and scarce resource competition (Aubert, 1963; Druckman and Zechmeister, 1973; Kelley and Thibaut, 1969; Thompson and Gonzalez, 1997). **Consensus conflict** occurs when one person's opinions, ideas, or beliefs are incompatible with those of another and the two seek to reach an agreement of opinion. For example, jurors' beliefs may differ about whether a defendant is innocent or guilty. Another example: Two managers may disagree about whether someone has project management skills.

Scarce resource competition exists when people perceive one another as desiring the same limited resources. The focus of this book is on conflicts of interest, or conflicts over scarce resources. **Conflicts of interest** concern people's preferences regarding various options and alternatives. For example, consider two managers in conflict over who has primary responsibility for expenditures on a particular project, roommates in conflict over phone bill charges, or spouses in conflict concerning child care and housework. In each of these cases, the people involved clash over the use, allocation, and control of resources. In some cases, resources are monetary—as in the case of phone bill charges. In many situations, however, resources are less tangible; they involve responsibility, control, time, services, and favors.

Resolution

The next level of the conflict tree identifies the mechanisms by which people may resolve conflicts of interest. Conflicts of interest may be resolved through various social justice mechanisms, such as changing a particular policy or rule or dividing resources on the basis of equality, equity, or need (Leventhal, 1976). Conflicts of interest may be resolved through a simple, strategic choice of behavior with each party acting in a unilateral fashion. Conflicts of interest may be resolved through negotiation. Finally, conflicts of interest may be resolved through various forms of alternative dispute resolution and third-party intervention such as mediation or arbitration. Third-party intervention will not be discussed further as this book focuses on negotiation.

CONDITIONS OF NEGOTIATION

Consider the situation that Tory is facing with the upcoming meeting in New York. Is it a real negotiation? What are the characteristics of negotiation situations?

Perceptions of Conflict

People who are involved in the same dispute may hold very different perceptions (Hastorf and Cantril, 1954; Thompson, 1995b). People may falsely believe they are in conflict—even when there is no objective basis. Although it may seem incredible that people could believe they have conflicting interests when in fact they don't, people frequently assume conflict exists when it doesn't (Thompson and Hrebec, 1996). This often results in **lose–lose outcomes:** both people want the same thing but settle for less because they believe they are in conflict.

For this reason, it is often useful to distinguish between objective conflict and perceptions of conflict (Thompson and Hrebec, 1996). Figure 1–2 illustrates four possibilities: In

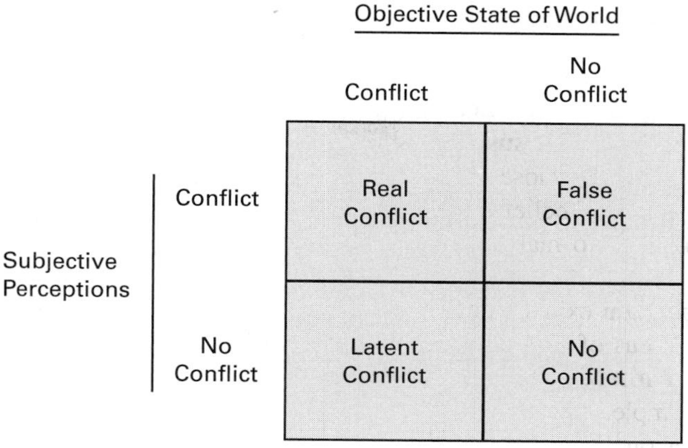

Objective State of World

	Conflict	No Conflict
Conflict	Real Conflict	False Conflict
No Conflict	Latent Conflict	No Conflict

Subjective Perceptions

FIGURE I–2. Perceptions of Conflict and Reality

veridical (or real) **conflict,** conflict actually exists between people and they perceive it as such. In **latent conflict,** conflict exists, but people do not perceive it. In **false conflict,** conflict does not exist between people, but they perceive conflict. Finally, in **no conflict,** conflict does not exist and is not perceived. We are especially concerned with instances of real conflict—that is, accurate perception of conflict—as well as false conflict—instances in which people perceive conflict that does not exist. It is obvious that Tory's firm and the New York supplier regard themselves as have differing interests that need to be worked out. Theirs is a case of real conflict.

Communication Opportunities

If people cannot communicate, they cannot negotiate. Most of us think of communication as involving unrestricted, face-to-face interaction with others. But communication may take many different forms, such as written messages, electronic mail, telephone calls, and reports from third parties or agents. There are two types of bargaining: explicit bargaining and tacit bargaining (Schelling, 1960). In **explicit bargaining,** people are able to communicate with one another; in **tacit bargaining,** people are unable to directly communicate but coordinate through their actions. In this book, our principal focus is on explicit bargaining. The purpose of Tory's trip to New York is to allow the parties to communicate in a direct fashion.

Intermediate Solutions or Compromises

If one party to a dispute must choose between total victory or yielding completely, no bargaining can occur. Only when intermediate solutions are possible can bargaining occur (Schelling, 1960). For example, if the supplier gave Tory an ultimatum, then no negotiation could occur. In chapter 2, we'll see why ultimatums and unwarranted threats are unwise strategies.

Interdependence

People are interdependent if their actions affect others' outcomes (Thibaut and Kelley, 1959). People in negotiation affect the actions each may take and the outcomes each receives. If one party has complete authority over the other party and is not affected by the actions of others, negotiation cannot occur. For instance, many, but certainly not most, parent–child interactions are not real negotiations because the parent ultimately has the final word. This is not to say that parties to real negotiations do not differ in power. Often, people negotiate with those of greater or lesser power. For example, an employee often has less power than his or her employer; nevertheless, such a situation is considered to be a negotiation because the employee could take actions that would affect the employer's welfare, such as quitting or initiating a lawsuit. Both Tory and the New York supplier are interdependent in that they can take actions that affect the other's welfare.

In the dyadic case, parties must agree to the outcome for negotiation to occur. Thus, each person has veto power in that he or she can leave the situation. In fact, we will see that "walk-away" alternatives are the basis of power in negotiation (see chapter 2). In the multiparty case, it is not always necessary that all parties reach mutual agreement for settlement to occur. Once three or more conflicting parties are involved, coalitions may form to wield influence over others and garner resources.

ELEMENTS OF NEGOTIATION

Negotiation may take any number of forms; no two negotiations are exactly alike. Given the complexity of players, issues, alternatives, and behaviors in many negotiations, it is important to know what main elements to look for. To return to Tory's plight introduced at the beginning of the chapter, how should Tory start to prepare for her negotiations with the New York supplier? The following framework is a good starting point for identifying the central elements of negotiation.

Parties

It is always important to identify who the players are in a negotiation. The people who negotiate are termed "parties" even if they represent only themselves. A **party** is a person (or group of persons with common interests), who acts in accord with his or her preferences. Parties are readily identified when they are physically present, but often, the most important parties are not present at the negotiation table. Such parties are known as the **hidden table** (Friedman, 1992).

We also need to distinguish the party of interest from his or her opponent. Following Raiffa (1982), we term the party of interest in our discussions the **focal negotiator;** the opponent is termed the other party or **target negotiator** (Raiffa, 1982). There is no common convention, however, used to refer to the "other party" in negotiations. When parties' interests are opposed, as in purely competitive negotiations, **opponent** is often used; when parties' interests are highly coordinated, **partner** may be used. In addition to the key players, also known as **principals,** there may be other parties to a negotiation, such as constituents, third parties, and so on. It is important to identify who these persons are and what their stake is in the negotiation.

Using this framework, Tory identified the main parties in the negotiation situation: herself; her manager, Dana (although not present, she was a central figure); the supplier; the supplier's constituents; and the supplier's union. In the negotiations, Tory was careful to be sensitive to each party's needs.

Issues

The **issues** are the resources to be allocated or the considerations to be resolved in negotiation. For example, in a land dispute, the issues may be particular plots, mineral and water rights, method of payment, development rights, and so on. In an employment negotiation, the issues may be salary, job responsibilities, health coverage, and so on. A central element of successful negotiation is identifying the issues.

Although it might seem that negotiations would be better for all involved if the issues were simplified and fewer in number, in fact, the opposite is true. The more issues, the better. More issues provide negotiators with more opportunities to construct tradeoffs among issues. For example, consider an employment situation in which the issue is hourly pay and the two parties have opposing preferences. That is, the employer wants to minimize wages; the employee wants high wages. At best, the two parties can reach a compromise agreement, leaving each of them perhaps moderately satisfied. However, if the same negotiation involves not only salary but job responsibilities and work hours, the parties may negotiate tradeoffs so that each benefits most on the issue that is most important to him or her. We will discuss such methods in more detail in chapter 4.

In her negotiations with the supplier, Tory identified the central issues from her own firm's perspective, but she also asked the supplier about the issues of concern to them. In this way, Tory expanded the **issue mix,** which provided more degrees of freedom in the negotiation.

Alternatives

The **alternatives** correspond to the choices available to negotiators for each issue to be resolved. For example, in the land dispute negotiation, the alternatives for the mineral rights may range from no rights to complete mining rights. In the employment negotiation, alternatives for medical coverage may include premiums, selection of health maintenance organizations, deductibles, dependent care, and so on. Again, just as negotiators identify the issues, they also identify and create alternatives; the more alternatives, the better. In her negotiations with the supplier, Tory sought to identify a number of feasible alternatives for each of the issues.

Interests and Positions

We've identified the issues and possible settlement options, but we have not yet determined how negotiators feel about the various options. **Positions** are the stated wants a negotiator has for a particular issue. **Interests** are the underlying needs that a negotiator has. For example, in an employment negotiation, salary is an issue. Requesting $75,000 is a position. The negotiator's underlying interest might be the ability to afford a home mortgage payment to be paid off in 15 years or to send children to college in 18 years. Usually, negotiators' needs may be met by a variety of positions. A key to successful negotiation is to move away from **positional bargaining** into a discussion of underlying interests and needs.

In her negotiation with the supplier, Tory did two things. First, she was careful to separate her own firm's interests from their position. Their interest was to cut stocking fees and to satisfy customers. Second, Tory designed questions, in advance of the meeting, to probe the supplier's interests. Tory correctly anticipated that negotiators often fail to separate their positions from their interests (Fisher, Ury, and Patton, 1991).

Negotiation Process

The **negotiation process** is the events and interaction that occur between parties before the outcome. The process of negotiation includes all of the verbal and nonverbal interchange among parties, the enactment of bargaining strategies, and the external or situational events affecting the interaction between negotiators. The negotiation process is also known as the **negotiation dance** (Raiffa, 1982).

The negotiation process includes the degree and level of concessions that each party makes, the use of threats and promises, and the medium of communication between negotiators. It is virtually impossible for a negotiator to reliably predict how the process will unfold. However, a negotiator can do three important things to better control process to his or her advantage. First, a negotiator may plan his or her opening statement or offer. In some instances, it is best to let the other party make the first offer, but even this should be planned. Second, a negotiator should think about which medium of communication is best from his or her perspective. We'll see later, for example, that some negotiators may not prefer face-to-face negotiations—with good reason. Finally, negotiators should have a good idea of the flow and pace of a negotiation. Is it important to resolve the situation today in this room? Often, in the heat of negotiation, parties feel pressure to resolve the situation, which may be to their disadvantage.

Tory thought about these three things and decided that she would like to make the opening statement in the negotiation, given that her firm's division had very clear goals. She realized that, although the negotiation was face-to-face, it may take longer than a single day. She prepared a plan for how discussions would continue, if necessary, in following days. This also allowed her to discuss the issues with Dana, prior to committing to anything.

Negotiation Outcome

The **negotiation outcome** is the product or endpoint of the bargaining. Negotiations may end in **impasse,** wherein parties do not reach a settlement. Such situations are also known as **stalemates** or **deadlocks.** In some cases, parties may elect to have a third party intervene and possibly impose a settlement. In other situations, parties mutually reach settlement. When settlement is achieved, we can examine the negotiators' performance and look for ways to improve it.

The analysis of negotiated outcomes does not stop with the attainment of mutual agreement. As we will see in chapter 10, negotiators have emotional reactions to negotiation. They sometimes feel satisfied; other times they feel cheated; they may even feel guilty. These feelings can dramatically affect the likelihood of settlement and the relationships and reputations of the parties.

WHY IS NEGOTIATION SO DIFFICULT?

Why do we need a whole book on negotiation if there exists a set of skills that can be effectively applied to a wide variety of negotiations? There are at least three reasons why negotiation is deceptively difficult to effectively master: cognitive hardwiring, feedback, and schematic frameworks.

Cognitive Hardwiring

We are barraged with an onslaught of information and stimuli. Fortunately, one of the wonderful things about our information processing system is that it is designed to simplify this information. We make shortcuts and simplifying assumptions to quickly process and apply information. Moreover, we have a need for **closure** (Kruglanski, Peri, and Zakai, 1991). That is, we desire to have immediate answers and resolutions to situations. We do not like ambiguity and uncertainty.

In most instances these simplifying procedures and our desire for closure serve us well. However, they can lead us astray if we make faulty assumptions. To be an effective negotiator, we have to actively fight against such simplifying assumptions. We must be willing to tolerate ambiguity and uncertainty, to test our assumptions in a disconfirmatory (rather than confirmatory) manner, and to think in different terms than those to which we may be accustomed. This book challenges the negotiator to do this.

Feedback

We noted earlier that unaided experience is not an effective teacher and that our egos tend to work against us. We recall our successes and forget our failures. When we bask in our glory, we don't focus on self-improvement. Further, even when we attempt to seek feedback about our performance, we seek **confirmatory feedback.** For example, we may ask our partner after a particularly contentious and acrimonious negotiation, "I was reasonable, right?" It rarely occurs to us, however, to ask the other side (or our own partner for that matter), "What aspects of my behavior seemed most unreasonable and aggressive?" The difference in wording seems subtle, if not trivial, but leads to dramatically different types of feedback. People will tell us what they think we want to hear, but that is not helpful for learning.

Schematic Frameworks

Most people don't have well-formulated frameworks for negotiation. When asked how they plan to negotiate, people say things like, "Well, I will see how things go, collect some information, and make decisions at that point." This is a poor substitute for effective negotiation planning. It can actually be more time- and energy-consuming for a negotiator to not have a framework than to carefully prepare a strategy. A naïve person may spend fruitless and frustrating hours in a negotiation situation that a skilled negotiator would have walked out on after five minutes upon realizing there was no potential for mutually beneficial agreement. This book provides a framework for approaching negotiation. Most of the important thinking and work in negotiation takes place prior to the negotiation.

NEGOTIATION: THE BIG PICTURE

In this book, we discuss many different types of negotiations that span a wide range of situations, for example: negotiations among managers in organizations, negotiations among colleagues, and negotiations among friends. Although there are certainly differences across these contexts, the basic characteristics and elements we discussed here are quite similar. Principles that describe negotiation in management–labor situations also characterize negotiations between spouses, roommates, and department heads.

Negotiation, like physics and biology, is a science. Just as the physicist uses theories, principles, and instruments rather than gut feeling and intuition to understand, predict, and control the physical world, the negotiator must use principles and informed analysis when making sense out of the social world.

There's a lot to learn about negotiation. For this reason, it is often helpful to have a "big picture" view when learning new skills. Figure 1–3 on page 12 is a schematic diagram of the most important elements involved in virtually all negotiation situations.

FIGURE 1–3. NEGOTIATION: The Big Picture

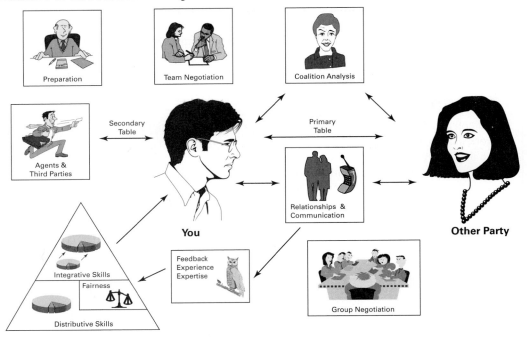

The most basic, fundamental negotiation involves two people facing one another at the bargaining table. This could be you and a potential employer, you and a car dealer, you and a house seller, or you and your business partner. This relationship is the **primary table.**

The first step in negotiation involves preparation. Most naïve negotiators fail to sufficiently prepare. The skilled negotiator focuses on two kinds of skills: integrative skills and distributive skills. Integrative skills involve enlarging the pie of available resources; distributive skills involve claiming resources. A key aspect of distributive negotiation is fairness.

As more parties enter the negotiation, the skills needed for successful negotiation become more complex. Team negotiation, coalitions, groups, agents, and third parties are common forms of negotiation.

The ability of negotiators to build and maintain a relationship, and communicate effectively, is critical for negotiation success. Finally, for a negotiator to become an expert, he or she must utilize feedback and experience wisely.

TAKE-AWAYS

- The best negotiators practice negotiation like a tennis pro practices her serve; negotiation skills do not come naturally to most people.
- We do not always see the world the way other people do; this can lead to conflict and lose–lose agreements.
- The starting point for analyzing any negotiation situation is to identify the parties, the issues, the alternatives and interests.
- Negotiation is difficult because we are cognitively hardwired to simplify information, we don't get timely and accurate feedback, and we lack schematic frameworks.

CHAPTER 2

Preparation: *What to Do Before Negotiation*

On a bright Saturday morning, two men entered a car dealership. One of them, Frank, had recently moved to the city and was in need of a car.

"Hello, gentlemen. Are you interested in buying a car today?" a salesman asked. Wanting to demonstrate firmness, Frank replied, "Possibly." After an hour or so of looking around the lot and a few test drives, Frank located his car of interest. The sticker price was $26,000. Gus, the salesman, offered, "I can let you have it for $25,200 today only."

"That's more than I wanted to spend," Frank replied. "How much did you want to spend?" "Well, uh, $23,000 or $24,000." Gus laughed, "Well, you can't get this car for that, but I can show you some other models in that price range," and gestured to the subcompacts in the back lot. Frank's friend started to move away, commenting, "Maybe we ought to look around some more." Suddenly, Gus offered, "I can go as low as $25,000 but that is all." The two men exchanged glances. Frank said, "I'll have to think about it."

During a lunch break, Frank's friend suggested the two of them drive 30 miles to the Belview dealership on the other side of town. At that dealership, they found the same car, similarly equipped, with the same sticker price. Before the salesman could open his mouth, Frank announced, "We can get this car at Lynnwood for $25,000."

The salesman replied, "That car—fine model—you can have it today for $24,600." After a brief huddle, Frank suggested to his friend that they continue to play this situation out. He asked the salesman, "Do you have a phone?" "Sure, right over there," he said, pointing to a desk. Frank looked up the phone number of the other dealership. "Is Gus there? Gus, my friend and I talked to you this morning about a car you were selling for $25,000, and we can get the same car at Belview for $24,600—is there any reason why we should buy it from you?"

Silence on the phone. Then, "Hold on a minute. Where are you again?" After a five-minute wait, Gus came back to the phone. "We can match that price."

"Match it? Can you do any better?" "No. We can match." Frank looked at his friend, "What should we do now? Looks like we pushed it as much as possible—right?" His friend replied, "I think so—let's just buy it here."

In any negotiation, we are left asking whether we could have done better—gotten the car or house for less, a higher salary for the job or more vacation days. In most circumstances, we never find out the answers to these questions because we are missing half of the story—namely, the goals, interests, and true bottom line of the "other side." In this chapter, we consider several negotiation situations that are based on information from both sides. We discuss methods for assessing information about an opponent.

DISTRIBUTIVE NEGOTIATION: WHO GETS HOW MUCH

In this chapter, we focus on the competitive aspect of negotiation, wherein each party tries to get the best deal he or she can from the other person. This desire has to be balanced against the possibility that one negotiator may leave the situation before agreement may be reached. Consider Terry, a second-year MBA student who is sitting on an offer from an advertising firm. Terry believes she can get a higher salary than the initial offer. However, if Terry proposes a counteroffer that is higher than the CEO of the company makes, Terry is not likely to be successful and, furthermore, runs the risk of insulting the recruiter and souring the negotiations. At the same time, if Terry accepts the first figure offered, it is possible that more could have been had. **Distributive negotiation** is about how negotiators claim resources. In short, it's about who gets how much. Every negotiation has a distributive component—no matter who we are dealing with and how altruistic we feel, the fact is, we must divide the pie. As we'll see, the key to effective distributive negotiation is preparation.

TARGET AND RESERVATION POINTS

A common assumption is that when people have conflicting goals, such as when a seller wants a high price for a good and a buyer wants a low price, each party makes concessions and they converge on a **compromise** or a midpoint agreement. This is not an accurate view. In all negotiations, it is true that parties have ideals they would like to achieve. Such ideal points are target points or target values (Raiffa, 1982; Walton and McKersie, 1965). A **target point** represents a negotiator's most preferred or ideal settlement. In many situations, negotiators may not have a specific target point. For example, buyers want to pay "as little as they can"; similarly, sellers want to charge "as much as possible." But it is unrealistic for a buyer to think she can buy a house for one cent, and unrealistic for a seller to believe he can get one million dollars for a used Toyota. So when we speak of target points, we focus on points that represent realistic appraisals. For example, in the opening example, Frank's target price for the car was $23,000. The dealer's target price was $26,000 (the sticker price for the car).

Typically, negotiators' target points do not positively overlap—for example, the seller wants more than the buyer is willing to pay.

In addition to target points, negotiators also have reservation points. A **reservation point** is the point at which a negotiator is indifferent between reaching a settlement and walking away from the bargaining table. As will become evident, the outcome of negotiation depends more on the relationship between parties' reservation points than on their target points.

Target points, also known as aspirations, goals, levels of aspiration (Siegel and Fouraker, 1960), and comparison levels (Thibaut and Kelley, 1959) are what negotiators commonly focus on when preparing for negotiation. However, it is one negotiator's reservation point that is essential for effective negotiation. Unfortunately, many negotiators fail to assess their reservation point when they prepare for negotiation. This fatal flaw can lead to two unfortunate outcomes: People may agree to terms that are worse for them than what they could attain by engaging in a different course of action, or people reject offers that are better than any other alternatives.

If a negotiator is unsure, how should he assess his reservation point? One method is to reason backward. This involves thinking about what you would do if the current negotiation deal fell through. For example, imagine that you are selling your house. You have already assessed your target price—in this case, $275,000. That is the easy part. The real question is: What is the lowest offer you would accept for your home? To answer this involves a four-step process to accurately assess your **BATNA,** *Best Alternative to a Negotiated Agreement* (Fisher, Ury, and Patton, 1991), and determine your reservation price, or the *least* amount of money for which you would agree to sell your home.

Step 1: Brainstorm Your Alternatives

Step 1 involves thinking about what you will do in the event that you do not get an offer of $275,000 for your house. Perhaps you may reduce the list price by $10,000 (or more); or perhaps you may stay in the house; or you may consider renting.

You should consider as many alternatives as possible. The only restriction is that the alternatives must be feasible—that is, realistic. This involves research on your part.

Step 2: Evaluate Each Alternative

In Step 2, you should order the various alternatives identified in Step 1 in terms of their relative attractiveness, or value, to you. If an alternative has an uncertain outcome, such as reducing the list price, you should determine the probability that a buyer will make an offer at that price. For example, suppose that you reduce the list price to $265,000. You assess the probability of a buyer making an offer of $265,000 for your house to be 70%, based on recent home sale prices in the area. Your reservation price is based on research, not hope. The best, most valuable, alternative should be selected to represent your BATNA.

Step 3: Attempt to Improve Your BATNA

Your bargaining position can be strengthened substantially to the extent that you have an attractive, viable BATNA. Unfortunately, this is the step that many negotiators fail to fully develop. To improve your BATNA in this case, you might contact a house rental company and develop your rental options, or you may make some improvements that have high return on investment (e.g., new paint). Of course, your most attractive BATNA is to have an offer in hand on your house.

Step 4: Determine Your Reservation Price

Once you have determined your most attractive BATNA, it is now time to identify your reservation price—the least amount of money you'd accept for your home at the present time. Once again, it is *not* effective negotiation strategy to pull this number out of thin air. It *must* be based on fact. For example:

Suppose that you assess the probability of getting an offer on your house of $265,000 (or higher) to be 60%. Suppose that you assess the probability that you will get an offer of $250,000 or higher to be 95%. You think there is a 5% chance that you won't get an offer of $250,000 and will rent out your house. We can use this information to assess our expected probabilities of selling our house:

Reduce the price of your home to $265,000	p_{sale}	$= .60\%$
Reduce the price of your home to $250,000	p_{sale}	$= .35\%$
Rent out the house	p_{rent}	$= .05\%$

The numbers in the right-hand column are probabilities, representing the chances that you think your house will sell at a particular price or will have to be rented. Thus, you think that if the list price of your house is reduced to $265,000, it is 60% likely that you will receive an offer of that amount within six weeks. If you reduce the price of your home to $250,000, you are 95% certain you will get an offer. (Note that we write this as 35% because it includes the 60% probability of receiving an offer of $265,000.) Finally, you think there is a 5% chance that you won't get an offer of $250,000 or more in the next six weeks and that you will have to rent your house—a value you assess to be worth only $100,000 to you at the present time.

Note that in our calculation, the probabilities always sum to exactly 100%, meaning that we have considered all possible events occurring. No alternative is left to chance. An overall value for each of these "risky" alternatives is assessed by multiplying the value of each option by its probability of occurrence:

Value of reducing price to $265,000 = $265,000 × .6 = $159,000
Value of reducing price to $250,000 = $250,000 × .35 = $87,500
Value of renting out the house = $100,000 × .05 = $5,000

As a final step, we add up all of the values of the alternatives to arrive at an overall evaluation:

.6 ($265,000) + .35 ($250,000) + .05 ($100,000) = $159,000 + $87,500 + $5,000 = $251,500

This value is our reservation price. It means that we would *never* settle for anything less than $251,500 in the next six weeks.[1] It also means that if a buyer were to make us an offer right now of $251,000, we would seriously consider it because it is so close to our reservation price. Obviously, we want to get a lot more than $251,500, but we are prepared to go as low as this amount at the present time.

The offers that we receive in the next six weeks can change our reservation point. Suppose a buyer offers to pay $260,000 for the house next week. This would be our reservation point by which to evaluate all subsequent offers.

---

[1] After six weeks, we may reduce price of home to $250,000.

THE PSYCHOLOGY OF RESERVATION POINTS

A negotiator's reservation point should be based upon objective assessment of the best possible alternative to reaching agreement. A person's reservation point should not change during the course of negotiations unless, for some reason, the objective situation has changed. For example, consider Frank's situation in buying the car. Suppose that his BATNA is to buy a stripped-down model of the same car that is one year older for $21,000. After two weeks of research, Frank has determined that the combined comfort, warranty, and long-term usability of the new car is worth $23,750 at the very most. This means that once in the heat of negotiation with Gus the salesman, Frank's walk-away point should not change; he should not under any circumstances pay more than $23,750 for the car. However, if he learns some objective information during the course of negotiation that affects his real BATNA (e.g., the stripped-down model has been sold or reduced in price), then it is appropriate to change his reservation price.

Bargainer Beware

Frank should be aware of a common bargaining ploy that salespersons often use. Many savvy negotiators attempt to talk negotiators out of their BATNA. Negotiators are most likely to fall prey to this ploy when they have not adequately prepared for the negotiation and have conjured up a BATNA not based on objective information. Imagine if Gus told Frank, "I couldn't bear to see you driving in an older car because it would hurt your image. You would surely regret your decision to buy last year's model once you saw your colleagues driving this year's model." Frank may very well be tempted to adjust his reservation price, but this would mean that he fell prey to Gus' persuasion attempt.

Clever negotiators appear to have our best interests in mind when actually they only have their own interests in mind. In a negotiation situation, the person who stands to gain most by changing our mind should be the least persuasive. Thus, it is important to develop a BATNA before commencing negotiations, and to stick to it during the course of negotiations. It is helpful to write your reservation point in ink on a piece of paper and put it in your pocket before negotiating. If you feel tempted to settle for less than your reservation price, that may be a good time to pull out the paper, call a halt to the negotiation process, and go home and engage in an objective reassessment.

Focal Points

Negotiators who make the mistake of not developing a reservation point before they negotiate often focus on an arbitrary value which masquerades as a reservation price. Such arbitrary points are **focal points.** Focal points can be salient numbers, figures, or values that appear to be valid, but have no basis in fact. A focal point might be a discount on a posted sticker price, or the price of a similar model car with fewer features. Negotiators tend to anchor on focal points during negotiation. A good example of the arbitrariness of focal points is provided by an investigation in which people made estimations about the number of African countries in the United Nations (Tversky and Kahneman, 1974). In the investigation, people stood before a wheel of fortune that was spun in front of them. After the wheel was spun and landed on a number, people were asked to indicate whether there were more or fewer African countries in the United Nations than the number shown on the wheel and then estimate the total number. People who landed on a high number estimated many more than those who had, by chance, landed on a low number. It would seem absurd to base judgments on the wheel-of-fortune number, but people did.

The Problem with Targets

Negotiators may often make the mistake of using their target point as a reservation point. When they are queried, they remark that the target is not "hard" and that they will move away a "little" from this point. Thus, the negotiator has a clear sense of what he or she would like to achieve but has not thought about the least acceptable terms he or she could live with. This is a poor negotiation strategy and can result in one of two fatal flaws. The negotiator who lacks a well-formed reservation point runs the risk of agreeing to a settlement that is worse than what he or she could do by following another course of action. In other cases, the negotiator may walk away from potentially profitable deals. Many home sellers turn down early offers on their house that exceed their reservation point only to be forced to accept an offer of less value after a considerable length of time.

The Not-so-even Split

A common focal point in negotiation is the "even split." In many negotiation situations, parties' offers do not overlap, such as in car and house-buying negotiations. Inevitably, one party has the bright idea of "splitting the difference." We can imagine Gus the salesman suggesting to Frank that instead of haggling over the price of the car that they simply split the difference. The concept of the even split has an appealing, almost altruistic flavor to it. To many of us, it seems unreasonable not to compromise or meet the other person halfway. So, what is the problem with even splits? The problem is that they are based on arbitrarily arrived-at values. Consider Frank's car situation. Suppose Frank initially offered $23,000 for the car, then $24,000, and then, finally, $24,500. Suppose the salesman initially requested $25,200, then reduced it to $25,000, and then to $24,600. The salesman then suggested that they split the difference at $24,550, arguing that an even split of the difference is "fair." However, the pattern of offers up to that point were not "even" in any sense. Frank made concessions of $1,500; Gus made concessions of $600. Further, even if the concessions were of equal magnitude, this is no guarantee that the middle value is a "fair" value. All this means is that it behooves a negotiator to begin with a high starting value and to make small concessions. Often, the person who suggests the even split is in an advantageous position. Before accepting or proposing an even split, make sure the values are favorable to you.

BARGAINING ZONE

The **bargaining zone,** or settlement zone, represents the region between parties' reservation points. We may reliably predict that the final settlement will fall somewhere above the seller's reservation point and below the buyer's reservation point. In our discussion of the bargaining zone, we use a buyer–seller example for simplicity; the same analysis applies to other negotiations that don't involve buyers and sellers. In the multiparty case, the bargaining zone is multidimensional, but the same analysis applies: The bargaining zone represents the region between parties' reservation points.

The bargaining zone is extremely important to assess, for it determines whether an agreement is feasible and whether it is worthwhile to negotiate. To assess the bargaining zone, a negotiator has to do two things. The first step is what we've already done in the house-selling example. A negotiator must assess his or her own reservation price, based upon his or her BATNA. This step, as we have seen, takes time and effort. The next step is equally important but much more difficult. It involves doing the *same analysis* for the other party. As you might guess, this is more difficult because we usually do not know the other party's alternatives. This requires research and analysis.

The bargaining zone may be either positive or negative (see Figures 2–1a and 2–1b). In a **positive bargaining zone,** parties' reservation points overlap. This means that it is possible for parties to reach mutual agreement. For example, consider the bargaining zone in Figure 2–1a. The seller's reservation point is $11; the buyer's reservation point is $14. The most the buyer is willing to pay is $3 greater than the very least the seller is willing to accept. The bargaining zone is between $11 and $14, or $3; if the two reach agreement, the settlement will be somewhere between $11 and $14. If parties fail to reach agreement in this situation, the outcome is an impasse and is **inefficient** because both parties are worse off by not reaching agreement than by reaching agreement. The negotiators leave money on the table.

The bargaining zone may be negative or nonexistent. For example, consider the bargaining zone in Figure 2-1b, in which the seller's reservation point is $14 and the buyer's reservation point is $12. The most the buyer is willing to pay is $2 less than the seller is willing to accept at a minimum. This is a **negative bargaining zone;** there is no positive overlap between parties' reservation points. In this situation, parties should exercise their best alternatives to agreement. Because negotiations are costly to prolong, it is to both parties' advantage to determine whether there is a positive bargaining zone. If there isn't, the parties should not waste time negotiating.

FIGURE 2–1A. Positive Bargaining Zone

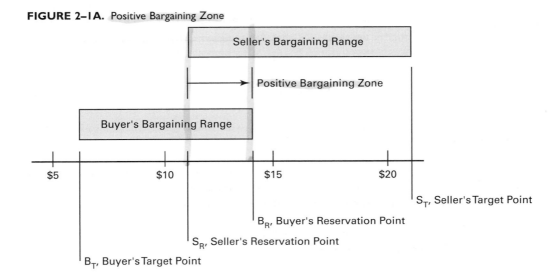

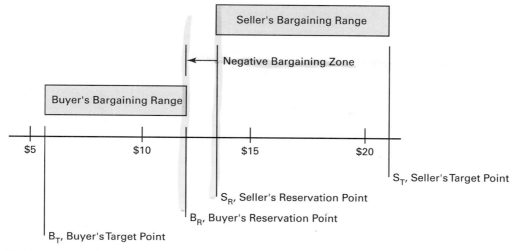

FIGURE 2–1B. Negative Bargaining Zone

BARGAINING SURPLUS

So far, we have made the point that mutual settlement is possible when parties' reservation points overlap and impossible when parties' reservation points do not overlap. **Bargaining surplus** is the amount of overlap produced by parties' reservation points. It is a measure of the size of the bargaining zone. The bargaining surplus is a measure of the value that negotiated agreement offers to both parties over the alternative of not reaching settlement. Sometimes this is very large; other times it is very narrow. Skilled negotiators know how to reach agreements when the bargaining zone is narrow.

NEGOTIATOR'S SURPLUS

We have noted that negotiated outcomes will fall somewhere in the bargaining zone. What determines where in this range the settlement will occur? Obviously, each party would like the settlement to be as close to the other party's reservation point as possible. In our example in Figure 2–1a, the seller would prefer to sell close to $14; the buyer would prefer to buy close to $11. The best possible outcome for the negotiator is one that just meets the other party's reservation point, thereby inducing the other party to settle, but allows the focal negotiator to reap as much gain as possible. This provides the focal negotiator with the greatest possible share of the resources to be divided. In the opening example, Frank wanted to figure out the lowest price he could pay for the car—he wanted to determine the dealer's reservation price. Similarly, in the house example, the seller would like to sell as close to $275,000 as possible.

The positive difference between the settlement outcome and the negotiator's reservation point is the **negotiator's surplus** (see Figure 2–2 on page 22). Notice that the total surplus of the two negotiators adds up to the size of the bargaining zone. Negotiators want to

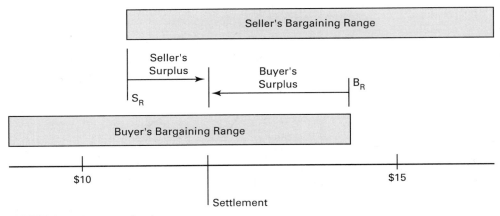

FIGURE 2–2. Bargaining Surplus

maximize their surplus in negotiations; surplus represents resources in excess of what is possible for negotiators to attain in the absence of negotiated agreement.

The fact that negotiated settlements fall somewhere in the bargaining zone and that each negotiator tries to maximize his share of the bargaining surplus illustrates the **mixed-motive** nature of negotiation. That is, negotiators are motivated to cooperate with the other party to ensure that settlement is reached if there is a positive bargaining zone, but they are motivated to compete with one another to claim as much of the bargaining surplus as they can.

THE ROLE OF INFORMATION

The most frequently asked question in negotiation is how one can achieve most of the surplus for oneself. The simple answer is to know the other party's reservation point and to offer the other party the option that represents his or her reservation point. For example, if we are a potential home buyer and we figure out that the seller's reservation point is $251,000, that is a perfect offer to make. But, this is easier said than done. How do we get this information? Most negotiators will never reveal their reservation point, but it never hurts to ask. Raiffa (1982) cautions negotiators not to reveal their reservation points and cites a humorous story wherein one party opens with a direct request for information about his opponent's reservation price: "Tell me the bare minimum you would accept from us, and I'll see if I can throw in something extra." The opponent, not to be taken in, quips, "Why don't you tell us the very maximum that you are willing to pay, and we'll see if we can shave off a bit?" (p. 40). This example illustrates the essence of negotiation: How do people make sure they reach agreement if the bargaining zone is positive but claim as much of the jointly available resources as possible?

There is another problem as well. Even if someone were to claim to reveal his reservation point, there is no way to verify that he is telling the truth. Negotiators who reveal their own reservation points cannot convince the other party that they are telling the truth; similarly, when the other party tells us his or her reservation point, we are faced with the dilemma of determining whether the information is trustworthy. The negotiator is always at an information deficit because the other party's reservation point is not verifiable.

Given that "private" information is inherently unverifiable, there would seem to be little point to negotiation. After all, if you can never tell if the other person is telling the truth, then communication would seem fruitless. Even so, we know that people negotiate all the time in the absence of such information. When people negotiate, they are constantly making judgments about the other person's reservation point and interests.

There may be some conditions that allow focal negotiators to be more confident about the other party's reservation point. For example, if the person with whom we are negotiating for possible hire shows us a signed letter from a competitor company containing an attractive salary offer, we can be fairly confident about the candidate's reservation point. If a person says something that is not in his or her interest, we may have more reason to believe it. For example, if a seller tells us she does not have another buyer and is under pressure to sell, we might believe her because this statement is not in her interest. This leads to an important cautionary note: It is not necessarily in your best interest to misrepresent your reservation point because you risk the possibility of disagreement. For example, imagine that you are trying to sell your used CD player because you have been given another, nicer model as a gift. You would be willing to accept $100 for the used model (your reservation point) based upon a pawnbroker's offer. But you would ideally like to get $200 (your target point). You place an ad and a potential buyer calls offering to pay $110. If you tell the caller that you have an offer of $120, you risk the possibility that the potential buyer will say "take it." It might be in your interest not to let potential buyers believe that your reservation price is $200 (see Farrell and Gibbons, 1989).

POWER

At the heart of distributive negotiation is **power.** Power can be based on many different factors in negotiation, including reward, punishment, status, attraction, and expertise (French and Raven, 1959) (see Table 2–1).

Reward power derives from a person's ability to influence the behavior of another person by providing or withholding rewards. Rewards may be tangible, like money, as well

TABLE 2–1. Five Bases of Power

Base of Power	Definition
Reward	Influence based on rewards offered to the target by the power holder contingent on compliance
Coercive	Influence based on punishments or threats directed toward the target person in the event of noncompliance
Legitimate	Influence based on the target's belief that the power holder has a justifiable right to demand the performance of certain behaviors
Referent	Influence based on the target's identification with, attraction to, or respect for, the power holder
Expert	Influence based on the target's belief that the power holder possesses superior skills and abilities

Source: Adapted from French, J. and B. Raven (1959). The bases of social power. In *Studies in social power.* D. Cartwright, ed. Ann Arbor: University of Michigan Press.

as less tangible, like opportunities, praise, acceptance, and status. For example, Sarah complies in her negotiations with a well-connected colleague because the colleague can provide important information for Sarah.

Coercive power derives from a person's ability to influence the behavior of others by punishing or threatening with punishment. Punishments may be tangible, such as fines and demerits, but can also be intangible, such as "faint praise." Consider Brian who is concerned about his negotiations with his office mate, Ned. The two need to work out how they will share resources. Brian is concerned because he has seen Ned slander other people and kill their chances for advancement by damning them with "faint praise."

Legitimate power derives from a person's authorization to tell another what to do. For example, in the military services, officers have a legitimate right to command those of lower rank. However, legitimacy is not always so clear cut, such as when a new hire is given the most boring and onerous tasks when working on a project with veterans in the organization.

Referent power derives from a person's respect and admiration for another. Oftentimes, this may be based on a person's status, such as when a middle-level manager acquiesces to a senior manager. However, referent power can be based on attraction for another, independent of rank. For example, Lorne has a deep respect for Carol, whom he regards as having successfully dealt with diversity and stereotyping issues in her organization.

Expert power derives from a person's knowledge, skills, and abilities. For example, the power of an expert witness in a trial can dramatically alter the course of events. However, experts in the same field are not always in perfect agreement. We know of an extremely powerful manager who prefaces every influence attempt by recounting his expertise in the field, (i.e., "I was one of the first managers to re-engineer our product development . . .").

There is no single basis of power that is uniformly effective in negotiation. However, reward and punishment power are less stable forms of power because they require constant maintenance. In contrast, status, attraction, and expertise are more intrinsically based forms of power.

ALTERNATIVES TO AGREEMENT

The most important source of power in negotiation is a person's alternative to negotiated agreements, or BATNA (Fisher, Ury, and Patton, 1991). The person who has a more attractive alternative option may effectively use that option to extract a larger share of the bargaining surplus. Negotiators who have an alternative are more likely to reap greater distributive gains and joint gains than negotiators who do not (Pinkley, Neale, and Bennett, in press). Further, the more attractive or valuable the alternative to negotiated agreement, the greater the benefits are for personal and joint outcomes. Finally, and perhaps most important, the better your own alternative relative to an opponent's alternative, the larger your piece of the resource pie. Clearly, the best way to enhance individual gain in negotiation is to enhance your BATNA.

Who needs to know about a BATNA for it to be effective? When a negotiator has an attractive BATNA, the size of the pie, or joint gain, increases. However, for a negotiator to receive a bigger slice of the pie, both parties must be aware that the other negotiator has an attractive BATNA (Pinkley, 1993). In summary, alternatives to agreement enhance distributive gains and promote integrative agreement when both parties are aware of the alternatives.

When to Walk and When to Stay

A negotiator should settle for outcomes that exceed his or her reservation point and walk away from negotiations that promise little or no chance of meeting his or her minimum terms. However, people frequently settle for outcomes that are worse than what they could have had by agreeing to another course of action. Furthermore, people often fail to reach agreement and exercise their BATNA when they are clearly better off reaching a mutual settlement. For example, most strikes are eventually settled on terms that could have been reached earlier, without parties incurring the costs that the strike imposes (Keenan and Wilson, 1993; Roth, 1993). Why is this? In the chapters to come, we'll examine some of the key reasons why negotiators behave in ways that work against their own interests.

Targeting for Success

We have been discussing the importance of BATNAs, or least acceptable terms. However, target points and goals also affect negotiations. In general, specific, challenging, and difficult goals result in greater profit for negotiators than do easy or nonspecific goals (Huber and Neale, 1986, 1987; Neale, Northcraft, and Earley, 1990). In many cases, non-specific or easy goals lead to compromise agreements. Adjusting the negotiator's perception of possible goals or limits may shape what a negotiator believes are attainable or even acceptable outcomes. There tends to be a self-regulating effect on goal development: Negotiators who are originally assigned easy goals set harder new goals. In spite of adjustments, however, their new goals are significantly easier than the easier goals chosen by the difficult-goal subjects.

Negotiator's Bargaining Range

A negotiator's bargaining range is the distance between his or her reservation point and target point. In some cases the distance may be broad, such as when a negotiator has an unattractive alternative to negotiation but nevertheless has high aspirations. In other cases, the distance may be narrow, as when a negotiator has attractive alternatives to negotiated agreement but modest aspirations. How does the negotiator's bargaining range affect settlements?

Negotiators with low minimum goals generally feel more successful than do those with higher minimum goals, even when the final settlement is identical (Thompson, 1995a). In a complementary fashion, negotiators with low aspirations feel more successful than do those with higher aspirations, even when the final settlement is identical. When the two are put to the test, aspirations influence negotiators' perception of success more than do minimum goals. And consequently, aspirations rather than reservation values determine the "final demands" made by negotiators. That is, negotiators with low minimum goals and high aspirations demand more from their opponents than do negotiators with high minimum goals and low aspirations. The message is that if you want to "feel successful," you should keep your aspirations in check.

CAPSTONE: A PREPARATION WORKSHEET

The most important aspect of negotiation occurs before negotiators ever sit down at the bargaining table. Preparation is the key to effective negotiation. Unfortunately, many negotiators do not adequately prepare for negotiation. This is not because they lack the motivation, but because it is not clear to them exactly how to prepare and *how* they should use this ever-precious time. A key mistake is to prepare by solely focusing on oneself. Preparation involves focusing on one's own issues and concerns as well as those of the other side.

What follows is a worksheet for a management student who is preparing for salary negotiations with potential employers. This is an extremely important negotiation, as it will affect one's livelihood and welfare for years to come. A misassumption at this point can have dramatic effects on one's personal and professional life. We have included an example to more concretely illustrate our principles. This preparation worksheet can be easily modified to suit any type of negotiation.

Step 1: Determine Your BATNA

A negotiator always has a BATNA. Some students who are beginning to negotiate with firms will agitatedly claim that they do not have a BATNA because they do not have any job offers in hand. What they are saying is that they do not have what they consider to be an *attractive* BATNA, but they inevitably have a plan of what they will do if they do not get a job offer. Perhaps they will travel in Europe; perhaps they will do freelance or volunteer work, take a research assistantship at a university, or search for a nonprofessional job while they continue their career search. All of these are BATNAs; they should be thought about and the best one focused upon and evaluated carefully.

Step 2: Improve Your BATNA

Our BATNAs are never as attractive as we'd like them to be. At the rare times when we have two or more fabulous job offers in hand, two bids on our house, and lucrative investment opportunities, we can afford to push for a lot more in negotiations.

Unfortunately, this does not characterize most negotiation situations. Often our BATNA is embarrassingly unattractive. Nevertheless, it is important to think about how we might improve upon our BATNA. Most negotiators do not spend adequate time attempting to improve their current situation. As a result, they approach negotiations feeling more desperate than they should.

Improving a BATNA is often difficult because it seems to be at odds with what a negotiator is trying to do. Consider Tom, a second-year student who, in May, still does not have a job lined up. He has an interview scheduled on Friday of next week with a major telecommunications company. Feeling somewhat desperate, Tom discussed the upcoming interview with a friend practiced in negotiation. The friend suggested that Tom attempt to line up a position as a research assistant in the marketing department of the business school. At first Tom resisted: "Why should I do that now? Shouldn't I do that if I strike out at the company? Then I can look for something here." Tom's friend then explained, "No, that is precisely the point; you will have a better interview (and subsequent negotiation) if you have alternative options." It took about three days of Tom's time to talk with two professors who were interested in hiring a research intern to work on a marketing project at a local company. They were delighted to have Tom's expertise and offered him a job that he was able to use as a BATNA in his negotiations with the telecommunications company, which eventually did offer him a position.

Step 3: Determine the Other Party's BATNA

Developing your own BATNA is only half of the work that needs to be done before the negotiation. The next step is to determine the other party's BATNA. Many people throw up their hands at this prospect, claiming that such a task is impossible. Such a task *is* possible, but it requires tapping into multiple sources of information and being creative. Consider Sal, who recently received an offer from a small progressive software firm that had been in operation for only two years. She was reasonably happy with the offer but wondered what would happen if she attempted to negotiate some of the terms, specifically the salary.

As a first step, Sal visited the career placement center and got all the printed information she could about the firm. This was not much because the company was so new. Next, Sal contacted some of the associates she had met while on her interview at the firm and suggested that they have a casual lunch. At the lunch, Sal was careful not to grill them for information but made inquiries into where the company was going and what problems there were to solve. This meeting revealed some important information about the firm's current situation. Sal then went to the World Wide Web and did a search on the company that revealed a lot of information about the company's current prospects. The website turned up the names of some individuals who, although not employed by the company, seemed to have an insider view. Sal contacted these people through the Internet. Finally, Sal had a friend contact the personnel department of the company. The friend explained that he was considering going to business school someday and wanted to find out about the company and its salary structure (all of this was true).

Through her search process, Sal was able to better determine the following important information about the company: the wage structure of the company, where the company falls in the distribution of players in its industry, its standard package, insurance, which elements were variable (e.g., bonus, vacation), recent staff problems and needs, and what candidate qualities were considered most important.

Step 4: Determine the Issue Mix

You've made your best assessment of the other party's BATNA. The negotiation is fast approaching. Now what? The next step is to determine the issues that are important to you in this negotiation. Do not make the mistake of letting the other party define the issues for you. Be ready to talk about your concerns and priorities.

After you have determined which issues are important from your perspective, go back through your list and attempt to create an even more detailed list, breaking each of the issues down into smaller and smaller subsets. For example, Andrew, in his negotiations with a Chicago firm, initially listed salary, signing bonus, vacation, and moving expenses as his key issues. On a second pass through his list, Andrew listed base salary, fringe benefits, commissions, vacation duration, paid vacation, and flextime opportunities as issues to discuss with the employer. Breaking the issues up into smaller and smaller issues does two things. First, it allows the negotiator to be much more specific about what is important (e.g., the paid aspect of a vacation or the number of days allowed off). Second, it provides much greater opportunity for creative agreements, as we'll see in chapter 4.

In addition to focusing on the issues and concerns of importance to you, anticipate the other party's perspective. Again, information and research can help here.

If you find yourself in the lucky position of having multiple offers, you are then faced with a choice. First, you should recognize this enviable position as an approach–approach conflict. How should you weigh the choices? The simplest way is to construct a grid where you list the choices along a row (e.g., firm x, firm y) and the relevant attributes along a column underneath (e.g., salary, fringe benefits, travel, vacation, bonus, etc.). Then, fill in the grid with the details of the offer and how they "stack up" compared to the others (on a 1 to 5 or 1 to 10 scale in your mind). Next, you can simply add down the columns to find a quick "winner." A more sophisticated version of this strategy is to multiply each grid value by how important it is before adding down columns (with importance defined on a 1 to 5 scale). For example, for most of us, salary is highly important (maybe a 5), whereas moving expenses are less important (maybe a 1 or 2). This gives a more fine-grained assessment. This assessment technique is known as **MAUT,** or **multiattribute utility technique.** We discuss it further in chapter 6.

Step 5: Think about the Best Way to Position and Present Your Opening Offer (or Counteroffer)

Remember to couch your offer in terms of a clear rationale. Use objective standards. Focus and select those standards that are favorable to you and be prepared to indicate why standards unfavorable to you are inappropriate.

Consider Marie, who landed a job offer in a consulting firm. Marie is on the young side for a senior management position and was offered a starting salary that was on the low side for senior management personnel. Marie did not have a particularly strong BATNA. In the next meeting with the employer, Marie carefully pointed out that she was indeed younger than most of the other senior management but that this was a great advantage for the company because she was young and energetic and on the upslope of what was sure to be a long and productive career. In short, Marie sold herself as having more to offer, rather than as having a lot of experience. The strategy worked.

Step 6: Think about Possible Tricks and How to Deal with Them

Negotiators have a million ways of asking people about their BATNAs. Asking a potential job recruit about their current salary and wage package is one of them. Remember that this is your business, not the recruiter's. If you are currently employed, you might want to redirect the discussion by indicating what it is going to take to move you (e.g., a more exciting job and a wage package commensurate with the job). If you are not employed, respond by explaining what it will take to hire you. Again, ward off direct attacks about previous wages by explaining that whether or not you will accept a position depends on the nature of the job offer and wage package.

You should be prepared to take the initiative in the conversation, especially for less structured interviews further along in the process of negotiation. Often it is helpful to practice by roleplaying.

If the employer attempts to get you to talk about why you are leaving a former job or why you are interested in leaving, avoid falling into the trap of trashing a former employer, even if you did have a miserable experience. It is a small world and things might come around. Even more importantly, the employer will probably get the wrong impression about you (e.g., regard you as a troublemaker or overly critical).

If you have not yet been offered the job but sense that the employer is wanting to find out what you would want in a job offer, avoid talking about salary or specific terms until you have a job offer. You are in a much weaker position to negotiate before you have a job offer than after you are offered a position. If you have been told that "things will work out" or that "a job offer is coming," express appreciation and inquire when you will receive formal notice. After that, schedule a meeting to talk about the terms.

While you are negotiating, you should assume that everything is negotiable. If you are told that some aspect of the job is "not negotiable," ask questions, such as whether everyone (new hires and veterans) receive the same treatment.

CONCLUSION

Proper preparation places the negotiator at a strategic advantage at the bargaining table. The negotiator who has analyzed his or her target and reservation points, rather than idealized them, is in a much better position to achieve his or her objectives. The negotiator who has prepared for a negotiation knows when to walk away and how much is reasonable to concede. The prepared negotiator is less likely to be tricked or duped by the other side. We have discussed the fundamentals and the finetuning of what to do prior to negotiation, but what should a negotiator do when actually seated at the negotiation table—especially when the other party may do or say some things that are not expected? This is the subject of our next chapter.

TAKE-AWAYS

- When preparing for negotiation, don't spend time thinking about what you'd like to have. Focus on what you'll do if you don't reach agreement.
- The essence of bargaining power is determined before a negotiator walks into the negotiation room. It is the power of (good) alternatives.
- A negotiator should not attempt to reach agreement at all cost. It is important to know when to walk away from the bargaining table.
- The most valuable information we can have in negotiation is knowing our opponent's best alternative to negotiating with us.

CHAPTER 3

The Conduct of Negotiation: *What to Do at the Bargaining Table*

Terry had just completed a final round of interviewing at a major consulting firm. She thought that the final interview, although grueling, had gone quite well. She was delighted to receive a phone call from the recruiter the following morning offering her a position in the company.

Terry was so relieved to get the offer that she blurted out, "Oh, that's great. I would love to work for your company." When the recruiter remarked, "I'm delighted that we don't have any competition to worry about," Terry realized her first mistake.

Terry hurriedly tried to regain her composure when the recruiter laid out the basic offer: a salary of $62,000, two weeks vacation, profit-sharing options, and standard health benefits. "Any questions?" asked the recruiter. Terry fumbled, "Can the salary be increased?" "What did you have in mind?" Terry offered $65,000. The recruiter said, "OK. We can do that. I will write up a final contract and put it in overnight mail. I'll also inform everyone you're on board." Terry hung up the phone, feeling a mixture of excitement but also a sinking feeling . . . she had not played her cards right at the bargaining table, and even more upsetting, it was not clear how she should have optimally handled the situation.

Y ou've analyzed the negotiation situation as best you can. You've thought about your own BATNA in a realistic fashion, developed a clear reservation point, and have used all available information to assess your opponent's BATNA. Now the time has come for real face-to-face negotiation. Now what? Who should make the first offer? How should you respond? How much should you concede the first time around? Things happened very fast for Terry, who was not ready when the recruiter began the negotiation. What should she have done? This chapter explores this question in detail.

The entire process of making a first offer and then ending up with a mutual settlement is known as the negotiation dance (Raiffa, 1982). Unfortunately, most of us have never taken lessons or know what to do. Should we lead? Follow? There are a few hard and fast rules of thumb, but there are many choices that the negotiator must make that are not so clear cut. We wrestle with these in this chapter.

OPENERS: WHO SHOULD MAKE THE FIRST OFFER AND WHAT SHOULD IT BE?

There are a number of factors to think about when considering whether to make the first offer. Contrary to popular thought, there is no reliable advantage for whomever makes the first offer in a negotiation situation. The ideal first offer is a proposal that barely exceeds the other party's reservation point. Such an offer will not be perceived by the opponent as "insultingly low" or "ridiculous" because, by definition, it is in the bargaining zone. Another wonderful feature of this offer is that if the other party accepts it, you are guaranteed all of the bargaining surplus. If you are highly confident of your opponent's reservation price, making the first offer can be advantageous.

Unfortunately, in most circumstances it is unlikely that we can nail down the other party's reservation point in such a precise fashion. When you don't know the other party's reservation point, you may overestimate his or her bargaining position and make too generous an offer. That is, a negotiator makes an offer well within the bargaining zone that gives away too much of the surplus. As a result, the negotiator loses bargaining ground. This is known as the **winner's curse** (Akerlof, 1970; Neale and Bazerman, 1991). If your first offer is immediately accepted by the other party, you have probably experienced the winner's curse. When this happens, it is difficult and awkward to attempt to retract your offer and offer less. As we'll see, you could be accused of bargaining in bad faith.

A sure-fire way to avoid the winner's curse is to make an offer that is so low or high (depending on whether you are a buyer or a seller, respectively) that it is virtually impossible that the other party will immediately accept it. Imagine, for example, that someone offered $5,000 for a car with a sticker price of $16,000, or that the person selling a $275,000 list-price home received an offer of $78,000. These offers certainly do not run the risk of being immediately accepted—they are likely to be laughed at, scoffed at, and irreparably sour the bargaining relationship. It is very difficult to recover from making a bad impression in negotiation. Negotiators should not substitute ridiculously low offers for thorough preparation.

As a general rule, whenever the other party has more information than you do, it is more risky to make the first offer. This does not mean that we should go through life never making a first offer. There are distinct advantages associated with making the first offer. The first offer that falls *within the bargaining zone* can serve as a powerful focal point. Recall in the previous chapter the example of the wheel of fortune and people's estimates of African nations in the UN. That was a case of insufficient adjustment from an arbitrary anchor. Making the first offer protects us against falling prey to a similar anchoring effect when we hear of the opponent's offer. Ideally, our first offer will act as an anchor for the opponent's counteroffer.

THE COUNTEROFFER

If you have made an offer to your opponent, then you should expect to receive some sort of counteroffer. Once you make an offer and put it on the table, be patient. It is time for your opponent to respond. In certain situations, patience and silence can be an important negotiation tool. Do not interpret silence on the other person's part to be a rejection of your offer. Wait to hear a response before making a concession.

Conversely, if your opponent has made you an offer, then the ball is in your court. It is wise to make a counteroffer in a timely fashion. This does two things. First, it diminishes the prominence of the opponent's initial offer as a key anchor. Second, it signals a willingness to negotiate.

A CLEAR RATIONALE

Negotiation does not simply consist of making offers back and forth. Rather, negotiators provide rationales and justifications for their proposals. Whereas it could be argued that it all comes down to dollars and cents, the way in which an offer is presented or framed can affect the course of negotiations. As a general rule, it is wise to present your offer with some rationale, and, ideally, your rationale should precede your offer.

To the extent that proposals are labeled as "fair" or "even splits" or "compromise" solutions, they appear to carry more weight. Round numbers and even divisions also seem to provide more rationale than arbitrary-appearing numbers.

CRYSTAL BALLS

If parties to a negotiation eventually concede, what is the point of going back and forth? Why can't negotiators just see the end of the road and immediately get there and save everyone a lot of time? In short, if we know something about parties' opening offers, can we predict the outcome of the negotiation?

The anecdotal answer appears to be yes. The best prediction of the final settlement of a negotiation is the midpoint between the first two offers on the table *that are within the bargaining zone* (Raiffa, 1982). The last part of the preceding statement is extremely important. Outlandish initial offers do not help negotiators to anchor on a final settlement that is more favorable to them.

By exchanging offers, negotiators may gain a sense of the bargaining zone. People need to feel a sense of control over the process of negotiation; immediately jumping to a final settlement robs people of this process. Whereas the final settlement may be a midpoint between the first two offers in the bargaining zone, this is certainly not always true: Patience and absence of time pressure can help the negotiator.

MAKING CONCESSIONS

First offers are "openers." It is rare (but not impossible) for a first offer to be accepted. Most negotiators expect to make concessions during negotiation. (One exception is a bargaining style known as **boulwarism,** after Boulware, former CEO of General Electric, who believed in making one's first offer one's final offer. As you might expect, this strategy is not very effective and often engenders hostility from the other side.) The question facing negotiators is what is the best way to make concessions so as to maximize their share of the bargaining zone. Two things to consider when formulating counteroffers and concessions are the **pattern of concessions** and the **degree of concessions.**

Pattern of Concessions

It is almost a law of the universe that concessions take place in a quid pro quo fashion, meaning that parties expect a back-and-forth exchange of concessions between the parties. People expect that concessions will be responded to with concessions in kind. Negotiators *should not* offer more than a single concession at a time to an opponent. Wait for a concession on the opponent's part before making further concessions. An exception to this would be a situation in which you felt that the opponent's offer was truly near his or her reservation point.

Degree of Concessions

Even though negotiators may exchange concessions in a back-and-forth method, this does not say anything about the degree of concessions made by each party. Thus, a second consideration when making concessions is to determine how much to concede. The usual measure of a concession is the amount reduced or added (depending upon whether one is a seller or buyer) from one's previous concession. It is unwise to make consistently greater concessions than one's opponent.

The graduated reduction in tension, or GRIT, model (Osgood, 1962) is a method whereby parties may avoid escalating conflict and reach mutual settlement. The GRIT model, based upon the reciprocity principle, calls for one party to make a concession and to invite the other party to reciprocate by making a concession. The concession offered by the first party is significant, but not so much that the offering party is tremendously disadvantaged if the opponent fails to reciprocate.

Hilty and Carnevale (1993) examined the degree of concessions made by negotiators over different points in the negotiation process (e.g., early on versus later). They compared black hat/white hat negotiators with white hat/black hat negotiators. BH/WH negotiators began with a tough stance and made few early concessions and later made larger concessions. WH/BH negotiators did the opposite: They began with generous concessions and then became tough and unyielding. The BH/WH concession strategy proved to be more effective than the WH/BH strategy in eliciting concessions from an opponent.

BARGAINING IN GOOD FAITH

"Good-faith bargaining" refers to the etiquette and ethics of negotiation. There are no prescribed rules, and there is often considerable disagreement about what constitutes appropriate behavior. Good-faith bargaining can mean many things. Often, it means that once an offer has been made by someone, it remains valid until the intended recipient rejects or accepts it. Sometimes, it means that if an offer has been made and rejected by an opponent, and if the opponent later wants to accept the offer, that the offer should still be available, even if previously rejected. Good-faith bargaining sometimes means that people should not falsify their intentions nor information to the other party.

Bargaining in good faith also means that if a negotiator makes demands on another person, which are granted, then the party will accept the terms offered and not ask for more—like Terry in the opening example.

With these differing definitions of good faith bargaining, it is easy to see how there could be considerable misunderstanding and violations. Violations of good-faith bargaining can lead to distrust and the breakdown of negotiating relationships. Violations of trust are extremely difficult to recover from, even when the party who breached the trust did not intend to violate any good-faith principle. Usually, violations of good-faith bargaining are traceable to "honest" misunderstandings between people. A good rule of thumb is to discuss expectations before negotiating so as to minimize later misunderstandings.

INFLUENCE

Whereas power refers to the basis of a person's influence over another in an interdependent context, influence refers to the method or strategy by which people exercise or use their power.

There are hundreds of different tactics that negotiators can use to attempt to influence the outcome of negotiation in a way favorable to themselves. According to Cialdini (1993), the majority fall within six basic categories, each guided by a fundamental social psychological principle that directs human behavior.

- Reciprocation
- Consistency
- Social proof
- Liking
- Authority
- Scarcity

Reciprocity: I'll Scratch Your Back and You Give Me a Massage

According to the **reciprocity principle,** we feel obligated to return in kind what others have offered or given to us. We referred to this powerful principle earlier as the law of the universe. This is not an overstatement, as all human societies subscribe to the rule permeating exchanges of all kinds (Gouldner, 1960). Feelings of indebtedness are so powerful that if unresolved, they carry on into the future and are passed on to the next generation to repay. People feel upset and distressed if they have received a favor from another person and are prevented from returning it. Not surprisingly, people are aware of the powerful grip that reciprocity has on them. Often people will turn down favors and rewards from others because they do not want to be obligated.

So far we have said that reciprocity is powerful. There seems to be nothing inherently illogical or dangerous with reciprocity with regard to negotiation. Usually, reciprocity pertains more to the pattern of concessions than to the degree of concessions. This means that if someone does us a favor or makes a concession, we feel obligated to return the favor or concession. However, unless we are careful, we could be victimized by an opponent who preys on our feelings of indebtedness.

For example, suppose the opponent provides us with a favor, gift, or service that we never invited and perhaps even attempted to avoid. Our attempts to return it have been denied and we are left with the unwanted gift. Even under these circumstances, the reciprocity rule may operate. Thus, we should beware of the unsolicited gift from our real estate agent, the courtesy token from our business associate, and the free lunch from the merger firm. When faced with these situations, we should acknowledge the favor and then, if we still feel indebted, return the favor on a similar level.

Consistency: I Always Do What I Say

The **consistency principle** is the fundamental need to appear to be consistent in our beliefs, feelings, and behaviors, not only to others, but also to ourselves. To contradict ourselves, whether in thought or in deed, is a sign of irrationality.

What are the implications of the consistency principle for the negotiator? If a negotiator agrees to something (i.e., particular set of terms, etc.) he or she is led by psychological forces to follow through. A common bargaining ploy of salespeople is to ask customers about their intentions to buy, for example, "Are you ready to buy a car today at the right price?" Most people would agree to this statement because it does not obligate them to any particular terms. However, powerful psychological commitment processes begin to operate once we acknowledge ourselves to be a "buyer."

The **foot-in-the-door technique** illustrates the power of commitment. In this technique, a person is asked to agree to a small favor (such as agreeing with a statement like the above, or signing a petition). Later, the same person is confronted with a larger request (e.g., buying a car or voting with a particular coalition in a departmental meeting). The probability that the person will agree to the larger request is tremendously increased when that person previously agreed to the smaller request. Why? According to the commitment principle, the smaller request is a public commitment to follow through. To not agree to the larger request would be an admission of inconsistency.

Social Proof: I'll Have What She's Having

In the movie *When Harry Met Sally,* Sally (Meg Ryan) is having lunch with Harry (Billy Crystal) and demonstrating how women can fake sexual pleasure. An older woman at a nearby table sees Sally moaning in ecstasy and tells the waitress, "I'll have what she's having." The woman used the principle of social proof to guide her own behavior.

According to the **social proof principle,** we look to the behavior of others to determine what is desirable, appropriate, and correct. This is sensible in many respects; if we want to get along with others, it only makes sense to know what they expect. However, this fundamental psychological process can work against us in negotiations if we look toward others—especially our opponent—to determine an appropriate offer or settlement.

The problem is that we do not realize the extent to which our behavior is influenced by those around us. Further, the more ambiguous the situation, the more likely we are to rely on situational cues and the behavior of others to tell us what to do.

Consider Peter, who was interested in buying an oriental rug for his new home. As a new home owner, Peter had never bought a rug before, much less an expensive oriental rug. Peter went into a rug dealership and inquired about the price of a rug that appeared to have no price tag. For that matter, none of the rugs had prominently displayed price tags. The salesperson replied that the rug was a Kashan and worth $3500. The salesperson lifted the rug and the sticker displayed its dimensions and value. Peter said he would buy it. At a cocktail party a week later, Peter listened with horror and shame as his colleagues talked about prices on oriental rugs with explicit discussions of the "marked price," which now became clear to Peter was never paid. Rather, it was customary to negotiate a price. Peter's feelings were driven by the social proof principle: his friends' behavior was proof that no one paid sticker price.

Liking: Flattery Can Get You Everywhere

The liking principle states that we are more agreeable with people whom we like. This is not too surprising. It would seem that our liking for people would be based on deep-seated values. However, our liking for people is often based on superficial, arbitrary factors (e.g., someone wearing a sweatshirt emblazoned with our college's name or with a haircut similar to ours). We like people whom we perceive to be similar to us. We tend to like people who are physically attractive. We also like people who appear to like us; in this sense, flattery is an effective social persuasion tool.

Negotiators are more likely to make concessions to people whom they like. It doesn't take too much to get someone to like us. Humor is one tactic. O'Quin and Aronoff (1981) examined the impact of humor on negotiators' willingness to agree to terms proposed by an opponent. When the "final" offer was prefaced by the joke, ". . . and I'll also throw in my pet frog," acceptance rates increased dramatically.

Negotiators in a good mood are more agreeable (Carnevale and Isen, 1986; Forgas and Moylan, 1996). Funny cartoons, unexpected little gifts, small strokes of fortune, and thinking positive thoughts all engender a good mood (see Isen and Baron, 1991, for a review). We know of a salesperson who has a smiling face on her business card. This serves two purposes: It engenders a good mood whenever people see her card, and, by the psychological process of association, it links positive feelings to the salesperson's name and company.

Negotiators are more likely to make concessions when negotiating with people they know and like. Savvy negotiators increase their effectiveness by making themselves familiar to the other party. Instead of having a single-shot negotiation, they suggest a preliminary meeting over drinks and follow with a few phone calls and unexpected gifts. By the time of the final negotiation, the target negotiator feels as though he or she is interacting with an old friend.

Authority: The Power of a White Coat

The **authority principle** states that we are inclined to accept the opinions, directions, and admonitions of people whom we consider to be legitimate authority figures. Again, this seems like perfectly reasonable behavior for the most part.

However, consider the commercials for pain reliever that starred actor Robert Young. Robert Young is not, nor ever was, a medical doctor. However, he played a doctor on the TV series *Marcus Welby, M.D.* In that show, he wore a white doctor's coat, a classic authority symbol. In the commercial, he played the role of a doctor. Despite the fact that the viewing audience knew he had no formal medical training, which he acknowledged himself, he still was a powerful authority figure.

The authority principle can lead the negotiator astray if the person with whom we are negotiating is not a real authority but merely acting as one. Remarkably and regrettably, most of us are swayed by salient signs or markers of authority (e.g., coat and tie, business card, portable phone, fast talk) more than real authority.

The power of authority is so strong that people will often do things that they later regret and even find abhorrent. The most dramatic illustration of the power of authority was demonstrated in a series of experiments at Yale University (Milgram, 1974). Imagine your-self in the following situation:

You answer an ad in the paper asking for participants in a study on memory and learning. When you arrive at the facility, you meet another participant, who is a 47-year-old, overweight, good-natured man. An experimenter in a white coat explains that one of you will play the role of a teacher and the other a learner. You randomly draw the role of the teacher. Your job, the ex-perimenter explains to you, is to teach the other participant a list of word pairs (e.g., blue-box, nice-day, etc.) and test him. The experimenter instructs you to deliver an electric shock to the learner whenever he makes a mistake so as to examine the effects of punishment on learning.

The learner is strapped into a chair in an adjacent room and electrodes are attached to his arm. You are seated in front of a shock generator that has 30 switches, from 15 to 450 volts. Each switch is labeled, beginning with "Slight Shock" to "Danger: Severe Shock" to an ominous "XXX" next to the highest levels. The experimenter tells you that the first time the learner makes a mistake, you should give him a shock of 15 volts (the smallest amount) and then increase to the next highest switch for each subsequent mistake. The experimenter gives you a sample shock of 45 volts, which is quite painful.

You then begin the testing phase. After a few minutes, the learner makes a mistake and you shock him. This continues until you get to the 75-volt level, and you hear him scream from the other room. You become concerned and ask the experimenter what you should do. The experimenter instructs you to "please continue." You go on and the screaming gets worse. Before reading further, stop and predict what you think most people do at this point.

When this question was posed to psychiatrists, they estimated that only about 1% of the population would continue to the maximum amount of 450 volts. As it happens, nearly 63% of the participants delivered the 450-volt shock amidst the agonizing screams and pleas of the learner to stop. The average amount of shock given was 360 volts.

Milgram (1963) describes a typical participant's response in the teacher role:

> I observed a mature and initially poised businessman enter the laboratory smiling and confi-dent. Within 20 minutes he was reduced to a twitching, stuttering wreck, who was rapidly approaching a point of nervous collapse. He constantly pulled his earlobe, and twisted his hands. At one point, he pushed his fist into his forehead and muttered, "Oh God; let's stop it." And yet he continued to respond to every word of the experimenter and obeyed to the end. (p. 377)

Most people read the report of Milgram's research studies with a mixture of horror and amazement. Virtually all believe that had *they* been in the situation, they would not have complied. Yet, several dozen follow-up studies indicated that people conform to the powerful voice of authority—even against their better judgment.

Most con artists know that people are influenced by the trappings of authority, and so they adopt these as part of their game. In negotiations, many people often fall into the trap of attempting to negotiate with persons who do not possess legitimate authority to make deci-sions. Unfortunately, this is usually revealed to us after we have made concessions and are consequently left with little bargaining power.

Scarcity: Available Only While They Last . . .

The **scarcity principle** states that we find more appealing those things which appear to be rare, hard to get, or in high demand. Think of the times when you've been in an unfamiliar city and have looked at the length of the waiting line to determine the quality of a restaurant.

The same principle holds in negotiation contexts. People become more interested and anxious when they feel that a deal has a limited time horizon or is a special "one-time" offer.

The phenomenon known as **psychological reactance** (Brehm, 1966), or more commonly, "reverse psychology," is the tendency of people to do the opposite of what someone is trying to get them to do. For example, consider the Blanes, who had two homes for sale in the same city. The Blanes' goal was to sell the more expensive home. Rather than making both homes appear equally attractive and available, the savvy real estate agent would show the lesser-priced home and strongly push its features. While showing this home, he would make vague references to the other home and remark, "You don't want to see that one; that's the one they would like to keep." At this point, almost all of his clients would insist on seeing the second house. The agent would adopt a very different demeanor when showing the second house, all the time making vague references to the owners' desire to keep this home. The reluctance to sell and the owners' passion for the home would generate excitement about the more expensive home. In terms of the scarcity principle, the second home was harder to get and, therefore, more desirable. When buyers indicated they wanted to make an offer on the second home, the realtor would attempt to talk the buyers out of making the offer on the second home and into the first home. This had the effect of magnifying the buyers' desire to own the second home—the psychological reactance effect. Of course, all along, the sellers and the agent, who earned a higher commission, desired to sell the more expensive home.

THE MOST COMMONLY ASKED QUESTIONS

Students and professional negotiators commonly wrestle with tough negotiation situations. There are about as many different answers to these questions as there are people with opinions. Next, we address some of the most common questions.

Should I Reveal My Reservation Price?

Revealing your reservation price is generally not a good strategy unless your reservation price is very good and you suspect that the bargaining zone is very narrow. If you reveal your reservation price, be prepared for the other party to offer you your reservation price.

As we saw earlier, the most valuable piece of information you could have about your opponent is his or her reservation price. This allows you to make your opponent an offer that barely exceeds his or her reservation price and claim all of the bargaining surplus for yourself. However, your opponent is no dummy and is not likely to reveal his or her reservation price. By the same token, if you reveal your reservation price, there is little to stop your opponent from throwing you a bone and claiming all of the surplus for him- or herself.

Some negotiators want to reveal their reservation price to show that they are bargaining in good faith and demonstrate trust in the other party. These negotiators rely on their opponent's good will and trust their opponent not to take undue advantage of this information. This is a flawed and ineffective strategy. Negotiation is not an issue of trust; it is an issue of strategy. The purpose of negotiation is to maximize your surplus, so why create a conflict of interest in the other party by "trusting" them with your reservation point?

In some cases, negotiators are seduced into revealing their reservation price when their opponent assumes that they do not have a good BATNA. Consider, for example, Lucille, a manager of a small advertising company that books events and shows. One of her hard-driving clients was trying to talk Lucille down from a quote for a children's show to be held at a major amphitheater. The client challenged Lucille by speculating that she did not have "any real overhead." Outraged, Lucille told the client in detail about where the advertising dollars were spent. After her harangue, the client agreed to pay just a fraction more than the overhead costs and "not a penny more." Negotiators, wanting to prove their worth, will offer their reservation price as a defensive tactic. Lucille was tricked by her opponent into revealing her BATNA. A better strategy would have been to redirect the discussion to different scenarios that might be worked out.

Should I Lie about My Reservation Price?

If negotiators do well for themselves by not revealing their reservation point, perhaps they might do even better by lying, misrepresenting, or exaggerating their reservation point. This is not advisable as a negotiation strategy for several important reasons.

First, lying about your reservation point reduces the size of the bargaining zone. This means that negotiations will sometimes end in impasse in situations in which the negotiator would prefer to reach an agreement. It is very difficult to attempt to save face or retract bold statements that are made by negotiators who lie about their reservation point. The most common lie in negotiation is, "This is my final offer." It is embarrassing to continue negotiating after making such a statement.

There is another problem with lying that is associated with your reputation. It is a very small world, and people in the business community develop reputations that quickly spread via electronic mail, telephone, and word of mouth. It is desirable to avoid being labeled as a negotiator who is more bark than bite and who misrepresents him- or herself at the negotiation table. Misrepresenting your reservation price is a poor substitute for preparation and developing strategy.

How Can I Smoke out a Bluffer? How Can I Tell Whether Someone Is Lying to Me?

The answer to this question depends on what is being lied about. There are many things to lie about in negotiation. Some lies may be complete falsifications (such as misrepresenting the inspection report on a building or pretending that another buyer will be calling at any moment with an offer); other lies may be exaggerations (exaggerating the appraisal value of a particular property; exaggerating the attractiveness of one's BATNA).

It is more difficult for liars to successfully carry off hard lies (i.e., complete falsifications of information) than to carry off easy lies (exaggerations). Consequently, it is easier for negotiators to detect complete falsifications.

What should you do to maximize the chances of catching a lie in negotiation? It is generally not an effective lie-detection strategy to ask someone whether they are lying. Usually, they will say no. So, what can you do? There are three steps the negotiator should take in this regard. First, the negotiator should test for consistency in the other party's statements. Detectives and lawyers ask people who they think might be lying several questions. The questions are designed so that inconsistencies will pop up if a person is lying. It is very difficult for even the best of liars to be perfectly consistent in all aspects of a lie.

Second, the negotiator should enrich the mode of communication. If negotiations have been proceeding by phone, written correspondence, or e-mail, the negotiator who wants to catch a lie should insist on a face-to-face interaction. It is much more difficult for liars to monitor themselves when the communication modality is multichanneled (as it is in face-to-face negotiations). Telltale signs of lying are often found in nonverbal "leakage," such as in the hands or body, rather than the face or words, which liars usually carefully monitor (Ekman, 1992).

Finally, the negotiator should ask to see *proof* or *evidence* other than the individual's word. For example, if the person with whom we are negotiating claims that the transmission in the car is less than a year old, we should ask to see receipts and contact the shop that replaced the transmission.

Should I Try to Talk the Other Party Out of Her Reservation Point?

Probably not. Assuming that the other party is reasonably intelligent, motivated, and informed (like you), he or she is not likely to fall prey to this readily transparent negotiation ploy. Remember the psychological reactance principle we discussed earlier. Such attempts may actually backfire, entrenching the party more steadfastly in his or her position.

Furthermore, you want to avoid the other negotiator's turning the tables on you with similar influence attempts. You probably would not fall for it, so why should they?

Some negotiators are inclined to use scare tactics such as, "If you don't sell your house to us, there won't be another buyer . . . ," or "You'll regret not buying this company from me in 10 years when I'm a billionaire. . . ." Scare tactics are not likely to be effective. Like the reactance principle, they will generally backfire or engender ill will.

Is It Better to Be a Tough or Soft Negotiator?

Negotiators often make the mistake of viewing themselves as having to choose between one of two completely different approaches: being tough or soft. The tough negotiator is unflinching, makes high demands, concedes very little, and holds out. In contrast, the soft negotiator typically offers the first magnanimous concession, reveals his or her reservation price, and is concerned with making sure the other party "feels good." Neither approach is effective. Both approaches are likely to lead to outcomes that negotiators regret or resent.

The tough negotiator is likely to walk away from a lot of profitable interactions and may gain a reputation for being stubborn. This may intimidate others, but it won't change the size of the bargaining zone, and it won't make the tough negotiator any richer.

The soft negotiator agrees too readily and never makes much of a surplus. The soft negotiator is liked by his or her opponents but is not respected. The constituents of the soft negotiator are typically angry and disgusted: "Why didn't you try to get more for us?"

The good news is that being tough or soft are not the only two choices. The approach recommended in this book is **strategic creativity.** That is, the negotiator should be strategic in terms of attempting to maximize his or her share of the resources, but also be creative about how to achieve this. The strategically creative approach shares features in common with Fisher, Ury, and Patton's (1991) principled negotiation approach and Bazerman and Neale's (1992) rational approach. The essence of this style of bargaining is that it is possible to get what you want and feel good about doing it. However, the approach takes work and skill. It is the subject of chapter 4.

Should I Attempt to Be Fair?

A typical negotiation situation usually involves two parties who each believe they are making whole-hearted, good-faith efforts to be fair and reasonable. Unfortunately, each party's idea of "fair and reasonable" seems worlds apart and conflict rages on. So what's going on?

Is one person lying? Are both people lying? No. Usually, both people are honestly putting forth "fair" settlement terms. The problem is that "fairness" is a vague concept that can be interpreted in many different ways.

There are about as many definitions of fairness as there are negotiators. Compounding this problem is the fact that most negotiators' ideas about fairness tend to be self-serving or egocentric (i.e., slanted in their own favor). Two people who are each committed to finding "higher ground" and a "fair" solution, but who have completely opposing viewpoints on how to do this, will experience conflict and difficulty negotiating.

The right question to ask in a negotiation situation is not *whether* to be fair, but *how* to be fair. Do you want to split resources evenly? equitably? or focus on people's needs? Be explicit and ask the other party to be explicit. If you find the other person making appeals to "fairness," recognize this as a bargaining ploy and ask the other party to clarify what he or she has in mind. It may be a surprise to realize that both of you desire a "fair" outcome, but have very different ideas about how to achieve this.

Should I Make a "Final Offer" or Commit to a Position?

In general, taking such a stance is not an effective negotiation strategy. Making an irrevocable commitment such as a "final offer" really should be done only when you mean it and you feel comfortable walking away from the bargaining table. Of course, you should only walk away from the bargaining table if your BATNA represents a more attractive option for you to pursue.

Making a commitment to intimidate the other side is risky. First, it is difficult to make "binding" commitments that appear to be credible. More important, it is difficult to reverse or take back such statements once they are made, at least without looking or feeling foolish.

What Do I Do if the Other Side Makes a Public Commitment and They're Reluctant to Budge?

You should recognize this as a negotiation ploy or strategy. Just because the opponent has told his or her spouse, boss, or the press that he or she is going to sell the company for a given amount does not mean that you are committed to this price. There are several steps you can take whenever the other person seems to be taking an irrevocable stance, such as labeling an offer as "final."

First, you may not want to recognize statements made by the other party in the heat of conflict. You might say, "Let me consider your offer and get back to you" rather than, "So if this is your final offer, I guess things are over." By not acknowledging the finality of their offer, you provide the other party with an "out" to later resume negotiations.

In other situations, you may have to help the other party by finding a face-saving strategy. Often, this can be achieved by relabeling some of the terms of the negotiation. An excellent example of face saving occurred in the General Motors–Canadian UAW strike talks. The Canadian union had insisted on a wage increase; GM wanted to institute a profit-sharing scheme but keep wages at a minimum. A solution was devised that allowed each party to believe that they had achieved their main objective.

FRATERNAL TWIN MODEL

Whereas all negotiation situations involve a distributive component, so that parties are in some degree of competition, all negotiations also involve a cooperative component, so that parties seek to determine whether mutual settlement is possible to reach and agreeable to both of them. At this point, some readers may be wondering where the discussion is that explains how the negotiator can successfully claim a larger share of the pie of resources to be divided. After all, isn't this what it means to be a successful negotiator? No. It is unreasonable to believe that you can perfect or master skills that will allow you to successfully claim a larger share of the bargaining surplus than your opponent. This hope is based on a faulty belief that the other party is less knowledgeable, less skilled, or has less information than you. Except in unusual circumstances, this belief is false and is strategically disadvantageous.

A useful metaphor for the negotiator who wants to improve his or her bargaining skills is to imagine that every opponent that he or she will face is his or her fraternal twin. Assuming your fraternal twin is every bit as smart and as knowledgeable as yourself, but has different predilections and tastes, you can quickly see that any hope of outsmarting or tricking your twin will only result in bargaining impasse and failed settlement. As we will see in chapter 8, such faulty beliefs are pervasive and rooted in basic principles of social perception. The optimal approach if you are negotiating with your twin is not to attempt to outsmart or trick the other or adopt a tough stance, but rather to focus on expanding the amount of available resources. By expanding the size of the pie, you can realistically hope to claim a larger slice than if the pie is small to begin with.

It is important to note that cooperation means only that the negotiator attempts to increase the amount of resources to ultimately be divided, not that the negotiator offers concessions or resources to the other party. The goal of claiming resources can best be achieved by expanding the amount of available resources. Chapter 4, examines how this may be achieved—even if the other party is not as enlightened as you.

CONCLUSION

We have reviewed how negotiators should "open" the negotiation, respond to the other party's offers, and attempt to influence the other party once at the bargaining table. Strategies that are designed to trick or intimidate the other party are not effective. Negotiators must assume that their opponent is as smart and motivated as they are.

TAKE-AWAYS

- Never reveal your BATNA or reservation price unless it is extremely attractive and you are prepared to have the other party just match it.
- The ideal opening offer is one that you are sure the other party won't immediately accept, but is serious enough that the other party will be forced to consider it.
- Be careful that your concessions are not greater and more frequent than those offered by the other party.
- Lying and making threats are not effective negotiation strategies; it is better to present a clear rationale.
- You may increase your bargaining power by using one or more of six social influence strategies: reciprocity, consistency, social proof, flattery, authority, and scarcity.

CHAPTER 4

Integrative Negotiation:
How to Be Strategically Creative

Sam, an automotive engineer, decided to start his own consulting business after working for a very large car company in Detroit and then at a smaller company on the West Coast for a couple of years. At this time, a large rift existed between academic research and the design of engines at car companies. Sam had contacts at the major car companies as well as links with academia. He spent several months drawing up a business plan built on some innovative ideas involving the development of engine models from cutting-edge academic research.

In order to build his models, Sam needed special software made by a company that was interested in reaching the lucrative automotive market, but that so far had made few inroads. Sam believed that the software company produced a better product than its main competitor, but the competitor currently had the lion's share of sales to industry and academia.

The price of the software—over $10,000—was way beyond Sam's budget. As a first step, Sam called the software company and asked whether they would consider giving him a copy because he was in business for himself. The salesman suggested that Sam just buy the $10,000 software. Disillusioned, Sam hung up and reflected on what he should do. He was convinced that both he and the software company could ultimately benefit by working out some arrangement.

Before reading further, stop and think about what you would advise Sam to do: Give up? Take out a large loan? Buy a less-expensive competitor's software? Try to work out some mutually beneficial agreement? If so, how? The early stages of most integrative negotiations look very much like Sam's dilemma. That is, it initially appears that there is a large road-block and that one of the parties must give in or nothing will come of the situation. Some people might even say that Sam has nothing to negotiate. Many people label such situations as "fixed-sum" or pure conflict. But situations like the one Sam faces contain potential for integrative agreement. This chapter can help you understand how to craft integrative agreements.

TWO EXTREMES AND A MIDDLE ROAD

Most negotiations are of one of three kinds: pure conflict, pure coordination, or mixed-motive.

Pure Conflict

In **pure conflict negotiations,** parties' interests are directly opposed: whatever one person wins, the other loses (see Figure 4–1). In Figure 4–1, the seller prefers 3.5 units of surplus (leaving the buyer –.5); the buyer prefers 3.5 units of surplus (leaving the seller –.5). Both of these options fall outside the bargaining zone (indicated by the shaded area in the figure). Note that all possible settlements in the bargaining zone sum to the same amount: $3. This represents the fixed-sum nature of pure conflict negotiations. In pure conflict, or fixed-sum situations, each party's interests are perfectly negatively correlated; there is complete divergence of interests. Any outcome that increases one party's satisfaction or utility decreases the

FIGURE 4–1. Pure Conflict

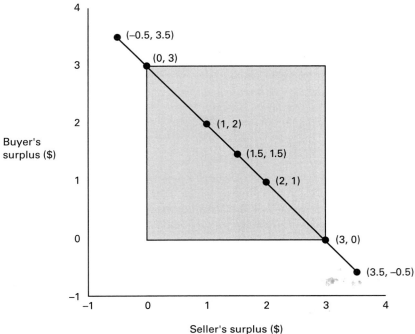

Note: numbers in parentheses are seller's and buyer's surplus, respectively.

other party's utility to the same extent. For example, two people bargaining over the price of a used car in which the seller wants more money and the buyer wants to pay as little as possible is a purely distributive negotiation situation. Pure conflict is relatively rare in negotiation situations, but, ironically, most people treat negotiations as fixed-sum enterprises.

Pure Coordination

The opposite of pure conflict is pure coordination. **Pure coordination** exists when parties' interests are perfectly compatible (Figure 4–2). Increasing one party's utility also increases the other party's utility. Parties' interests are perfectly positively correlated—they win or lose together—and their preference functions are identical. In Figure 4–2, the seller prefers three units of surplus (leaving the buyer three units); the same is true for the buyer. Note that all possible agreements in the bargaining zone sum to different amounts. The settlement point (3,3) is the one that maximizes the parties' joint outcomes. Pure coordination negotiations are relatively rare, however.

Mixed-motive Negotiation

The most common type of negotiation situation is mixed-motive negotiation. In Figure 4–3 on page 46, the seller's most preferred settlement point (3.5, −.5) is outside of the bargaining zone, as is the buyer's most preferred settlement point (−.5, 3.5). At first glance, the situation seems to be very much like the pure conflict case. But in this situation, there are

FIGURE 4–2. Pure Coordination

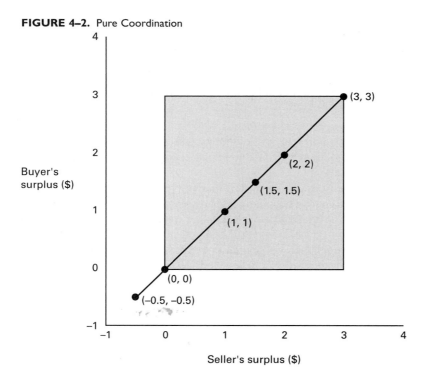

Note: numbers in parentheses are seller's and buyer's surplus, respectively.

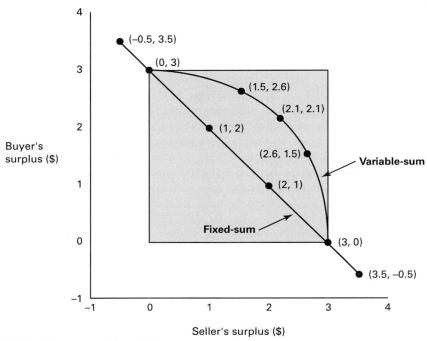

FIGURE 4–3. Mixed-motive Negotiation

more possible settlement points in the bargaining zone (shaded area). Some of these possible settlement points are better for *both* parties than are others. For example, both the seller and the buyer prefer the settlement point (2.1, 2.1) over settlement points (1,2) and (2,1).

The joint profit for the (2.1, 2.1) settlement is 4.2, compared to a joint profit of only 3 in the (2,1) and (1,2) cases—a 40% increase in joint profit. The **integrative potential** of negotiation is the increase in joint profit available to negotiators over and above the joint profit afforded by a fixed-sum solution.

Most negotiation situations are the mixed-motive type and contain potential for integrative agreement. In mixed-motive negotiations, parties' interests are neither completely opposed nor purely compatible. Rather, their interests are imperfectly correlated with one another. The gains of one party do not represent equal sacrifices by the other. For example, consider a negotiation between two collaborators concerning a joint project: one is risk-averse and values cash up front more than riskier long-term payoffs; the other is more interested in long-term value than in current gains. The two may settle on a contract in which a large lump sum is paid to the risk-averse negotiator and the other party reaps most of the (riskier) profits in the long term. Few conflicts are win-or-lose enterprises (Deutsch, 1973). Nevertheless, despite the abundance of integrative negotiation opportunities, people often fail to realize this and settle for suboptimal settlements.

The real question, then, for the negotiator is how to maximize the integrative potential of negotiation. Unfortunately, integrative negotiation agreements are much easier to see in hindsight than to create at the outset.

DISTRIBUTIVE AND INTEGRATIVE NEGOTIATION

There are two important elements to every negotiation situation: distributive and integrative. The distributive element is how negotiators divide or distribute resources amongst themselves. In short, the distributive element focuses on how much of the pie a negotiator claims for him- or herself. This is what we discussed in the previous chapter.

The **integrative** element concerns how negotiators expand the pie of resources to be divided. Why would a negotiator try to expand the pie? By expanding the pie of resources, there are more resources to go around. Most negotiations contain potential for integrative agreements, meaning that it is possible to create additional resources. Unfortunately, most negotiators fail to realize this because they have a **fixed-pie perception** (Bazerman and Neale, 1983; Thompson and Hastie, 1990). The fixed-pie perception can lead to unsatisfying outcomes, impasses, and **lose–lose agreements** or the unnecessary waste of resources (Thompson and Hrebec, 1996). The purpose of this chapter is to examine how negotiators can create more resources in situations where it appears that they have completely opposing interests. We call such skills strategic creativity.

A Pyramid Model

Integrative negotiation refers to both a process and an outcome of negotiation. Parties to negotiation may engage in behaviors designed to integrate their interests, but that is no guarantee they will reach an integrative outcome. An **integrative agreement** is a negotiated outcome that leaves no resources unutilized.

The pyramid model presented in Figure 4–4 depicts three "levels" of integrative agreements. Beginning at the base, each successive level subsumes the properties of the levels below it. Ideally, negotiators should always strive to reach level 3 integrative agreements. Higher levels are progressively more difficult for negotiators to achieve, but are more beneficial to negotiators.

Level 1 integrative agreements are agreements that exceed parties' no-agreement possibilities, or reservation points. Reaching an agreement that exceeds parties' no-agreement possibilities creates value relative to the best alternative. Parties create value by reaching settle-

FIGURE 4–4. A Pyramid Model of Integrative Agreements

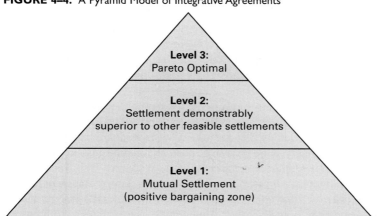

Level 3:
Pareto Optimal

Level 2:
Settlement demonstrably
superior to other feasible settlements

Level 1:
Mutual Settlement
(positive bargaining zone)

ments that are better than their reservation points, or disagreement alternatives. If Sam's best alternative is buying the competitor's software, priced 15 percent cheaper, and the company's reservation point is selling the software at a 20 percent educational discount, then there is room for agreement between the two parties.

Level 2 integrative agreements are agreements that are better for both parties than are other feasible negotiated agreements. That is, negotiators create value with respect to one negotiated outcome by finding another outcome that all prefer. For example, suppose that Sam and the company representative both conclude that giving the software to Sam on a six-month trial basis with the understanding that Sam will supply contacts at universities and industries is better than selling the software to Sam at a 20 percent academic discount. The first arrangement is demonstrably superior to the second alternative in the eyes of both parties, and so it is a level 2 integrative agreement.

The existence of such agreements, by definition, implies that the bargaining situation is not purely fixed-sum: Some agreements yield higher joint gain than do others. Recall that in purely fixed-sum situations, all agreements sum to the same joint amount, and, therefore, no alternative agreement exists that improves one party's outcome while simultaneously improving or not reducing the outcome of the other party. If negotiators fail to reach agreement in a fixed-sum negotiation when the bargaining zone is positive, they have failed to reach a level 1 agreement. Unlike the pure fixed-sum case, integrativeness is much more difficult to assess in the more common mixed-motive case.

Level 3 integrative agreements are those that are impossible to improve upon from the perspective of *both* parties. Technically speaking, level 3 integrative agreements are settlements that lie along the **pareto-optimal frontier** of agreement; meaning that no other feasible agreement exists that would improve one party's outcome while simultaneously not hurting the other party's outcome. This means that *any* agreement reached by negotiators in a purely fixed-sum situation is level 3—that is, there is no way to improve any negotiator's outcome without making the other party worse off. In reality, it is difficult to determine whether an agreement is level 3, but we will present some suggestive techniques.

The Problem with Win–Win Agreements

In many instances, manufacturers and retailers, management and union, and buyers and sellers will proudly describe their negotiation outcomes to be "win–win." However, closer inspection usually reveals that money was squandered, resources wasted, and potential joint gain untapped. Clearly, these negotiators' hearts were in the right places, but they did not achieve what they wanted—an efficient (level 3) agreement. What went wrong? Integrative agreements are often used interchangeably with the term "win–win" agreement. However, the term "win–win" is problematic for many reasons. Win–win often implies that parties to the negotiation distribute the bargaining surplus equally among themselves. However, allocation of resources is a distributive issue and in no way ensures that an integrative agreement has been reached. Win–win is often used to mean that negotiators are happy or satisfied with the outcome. However, happiness is no guarantee that money and resources have not been squandered; many "happy" negotiators needlessly waste resources (see Thompson, Valley, and Kramer, 1995). Finally, win–win is a term often used to describe negotiations between persons who are interested in the welfare of each other, which implies that genuine interest in the other party's outcomes is necessary for integrative agreement. It is unreasonable to think that a requirement for integrative agreements is to have a strong, intrinsic interest in the other party's welfare. It is nice when it happens, but it is no guarantee for reaching a pareto-optimal outcome.

Lose–Lose Agreements

In 1990, Thompson and Hastie uncovered a particularly insidious and widespread effect in negotiations: the lose–lose effect. They constructed a negotiation situation in which the parties involved had compatible interests on a subset of the negotiation issues. That is, both parties wanted the same outcome. At first, it seemed absurd to imagine any other outcome occurring other than the parties settling for what was obviously the best solution for themselves and the other person. However, a substantial number of negotiators not only failed to realize that the other person had interests that were completely compatible with their own but reached settlements that were less optimal for both parties than some other readily available outcome. A situation in which two people fail to capitalize on compatible interests is a lose–lose agreement (Thompson and Hrebec, 1996). In an analysis of 32 different negotiation studies across over 5,000 people, Thompson and Hrebec (1996) found that negotiators failed to realize compatible issues about 50 percent of the time and fell prey to the lose–lose effect about 20 percent of the time. Lose–lose agreements are perhaps the most heartbreaking type of negotiation outcome.

What should negotiators do to avoid lose–lose agreements? First, negotiators should be aware of the fixed-pie perception and not automatically assume that their interests are opposed to the other party. Second, negotiators should avoid making **premature concessions** to the other party (i.e., making concessions on issues before they are even asked for). Finally, negotiators should develop an accurate understanding of the other party's interests—a skill we'll explore soon.

HOW DO NEGOTIATORS EXPAND THE PIE OF RESOURCES?

The complexity and value of reaching integrative agreements is best understood through an example. Consider a negotiation between a buyer, the Windy City Theater (WCT), and a seller, POP Productions (POP). Imagine you are Gene Girard, general manager of the WCT. You would like to bring the Broadway musical, *Oceania!*, to the WCT for a week next April. *Oceania!* is represented and managed by POP Productions, one of the largest producers of live entertainment in New York. You have a talk scheduled this afternoon with Nat Ryan, sales representative for POP. As general manager of WCT, you are committed to bringing quality live entertainment to the theater and structuring deals that are profitable for WCT. What steps should you take to maximize your profits?

Before Negotiation

In preparation for your negotiation with Nat, you make a list of the relevant issues to discuss:

1. Profit sharing of ticket revenues (typically, the theater and production company share ticket revenues, but the exact percentage is a matter of negotiation)
2. Salaries for the cast and crew (the theater pays a lump-sum salary to POP productions for the cast and crew)

3. The number of shows to be offered during the week (the typical number of shows is nine: five evening performances and four weekend matinees; however, the total number of shows could be reduced to seven or increased to add two weekday matinees)

4. Lodging and meal costs for the cast and crew (lodging and board for the 100-member cast and crew for the week-run show can be expensive—who should pick up the tab?).[1]

You spend the next week determining your reservation point and your best assessment of Nat Ryan's reservation point. Specifically, you make the assessments listed in Table 4–1. Note that in this negotiation, WCT has a reservation point for *each* issue (as opposed to a general, summary R.P).

First Meeting

You make a strategic decision to let your opening offer represent what you believe to be Nat's reservation point for each of the negotiation issues. You bring up these issues with Nat and clearly state your preferences for each (see Table 4–2).

Not surprisingly, Nat rejects your opening proposal and counters by proposing a set of terms that represent your reservation point (Table 4–2, POP's opening offer). Obviously, Nat has done her homework! You use the flipchart in the room to make a sketch of the proposals that looks like Table 4–2. A quick inspection of Table 4–2 reveals that your interests appear to be primarily opposed: POP wants 50 percent of net ticket revenues, and bigger salaries than WCT wants to pay; POP wants to contract for fewer performances and desires complimentary lodging and board. You are feeling a little downtrodden. Nat then suggests that the two of you compromise by splitting the difference halfway on each of the issues. Nat proposes the following:

Profit sharing:	60–40 (WCT/POP)
Cast and crew salaries:	$225,000/week
Performances:	9
Lodging:	WCT pays for hotel; POP pays for meals

You are pleased by Nat's reasonable offer. It clearly punctures your reservation price for each issue, and so you seriously consider accepting it on the spot and concluding the negotiation. You call your financial advisor, who gives you an assessment of the expected value

TABLE 4–1. WCT Reservation and Target Points (Columns 2 and 3); WCT's Assessment of POP's Reservation and Target Points (Columns 4 and 5).

To-Be-Negotiated Issue	WCT RP	WCT Target	POP RP*	POP Target*
Profit sharing (WCT/POP)	50–50	70–30	70–30	50–50
Salaries for cast and crew	$250,000/week	$175,000/week	$200,000/week	$275,000/week
Number of performances	9	11	11?	7
Lodging and board arrangements	WCT expense	POP expense	POP expense	WCT expense

* *Note*: WCT does not know POP's reservation or target points, but this is Gene's best estimate.

[1] This negotiation has been simplified to illustrate key points. Case available from Dispute Resolution Research Center, Kellogg Graduate School of Management, Northwestern University; email: drrc@kellogg.nwu.edu.

TABLE 4–2. WCT Opening Offer; POP's Opening Offer.

To-Be-Negotiated Issue	Windy City Theater's Opening Offer	POP Production's Opening Offer
Profit sharing (WCT/POP)	70–30	50–50
Salaries for cast and crew	$200,000/week	$250,000/week
Number of performances	11	7
Lodging and board arrangements	POP expense	WCT expense

of Nat's latest proposal, about $236,000.[2] You are unsure exactly how much the proposal is worth to Nat, but it is an obvious improvement over your opening offer to her. You guestimate that the proposal has a net value of $549,000 to Nat (40% of $885,000 in ticket revenues = $354,000, plus $225,000 in salaries = $579,000 less $30,000 for food = $549,000. Graphically, this is point A plotted in Figure 4–5.) Nat has her legal expert draw up the paperwork and you are about to sign off. However, you decide to wait until morning.

That night, you call your financial advisor, who gives you more details about the projected profits figure. She explains that the added revenue from each additional show to the regularly scheduled nine performances would be $98,000 per performance. This means that if you add two matinee performances to the run of *Oceania!*, you could increase your profits by nearly $200,000! You speculate that lodging and food expenses for POP would be more expensive than adding additional performances, since their cast and crew are already in town.

FIGURE 4–5. Gene's First Assessment of Profit to WCT and POP

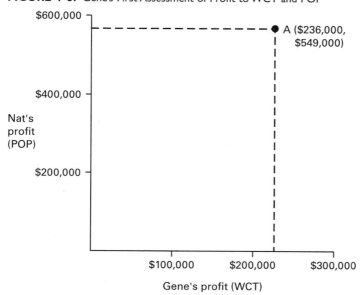

[2] This figure is based upon financial calculations that include ticket revenues from expected sales: i.e., 60% of $885,000 in ticket sales, less $225,000 for salary, and less $70,000 in hotel bills (quote from hotel for block of rooms).

You decide to suggest a tradeoff: You pay for the cast and crew's lodging and meals for the entire week (cost to you = $95,000); in exchange, POP adds two weekday matinee performances to the run. This would mean an increase in value to you of over $120,000 over the previous deal (or $356,000).

Second Meeting

The next morning, you propose the following offer (point B on Figure 4–6) to Nat:

Profit-sharing:	60–40 (WCT/POP)
Cast and crew salaries:	$225,000/week
Performances:	11
Lodging:	WCT pay for hotel/lodging (no charge to POP)

Nat is clearly pleased. You estimate that Nat's profits have increased by about $40,000—the savings she made on meals. In addition, it represents added value for you. This means that you have moved from a level 1 integrative agreement to a level 2 integrative agreement (see point B in Figure 4–6). Nat's attorney prepares another contract for you to sign. However, you are still reluctant to sign a contract. You feel that the terms are acceptable, but shudder at the thought that you nearly failed to realize the additional $120,000 in profit. You wonder: Is there more hidden value in this negotiation? You recall in your first meeting with Nat that you also discussed another POP Productions Broadway show, *Bugles*. You discussed the possibility of bringing *Bugles* to WCT with your board of directors, who agreed that it would be considered profitable if cast and crew salaries were $100,000 or less. You decide to ask Nat about her plans for *Bugles*.

FIGURE 4–6. Gene's Second Assessment of Profit to WCT and POP

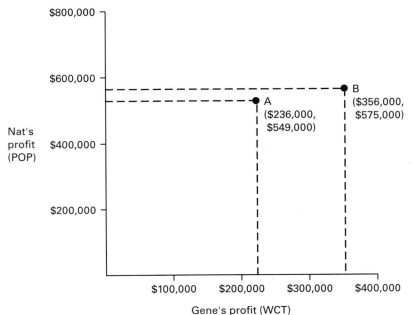

Third Meeting

When you mention *Bugles* to Nat, her eyes light up and she says that she has received a lot of feelers about *Bugles*, but has not signed a contract. You ask Nat point blank about cast and crew salaries, and she says POP is targeting $100,000 per week with a bottom line of $75,000. You offer Nat $80,000 for *Bugles* at WCT. She accepts, and you have added another $20,000 of value to the deal for WCT! In addition, POP's profits have increased by at least $5,000 (see point C in Figure 4–7). Nat phones her lawyer, and *Bugles* is written into the contract. Again, you delay closing the deal, suggesting that the two of you meet for coffee the next morning.

You go home to think about the deal. You are unsure how to add additional value without renegotiating the terms that you have already agreed to. You feel that it would be bargaining in bad faith to renegotiate the profit sharing of 60–40 WCT/POP. However, you remember Nat saying she expected ticket sales for *Oceania!* to be about 85 to 90 percent of the house for the week-long run of *Oceania!* In contrast, you are less optimistic about the show's likely success. In fact, your marketing manager projects sales of 75 percent of the house. Clearly, the two of you have very different beliefs about the success of the show. You wonder if Nat would be willing to bet on it.

Fourth Meeting

You open up the meeting by telling Nat you are more pessimistic about the show than she is. You explain that it is highly unlikely that ticket sales will be over 75 percent of the house, and project $885,000 of net ticket sales. Nat shakes her head in disagreement and claims that *Oceania!* will sell 85 percent of the house across all performances, which would mean net

FIGURE 4–7. Gene's Third Assessment of Profit to WCT and POP

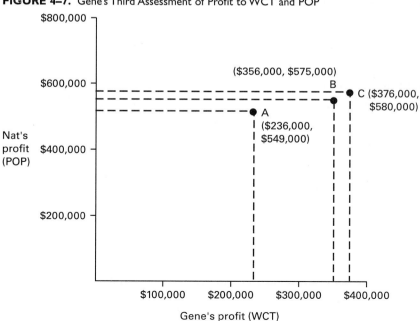

ticket revenues in excess of $1 million. The two of you argue about this unproductively. You realize there is no changing her mind, and you propose the following offer to Nat:

- If ticket sales are less than $900,000, WCT takes 70 percent of the profits.
- If ticket sales are between $900,000 and $1 million, WCT takes 60 percent of the profits (original deal).
- If ticket sales are greater than $1 million, WCT takes 40 percent of the profits.

Nat is very receptive and accepts the bet (point D in Figure 4–8). How valuable is this proposal to you? You are 80 percent sure that ticket sales will be under $900,000. You estimate there is a 10 percent chance that ticket sales will be between $900,000 and $1 million. You estimate there is a 10 percent chance that ticket sales will be greater than $1 million. You compute your expected value, using the expected utility principle:

$$.8(\$630,000) + .1(\$560,000) + .1(\$400,000) = \$504,000 + \$56,000 + \$40,000 = \$600,000$$

$600,000 is clearly better than the original deal—the value of the deal to WCT has increased by $70,000 since your last meeting with Nat. You estimate that Nat's value increased by at least the same amount. Graphically, this is shown as point D in Figure 4–8. You now feel confident that you have negotiated a good deal for the WCT. Further, it is clear that the integrative negotiation process has had a positive impact on your relationship with Nat.

Analysis

In Gene's negotiations with Nat, the value of both parties' outcomes improved steadily. Figure 4–8 reflects the value (in thousands of dollars) of each successive proposal. Through a

FIGURE 4–8. Gene's Fourth Estimate of the Profit to WCT and POP

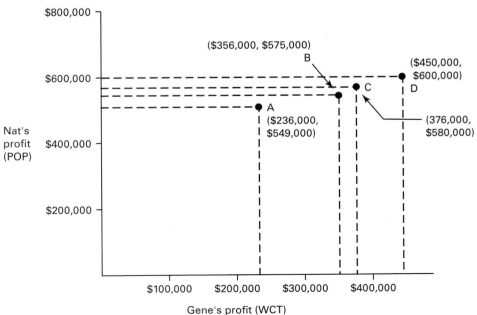

combination of logrolling, bridging interests, and betting on different expectations, Gene successfully moved the negotiation from a level 1 integrative agreement to a level 3 integrative agreement.

THE ROLE OF INTERESTS

As Gene and Nat's situation illustrates, unlocking the integrative potential of negotiation hinges on understanding parties' interests for alternatives among negotiation issues. Three important components to this assertion reflect the fundamental "elements" of negotiation we outlined in the first chapter: interests, issues, and alternatives. In the example above, Gene found a maximally integrative agreement by examining parties' preferences for the alternatives for each issue.

This sounds easy enough, but there is a problem: Interests cannot be seen or measured objectively. Rather, we make inferences about someone's preferences based on his or her behavior or responses.

In negotiation, people reveal their positions rather than their interests (Fisher, Ury, and Patton, 1991). Positions are a negotiator's stated demands. Interests are a person's underlying goals. Often, negotiators' stated positions may be in complete conflict, but their underlying interests may be compatible.

The Importance of Differences

Negotiators not only have differences in interest and preference, but they view the world differently. Nat thinks the show is going to be a near sell-out performance; Gene expects 25 percent of the tickets to go unsold. Different interpretations of the facts may threaten already tenuous relations. Attempts to persuade the other person may be met with skepticism, hostility, and an escalating spiral of conflict. The surprising fact is that differences in beliefs—or expectations about uncertain events—pave the way toward integrative agreements.

Because negotiators are not identical in their tastes, forecasts, and endowments, they have something to offer that is relatively less valuable to them than to those with whom they negotiate. Lax and Sebenius (1986) note five dimensions of difference that negotiators may exploit to capitalize on integrative agreement:

- differences in valuation of the negotiation issues
- differences in expectations of uncertain events
- differences in risk attitudes
- differences in time preferences
- differences in capabilities

Differences in Valuation

Negotiators have different strengths of preference for each issue. For example, even though Gene and Nat's preferences were opposed on the lodging/meals and number of performances, Gene had the most to gain by adding two matinee performances while Nat was able to substantially cut lodging and meal expenses. By trading off these issues, both were better off than by simply compromising on each issue. The strategy of trading off so as to capitalize on different strengths of preference is **logrolling** (Froman and Cohen, 1970).

Differences in Expectations: Forming Contingent Contracts

Because negotiation often involves uncertainty, negotiators differ in their forecasts, or beliefs, about what will happen in the future. Consider the case of a woman and her brother who inherited a tool store from their father. The sister expected the profitability of the store to decline steadily; the brother expected the store to succeed. The sister wanted to sell the store; the brother wanted to keep it. A contingent contract was constructed: The brother agreed to buy his sister's share of the store over a period of time at a price based on her bleak assessment of its worth. The sister is guaranteed a certain return; the brother's return is based on how well the store does.

Consider another example. A city planner contracted with a building corporation to build and manage a condominium/retail center. The city's assessment of the likely sales was bleak, and so the city wanted to tax the units heavily. The corporation did not like the prospect of high taxes and believed that sales would be high in the coming year. A contingent contract was developed. The city promised the corporation a tax cap over ten years as a function of yearly sales: Higher sales meant a lower tax cap; lower sales meant a higher tax cap. Each party was confident that his or her "best case" scenario would come to pass.

Differences in Risk Attitudes

In other situations, parties agree on the probability of future events but feel differently about taking risks. For example, two colleagues may undertake a collaborative project, such as writing a novel, for which they both agree that the probability of success is only moderate. The colleague with an established career can afford to be risk-seeking; the struggling young novelist may be risk-averse. The two may capitalize on their different risk-taking profiles with a contingent contract: The more risk-averse colleague receives the entire advance on the book; the risk-seeking colleague receives the majority of the risky profits after the publication of the novel.

Differences in Time Preferences

People may value the same event quite differently depending on *when* it occurs. If one party is more impatient than the other, mechanisms for optimally sharing the consequences over time may be devised. Two partners in a joint venture might allocate the initial profits to the partner who has high costs for time, whereas the partner who can wait will achieve greater profits over a longer, delayed period.

Differences in Capabilities

People differ not only in their tastes, probability assessments, and risk preferences; they differ in their capabilities, endowments, and skills. Consider two managers who have different resources, capital, and support staff. One manager has strong quantitative, statistical skills and access to state-of-the-art computers; the other has strong marketing and design skills. Together, they may combine their differing skills and expertise in a mutually beneficial way, such as in the design of a new product concept. The development of successful research collaborations are fostered by differences in skills and preferences (Northcraft and Neale, 1993).

Cautionary Note

Capitalizing on differences often entails **contingency contracts,** wherein negotiators make bets based upon different states of the world occurring. Gene and Nat's bet on expected ticket revenues is an example of a contingency contract. For contingency contracts to be effective, they should be able to be readily evaluated, leaving no room for ambiguity of interpretation (e.g., ticket sales are readily assessed). Conditions and measurement techniques should be spelled out in advance (e.g., Gene and Nat should decide whether to include all ticket sales, only those for regularly scheduled performances, etc.). Further, a date or timeline should be mutually agreed upon.

A STRATEGIC FRAMEWORK FOR REACHING INTEGRATIVE AGREEMENTS

The discovery and creation of integrative agreements is much like problem solving. Problem solving requires creativity. Integrative agreements are devilishly obvious after the fact, but not before. At least two factors make the discovery and creation of integrative agreements complex and, often, seemingly impossible—the hindsight bias and functional fixedness.

The **hindsight bias** refers to a pervasive human tendency for people to be remarkably adept at inferring a process once the outcome is known, but unable to predict outcomes when only the processes and precipitating events are known (Fischhoff, 1975). The hindsight bias, or the "I knew it all along" effect, makes integrative solutions to negotiation situations appear to be obvious when we see them in retrospect, although before they were discovered, the situation appeared to be fixed-sum.

Functional fixedness occurs when a problem-solver bases a strategy on familiar methods (Adamson and Taylor, 1954). The problem with functional fixedness is that previously learned problem-solving strategies hinder the development of effective strategies in new situations. The person fixates on one strategy and cannot readily switch to another method of solving a problem. That is, experience in one domain produces in-the-box thinking in another domain. Reliance on compromise as a negotiation strategy may produce functional fixedness.

Because negotiation is an ill-structured task, with few constraints and a myriad of possible "moves," a royal road for reaching integrative agreement does not exist. The closest we come to a generic "bag of tricks" is the presentation of a decision-making model of integrative negotiation. The model is prescriptive; that is, it focuses on what negotiators *should* do to reach agreement, not what they *actually* do.

The decision-making model of integrative negotiation is depicted in Figure 4–9. The model has five major components: resource assessment, assessment of differences, construction of offers and tradeoffs, acceptance/rejection of decision, and renegotiation.

Resource Assessment

Resource assessment involves the identification of the bargaining issues and alternatives. For example, consider an employment negotiation. The bargaining issues may be salary, vacation, and benefits. The feasible salary range may be $60,000 to $100,000; vacation time may be 1 to 5 weeks, and benefits may include stock options or a company car. In this stage, parties identify the issues that are of concern to them in the negotiation. A superset emerges from the combination of both parties' issues.

In our earlier example, Gene considered the profit sharing, salaries, and number of performances to be the central issues; Nat considered crew and cast lodging as an important issue. The union of both parties' issue sets forms the issue mix of the negotiation. In addition to specifying the issue mix, parties also define and clarify the alternatives for each issue. For

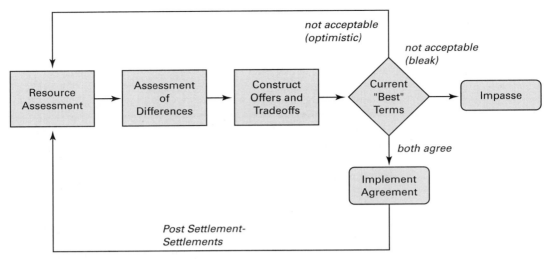

FIGURE 4–9. Decision-making Model of Integrative Negotiation

example, Gene may consider between nine and eleven performances; Nat may consider be-tween seven and nine. The ultimate set of options for each issue is a superset of both parties' alternatives.

Later stages of resource assessment move beyond the mere identification of issues and alternatives to two higher-order processes: the **unpacking** of issues and alternatives, and the addition of new issues and alternatives. Unpacking or unbundling (Lax and Sebenius, 1986) of issues is important in negotiations that center around a single issue. Because mutually benefi-cial tradeoffs require a minimum of two issues, it is important to fractionate conflict into more than one issue. In other instances, it may be necessary to add new issues and alternatives. The process of adding issues and alternatives is facilitated through the discussion of parties' needs.

Assessment of Differences

Once the issue mix and set of alternatives are identified, parties should focus on assessing their differences in valuation, probability assessment, risk preferences, time constraints, and capabilities.

Two concerns should guide the assessment of interdependencies. First, each party should focus on his or her most important issues. Second, parties should focus on issues that are of high value to one party and of low cost for the other party to provide. For example, in Sam's case, his high-value issue (obtaining a copy of the software) is a relatively low-cost item for the software company. Similarly, sales and training are high-cost issues for the com-pany but are low-cost issues to Sam. In Gene's case, lodging is relatively low cost in compar-ison to the additional revenues from weekday matinees.

Offers and Tradeoffs

Pruitt and Rubin (1986) outline five methods for pursuing integrative agreement:

- expanding the pie
- nonspecific compensation

- logrolling
- cost-cutting
- bridging

When negotiators **expand the pie,** they increase the amount of available resources. To take Sam's case, perhaps Sam might get a grant to buy the software he needs. In many cases, though, it is not possible to create additional resources. **Nonspecific compensation** involves one party receiving his or her most desirable alternative; the other party is repaid in some unrelated coin. For example, the software company might give Sam the software; in return, Sam might provide training seminars for the company using the software. When parties logroll, they make mutually beneficial tradeoffs among issues. Each party concedes on a low-priority issue in exchange for his or her most preferred alternative on a high-priority issue. For example, Sam's most important priority may be obtaining the software; the company's most important priority may be expanding its customer base. They may logroll their interests so that Sam receives the software in return for locating five new clients. When parties **costcut,** one party gets what he or she wants and the other's costs are reduced or eliminated. For example, Sam might receive the software free of charge in exchange for paying packaging fees, shipping fees, cost of manuals, and technical support. **Bridging** involves the creation of a new option that satisfies both parties' key interests. For example, the company might agree to provide Sam with a beta (prerelease) version of the software; in return, Sam provides the company with extensive feedback about usability and potential improvements.

In this phase, parties should consider several potential tradeoffs among valuations, forecasts, risks, time preferences, and capabilities, and eliminate those dominated by other alternatives. There is no sense in making a tradeoff unless what you are offering the other party is more valued by him or her than it costs you to provide.

Acceptance/Rejection Decision

At some point, negotiators may land on an outcome both find minimally acceptable: It exceeds both parties' reservation points, and constitutes a level 1 integrative agreement. Parties may end negotiations with this agreement, as Nat was inclined to do after the first meeting with Gene. But the identification of a minimally acceptable agreement does not necessarily mean that settlement is efficient. Like Gene, negotiators should continue to explore the possibilities, depending on their costs for time and their subjective assessments of the likelihood of reaching a superior solution. Negotiators' aspirations and goals may influence the search process in negotiation; negotiators who set specific, challenging goals are more likely to continue to search for integrative agreements than do those who do not set goals or who set easy goals (Huber and Neale, 1986).

Prolonging Negotiation and Renegotiation

Two feedback loops emanate from the decision stage: the decision to prolong negotiations and the decision to renegotiate.

Negotiators should prolong negotiations when the best agreement on the bargaining table fails to meet both parties' reservation points. Negotiators should reassess the resources by unpacking the initial set of issues and breaking them down to smaller issues that may be traded off. In addition to unpacking issues, negotiators may add issues and alternatives to the bargaining mix. If parties have identified all the issues and alternatives, identified differences to tradeoff, and a mutually agreeable solution has not been found, then they should call a halt to the negotiation and pursue their best identified alternatives.

In some instances, parties may decide to renegotiate after a mutually agreeable settlement has been reached. It may seem counterintuitive or counterproductive to resume negotiations once an acceptable agreement has been reached. But the strategy of **postsettlement settlements** is remarkably effective in improving the quality of negotiated agreements (Bazerman, Russ, and Yakura, 1987) and moving an agreement from a level 1 agreement to a level 2 or 3 agreement. In the postsettlement settlement, negotiators agree to explore other options with the goal of finding another that both prefer more than the current one (Raiffa, 1982). The current settlement becomes both parties' new reservation point. For any future agreement to be binding, both parties must agree to the new terms.

The postsettlement settlement strategy allows both parties to reveal their preferences without fear of exploitation, because they can safely revert to their previous agreement. If better terms are found, parties can be more confident they have reached a level 2 or 3 settlement. If no better agreement is found, the parties may be more confident that the current agreement is level 3.

THE ROLE OF INFORMATION

Central to the decision-making model is information about parties' interests and priorities. Lax and Sibenius (1986) specify four areas to examine when assessing another party's interests in organizational negotiations.

- past behavior
- training and professional affiliation
- organizational position and affiliation
- relevant authorities

Of course, assessment of the other party's interests is important to do during negotiation as well. There are a variety of ways of acquiring such information, which may be generally classified as direct and indirect methods.

Direct Methods: Asking Questions and Providing Information

It is a fallacy to believe that negotiators should never provide information to the opponent. Negotiations would go nowhere if parties did not communicate their interests to the other party. Remember: You should negotiate as you would with your fraternal twin. If you don't provide information, neither will the other party. The important question is not *whether* to provide information, but *what* information to reveal.

Direct methods involve posing questions to the other party about his or her interests and preferences. A negotiator who asks the other party about preferences is much more likely to reach integrative agreements than negotiators who do not ask the opponent about priorities (Thompson, 1991). The disappointing news, however, is that left to their own devices, negotiators do not seek information. Only 7 percent of untrained negotiators seek information about the other party's preferences during negotiation (Thompson, 1991).

In addition to seeking information about the other party, negotiators may provide information about their own interests. Negotiators who provide information to the other party about their priorities are more likely to reach integrative agreements than negotiators who do not provide this information (Thompson, 1991). Further, there is no evidence to suggest that the "disclosing" negotiator is disadvantaged. The disclosing negotiator does not earn significantly more or less resources than his or her opponent.

Indirect Methods: The Strategy of Multiple Offers

In some cases, negotiators are disappointed and frustrated to find that their attempts to provide and seek information are not effective. This happens most commonly in the face of high distrust and less than amicable relations. Now what? Is all hope lost? Is there anything the negotiator can do? Fortunately, there is. The strategy of **multiple offers** can be effective even with the most uncooperative of negotiators. The strategy involves presenting the other party with at least two (and preferably more) proposals of *equal* value to oneself. The other party is asked to indicate which of the two (or more) proposals he or she prefers. By listening to the opponent's response, the negotiator learns about the other party's preference. Thus, the negotiator plays "detective" by drawing conclusions based upon the negotiator's responses to the multiple offers. The multiple-offer strategy has psychological benefits as well: When people perceive themselves as having more choices (as opposed to only one), they may be more likely to comply. The strategy can reveal valuable information about which issues are important to the other party.

DON'T FORGET ABOUT CLAIMING!

Sometimes, when negotiators learn about integrative agreements and expanding the pie, they walk off into the sunset and forget about the distributive element of negotiation. It is *not* an effective negotiation strategy to solely focus on expanding the pie; the negotiator must simultaneously focus on claiming resources. After all, if a negotiator just focused on expanding the pie, he or she would be no better off, because the other party would claim all the added value.

Sometimes negotiators will regard this advice as callous and state that they "trust" that the other party will want to be "fair" in the negotiations. This is a nice thought but doesn't square with reality. Negotiation is not a game of trust—so why tempt your opponent? Negotiators can successfully build and maintain collaborative, mutually beneficial relationships if they both focus on claiming as well as expanding the pie.

Sins of Omission and Co-mission

Quite often, negotiations contain issues for which negotiators have completely compatible interests. We have discussed the sad case of what happens when *both* negotiators fail to realize this—they frequently end up with a lose-lose settlement (Thompson and Hrebec, 1996). What about the situation in which one party is aware of the compatible issue, but the other is not? We have the makings for a devious strategy: the misrepresentation of common interests (O'Connor and Carnevale, in press).

Consider the following situation: You and another person have been hired to act as a project team in a company that makes children's toys. You and your associate are given a large office to share and arrange your workplace. There are two desks and the only window can be enjoyed from one of the desks. During a conversation with your colleague, it is obvious that he wants the desk with the window view and is ready to make sacrifices on other joint resources to get this—like giving up the close parking space and the storage areas. Unbeknownst to your colleague, you have a terrible fear of heights; the window overlooks a steep precipice outside, and frankly, you would prefer the other desk that is near an attractive tropical plant. You consider not mentioning your true preference, hoping that you can *appear* to make a sacrifice, and so extract more of the other resources. This strategy is known as **passive misrepresentation** because a negotiator does not mention her true preferences and allows the other party to arrive at an erroneous conclusion.

Suddenly, your colleague startles you by asking you point blank which desk you prefer—the one by the windows or the plant. Do you lie about your preferences? If so, this is an act of **active misrepresentation** in that you deliberately mislead your opponent.

The strategic manipulation ploy is used about 28% of the time (O'Connor and Carnevale, in press). We do not advocate strategic misrepresentation of compatible issues as a bargaining ploy. It can backfire; you can be "caught" in a lie and can potentially engender ill will. Our advice is to be wary when expressing your preferences so that you don't become an unwitting victim of a strategic manipulation.

THE NEGOTIATOR'S DILEMMA

It would seem that reaching integrative agreement would be straightforward if negotiators simply revealed their preferences to the other party. Is this wise to do? If you completely reveal your interests to the other party, you may pave the way toward integrative agreement. But you risk giving away all of the bargaining surplus to the other party. In short, the final agreement may be highly integrative (level 3), but it may allocate most of the bargaining surplus to the opponent, rather than to you.

For example, suppose Gene told Nat that he was most concerned about the number of performances, moderately concerned about cast and crew salaries, and much less concerned about lodging and meal expenses. Nat might strategically respond by saying, "That's interesting. I am less concerned about the number of performances than the lodging issue, but salaries are also important to me. So, how about we increase the number of performances, but you pay for all lodging and meals and give us a high salary?" Such an agreement is a level 3 integrative agreement, but Nat receives the lion's share of the resources.

The **negotiator's dilemma** refers to the fact that revealing information about your interests may maximize joint gain but may put you at a strategic disadvantage (Babcock, Thompson, Pillutla, and Murnighan, 1997). This dilemma speaks to the inherent, inevitable tension between the distributive and integrative aspects of negotiation. So, given the tension, what should a negotiator do? As a general rule, it is not detrimental for a negotiator to reveal his or her **priorities** among issues. A simple rank ordering of the issues does not hinder individual gain (Thompson, 1991). In contrast, revealing preferences for specific alternatives on particular issues may in certain instances (i.e., when the other party is experienced) lead to a disadvantage (Thompson, 1990a).

AN APPLICATION

Sam used many of the principles discussed in this chapter to forge an integrative agreement with the software company. Through a thorough analysis of both parties' high-value needs as well as the resources that were relatively inexpensive for each to provide, an integrative agreement was carved out (see Table 4–3).

TABLE 4–3. Sam's Negotiation with the Software Company

	Sam	*Software Company*
High-value needs	• Software package ($10,000) • Promotion of business	• Training seminars on software • Advertising (third-party endorsements) • Contacts: industry and academia • More customer loyalty
Low-cost capabilities	• Time investment • Training seminars • Making contacts	• Price of software ($50)

After several weeks of his time, involving research, letter writing, and phone calls, Sam received more than $16,000 of software free of charge and more than $40,000 in advertising for his own business through the company—an unexpected benefit that emerged through an evaluation of both parties' needs. In turn, the company made valuable inroads into both the automotive industry and the academic network through Sam's contacts. By giving Sam the software, the company achieved many valuable goals. First, it induced Sam to become committed to using the company's software, rather than its competitor's. The price of the software to the company is trivial—about $50 worth of diskettes and manuals. By providing Sam with a relatively cheap item, the company saved hundreds of thousands of dollars in sales and training costs, for Sam acts as both a salesperson and a training repre-sentative for the company in the development of his models. Further, with Sam as a representative, the company gains a valuable endorsement for their product from an external source.

WHERE DO INTEGRATIVE AGREEMENTS REALLY COME FROM?

Now that we know how differences among parties pave the way for integrative agreement, we may ask how differences come about. There are two views on how integrative agreements occur, which correspond to the classic "nature versus nurture" debate about human behavior.

Nature View

According to the **nature view,** negotiators' preferences are the "givens" in a negotiation. To reach integrative agreements, negotiators must "discover" the potential that underlies their preferences. The act of negotiation and the search process that it entails do not change negotiators' preferences. The key to the attainment of integrative agreements is the search for and discovery of differences in preferences and risk attitudes. Imagine two negotiators standing atop a field rich with oil. The oil is valuable and represents the integrative potential available to the two negotiators. Like most negotiation situations, the parties are unaware of the full potential in the situation. The question facing the negotiators is how to drill for the oil. Obviously, it is not cost effective for negotiators to place an oil well on every square inch of the land. How do they decide which is the most promising spot?

Nurture View

According to the **nurture view,** negotiators construct and develop integrative potential through their evolving and changing preferences. According to this view, preferences are not necessarily well-formed, stable, and exogenously determined, but are malleable, unstable, and often unknown.

How do negotiators modify their opponents' perceptions of their own preferences? According to Walton and McKersie (1965), each party to a negotiation attempts to force the other person to reappraise the utility of a given issue. These attempts are based on the principle of uncertainty about outcomes and preferences. In many circumstances, individuals' preferences are unknown to them, and it is only through the process of negotiation that their preferences are defined. Preferences may change not merely as a function of an opponent's deliberate influence attempt, but as a negotiator learns and becomes more familiar with his or her tastes and preferences.

How do our preferences evolve and change? We identify three key processes: mere exposure, thought-induced affect, and reactive devaluation.

- **Mere exposure effect.** The more we are exposed to something—an image, item, or idea, the more we come to like it. The mere exposure effect (Zajonc, 1968) is extremely powerful and occurs below the level of our awareness. Advertisers know about the mere exposure effect. Why do you think that television ads are repeatedly shown to an audience? The more we are exposed to the ad, the more we come to like the product—up to a point.

- **Thought-induced affect.** Merely thinking about something or someone can polarize our feelings, a phenomenon known as thought-induced affect (Tesser, 1978). For example, people who are asked why they like a particular type of cereal will have stronger feelings about the cereal than people who are not asked to think about the cereal. The same is true when thinking about political candidates—or virtually anything else: Thinking about something polarizes our views about it. Further, thinking about the *reasons* for our preferences may change our preferences (Wilson and Dunn, 1986).

- **Reactive devaluation.** The mere act of offering an opponent a concession can lead to reactive devaluation—reduced preference for an option previously considered to be more attractive (see Ross and Stillinger, 1991). For example, in the mid-1980s, students in American universities were very concerned about divestiture from South Africa, and staged many protests. Imagine that you are a student and the university administration has proposed two different divestment packages, A and B, both rather highly complex economic packages. You and the entire student body are asked which of the packages is most preferable. Imagine that your university has offered to put policy A into place. What are your reactions? When policy A is offered by the administration, students protest and demand policy B. When policy B is offered, students protest and demand A. In the absence of a concession, the students are split in their preferences (from Ross and Stillinger, 1991).

  What is going on here? The phenomenon of reactive devaluation is the tendency of an opponent to devalue proposals offered by the other side. Why? Obviously, not on the proposals' intrinsic merits, but rather, as a mere consequence of their having been offered. The phenomenon stems from a basic trust issue: If we negotiate with someone about something we don't know that much about, a simple heuristic is to distrust anything they offer in the way of a concession. This pattern can lead to comic–tragic results, as when two opponents cycle through a never-ending trade of concessions that are offered—refused—reneged, ad infinitum.

All of these examples suggest that preferences in negotiation are not necessarily fixed but may be manipulated, modified, changed, and discovered.

A Balanced View

Just as human personality and behavior are a function of both nurture and nature, the same holds true for negotiation: Preferences are often stable but at times subject to change, either through direct manipulation or through natural interaction with others. The real task is to understand the conditions and contexts that tend to favor each view.

BENEFITS OF INTEGRATIVE AGREEMENT

Integrative agreements, like Sam's, result in a number of beneficial effects that extend well beyond the immediate parties. The creation of integrative agreement between two parties is like dropping a pebble in a pond: There is a ripple effect. Figure 4–10 illustrates the ever-widening beneficial effects of integrative agreements.

Immediate Parties

Integrative agreements are beneficial for the parties involved. Both Sam and the software company gained thousands of dollars' worth of value through their mutual agreement. Integrative agreements often allow negotiators to avoid impasse, deadlock, and stalemate (Pruitt and Rubin, 1986). For example, if both parties' reservation points are high (i.e., both have attractive alternatives to negotiated agreement) and the bargaining zone is very small but positive, it may be difficult for parties to resolve the conflict unless a way can be found to join their interests. Of course, level 2 and 3 agreements provide even greater rewards for negotiators.

Negotiators' Relationship

Because integrative agreements are mutually rewarding, they tend to strengthen the relationship between parties and pave a path of good relations (Pruitt and Rubin, 1986). Negotiators often view themselves as partners rather than opponents. Sam built a rewarding and prof-

FIGURE 4–10. Benefits of Integrative Agreement

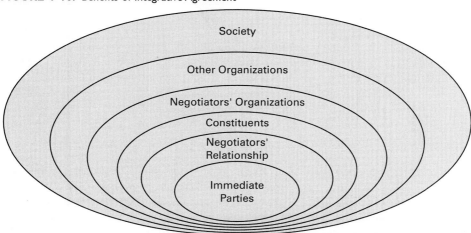

itable relationship with the software company. Through their joint problem solving, both have avoided costly attorney fees. For this reason, integrative agreements tend to be stable—people are less likely to renege on an agreement (Pruitt and Rubin, 1986).

Constituents

Negotiators' constituencies also profit from integrative agreements. For example, Sam's contacts in industry and academia have benefited from his relationship with the software company.

Negotiators' Organizations

Firms will usually reap benefits as a whole if their departments reconcile their differences effectively. Both Sam's consulting business and the software company profit as a result of their departments' integrative agreement.

Other Organizations

The beneficial effects of integrative agreements extend to organizations outside the immediate negotiations. For example, Sam's negotiations with the software company led several automotive companies and academic departments to purchase software from the company (an organizational benefit) as well as hardware from other companies (an extraorganizational benefit).

Society

Disputes are costly to the parties, their constituencies, organizations, society, and families. For example, a Greyhound strike is harmful to the broader community because of the inconvenience caused to travelers. Service providers, such as travel agents, who are not on strike but in related industries, often suffer as much as customers and clients. On a broader scale, Sam's integrative agreement with the software company will ultimately improve the way automotive engines are developed for consumers in years to come.

DO INTEGRATIVE AGREEMENTS REALLY EXIST?

Whereas researchers and practitioners agree that integrative potential exists in just about every negotiation situation, negotiators are often skeptical, especially when in the throes of negotiation: "Your research examples are cute, but they don't pertain to my real life negotiations in buying my house or car, or negotiating my job—those are really fixed-sum situations!" Most people don't immediately see the opportunity for integrative agreement, and therefore believe the situation is fixed-sum. Hindsight in negotiation is not 20–20. That is, even when we look back on our negotiations, we remain convinced that they were fixed-sum.

Most negotiation situations involve more than one issue. The probability that negotiators will have identical preferences across the set of issues to be negotiated is very small. As we have seen, integrative potential exists when negotiators have different strengths of preference among negotiation issues, even if their preferences within issues are in opposition. Differences in preferences, beliefs, and capacities may be profitably traded off to create joint gain.

The more interesting question concerns *how much* potential exists and how it may be identified by negotiators. A widespread fallacy about negotiation is the belief that people fail to reach integrative agreements because they take too much time and effort. Lack of time and effort do not explain ineffective negotiation. The biggest detriment to the attainment of integrative agreements are the faulty assumptions we make about our opponent and the negotiation situation. We explore these faulty assumptions in detail in chapters 6, 7, and 8.

CONCLUSION

Integrative agreements are forged from information sharing, decision making, and creativity. We focused on the substantive basis for achieving joint gains rather than on personality and simple tricks. People's preferences and problem-solving strategies are the key skills a negotiator needs to have to be effective. Some people believe that integrative agreement requires parties to be concerned with one another and to seek to further each other's interests. To be sure, negotiators may have warm feelings and express genuine concern for the other party, but these are not necessary ingredients for integrative agreement. Furthermore, they are no guarantee for the attainment of integrative agreement (not to mention unrealistic expectations in many business negotiations). As we have seen in this chapter, you need not have any altruistic or cooperative orientation toward the other party other than the desire to secure an agreement with him or her so that your own needs can be met. It certainly is true that many negotiators, like Sam, desire to foster good relations with the other party. These concerns do not necessarily reflect basic altruism, but rather, rational thought. We now turn to an analysis of normative models of negotiation, which are based on axioms of rationality. Rational models provide tools for analyzing negotiation situations and predicting the best outcomes of negotiations.

TAKE-AWAYS

- In most negotiation situations, parties' interests are neither completely opposed nor compatible, but rather, they have *mixed motives*—an incentive to reach a (profitable) agreement with the other party and a desire to maximize their own gains.
- The most effective way to reach an integrative agreement is to assess the other party's interests and capitalize on *differences* of interest, time preference, and risk attitudes.
- Asking direct questions, providing information, making multiple offers, and exploring postsettlement settlements should be part of every negotiator's repertoire.
- Integrative bargaining is intimately related to distributive negotiation: Do not expand the pie without thinking of your own interests. This is what it means to be *strategically creative.*

CHAPTER 5

Rational Behavior:
A Prescriptive Approach

Pat is a young middle-level manager at a large utility company on the West Coast. At the beginning of her fourth year at the company, a prestigious consulting firm in the Midwest makes Pat a job offer. The salary offer is very attractive, representing a 60 percent increase over her current salary. Although salary is important, especially since Pat recently started a family and bought a house, other considerations are also important. For example, she is interested in job security. Pat's promotion decision for senior manager at the utility company is coming up soon, whereas the consulting firm has a significantly longer career advancement ladder. Quality of life is also important. Pat is an avid skier and mountain climber, which makes the West Coast much more attractive than the Midwest. Nevertheless, the consulting firm is stronger in resources, opportunities, and colleagues.

To complicate matters, there is the consideration of Pat's spouse, Marty, who has a career in social services. Marty is reluctant to leave a job that was difficult to find and is rewarding. However, Marty has recently thought about returning to school for a higher degree; the programs in the Midwestern location are better than those in their West Coast vicinity.

Although Pat is happy to have the offer, both she and Marty are in a state of anguish concerning the decision, which has to be made soon.

Like Pat and Marty, we make decisions every day of our lives. Sometimes our decisions are trivial, such as whether to have chocolate cake or cherry pie for dessert. Other times, our decisions are of great consequence, such as when we choose a career or a spouse. Pat's career decision illustrates the two major types of decision making: individual and joint (or interdependent). Pat must decide whether she prefers the new job to her current one. She must then negotiate with her spouse concerning a possible move. Our decision of what to have for dessert or which job offer we should take is an example of individual decision making. When we negotiate with an employer to decide what our salary will be or with a spouse to decide on dual career paths, this is interdependent decision making. Negotiation is interdependent decision making.

What is the right job for Pat to choose? To answer this, we begin with a discussion of **expected utility theory,** which characterizes a decision rule for rational decision making. Expected utility theory is a theory of rational behavior. We then use the principles of expected utility theory to analyze two-party decision making, or negotiation.

Why is it important for a negotiator to know the principles of rational behavior? For that matter, is it important to be rational in negotiation? Perhaps if we behave irrationally, we might confuse our opponent and reap greater surplus for ourselves; or we might simply be better off by following intuition rather than logic.

An understanding of rational behavior is extremely important for four reasons. First, models of rational behavior are based upon the principle of **maximization** such that the course of action followed guarantees that the negotiator will maximize his or her interests (whether that may be monetary gain, career advancement, prestige, etc.). In short, there is no better way to maximize one's interests than by following the prescriptions of a rational model.

As we have seen, it is not an effective bargaining strategy to attempt to outsmart or trick your opponent. Rational models assume that the opponent is rational. However, this is not often the case, so often a rational negotiator might perform poorly because she fails to anticipate irrationality on the part of her counterpart.

A third advantage of rational models is that, if followed correctly, our behavior will be consistent. Consistency is important for several reasons. Inconsistency in our behavior can inhibit learning. Furthermore, it can send our opponent ambiguous messages. When people are confused or uncertain, they are more defensive and trust diminishes.

Rational models provide a straightforward method for making decisions. However, the decision maker must make some tough assessments of how to weigh elements of the decision. To illustrate the important concepts of rational expectations theory, we will focus on Pat's career decision.

EXPECTED UTILITY THEORY

Probability theory has a long history, dating back to the sixteenth century when French noblemen commissioned their court mathematicians to help them gamble. Modern utility theory is expressed in the form of gambles, probabilities, and payoffs. Why do we need to know about gambling to be effective negotiators? Virtually all negotiations involve choices, and many choices involve uncertainty, which makes them gambles. Before we can negotiate effectively, we need to be clear about our own preferences. Utility theory helps us do that.

Background and Purpose

Expected utility theory is a theory of choices made by an individual actor (von Neumann and Morgenstern, 1947). It prescribes a theory of **"rational behavior."** Behavior is rational if a person acts in a way that maximizes his or her decision utility, or the anticipated satisfaction from a particular outcome. In other words, Pat's career decision either to stay in the current job or to move would be rational if the choice maximizes what is important to Pat and her overall satisfaction. The maximization of utility is often equated with the maximization of monetary gain. But there are many nonmonetary kinds of satisfaction. Obviously, people care about things other than money. For example, weather, culture, quality of life, and personal esteem are all factors that bear on Pat's decision, in addition to salary.

Expected utility theory is based on **revealed preferences.** People's preferences or utilities are not directly observable but must be inferred from their choices and willful behavior. To understand what Pat really wants and values, we have to see what choices she makes. Actions speak louder than words. In this sense, utility maximization is a tautological statement: A person's choices reflect his or her utilities; therefore, all behaviors may be represented by the maximization of this hypothetical utility scale.

How, then, do we make rational decisions in negotiation? Expected utility theory is based on a set of axioms about preferences among gambles. The basic result of the theory is summarized by a theorem stating that if a person's preferences satisfy the specified axioms, then his or her behavior maximizes his or her expected utility. In this chapter, we examine the kinds of choices we make in some risky situations involving gambles. Expected utility theory allows us to examine the rationality of our choices concerning dessert selection, job opportunities—anything involving decisions.

Utility Function

A **utility function** is the quantification of a person's preferences with respect to certain objects such as jobs, potential mates, and ice cream flavors. Utility functions assign numbers to objects and gambles that have objects as their prizes (e.g., flip a coin and win a trip to Hawaii or free groceries). For example, Pat's choice to stay at her current company could be assigned an overall value, say a "7" on a 10-point scale. Her option to take the new job might be assigned a value of either "10" or "2," depending on how things work out for her at the new job. Pat's current job is the sure thing; the second job, because of its uncertainty, is a gamble. How should Pat rationally make a decision between the two?

We first need to examine Pat's utility function. The following seven axioms guarantee the existence of a utility function. The axioms are formulated in terms of preference-or-indifference relations defined over a set of outcomes (see also Coombs, Dawes, and Tversky, 1971). As will become clear, the axioms described below provide the foundation for individual decision making (such as Pat's career) as well as negotiation, or joint decision making.

Comparability

A key assumption of expected utility theory is that everything is comparable. That is, given any two objects, a person must prefer one to the other or be indifferent to both; no two objects are incomparable. For example, a person may compare a dime and a nickel or a cheeseburger and a dime. Pat should compare the offer in the Midwest to her current job on the West Coast. Utility theory implies a single, underlying dimension of "satisfaction" associated with everything. People are rational if they make choices that maximize their satisfaction.

Closure

The **closure property** states that if x and y are available alternatives, then so are all the gambles of the form (x,p,y) that can be formed with x and y as outcomes. In this formulation, x and y refer to available alternatives; p refers to the probability that x will occur. Therefore (x,p,y)

states that x will occur with probability p, otherwise y will occur. The converse must also be true: $(x,p,y) = (y,1-p,x)$, or y will occur with probability $(1-p)$, otherwise x will occur.

As an example, imagine that Pat assesses the probability of receiving a raise from her current employer to be about 30 percent. The closure property states that the situation expressed as a 30 percent chance of receiving a raise (otherwise, no raise) is identical to the statement that Pat has a 70 percent chance of not receiving a raise (otherwise, receiving a raise).

So far, utility theory may seem to be so obvious and simple as to be absurd to spell out in any detail. However, we will soon see how people violate basic "common sense" all the time.

Transitivity

Transitivity means that if we prefer x to y and y to z, then we should prefer x to z. Similarly, if we are indifferent between x and y and y and z, then we will be indifferent between x and z.

Suppose your employer offers you one of three options: a transfer to Seattle, a transfer to Pittsburgh, or a raise of $5,000. You prefer a raise of $5,000 over a move to Pittsburgh, and you prefer to move to Seattle more than a $5,000 raise. The **transitivity property** states that you should therefore prefer a move to Seattle over a move to Pittsburgh. If your preferences were not transitive, you would always want to move somewhere else. Further, a third party could become rich by continuously "selling" your preferred options to you.

Reducibility

The **reducibility axiom** refers to a person's attitude toward a compound lottery, in which the prizes may be tickets to other lotteries. According to the reducibility axiom, a person's attitude toward a compound lottery depends only on the ultimate prizes and the chance of getting them as determined by the laws of probability; the actual gambling mechanism is irrelevant, $(x,pq,y) = [(x,p,y),q,y)]$.

Suppose that the dean of admissions at your first-choice university tells you that you have a 25 percent chance of getting accepted to the graduate MBA program. How do you feel about the situation? Now, suppose the dean tells you that there is a 50 percent chance that you will not get accepted and a 50 percent chance that you will face a lottery-type admission procedure, wherein half the applicants will get accepted and half will not. Which situation do you prefer to be in? According to the reducibility axiom, both situations are identical. Your chances of getting admitted into graduate school are the same in each case: exactly 25 percent. The difference between the two situations is that one involves a **compound gamble** and the other does not.

Compound gambles differ from simple ones in that their outcomes are themselves gambles rather than pure outcomes. Furthermore, probabilities are the same in both gambles. If people have an aversion or attraction to gambling, however, these may not seem the same. This axiom has important implications for negotiation; the format by which alternatives are presented to negotiators—in other words, in terms of gambles or compound gambles— strongly affects our behavior.

Substitutability

The **substitutability axiom** states that gambles that have prizes about which people are indifferent are interchangeable. For example, suppose one prize is substituted for another in a lottery but the lottery is left otherwise unchanged. If you are indifferent between the old and the new prizes, you should be indifferent between the lotteries. If you prefer one prize to the other, you will prefer the lottery that offers the preferred prize.

As an illustration, imagine you work in the finance division of a company and your supervisor asks you how you feel about transfering to either the marketing or sales division in your company. You respond that you are indifferent between the two. Then your supervisor presents you with a choice: You can either be transferred to the sales division or you can move to a finance position in an out-of-state parent branch of the company. After wrestling with the decision, you decide that you prefer to move out of state rather than transfer to the sales division. A few days later, your supervisor surprises you by asking whether you prefer to be transferred to marketing or to be transferred out of the state. According to the substitutability axiom, you should prefer to transfer because, as you previously indicated, you are indifferent to marketing and sales; they are substitutable choices.

Betweenness

The **betweenness axiom** asserts that if x is preferred to y, then x must be preferred to any probability mixture of x and y, which in turn must be preferred to y. This principle is certainly not objectionable for monetary outcomes. For example, most of us would rather have a dime than a nickel and would rather have a probability of either a dime or a nickel than the nickel itself. But consider nonmonetary outcomes, such as skydiving, Russian roulette, and Bungee jumping. To an outside observer, people who skydive apparently prefer a probability mixture of living and dying over either one of them alone; otherwise, one can easily either stay alive or kill oneself without ever skydiving. People who like to risk their lives appear to contradict the betweenness axiom. A more careful analysis reveals, however, that this situation, strange as it may be, is not incompatible with the betweenness axiom. The actual outcomes involved in skydiving are: (1) staying alive after skydiving; (2) staying alive without skydiving; (3) dying while skydiving. In choosing to skydive, therefore, a person prefers a probability mix of (1) and (3) over (2). This analysis reveals that "experience" has a utility.

Continuity or Solvability

Suppose that of three objects, A, B, and C, you prefer A to B and B to C. Now, consider a lottery in which there is a probability, p, of getting A and a probability of $1 - p$ of getting C. If $p = 0$, the lottery is equivalent to C; if $p = 1$, the lottery is equivalent to A. In the first case, you prefer B to the lottery; in the second case, you prefer the lottery to B. According to the **continuity axiom,** there is a value, p, between 0 and 1 for which you are indifferent between B and the lottery. Sounds reasonable enough.

Now consider the following example from von Neumann and Morgenstern involving three outcomes: receiving a dime, receiving a nickel, and being shot at dawn. Certainly, most of us prefer a dime to a nickel and a nickel to being shot. The continuity axiom, however, states that there is a point of inversion at which some probability mixture involving receiving a dime and being shot at dawn is equivalent to receiving a nickel. This derivation seems particularly disdainful for most people, as no price is equal to risking one's life. However, the counterintuitive flavor of this example stems from an inability to understand very small probabilities. In the abstract, people believe they would never choose to risk their life but, in reality, people do so all the time. For example, we cross the street to buy some product for a nickel less, although by doing so we risk getting hit by a car and killed.

In summary, whenever these axioms hold, a utility function exists that (1) preserves a person's preferences among options and gambles, and (2) satisfies the expectation principle: The utility of a gamble equals the expected utility of its outcomes. This utility scale is uniquely determined except for an origin and a unit of measurement.

Bargaining Situation

In our discussion of reservation points, bargaining zones, and integrative bargaining, we assumed that people had preferences. The analysis of these axioms gives us a basis for preferences. Each outcome in a negotiation situation may be identified in terms of its utility for each party. In Figure 5–1, for example, party 1's utility function is represented as $u1$; party 2's utility function is represented as $u2$. Remember that utility payoffs represent the **satisfaction** parties derive from particular commodities or outcomes, not the actual monetary outcomes or payoffs themselves. A bargaining situation like that in Figure 5–1 has a feasible set of utility outcomes, or F, defined as the set of all its possible utility outcomes for party 1 and party 2 and by its conflict point, c, where $c = (c1, c2)$. C represents the point at which both parties would prefer not to reach agreement—the reservation points of both parties.

Individual Rationality and Joint Rationality

So far, we have made two points about rationality: (1) **individual rationality**—individuals should not agree to a utility payoff smaller than their reservation point; and (2) **joint rationality**—two negotiators should not agree on an outcome if another outcome exists that is pareto-superior (i.e., one that is more preferable to one party and does not decrease utility for the other party) (e.g., level 3 integrative agreements).

For example, in Figure 5–1, the area F is the feasible set of alternative outcomes expressed in terms of each negotiator's utility function. The triangular area bcd is the set of all points satisfying the individual rationality requirement. The upper-right boundary $abde$ of F is the set of all points that satisfy the joint rationality requirement. The intersection of the area bcd and of the boundary line $abde$ is the arc bd: It is the set of all points satisfying both rationality requirements. As we can see, b is the least favorable outcome party 1 will accept; d is the least favorable outcome party 2 will accept.

The individual rationality and joint rationality assumptions do not tell us how negotiators should divide the pie. Rather, they tell us only that negotiators should make the pie as big as possible before dividing it. How much of the pie should you have?

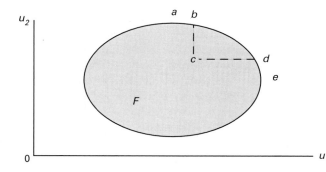

FIGURE 5–1. Set of Feasible Bargaining Outcomes for Two Negotiators.

Source: Adapted from Harsanyi, J. C. (1990). Bargaining. In *The new palgrave: A dictionary of economics*. J. Eatwell, M. Milgate, and P. Newman, eds. New York: Norton: 54–67.

NASH'S BARGAINING THEORY

Nash's (1950; 1953) bargaining theory specifies how negotiators should divide the pie, which involves "a determination of the amount of satisfaction each individual should expect to get from the situation or, rather, a determination of how much it should be worth to each of these individuals to have this opportunity to bargain" (p. 155). Nash's theory makes a *specific* point prediction of the outcome of negotiation, the **Nash solution,** which specifies the outcome of a negotiation if negotiators behave rationally.

Nash's theory makes several important assumptions: Negotiators are rational; that is, they act to maximize their utility. The only significant differences between negotiators are those included in the mathematical description of the game. Further, negotiators have full knowledge of the tastes and preferences of each other. (This rather unrealistic assumption eliminates the problem discussed earlier concerning incomplete information.)

Nash's theory builds on the axioms named in expected utility theory by specifying additional axioms. By specifying enough properties, we exclude all possible settlements in a negotiation, except one. Nash postulates that the agreement point, u, of a negotiation, known as the Nash solution, will satisfy the following five axioms: uniqueness, pareto-optimality, symmetry, independence of equivalent utility representations, and independence of irrelevant alternatives.

Uniqueness

The **uniqueness axiom** states that there is a unique solution to each bargaining situation. Simply stated, one and only one best solution exists for a given bargaining situation or game. In Figure 5–2, the unique solution is denoted as u.

Pareto-optimality

The bargaining process should not yield any outcome that both people find less desirable than some other feasible outcome. The pareto-optimality (or efficiency) axiom is simply the joint rationality assumption made by von Neumann and Morgenstern and the level 3 integrative agreement discussed in chapter 4. The **pareto-efficient frontier** is the set of outcomes

FIGURE 5–2. Set of Feasible Bargaining Outcomes. *U* Is Unique Point, Representing Midpoint on Pareto-efficient Frontier.

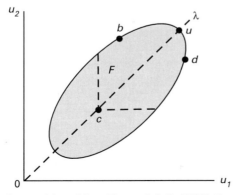

Source: Adapted from Harsanyi, J. C. (1990). Bargaining. In *The new palgrave: A dictionary of economics.* J. Eatwell, M. Milgate, and P. Newman, eds. New York: Norton: 54–67.

corresponding to the entire set of agreements that leaves no portion of the total amount of resources unallocated. A given option, x, is a member of the pareto frontier if, and only if, no option y exists such that y is preferred to x by at least one party and is at least as good as x for the other party.

Consider Figure 5–2: Both people prefer settlement point u ($u1,u2$), which eliminates c ($c1,c2$) from the frontier. Therefore, settlement points that lie on the interior of the arc bd are said to be pareto-inefficient. Options that are not on the pareto frontier are dominated; settlements that are dominated clearly violate the utility principle of maximization. The resolution of any negotiation should be an option from the pareto-efficient set because any other option unnecessarily requires more concession on the part of one or both negotiators.

Another way of thinking about the importance of pareto optimality is to imagine that in *every* negotiation, whether it be for a car, a job, a house, a merger, etc., there is a table with hundreds, thousands, and in some cases, millions of dollars sitting on it. It is yours to keep, provided that you and the other party (e.g., a car dealer, employer, seller, business associate, etc.) agree how to divide it. Obviously, you want to get as much money as you can— this is the distributive aspect of negotiation. Imagine, for a moment, that you and the other negotiator settle upon a division of the money that both of you find acceptable. However, imagine that you leave half or one third or some amount of money on the table. A fire starts in the building and the money burns. This is equivalent to failing to reach a pareto-optimal agreement. Most of us would never imagine ever allowing such an unfortunate event to happen. However, in many negotiation situations people do just that—they leave money to burn.

Symmetry

In a symmetric bargaining situation, the two players have exactly the same strategic possibilities and bargaining power. Therefore, neither player has any reason to accept an agreement that yields a lower payoff than that of the opponent.

Another way of thinking about symmetry is to imagine interchanging the two players. This should not change the outcome. In Figure 5–2, this means that $u1$ will be equal to $u2$. The feasible set of outcomes must be symmetrical with respect to a hypothetical 45-degree line, λ, which begins at the origin 0 and passes through the point c, thereby implying that $c1 = c2$. If we extend this line out to the farthest feasible point, u, that is the Nash point, wherein parties' utilities are symmetric.

The symmetry principle is often considered to be the fundamental postulate of bargaining theory (Harsanyi, 1962). When parties' utilities are known, the solution to the game is straightforward (Nash, 1950). As we have noted, however, players' utilities are usually not known. This uncertainty reduces the usefulness of the symmetry principle. That is, symmetry cannot be achieved if a negotiator has only half of the information (Schelling, 1960).

The pareto-optimality and symmetry axioms uniquely define the agreement points of a symmetrical game. The remaining two axioms extend the theory to asymmetrical games in which the bargaining power is asymmetric.

Independence of Equivalent Utility Representations

Many utility functions can represent the same preference. Utility functions are behaviorally equivalent if one can be obtained from the other by an order-preserving linear transformation—for example, by shifting the zero point of the utility scale or by changing the utility unit. A distinguishing feature of the Nash solution outcome is that it is independent of the exchange rate between two players' utility scales; it is invariant with respect to any fixed weights we might attach to their respective utilities.

The solution to the bargaining game is not sensitive to positive linear transformations of parties' payoffs because utility is defined on an interval scale. Interval scales such as temperature preserve units of measurement but have an arbitrary origin (i.e., zero point) and unit of measurement. The utility scales for player 1 and player 2 in Figure 5–2 have an arbitrary origin and unit of measurement.

For example, suppose that you and a friend are negotiating to divide 100 poker chips. The poker chips are worth $1 each if redeemed by you and worth $1 each if redeemed by your friend. The question is: How should the two of you divide the poker chips? The Nash solution predicts that the two of you should divide all of the chips and not leave any on the table (pareto-optimality principle). Further, the Nash solution predicts that you should receive 50 chips and your friend should receive 50 chips (symmetry principle). So far, the Nash solution probably sounds fine. Now, suppose that the situation is slightly changed. Imagine that the chips are worth $1 each if redeemed by you, but they are worth $5 each if redeemed by your friend. (The rules of the situation do not permit any kind of side payments or renegotiation of redemption values.) Now, how should the chips be divided? All we have done is transform your friend's utilities using an order-preserving linear transformation (multiply all her values by 5) while keeping your utilities the same. The Nash solution states that you should still divide the chips 50–50 because your friend's utilities have not changed; rather, they are represented by a different, but nevertheless equivalent, linear transformation.

Some people have a hard time with this axiom. After all, if you and your friend are really "symmetric," one of you should not come out richer in the deal. But consider the arguments that could be made for one of you receiving a greater share of the chips. One of you could have a seriously ill parent and need the money for an operation; one of you might be independently wealthy and not need the money; or one of you could be a foolish spendthrift and not deserve the money. Moreover, there could be a disagreement: One of you regards yourself to be thoughtful and prudent but is regarded as silly and imprudent by the other person. All of these arguments are outside the realm of Nash's theory because they are **indeterminate.** Dividing resources to achieve *monetary* equality is as arbitrary as flipping a coin.

But wait a minute. In negotiation, doesn't everything really boil down to dollars? No. In Nash's theory, each person's utility function may be normalized on a 0 to 1 scale so that his or her "best outcome" = 1 and "worst outcome" = 0. Therefore, because the choices of origin and scale for each person's utility function are unrelated to one another, actual numerical levels have no standing in theory, and no comparisons of numerical levels can affect the outcome.

This axiom has serious implications. By permitting the transformation of one player's utilities without any transformation of the other player's, it destroys the possibility that the outcome should depend on interpersonal utility comparisons. Stated simply, it is meaningless for people to compare their utility with another. The same logic applies for comparing salaries, the size of offices, or anything else.

However, as we shall see, people do engage in interpersonal comparisons of utility (chapter 11). The important point is that interpersonal comparisons and arguments based on "fairness" are inherently subjective. There is no rational method for fair division.

Independence of Irrelevant Alternatives

The **independence of irrelevant alternatives** axiom states that the best outcome in a feasible set of outcomes will also be the best outcome in any smaller subset of feasible outcomes that still contains that outcome. For example, a subset of a bargaining game may be obtained by excluding some of the irrelevant alternatives from the original game, without excluding the original agreement point itself. The exclusion of irrelevant alternatives does not change the settlement.

Consider Figure 5–2: The Nash solution is point *u*. Imagine that the settlement options in the half-ellipse below the 45-degree line are eliminated. According to the independence of irrelevant alternatives axiom, this should not affect the settlement outcome, which should still be *u*.

This axiom allows a point prediction to be made in asymmetric games by allowing them to be enlarged to be symmetric. For example, imagine that the game parties play is an asymmetric one like that described above (that is, the half-ellipse below the 45-degree line is eliminated). Such a bargaining problem would be asymmetric, perhaps with player 2 having an advantage. According to Nash, it is useful to expand the asymmetric game to be one that is symmetric—for example, by including the points in the lower half of the ellipse that mirrors the half-ellipse above the 45-degree line. Once these points are included, the game is symmetric and the Nash solution may be identified. Of course, the settlement outcome yielded by the new, expanded game must also be present in the original game.

The independence of irrelevant alternatives axiom is motivated by the way negotiation unfolds (Harsanyi, 1990). Through a process of voluntary mutual concessions, the set of possible outcomes under consideration gradually decreases to just those around the eventual agreement point. This axiom asserts that the winnowing process does not change the agreement point.

In summary, Nash's theorem states that there is a unique solution that possesses these properties. Nash's solution selects the unique point that maximizes the geometric average (i.e., the product) or the gains available to people as measured against their reservation points. For this reason, the Nash solution is also known as the Nash product. If all possible outcomes are plotted on a graph whose rectangular coordinates measure the utilities that the two players derive from them, as in Figures 5–1 and 5–2, the solution is a unique point on the upper right boundary of the region. The point is unique because, if there were two, the two could be joined by a straight line representing available alternative outcomes achievable by mixing, with various odds, the probabilities of the original two outcomes, and the points on the line connecting them would yield higher products of the two players' utilities. In other words, the region is presumed convex by reason of the possibility of probability mixtures, and the convex region has a single maximum-utility-product point, or "Nash point."

LIMITATIONS OF RATIONAL THEORY

We have presented the Nash bargaining model to illustrate the precision and quantification of negotiation theory and introduce important terms and concepts that pervade virtually all descriptive analyses of negotiation. This model provides a way of thinking about optimal outcomes to attain in virtually any negotiation situation.

Rational models are often built on the assumption that people have complete and perfect information. However, this is rarely the case. Under conditions of incomplete, private information, normative models predict a certain amount of inefficiency in negotiations (see Myerson and Satterthwaite, 1989). That is, not all outcomes are expected to be pareto-efficient as in the perfect information situation.

FIGURE 5–3.

Source: Drawing by Ged Melling. *The Economist*, December 24, 1994—January 6, 1995. Used with permission.

Rational theories of negotiation were formulated as models of what people should do and how they actually behave. However, examinations of actual bargaining behavior depart from rational theory and violate the fundamental axioms of normative models. This suggests that people are not purely rational. Given the failure of rational models to explain actual negotiation behavior, what is their value for our understanding negotiation? What use are they if they don't predict behavior?

Traditionally, economic models were based on principles of rational behavior. As the cartoon (Fig. 5–3) suggests, people's behavior is not always rational. Even so, principles and assumptions derived from rational models are still a fundamental part of our "mix" for understanding human behavior.

VALUE OF RATIONAL THEORY

Rational models of negotiation behavior offer a number of important advantages for the negotiator interested in understanding, prediction, and control. First, rational models have intuitive appeal. The axioms of Nash's bargaining theory and expected utility theory are compelling in their internal consistency, logic of prediction, and precision. No descriptive theory makes such precise predictions. Rational models make clear and definitive predictions that are falsifiable, in contrast to many descriptive theories, which are often vague and subject to a variety of interpretations.

Second, rational models provide a measure of perfection or optimality. If rational models did not exist, we would have no way of evaluating how well people perform in negotiation nor what they should strive to do. We would not be able to offer any advice to negotiators because we would not have any consensus about what a "good" outcome is. Rational models provide an ideal.

Finally, rational models serve a useful diagnostic purpose because they often reveal where negotiators make mistakes. Because rational models are built on a well-constructed theory of decision making, they offer insight about the mind of the negotiator.

CONCLUSION

A solid understanding of rational models of negotiation is essential for the negotiator who wants to understand, predict, and control negotiation situations. With rational expectations theory as a basis for our analysis of negotiations, we are now ready to examine actual bargaining behavior. We move from a primarily rational analysis of negotiation to a descriptive focus. We have poured the "rational behavior" ingredients into the mix; now we are ready to examine "character defects."

TAKE-AWAYS

- If the decisions we make about our own lives are not rational (i.e., transitive, etc.), the decisions that we make when negotiating with others will also be flawed.
- A good way to examine the soundness of our own thinking and decision making is to frame choices in many different ways (e.g., as a gamble or sure thing). If we come up with the same answer each time, we can be more confident about our decisions.
- Most negotiators fail to obtain pareto-optimal agreements—in short, they leave money on the table.
- It's valuable to understand rational decision theory and the Nash bargaining model, so we can learn where we are making mistakes and avoid being taken advantage of at the bargaining table.

CHAPTER 6

Judgment and Decision Making:
Deciding among Sure Things and Risky Prospects

The couple stood by the sweeping sectional couch. "I really like it," said Kerry. "It will look great in the house," agreed Jo. "I hope the salesman agrees to lower the price on the ottoman as well as the rest of the pieces."

David, the salesman, returned beaming, "Good news. The manager said he would lower the price on the ottoman as well. So, you can get the entire grouping for $4,500."

After a brief discussion, the couple told the salesman that they would buy the couch. They approached the counter and filled out the paperwork. "I assume that the cost of the fabric protector is already included in the price since this is a floor model?" asked Kerry. David replied that this was not included and that the charge would be an additional $75. "Well, don't you think you could include the protection as part of the package?" Jo offered. "Actually, it is a separate company that does the protection, so we really can't," David explained.

Kerry started to get indignant. The salesman then explained that the ottoman—had it not been reduced—would have been an additional $80. "So, you see, you actually made $5." "Hmm, I guess I can live with that. That is pretty good. Here's my credit card," said Kerry.

The couch-buying example illustrates a common observation in most negotiation situations: the presence of multiple reference points. Kerry viewed the couch purchase to cost $75 more than expected. However, according to the salesman, the couple saved $5. In both cases, the objective outcome is the same: The couple goes home with a new couch with fabric protection for $4,575. However, the way the situation is framed dramatically affects how we make decisions.

Negotiation is a decision-making task in which people choose among alternative courses of action. Decision-making tasks can be "solved" by applying normative models, which guarantee rational choices. To make judgments, negotiators use **heuristics, or rules of thumb** to guide their decision making. (Heuristics may be contrasted with algorithms, which are formal logical processes that guarantee a correct solution.) Although heuristic processes often produce satisfactory responses, they occasionally lead to systematic and dramatic errors that have serious consequences for negotiators.

To understand how decision heuristics guide our behavior, it is necessary to examine rational decision-making models. After all, we cannot understand why decisions are faulty unless we know how to make good decisions. Therefore, we begin by covering the basics of individual decision theory. Because the roots of decision theory are primarily normative, prescribing how decision makers should make decisions (Keeney and Raiffa, 1976), we build on the basic principles covered in chapter 5 in our discussion.

DECISION MAKING

We make many types of decisions. Our decisions about how to spend the weekend may seem fundamentally different from deciding what to do with our entire life. There are, however, generalities that cut across domains. Rational-decision making models provide the tools necessary for analyzing trivial decisions as well as those of monumental importance. Generally speaking, there are three main types of decisions: riskless choice, decision making under uncertainty, and risky choice.

Riskless Choice

Riskless choice, or choice under certainty, involves choosing between two or more readily available options. For example, a choice between two apartments is a riskless choice, as is choosing among 31 flavors of ice cream or selecting which book to read. Often, we do not consider these to be decisions because they are so simple and easy. However, at other times it is difficult to make such choices. We find ourselves in a state of indecision and wonder what the best choice is.

The study of decision making provides a way of thinking about decisions and a way of choosing among options which, if followed correctly, will produce the "best" outcome for the chooser, maximizing his or her own preferences.

Imagine that you have received acceptance letters for graduate study from your top two universities, X and Y. From chapter 1, you recognize this enviable situation to be a classic approach–approach conflict. You have to make a final decision in the next week. On your coffee table is a large stack of brochures, descriptions, and information about the schools. How should you begin to analyze your situation?

To analyze this decision situation, we will employ a method known as **multiattribute utility technique,** or MAUT (see Baron, 1988, for an overview). According to MAUT, there are four main tasks to do: (1) identify the alternatives, (2) identify dimensions or attributes of the alternatives, (3) evaluate the utility associated with each dimension, and (4) weight or prioritize each dimension in terms of importance.

Identification of Alternatives

The first step is usually quite simple. The decision maker simply identifies the relevant alternatives. For example, you would identify the schools to which you had been accepted. In other situations, the alternatives may not be as obvious. For example, in chapter 4 we saw that the identification of alternatives often requires complex problem solving. Also, in the case that you did not get any acceptance letters, you must brainstorm about what to do with your life.

Identification of Attributes

The second step is more complex and involves identifying the key attributes of the alternatives. The attributes are the features of the alternatives that make them appealing or unappealing. For example, when choosing among schools, relevant attributes might include the cost of tuition, reputation of the program, course requirements, placement options, weather, cultural aspects, family, and faculty. There is no limit to the number of attributes that you may identify as relevant to your decision.

Utility

The next step is to evaluate the relative utility or value of each alternative for each attribute. For example, we might use a 1 to 5 scale in the school decision. You might evaluate the reputation of university X very highly (+5) but the weather as very unattractive (+1); you might evaluate university Y's reputation to be moderately high (+3) but the weather to be fabulous (+5). MAUT assumes preferential independence of attributes (i.e., the value of one attribute is independent of the value of others).

Weight

In addition to determining the evaluation of each attribute, the decision maker also evaluates how important that attribute is to him or her. The importance of each attribute is referred to as weight in the decision process. Again, we can use a simple numbering system, with 1 representing relatively unimportant attributes and 5 representing very important attributes. For example, you might consider the reputation of the school to be very important (+5), but the cultural attributes of the city to be insignificant (+1).

Making a Decision

The final step in the MAUT procedure is to compute a single, overall evaluation of each alternative. To do this, first multiply the utility evaluation of each attribute by its corresponding weight, and then sum the weighted scores across each attribute. Finally, select the option that has the highest overall score. An example of this procedure is illustrated in Figure 6–1.

We can see from the hypothetical example in Figure 6–1 that university X is a better choice for the student compared to university Y. However, it is a close decision. If the importance of any of the attributes were to change (e.g., tuition cost, reputation, climate, or cul-

FIGURE 6–1. Multi-attribute Decision Making

Attribute (weight)	University Y (evaluation)	University X (evaluation)
Tuition cost (4)	Low (5)	High (1)
Reputation (5)	Medium (3)	High (5)
Climate (3)	Lousy (1)	Great (5)
Culture (1)	Good (4)	Lacking (1)

Utility of University $(Y) = (4*5) + (5*3) + (3*1) + (1*4) = 42$

Utility of University $(X) = (4*1) + (5*5) + (3*5) + (1*1) = 45$

ture), then the overall decision could change. Similarly, if the evaluation of any attributes changes, then the final choice may change. Decision theory can tell us how to *choose*, but it cannot tell us how to weigh the attributes that go into making choices.

Decision Making under Uncertainty

Sometimes we must make decisions when the alternatives are uncertain or unknown. These situations are known as decision making under uncertainty or decision making in ignorance (Yates, 1990). In such situations, the decision maker has no idea about the likelihood of events. Consider, for example, a decision to plan a social event outdoors or indoors. If the weather is sunny and warm, it would be better to hold the event outdoors; if it is rainy and cold, it is better to plan the event indoors. The plans must be made a month in advance, but the weather cannot be predicted a month in advance. The distinction between risk and uncertainity hinges upon whether probabilities are known exactly (e.g., as in games of chance) or whether they must be judged by the decision maker with some degree of imprecision (e.g., almost everything else). Hence, "ignorance" might be viewed merely as an extreme degree of uncertainty where the decision maker has no clue (e.g., probability that the closing price of Dai Ichi stock tomorrow on the Tokyo stock exchange is above 1600 yen).

Risky Choice

Whereas in decision making under uncertainty the likelihood of events is unknown, in risky choice situations the probabilities are known. As we will see below, most theories of decision making are based on an assessment of the probability that some event will take place. Because the outcomes of risky choice situations are not fully known, outcomes are often referred to as prospects.

Negotiation is a risky choice situation because parties cannot be completely certain about the occurrence of a particular event. For instance, a negotiator cannot be certain that mutual settlement will be reached because negotiations could break off as each party opts for his or her BATNA. To understand risky choice decision making in negotiations, it is useful to first study one-party decision making, then move to more complex two-party or multiparty decision making.

DOMINANCE PRINCIPLE

In our discussion of riskless choice, we introduced the MAUT model of decision making, which specified alternatives, dimensions, utilities, and weights as well as a method of combining judgment to yield choice among options. How should you choose among risky options?

According to the **dominance principle,** one alternative *dominates* another if it is strictly better on at least one dimension and at least as good on all others. For example, imagine if university *Y* had been evaluated as a 5 in terms of tuition cost, a 5 in ranking, a 4 in climate, and a 4 in culture; and university *X* had been evaluated as a 1, 5, 4, and 3, respectively. In this case, we can quickly see that university *Y* is just as good as university *X* on two dimensions (reputation and climate) and better on the two remaining dimensions (tuition cost and culture). Thus, university *Y* dominates university *X*. Identifying a dominant alternative greatly simplifies decision making: If one alternative dominates the other, we should select the dominating option.

The example seems simple enough. In many situations, however, we are faced with considering many more alternatives, each having different dimensions. It may not be easy for us to spot a dominant alternative when we see one. What should we do in this case? The first step is to eliminate from consideration all options dominated by others, and choose among only the nondominated alternatives that remain. The dominance principle can also be applied to risky-choice situations that involve probability: Pick a prospect that has a greater probability over an equally valued but less likely prospect. The dominance principle in individual decision making is analogous to the concept of pareto-optimality in negotiation.

The dominance principle as a method of choice seems quite compelling, but it applies only to situations in which one alternative is clearly superior to others. It does not help us with the agonizing task of choosing among options that involve tradeoffs among highly valued aspects. We now turn to situations which defy MAUT and dominance detection.

EXPECTED-VALUE THEORY

Imagine that you have a rare opportunity to invest in a highly innovative start-up company. The company has developed a new technology that allows cars to run without gasoline. The cars are fuel efficient, environmentally clean, and less expensive to maintain than regular gasoline-fueled cars. On the other hand, the technology is new and unproven. Further, the company does not have the resources to compete with the major automakers. Nevertheless, if this technology is successful, an investment in the company at this point will have a 30-fold return. Suppose you just inherited $5,000 from your aunt. You could invest the money in the company and possibly earn $150,000—a risky choice. Or you could keep the money and pass up the investment opportunity. You assess the probability of success to be about 20 percent. (A minimum investment of $5,000 is required.) What do you do?

The dominance principle does not offer a solution to this decision situation because there are no clearly dominant alternatives. But the situation contains the necessary elements to use the **expected-value principle.** The expected-value principle applies when a decision maker must choose among two or more prospects, as in the example above. The "expectation" or "expected value" of a prospect is the sum of the objective values of the outcomes multiplied by the probability of their occurrence.

To see how the expected-value principle works, let's evaluate the expected value of this risky choice. An expected value requires us to compute an overall value for the decision alternatives. This can be done by multiplying the value of the alternative by its probability. For example, suppose you are offered a choice between earning a $50,000 salary or a salary based on profit sharing, such that there is a 20 percent chance your salary would be $20,000; a 20 percent chance of $35,000; a 20 percent chance of $50,000; a 20 percent chance of $75,000; and a 20 percent chance of $100,000. Which salary structure should you take? The overall value of the profit-sharing salary may be computed as follows:

Overall value of profit-sharing salary = .20($20,000) + .2($35,000) + .2($50,000) + .2($75,000) + .2 ($100,000) = $4,000 + $7,000 + $10,000 + $15,000 + $20,000 = $56,000

If we compare the flat salary of $50,000 to the profit-sharing salary's expected value ($56,000), it is easy to see that the profit-sharing salary has a higher expected value.

Now, what about our investment option? For a variety of reasons, you believe there is a 20 percent chance that the investment could result in a return of $150,000, which mathematically is .2 × $150,000 = $30,000 or $30,000 − $5,000 (initial investment) = $25,000. There is an 80 percent chance that the investment could result in a complete loss of your money, which mathematically is .8 × −$5,000 = −$4,000, or −$4,000. We can now compute the expected value of the risky choice by summing these values, or $25,000 − $4,000 = $21,000. Thus, the expected value of this gamble is $21,000.

The expected value of the certain option, not investing the money, may be computed the same way. In this case, it is certain (100 percent probability) that you can keep the money if you do not invest; therefore the calculation is $5,000 × 1 = $5,000. The expected-value principle dictates that the decision maker should select the prospect with the greatest expected value. In this case, the risky option (with an expected value = $21,000) has the greater expected value than the sure option (expected value = $5,000).

A related principle applies to evaluation decisions, or situations where decision makers must state, and be willing to act upon, the subjective worth of a given alternative. Suppose you could choose to "sell" your opportunity to invest to another person. What would you consider to be a fair price to do so? According to the expected-value evaluation principle, the evaluation of a prospect should be equal to its expected value. That is, the "fair price" for such a gamble would be $21,000. Similarly, the opposite holds: Suppose that your next-door neighbor held the opportunity but was willing to sell the option to you. According to the expected-value principle, people would pay up to $21,000 for the opportunity to gamble.

Prescriptive Value

The expected-value principle is intuitively appealing, but should we use it to make decisions? To answer this question, it is helpful to examine the rationale for using expected value as a prescription. Let's consider the short-term and long-term consequences (Yates, 1990). Imagine that you will inherit $5,000 every year for the next 50 years. Each year you must decide whether to invest the inheritance (the risky choice) or keep the money (the sure choice). The expected value of a prospect is its long-run average value. This principle is derived from a fundamental principle: **the law of large numbers** (Feller, 1968; Woodroofe, 1975). The law of large numbers states that the mean return will get closer and closer to its expected value the more times a gamble is repeated. Thus, we can be fairly sure that after 50 years of investing your money, the average return would be about $21,000. Some years you would lose, others you would make money, but on average, your return would be $21,000. When you look at the gamble this way, it seems reasonable to invest.

Now imagine that the investment decision is a once-in-a-lifetime opportunity. In this case, the law of large numbers does not apply to expected-value decision principle. You will either make $150,000, make nothing, or keep $5,000. There is no in-between. Under such circumstances, there are often very good reasons to reject the guidance of the expected value principle (Yates, 1990). For example, suppose that you need a new car. If the gamble is successful, buying a car is no problem. But if the gamble is unsuccessful, you will have no money at all. Therefore, you may decide that buying a used car at or under $5,000 is a more sensible choice.

Risk Attitudes

The expected-value concept is the basis for a standard way of labeling risk-taking behavior. For example, in the situation above you could either take the investment gamble or receive $21,000 from selling the opportunity to someone else. In this case, the "value" of the sure thing (i.e., receiving $21,000) is identical to the expected value of the gamble. Therefore, the "objective worths" of the alternatives are identical. What would you rather do? Your choice reveals your **risk attitude.** If you are indifferent to the two choices and are content to decide on the basis of a coin flip, you are **risk neutral or risk indifferent.** If you prefer the sure thing, then your behavior may be described as **risk averse.** If you choose to gamble, your behavior is classified as **risk seeking.**

Although there are some individual differences in people's risk attitudes, individuals do not tend to exhibit consistent risk-seeking or risk-averse behavior (Slovic, 1962; 1964). Rather, risk attitudes are highly context dependent. The fourfold pattern of risk attitudes predicts that people will be risk averse for moderate to high probability gains and low probability losses, and risk seeking for low probability gains and moderate to high probability losses (Tversky and Kahneman, 1992; Tversky and Fox, 1995).

St. Petersburg Paradox

How much money would you be willing to pay to play a game with the following two rules: (1) An unbiased coin is tossed until it lands on heads; (2) The player of the game is paid $2 if heads appears on the opening toss, $4 if heads first appear on the second toss, $8 on the third toss, $16 on the fourth toss, and so on. Before reading further, indicate how much you would be willing to pay to play the game.

To make a decision based upon rational analysis, let's calculate the expected value of the game by multiplying the payoff for each possible outcome by the probability of its occurring. Although the probability of the first head appearing on toss N becomes progressively smaller as N increases, the probability never becomes zero. In this case, note that the probability of heads for the first time on any given toss is $(1/2)^n$; and the payoff in each case is ($\$2^n$); hence, each term of the infinite series has an expected value of $1. The implication is that the value of the game is infinite! (Lee, 1971). Even though the value of this game is infinite, most people are seldom willing to pay more than a few dollars to play it. Most people believe that the expected value principle in this case produces an absurd conclusion. The observed reluctance to pay to play the game, despite its objective attractiveness, is known as the **St. Petersburg paradox** (Bernoulli, 1738/1954).

How can we explain such an enigma? We might argue that expected value is an undefined quantity when the variance of outcomes is infinite. Because, in practice, the person or organization offering the game could not guarantee a payoff greater than its total assets, the game was unimaginable, except in truncated and therefore finite form (Shapley, 1977). So what do we do when offered such a choice? We have decided that to regard it as "priceless" or even to pay hundreds of thousands of dollars would be absurd. So, how should managers reason about such situations?

EXPECTED UTILITY THEORY

The reactions people have to the St. Petersburg game are consistent with the proposition that people decide among prospects not according to their expected objective values, but rather according to their expected subjective values. That is, the psychological value of money does not increase proportionally as the objective amount increases. To be sure, virtually all of us like more money than less money, but we don't necessarily like $20 twice as much as $10. And the difference in our happiness when our $20,000 salary is raised to $50,000 is not the same as when our $600,000 salary is raised to $630,000. Bernoulli proposed a logarithmic function relating the utility of money, u, to the amount of money, x. This function is **concave,** meaning that the utility of money decreases marginally. Constant additions to monetary amounts result in less and less increased utility. The principle of **diminishing marginal utility** is related to a fundamental principle of psychophysics, wherein good things satiate and bad things escalate. The first bite of a pizza is the best; as we get full, each bite brings less and less utility.

The principle of diminishing marginal utility is simple, yet profound. It is known as "everyman's utility function" (Bernoulli, 1738/1954). According to Bernoulli, a fair price for a gamble should not be determined by its expected (monetary) value, but rather by its expected utility (see Figure 6–2). Thus, the logarithmic utility function in Figure 6–2 yields a finite price for the gamble.

According to expected utility theory, each of the possible outcomes of a prospect has a utility (subjective value) that is represented numerically. The more appealing an outcome is, the higher its utility. The expected utility of a prospect is the sum of the utilities of the potential outcomes, each weighted by its probability. According to expected utility theory, when choosing among two or more prospects, people should select the option with the highest ex-

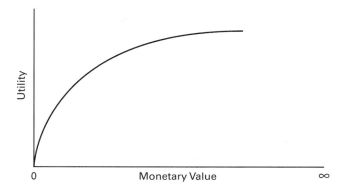

FIGURE 6–2. Utility as a Function of Value

pected utility. Further, in evaluation situations, risky prospects should have an expected utility equal to the corresponding "sure choice" alternative.

Expected utility (EU) principles have essentially the same form as expected value (EV) principles. The difference is that expectations are computed using objective (dollar) values in EV models as opposed to subjective values (utility) in EU models.

Utility Function Shape and Risk Taking

A person's utility function for various prospects reveals something about their risk-taking tendencies. If a utility function is concave, a decision maker will always choose a sure thing over a prospect whose expected value is identical to that sure thing. The decision maker's behavior is risk averse (Figure 6–3a). The risk-averse decision maker would prefer a sure $5 over a 50–50 chance of winning $10 or nothing—even though the expected value of the gamble [.5 ($10) + .5($0) = $5] is equal to that of the sure thing. If a person's utility function is convex, he or she will choose the risky option (Figure 6–3b). If the utility function is linear, his or her decisions will be risk neutral and of course, identical to that predicted by expected value maximization (Figure 6–3c).

Allais Paradox

If most managers' utility for gains are concave (i.e., risk averse), then why would people ever choose to gamble? Bets that offer small probabilities of winning large sums of money (e.g., lotteries, roulette wheels) ought to be especially unattractive, given that the concave utility function that drives the worth of the large prize is considerably lower than the value warranting a very small probability of obtaining the prize.

Imagine that, as a manager, one of your subordinates comes to you with the following prospects based upon the consequences of a particular marketing strategy:

Strategy *A*:   80 percent probability of earning $40,000 or nothing

Strategy *B*:   earn $30,000 for sure

Which do you choose? Only a small minority of managers (20 percent) choose strategy *A* over strategy *B*. Meanwhile, suppose that another associate on a different project presents you with the following two plans:

Strategy *C*:   20 percent probability of earning $40,000 or nothing

Strategy *D*:   25 percent probability of earning $30,000 or nothing

FIGURES 6–3a, b, and c. Risk Attitudes

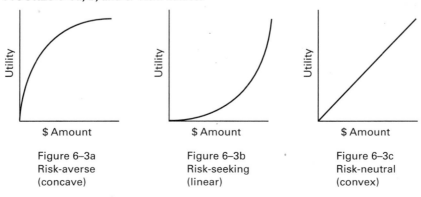

Figure 6–3a
Risk-averse
(concave)

Figure 6–3b
Risk-seeking
(linear)

Figure 6–3c
Risk-neutral
(convex)

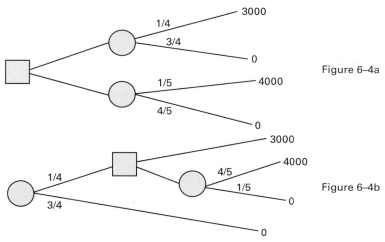

FIGURE 6–4. Allais Paradox Decision Tree

Source: Adapted from Kahneman, D. and A. Tversky (1979). Prospect theory: An analysis of decision under risk. *Econometrica* **47**: 263–291. Copyright © by The Econometric Society.

Faced with this choice, a clear majority (65 percent) choose strategy *C* over strategy *D* (the smaller, more likely prize) (adapted from Kahneman and Tversky, 1979).

However, in this example, the manager's choice behavior violates expected-utility theory, which requires consistency between the *A* versus *B* choice and the *C* versus *D* choice. In Figure 6–4b, *C* versus *D* should be treated the same as a two-stage lottery because the theory considers final states of wealth rather than incremental changes (see Figure 6–4a). In the first stage, there is a 25 percent chance of surviving to a second stage offering *A* versus *B*. When the ratio of the value of the two lottery prizes is fixed, the preference between respective options should be completely determined by the ratio of the probability of winning the prizes.

In the *A* versus *B* and *C* versus *D* choices above, the ratio is the same: (.8/1) = (.20/.25). However, managers' preferences usually reverse. According to the **certainty effect,** people have a tendency to overweight certain outcomes relative to outcomes that are merely probable. The reduction in probability from certainty (1) to a degree of uncertainty (.8) produces a more pronounced loss in attractiveness than a corresponding reduction from one level of uncertainty (.2) to another (.25). Managers do not think rationally about probabilities. Those close to 1 are often (mistakenly) considered sure things. On the flip side is the possibility effect: the tendency to overweight outcomes that are possible relative to outcomes that are impossible.

PROSPECT THEORY

Prospect theory is a descriptive theory of how people make decisions (Kahneman and Tversky, 1979). There are two key pharses in a decision process: editing and evaluation. The editing phase consists of "coding," "combination," "segregation," and "cancellation." The evaluation phase consists of associating a utility with a prospect.

Main Elements

The main elements of prospect theory are decision weights, subjective value, combination rules, and decisions.

Decision Weights

In contrast to expected utility theory, probabilities do not combine directly with values in prospect theory. Instead, the decision maker transforms probabilities into psychological decision weights. The decision weights are then applied to the subjective values. Prospect theory proposes a relationship between the probabilities' potential outcomes and the weights those probabilities have in the decision process.

Figure 6–5 illustrates the probability weighting function proposed by cumulative prospect theory. It is an inverted–S function that is concave near 0 and convex near 1. There are several noteworthy features of the probability–weighting function.

Extremity Effect   Low probabilities tend to be overweighted, and high probabilities are underweighted.

Crossover Point   The **crossover probability** is the point at which objective probabilities and subjective weights coincide. Prospect theory does not pinpoint where the crossover occurs, but it is definitely lower than 50 percent.

Subadditivity   Adding two probabilities, $p1$ and $p2$, should yield a probability $p3 = p1 + p2$. For example, suppose you are an investor considering three stocks, A, B, and C. You assess the probability that stock A will close two points higher today than yesterday to be 20% and you assess the probability that stock B will close two points higher today than yesterday to be 15%. The stocks are two different companies in two different industries and are completely independent. Now consider the price of stock C, which you believe has

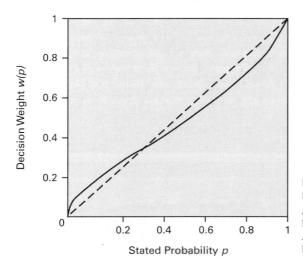

FIGURE 6–5. A Weighting Function for Decision Under Risk

Source: Fox, C.R. and A. Tversky. A belief-based model of decision under uncertainty. *Management Science,* in press. Copyright © by The Econometric Society.

a 35% probability of closing two points higher today. The likelihood of a two-point increase in either stock A or B should be identical to the likelihood of a two-point increase in stock C. The probability–weighting relationship proposed by prospect theory, however, does not exhibit additivity. That is, for small probabilities, weights are subadditive, as we see from the extreme flatness at the lower end of the curve. This means that most decision makers consider the likely increase of either stocks A or B to be less likely than an increase in stock C.

Subcertainty   Except for guaranteed or impossible events, prospect theory asserts that weights for complementary events do not sum to 1. One implication of the **subcertainty** feature of the probability–weight relationship is that for all probabilities, p, with $0 < p < 1$, $\pi(p) + \pi(1 - p) < 1$.

Regressiveness   According to the **regressiveness principle,** extreme values of some quantity do not deviate very much from the average value of that quantity. The relative flatness of the probability–weighting curve is a special type of regressiveness suggesting that people's decisions are not as responsive to changes in uncertainty as are the associated probabilities. Another aspect is that nonextreme high probabilities are underweighted and low ones are overweighted.

Subjective Value

The subjective value associated with a prospect depends on the decision weights and the subjective values of potential outcomes. The theory makes specific claims about the form of the relationship between various amounts of an outcome and their subjective values. Figure 6–6 illustrates the generic prospect theory value function.

There are three noteworthy characteristics about the value function. The first pertains to the decision maker's **reference point.** According to prospect theory, there is a focal amount of the pertinent outcome at which smaller amounts are considered losses and larger amounts gains. That focal amount is the manager's reference point. For example, Kerry's reference point for the couch was $4,500; when he had to pay $75 extra, he was angry, because he viewed this as a $75 loss. The savvy salesman quickly provided another reference, $4,580 less a discount of $5, which appears to be a savings. According to prospect theory, people are sensitive to *changes in wealth*; in contrast, expected utility theory argues that people evaluate outcomes with respect to *impact on final assets.*

A second feature is that the shape of the function changes markedly at the reference point. For gains, the value function is concave, exhibiting diminishing marginal value. As the starting point for increases in gains becomes larger, the significance of a constant increase lessens. A complementary phenomenon occurs in the domain of losses: constant changes in the negative direction away from the reference point also assume diminishing significance the farther from the reference point the starting point happens to be.

Finally, the value function is noticeably steeper for losses than for gains. Stated another way, gains and losses of identical magnitude have different significance for people; losses are considered more important. We are much more disappointed about losing $75 than we are happy about making $75.

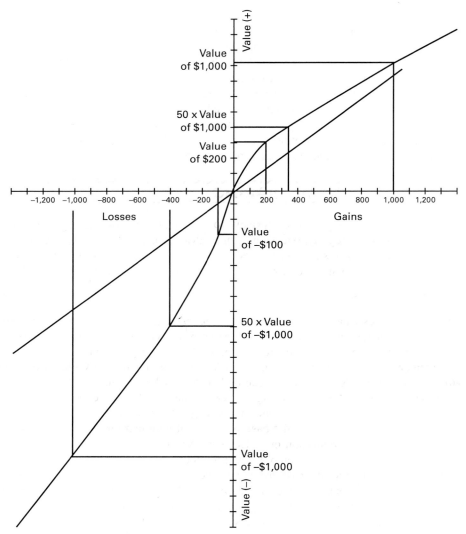

FIGURE 6–6. A Hypothetical Value Function

Source: Kahneman, D. and A. Tversky (1979). Prospect theory: An analysis of decision under risk. *Econometrica* 47:263–291. Copyright © by The Econometric Society.

Combination Rules

How do decision weights and outcome values combine to determine the subjective value of a prospect? The amounts that are effective for the decision maker are not the *actual* sums that would be awarded or taken away, but are instead the *differences* between those sums and the decision maker's reference point.

Decisions

Once a manager determines subjective values for the given prospects, those values should be used to make the decision. This analysis of prospect theory tells us how managers make decisions and how such decisions may sometimes be faulty or not rational if probabilities are not carefully considered. A manager's way of assessing probabilities affects how he or she negotiates. Clever managers are aware of how their *own* decisions may be biased, as well as how the decisions of others may be manipulated to their own advantage. Now that we know about how individuals make decisions, we are ready to explore multiparty, or interdependent, decision making. Next, we consider how our negotiation behavior is affected by the quality and rationality of our judgments. We explore the major flaws made by negotiators and how to correct them.

INTERDEPENDENT DECISION MAKING

The theories discussed above pertain exclusively to individual decision making. As noted earlier, negotiation is the multiparty extension of individual decision making. Below, we discuss the four major impediments to effective decision making in negotiation: reference point effects, elicitation effects, violations of consequentialist reasoning, and overconfidence.

Reference Point Effects

A reference point defines what a person considers to be the status quo, such as one's current wealth. Outcomes that fall short of one's reference point are regarded as losses; outcomes that exceed one's reference point are regarded as gains. Whether a given outcome is viewed as a loss or gain dramatically affects our behavior. Manipulation of a person's reference point can produce paradoxical judgment: People can be led to be risky or cautious, depending on whether they view themselves as maximizing gain or minimizing loss. For example, consider Syd, a sales manager. It was company policy for young salespersons to work either based solely on commission or to receive a flat base pay without commission. Syd wanted all of her employees to work on commission only. However, because she could not enforce this, Syd would skillfully manipulate her employees' reference points. She would describe the two choices as, "If you go with the base-pay option, you are sure to earn less than the managers in the upper 25th percentile. However, if you go with the commission pay, you could earn quite a bit more than those on the base-pay plan although there is some possibility that you would earn even less. Thus, you can: take a sure loss by going with the base-pay plan, or you can try to maximize your gains by trying the commission plan." Syd correctly realized that people are risk-seeking for (moderate) losses and thereby used reference points to induce people to choose the riskier course of action.

Risk Seeking and Risk Aversion

A negotiator's reservation point can act as a reference point in negotiation from which everything above it is viewed as a gain; proposals that fall short are viewed as losses. For example, in a management–labor situation, negotiators were led either to view the outcomes they received in negotiations as gains (positive departures from a reference point) or losses (negative departures from a reference point). Thus, some negotiators were told that their payoffs in the negotiation represented net profits; others were told that their goal was to minimize expenditures, which would be subtracted from a starting budget value of $8,000. In both cases, the situation facing the negotiators was objectively identical.

The different reference points dramatically influenced behavior. Negotiators who were instructed to minimize their losses made fewer concessions, reached fewer agreements, and perceived the settlements that were reached to be less fair, compared to those in the "gain" frame. In short, these negotiators adopted more risky bargaining strategies, preferring to hold out for a better, but more risky, settlement. When they did reach agreements, their deals were more profitable. In contrast, positive departures from reference points led to more concession (cf. Bazerman, Magliozzi, and Neale, 1985; Neale and Northcraft, 1986; Neale, Huber, and Northcraft, 1987; for reviews, see Neale and Bazerman, 1991).

Obviously, negotiators should carefully examine their reference points. Be wary when an opponent attempts to manipulate your reference point. Kerry should have been suspicious of the salesman's remark about saving $5.

The effect of reference points on negotiation behavior may depend on the risk of the negotiated settlement versus the impasse alternative (Schuur, 1987). We have considered the situation in which negotiators bargain over "certain" outcomes versus a "risky" alternative (i.e., to hold out and possibly have to accept one's BATNA). However, what about the situation in which negotiators bargain over "risky" gains and losses and the reference point represents a "sure" outcome? In this situation, it is possible for negotiators to reach a settlement that is worse than their impasse alternative. In this case, positively framed negotiators are *more* likely than negatively framed negotiators to hold out for less risky outcomes (Schuur, 1987).

The observation that positively framed negotiators are more effective than negatively framed negotiators is inconsistent with the central tenets of bargaining theory, which hold that risk aversion is disadvantageous (von Neumann and Morgenstern, 1947). That is, positive framing should be unilaterally disadvantageous because a negotiator's alternatives to settlement will be viewed as less attractive, leaving negotiators susceptible to exploitation by the less risk-averse negotiator. Of course, if both negotiators are risk averse, they may succeed in avoiding contentious behavior and reach a mutually beneficial agreement.

Should a Negotiator View the Glass as Half Empty or Half Full? Which negotiator has the advantage at the bargaining table—the negotiator who views the glass as half empty or the negotiator who views the glass as half full? Before reading further, make an argument for a particular side. Negotiators who have positive frames (view the glass as half full) are more likely to engage in the mutual problem solving necessary for integrative agreement, but they are also more likely to agree to less favorable terms and risk being exploited than are negotiators who view the glass as half empty. When both negotiators have a negative frame (view the glass as half empty), impasse is likely. Conversely, when both negotiators have a positive frame, agreements of high joint value are likely. If one negotiator has a negative frame and the other has a positive frame, the negotiator with the negative frame reaps a greater share of the resources. Thus, positive frames in negotiation can be a liability in distributive and integrative bargaining (Bottom and Studt, 1993). Risk aversion is advantageous only in situations in which settlement involves greater risk taking than impasse (see Schuur, 1987).

Is the Opponent's Glass Half Empty or Half Full? Negotiators' behavior might be influenced not only by their own reference point, but also by the other party's reference point. To investigate this possibility, negotiators were given either a positive or a negative frame and then given information about the other party's frame (the other party was actually a computer program) (deDreu et al., 1992). When both parties had a gain frame, negotiators made lower demands and higher concessions than when either negotiator had a loss frame. The results are consistent with a "frame adoption" hypothesis, suggesting that negotiators' frames develop and change as a function of their opponents' communicated frame (deDreu et al., 1992).

Risky Business   In many negotiation situations, settlement outcomes are determined without uncertainty at the time of settlement. For example, we know that we'll drive home in a new car or earn a particular salary once the deal is negotiated. However, some negotiations contain an element of risk. For example, consider buying a piece of real estate. Depending upon the market, the land might be worth much more than what we pay or much less. This situation is known as **contractual risk.**

The Mitsubishi Estate Company provided a dramatic example of the risk of erroneous estimates in negotiation (Bottom, 1996). In October of 1989, Mitsubishi agreed to pay the Rockefeller family trust $846 million in exchange for a controlling interest in the Rockefeller Group, Inc., which owns Rockefeller Center. Unfortunately, Mitsubishi, along with many others, failed to foresee the collapse of the New York real estate market, which dramatically lowered the value of the acquisition. In May of 1995, Mitsubishi Estate Company was forced to seek bankruptcy protection primarily in an attempt to stem the $600 million in losses they had incurred on the investment (Pacelle, 1995; Pacelle and Lipin, 1995). Clearly, the Mitsubishi negotiators expected a much better payoff when they signed the original agreement to acquire control of the property.

How does such contractual risk affect negotiator behavior? Under contractual risk, negotiators with negative frames are more likely to reach integrative agreement than those with positive frames. Why? The only route capable of attaining high aspirations entails some creative risk. Thus, if integrative negotiation outcomes involve "sure things," positive frames are more effective; however, if the integrative outcomes require negotiators to "roll the dice," negative frames are more effective.

Package Deal or Piecemeal?   Is a negotiator better off treating the issues to be negotiated (i.e., the issue mix) in terms of a package, lump-sum value or on an issue-by-issue basis? According to prospect theory, people should prefer segregated gains to integrated gains, because of the diminishing returns principle. In contrast, integrated losses should be preferred to segregated losses because losses tend to mount. For example, would you prefer to receive seven pieces of good news (e.g., a raise, promotion, lottery payoff, unexpected call from a friend, etc.) all in one day or over the span of a week? Most people like to spread out good news. Now imagine the same situation for bad news (e.g., a parking ticket, a bounced check, car trouble, rain, etc.). Would you want to spread these things out over time or be hit with them all at once? Most people prefer to receive bad news all at once. Negotiators with positive frames are more likely to reach agreement than those with negative frames in traditional segregated, multi-issue outcome situations. The opposite is true when outcomes are integrated (Carnevale, O'Connor, and McCusker, 1993).

Escalation of Commitment: When Things Go from Bad to Worse

Suppose that you make a small investment in a start-up company with great potential. After the first quarter, you learn that the company suffered an operating loss. You can't recover your investment; your goal is to maximize your long-term wealth. Should you continue to invest in the company? Consider two possible ways you might look at this situation: Suppose that you consider the performance of the company during the first quarter to be a loss, and view continued investment as a choice between: (1) losing the small amount of money you've already invested, or (2) taking additional risk by investing more money in the company, which could turn around or plummet even further. Prospect theory would predict that you will continue to invest in the company because you've already adopted a "loss frame" based upon your initial investment. Negotiators are risk seeking when situations are framed as losses.

Suppose that you recognize that the company did not perform well in the first period and consider your initial investment to be a sunk cost—that is, water under the bridge. In short, you adapt your reference point. Now ask yourself whether it would be wiser (1) not to invest in the company at this point (a sure outcome of $0), or (2) to take a gamble and invest more money in a company that has not shown good performance in the recent past. Under these circumstances, prospect theory predicts that you will not invest in the company because you would rather have a sure thing than a loss.

This investment scenario illustrates an important point: Identical situations may be framed as either a loss or a gain, depending upon one's perspective. In many situations, decision makers fail to adapt their reference point and continue to make risky decisions, which often prove unprofitable. **Escalation of commitment** or **psychological entrapment** (Staw and Ross, 1987; Brockner and Rubin, 1985) explains why some people literally gamble their lives away. The same phenomenon happens in management. In fact, when the top management of companies who have suffered substantial losses are replaced with new management, new management is much more likely to disinvest and improve company performance. It is worth mentioning that people sometimes commit the reverse fallacy of premature deescalation of commitment (Heath, 1995).

Obviously, a critical question concerns how to get people to make cost-benefit decisions "on the margin," neglecting sunk costs or predetermined budgets. This idea is related to **mental accounting** (Thaler, 1985) wherein decision makers have mental "budgets" for various items. To the extent that the new decision situation is treated as a different budget, then the decision maker might not fall prey to the escalation-of-commitment trap.

Endowment Effects: A Mug Only Your Mother Could Love

According to basic principles of expected utility theory, the value or utility we associate with a certain object or outcome should not be influenced by irrelevant factors, such as who owns the object. Simply stated, the value of the object should be about the same, whether we are a buyer or a seller. (*Note*: Buyers and sellers might want to adopt different bargaining positions for the object, but their private valuations for the object should not differ as a consequence of who has possession of it.) But negotiators' reference points may lead buyers and sellers to have different valuations for objects. Someone who possesses an object has a reference point that reflects his or her current endowment. When someone who owns an object considers selling it, he or she may view the situation as a loss. The difference between what sellers demand for the mug and what buyers are willing to pay is a manifestation of loss aversion, coupled with the rapid adaptation of the reference point. Therefore, on the basis of prospect theory, we should expect that sellers will demand more for objects than buyers are willing to pay.

To investigate this idea, students in an MBA class were "endowed" with coffee mugs worth $6 as charged by the university bookstore (Kahneman, Knetsch, and Thaler, 1990). The students who were not given a coffee mug were told that they had the opportunity to buy a mug from a student who owned the mug, if the student who owned the mug valued it less. The buyers' willingness to pay for the mug and the sellers' willingness to sell the mug were inferred from a series of choices (e.g., "receive $9.75" versus "recieve mug," "receive $9.50 versus a mug," etc.). Now consider two theories we have talked about. Expected utility theory would predict that about half of the buyers will value the mug more than the seller and therefore trade will occur; similarly, about half of the sellers will value the mug more than the buyer and trade will not occur. Prospect theory, on the other hand, predicts that because of the loss-aversion behavior engendered by the seller's loss frame, trade will occur less than expected. Indeed, although 11 trades were expected, on average only four took place. Sellers demanded in excess of $8 to part with their mugs; prospective buyers were only willing to pay list price (Kahneman, Knetsch, and Thaler, 1990).

If sellers are risk seeking by virtue of their endowment, how can it be that horses, cars, furniture, companies, and land are bought and sold every day? The endowment effect operates only when the seller regards himself or herself to be the owner of the object. If a seller expects to sell a good for a profit and views the good as currency, the endowment effect does not occur. For example, when MBA students are endowed with tokens rather than coffee mugs, the endowment effect does not occur.

Regret: Thinking about the Road Not Taken

People evaluate reality by comparing it to its salient alternatives (Kahneman and Miller, 1986). Sometimes we feel we made the "right" decision when we think about alternatives. Other times, we are filled with regret. What determines whether we feel we did the right thing (e.g., took the right job, married the right person) or whether we feel regret? An important component in determining whether a person experiences regret is counterfactual thinking (Gilovich and Medvec, 1994). **Counterfactual thinking,** or thinking about what might have been but did not occur, may act as a reference point for the psychological evaluation of actual outcomes.

As an example, consider feelings of regret experienced by athletes in the Olympic games (Medvec, Madey, and Gilovich, 1995). Although silver medalists should feel happier than bronze medalists because their performance is objectively superior, counterfactual reasoning might produce greater feelings of regret and disappointment in silver medalists than in bronze. Specifically, the bronze medalist's reference point is that of not placing at all, so winning a medal represents a gain. In contrast, the silver medalist views him- or herself as just missing the gold. With the gold medal as the referent, the silver medalist feels a loss. Indeed, videotapes of medalists' reactions (with the audio portion turned off) reveal that bronze medalists are perceived to be happier than silver medalists (Medvec, Madey, and Gilovich, 1995). Further, silver medalists report experiencing greater feelings of regret than do bronze medalists.

Elicitation Effects: The Answer Depends on How You Ask the Question

A fundamental principle of expected utility theory is **procedure invariance,** which requires that strategically equivalent methods of elicitation should yield the same preference order (Tversky, Sattath, and Slovic, 1988). Whether a person is asked to indicate a choice by judgment, evaluation, or actual decision, his or her behavior should be consistent. However, subtle differences in the way choice is elicited sometimes lead to dramatic reversals of preference. This has implications for how we ask our opponent to evaluate our proposals in negotiation and vice versa.

Preference Reversals

Your business associate comes into your office filled with excitement. She explains that you've got a great opportunity to invest in a rail transport company. It appears that two companies are for sale: company *X* and company *Y*. If profitable, company *X* could be worth $2 million. Your colleague estimates the chances to be 60 percent. Company *Y* could be worth $2.5 million, but the chances are only 40 percent. Which company should you invest in? Before reading further, pick which company you find to be the better investment.

A week later your associate bursts into your office with another proposition. Again, the proposition involves two transport companies, but this time your associate wants you to put a dollar value on what you think they are worth. Company *X* has a 30 percent chance of success and, if successful, will be worth $4 million. Company *Y* has a 20 percent chance of success and, if successful, will be worth $5 million. What do you think is a fair price to pay for company *X*? Company *Y*?

When faced with decisions like the ones above, managers tend to be inconsistent. That is, in the first situation, they choose company *X* over company *Y*. However, in the second situation, they put a higher price tag on company *Y* than company *X*. In fact, your associates' second proposition is identical to the first proposition when all values/probabilities are divided/multiplied by 2.

Preference reversals are inconsistencies in choice. For example, people choose gambles that offer a greater chance to win over another gamble that offers a higher payoff but a lower chance to win, but then assign a higher price (value) to the gamble offering the higher payoff than to the one with the greater chance to win (Slovic and Lichtenstein, 1983). This pattern of preferences violates basic principles of decision theory and has been observed in several contexts, including professional gamblers in Las Vegas casinos (Lichtenstein and Slovic, 1971). Why does intransitive choice happen?

The reason has to do with the aspects of the alternative that are salient to the decision maker. The prices of gambles are expressed in dollars, and, therefore, when evaluating the value of the gamble, people focus on the money they could win. In contrast, when gamblers choose between two gambles, the likelihood of winning is salient. In another example, people were presented with pairs of hypothetical students who had taken two courses. Their grades in one course and ranks in the other were shown: One student had a higher grade in one course, and the other student had a higher rank in the second. Some people were asked to predict which student would acheive a higher grade in a third course; others were asked to predict which student would receive a higher rank in a third course. The student with the higher grade was expected to perform better 56% of the time by the grade group and only 49% of the time by the rank group.

Choosing versus Rejecting: What to Keep and What to Throw Away

Decision making is difficult because people often do not know how to trade off one attribute (e.g., salary) with another (e.g., quality of life) in a job choice. Elicitation not only reveals preferences; it also constructs preferences. Decisions are often reached by focusing on considerations that justify the selection of one option over others (Simonson, 1989; Tversky and Shafir, 1992; Shafir and Tversky, 1992; Shafir, Simonson, and Tversky, 1993).

In one investigation, people were presented with pairs of options. The option pairs were created so that one was an "enriched" option (included more positive and more negative aspects) and the other was "impoverished" (included fewer positive and negative aspects). For example, one option pair concerned a child custody decision, wherein one parent had both positive and negative aspects (e.g., very close relationship to the child but much work-related travel); the other parent had fewer positive and negative aspects (reasonable rapport with child, average working hours). Some people were asked to indicate to which parent they would award custody, whereas others were asked to which parent they would deny custody. According to decision theory, the two choices are objectively identical and therefore there should be no difference in decisions when people are asked to choose or reject one parent. Nevertheless, the "enriched" parent was the modal choice for both being awarded and denied custody of the child. Why does this happen? The reason has to do with the "salience" idea discussed earlier. The reasons for awarding and denying the "enriched" parent are more salient.

The implications for negotiation behavior are extremely serious. Remember from chapter 4 the multiple offer strategy in which a negotiator presents the opponent with several offers (all of equal value) from which to choose. The opponent's response may be dramatically different if asked to reject one of the options. The message? Be cognizant of how you present choices to your opponent and how your opponent presents choices to you. Before making a commitment, ask yourself whether your answer would have been the same if you were to either choose or reject an offer.

Violations of the Sure Thing Principle

Imagine that you face a decision between going to graduate school X on the East Coast or graduate school Y on the West Coast. You must make your decision before you find out whether your start-up company has received funding from a venture capitalist. In the event you get the funding, the East Coast provides access to many more of your potential customers. In the event the funding does not come through, by going to the East Coast you would be closer to your family, who could help you with finances. This sounds pretty straightforward so far: X is your dominant choice no matter what the venture capitalist does. In other words, you have chosen school X regardless of whether you get funding. Making a decision between X and Y should not be hard—or should it?

When faced with uncertainty about some event occurring (such as whether your company will be funded), people are often reluctant to make decisions and will even pay money to delay decisions until the uncertain event is known. This is paradoxical because, no matter what happens, people choose to do the same thing (Tversky and Shafir, 1992). Consider a situation in which a student has just taken a tough and exhausting qualifying examination (see Shafir, 1994). The student has the option of buying a very attractive five-day Hawaiian vacation package. The results of the exam won't be available for a week, but the student must decide whether to buy the vacation package now. Alternatively, she can pay a nonrefundable fee to retain the right to buy the vacation package at the same price the day after the exam results are posted. When presented with these three choices, most respondents (61 percent) choose to pay a nonrefundable fee to delay the decision. Two other versions of the scenario are then presented to different groups of participants. In one version, the student passed the exam, and in the other version, the student failed. In both of these situations, respondents overwhelmingly preferred to go on the vacation. Thus, even though we decide to go on the vacation no matter what the results of the exam, we are willing to pay to delay making this decision.

This behavior violates one of the basic axioms of rational theory of decision making under uncertainty: the **sure thing principle** (Savage, 1954). According to the sure thing principle, if alternative X is preferred to Y in the condition that some event, A, occurs, and if X is also preferred to *Y* in the condition that some event, *A*, does not occur, then *X* should be preferred to *Y*, even when it is not known whether *A* will occur.

Why would people pay a fee to a consultant or intermediary to delay the decision when they would make the same choice either way? Violations of the sure thing principle are rooted in the *reasons* people use to make their decisions. In the example above, people have different reasons for going to Hawaii for each possible event. If they pass the exam, the vacation is a celebration or reward; if they fail the exam, the vacation is an opportunity to recuperate. When the decision maker does not know whether he or she has passed the exam, he or she may lack a clear reason for going to Hawaii. In the presence of uncertainty, people may be reluctant to think through the implications of each outcome and, as a result, they violate the sure thing principle.

Overconfidence

Consider a situation in which you are assessing the probability that a particular company will be successful. Some people might think the probability is quite good; others might think the probability is low; others might make middle-of-the-road assessments. For the decision maker, what matters most is making an assessment that is accurate. How accurate are people in judgments of probability? How do they make assessments of likelihood, especially when full, objective information is unavailable?

Judgments of likelihood for certain types of events are often more optimistic than is warranted. The **overconfidence effect** refers to unwarranted levels of confidence in people's judgment of their abilities and the occurrence of positive events and underestimates of the likelihood of negative events. For example, in negotiations involving third-party dispute resolution, negotiators on each side believe the neutral third party will adjudicate in their favor (Farber and Bazerman, 1986, 1989; Farber, 1981). Obviously, this can't happen; the third party can't adjudicate in favor of both parties. Similarly, in final-offer arbitration, wherein parties each submit their final bid to a third party who then makes a binding decision between the two proposals, negotiators consistently overestimate the probability that the neutral arbitrator will choose their own offer (Neale and Bazerman, 1983; Bazerman and Neale, 1982). Obviously, there is only a 50 percent chance of all final offers being accepted; nevertheless, typically, both parties' estimates sum to a number greater than 100 percent. The message is to beware of the overconfidence effect. When we find ourselves to be highly confident of a particular outcome occurring (whether it be our opponent caving in to us, a senior manager supporting our decision, etc.), it is important to examine why.

CONCLUSION

People consistently violate axioms of normative models. Inconsistent and intransitive behavior can lead to feelings of regret and make the decision maker vulnerable to exploitation. Negotiators profit economically and psychologically by understanding ways that they are victimized by their own well-intentioned judgment processes.

Whereas the judgment and decision-making approach points to *how* judgments deviate from optimal behavior, its analysis of *why* negotiators' judgments are often flawed is less obvious. It certainly can't be the case that people are ignorant or unmotivated. Most negotiators are highly motivated. So, what is going on? To better understand negotiators' judgment processes, we explore the mind of the negotiator in chapter 7.

TAKE-AWAYS

- Most of our important decisions involve some risk. People tend to be risk averse when thinking about gains and risk seeking when considering losses.
- Whether a person is risk seeking or risk averse depends upon his or her reference point. Like the old adage, any situation can be viewed in terms of a gain or a loss.
- People can throw away good money after bad in an escalating fashion if they fail to update their reference point and do not recognize sunk costs.
- Inconsistency in decision making can lead to unnecessary squandering of resources to parasitic third parties.
- Most people are overly confident and under-accurate in their judgments.

CHAPTER 7

Social Cognition: *A Look Into the Mind of the Negotiator*

Paul was in his last year of an MBA program and had aspirations of getting a position in a consulting firm. He was an older student and had many experiences that created breaks in his record. Furthermore, Paul had taken two years off and had not really done anything during that time that seemed to fit the relevant categories of academic and job experience. He had two weeks before he needed to develop a résumé to send to the employers of his "dream" companies. He was not sure how to best present his experiences.

That evening on the radio, Paul listened to a program on "hiring the best people." The featured speaker on the show, a personnel and management consultant for several companies, explained his views on hiring: "What I look for is the person who went to U.C. Berkeley for three years as a computer science major and then dropped out unexpectedly for a couple of years. Her résumé doesn't explain what the hell she was doing during that time—she coulda been feeding starving children in the streets or knocking over 7–11 stores—we don't know! What that gap tells me, though, is that she is a person who has taken time out to question authority and to find out who she is. We need managers like her for the next decade, rather than the guy who has a résumé that can account for every minute of his life since he was three years old!"

Paul was ecstatic to learn that what he viewed as a weakness could actually be a strength for him in the job market. After a night of working on his résumé, he brought it over to the placement center, where he had an appointment with a career advisor. The advisor read Paul's résumé with knitted brows. She put it down and sighed, "You're going to have to do something about accounting for those gaps in your academic experience. Is there anything you did during that time that could fit into academic learning or job experience? Employers will not look favorably on this."

Paul explained about the manager's views on the radio show. The counselor shook her head. "That's not how I view it!" she remarked.

One employer interprets a two-year hiatus on an applicant's résumé to be a sign of "self-exploration and discovery," whereas another regards the applicant to be "unmotivated and lacking direction." How could two people interpret the same résumé completely differently?

Every day, we encounter discrepancies between our views of a situation and those of others. A presidential debate is aired, and both sides claim victory. In another instance, we find ourselves disagreeing with a business associate about a financial portfolio, yet the objective information is identical. What explains why people interpret events and information so differently? Given the importance of information for effective negotiation, it is imperative to understand how we process information during negotiation. This chapter is concerned with how we gain knowledge about our world and how we use our knowledge to guide our decisions and perform effective actions in negotiation.

This chapter explores the mind of the negotiator. We review the key mechanisms of social perception and human memory. Then we apply these principles to an analysis of a negotiation. Next, we review the main types of processing mechanisms we use to make sense of people and situations and the mental pictures that we create to represent our social world. Finally, we discuss how our information processing system influences our thoughts, feelings, and behaviors, often in surprising ways.

THE MIND OF THE NEGOTIATOR

As the opening example suggests, the human mind is not a tabula rasa and our behavior is not just a response to external stimuli; rather, we impose meaning on stimuli. Therefore, we need a model of the mind to describe how we represent and process information in negotiation. This model provides an account of the information that we attend to, remember, and use to make judgments in negotiation.

Consider a negotiation situation in which a client from a medical facility makes an opening offer for your software system. When you receive the client's bid, you assess the information you have about the client and his or her needs, as well as your own interests. You might think about previous negotiations you've had with the client as a way of determining whether he or she is serious or just throwing out a low-ball figure. In short, the information you have about this particular client, as well as your general knowledge of the medical community, allows you to evaluate her opening offer.

Understanding how the mind works allows people to better utilize its capabilities and avoid its shortcomings. Further, understanding how the mind works helps us predict and understand the judgment and behaviors of our partners and opponents in negotiation.

Information Processing

Humans have the capacity to process the world's enormous complexity, but if they do, they become "slaves to the particular," and so they develop mental shortcuts and other strategies that reduce processing demands (Bruner, Goodnow, and Austin, 1956). Before we understand what can go wrong with our information processing, it is useful to understand the basic operations of the human mind.

The **information-processing approach** assumes that cognitive activity may be analyzed conceptually in terms of a series of stages during which information is transformed or recoded by particular components or mechanisms. In each stage the information that was coded in the previous stage as input is condensed, abstracted, recoded, or elaborated upon, and passed on to the next stage. The causal order of these processes is represented by blocks in a flow diagram in Figure 7–1. The interconnections between components are specified by arrows that suggest the direction of action and control. As may be seen in Figure 7–1, our information-processing system consists of sensory buffers, a response generator, memory systems, and a central processor (Newell and Simon, 1972). The central processor, or executive monitor, controls the active processes which coordinate memorization, thinking, evaluation, and decision making. Below, we describe the basic components and processes in Figure 7–1, beginning with the perception of stimulus events.

Perception: One Percent

In negotiations, we are bombarded with stimuli—the opponents' physical appearance, his or her opening remarks, hearsay knowledge, nonverbal behavior, and so on. Do we notice all of this information? No. We perceive about one percent of all information in our stimulus field (Kaplan and Kaplan, 1982). We perceive only a tiny fraction of what happens in the negotiation room. How do we know if we are paying attention to the right cues?

The basic function of our sensory information buffers is to parse and code stimulus information into recognizable symbols. Because external stimuli cannot get directly inside our heads, we cognitively represent stimuli as internal symbols and their interrelations as symbol structures. The sensory buffers—visual, auditory, and tactile—maintain the stimulus as an image or icon while its features are extracted. This activity occurs very rapidly and below our threshold of awareness. The features extracted from a given stimulus object comprise a coded description of the object. For example, our interaction with a colleague concerning a joint venture is an event that is real, but our minds are not video cameras that record everything; rather, we use a process known as **selective attention.**

Following the feature extraction stage, there is an identification stage, in which the stimulus object is classified by matching its feature list with a likely set of prototypes contained in long-term memory. For example, when someone gives us his or her phone number and we try to read the scrawl to decide whether the last digit is a "2" or a "7," we compare the features of the stimulus (the person's scrawl) to our mental prototypes of the numbers 2 and 7. A meaningful stimulus is identified more easily if an associated semantic context has been activated near the time the stimulus appears. For example, we can more accurately and quickly identify a high school photo of someone if we have been thinking about our hometown.

Short-term Memory: Seven Plus-or-Minus Two

Short-term memory is the part of our central processor that holds the symbols currently in the focus of attention and conscious processing. The central processor has rapid access to the items in short-term memory in contrast to long-term memory. However, short-term memory has severely limited capacity; only about five to nine symbols or coded items may be currently active. The "seven plus-or-minus two" rule extends to just about everything we try to remember (Miller, 1956). Consider, for example, an interaction you might have with the president of a company concerning the details of a consulting project. The president tells you many facts about her company; you will recall, on average, five to nine pieces of information. Without deliberate rehearsal, the information in your short-term memory will disappear and be replaced with new information perceived by your sensory registers. Obviously, we perceive much more information than we ultimately store and remember.

FIGURE 7–1. Basic Information Processing Model

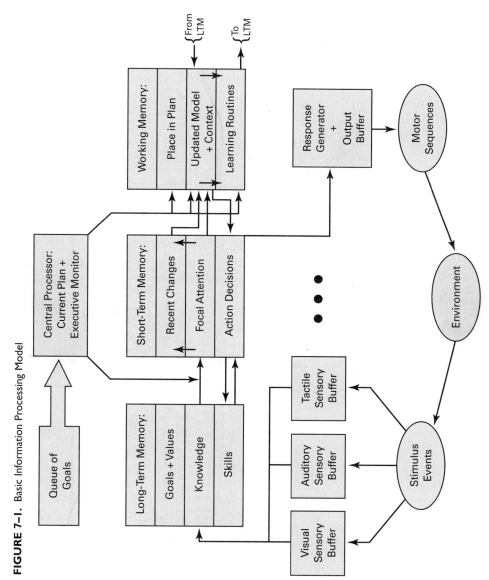

Source: Newell, A. and H. A. Simon (1972). *Human Problem Solving.* Englewood Cliffs, NJ, Prentice Hall.

Working Memory: Top of the Head

Our **working memory** maintains information about the local context, which is neither in the focus of our active memory nor in the recesses of our long-term memory. One of the primary functions of working memory is to construct and maintain an internal model of the immediate environment. We may think of our working memory as containing a description of the setting, framework, or context within which the more dynamic aspects of the stimulus environment are occurring. Working memory serves as a context for perception and, in so doing, calls upon information stored in our long-term memory concerning the nature of objects and spatial relationships. For example, if we see an overnight mail envelope in our mailbox, we are not startled to see someone walking swiftly away in a uniform toward an illegally parked van because our contextual model makes such events plausible. It is on the basis of long-term memory that we know that the large symbols suddenly appearing on the wall are produced by an overhead projector on the adjacent table and not a supernatural apparition. Therefore, we are prepared to see certain things and expect certain changes if we take certain actions (e.g., when we hit a key on a keyboard, we expect the screen to change on the monitor). Perception is very much a matter of "predicting" the results of our interactions with the environment. Our world model enables us to bring the appropriate knowledge to bear on the issue.

Long-term Memory: The Mind's Files

Long-term memory is the repository of our more permanent knowledge and skills, including beliefs about physical relationships in the environment, properties of objects, people, ourselves, organizations, and motor and perceptual skills (Bower, 1977). Long-term memory contains two types of information, episodic and semantic. **Episodic memory** contains specific events and concrete experiences. Episodic memory is stored in a temporal code. For example, your meeting today with the manager of the health care organization is stored as episodic memory. In contrast, **semantic memory** contains the meaning of concepts. Your knowledge of the healthcare industry is stored as semantic memory. The distinction between episodic memory and semantic memory is similar to the difference between a diary (which records and organizes events by their date of occurrence) and a dictionary (which associates concepts with their meaning).

Response Generation: Taking Action

Once we decide which action to take, a central plan is drawn from our long-term memory for that action and is initialized for the current situation in which the response is to be executed. Most skilled actions may be analyzed in terms of a multilevel hierarchy with various tests in the plan which compare accomplished with anticipated results.

At different times and in different situations, people have different goals that they try to achieve. In your organization, you may want a promotion but simultaneously also look at other firms for a possible switch. An executive monitor controls our information-processing system as it attempts to carry out our goals and plans. The information-processing system tends to behave economically to accomplish our goals by expending a minimum amount of time and processing resources. This tendency gives rise to heuristics or cognitive shortcuts that facilitate information processing but often produce inaccurate judgments and biases (Tversky and Kahneman, 1974).

Most of us take our information-processing capacities for granted. However, imagine for a moment that you are unable to recall the events of your day. Imagine, also, that you are unable to recall the names of your key clients. Your career would probably suffer some serious consequences. Clearly, we rely on both our episodic and semantic memory for successful, strategically effective interactions, such as negotiation. In most negotiation situations, people seldom take notes or record the interaction, believing that they will effortlessly and accurately recall the contents of the interaction. Failing to remember a conversation or a name, or falsely remembering something that did not occur, is only one aspect of the fallibility and creativity of human memory.

PROCESSING MECHANISMS: HOW DO WE USE INFORMATION?

Now that we know how information gets into memory, how do we use it? How do we operate on information that we have stored?

Drawing Inferences: How Our Memory Plays Detective

To see how our information-processing system is essential for negotiation, consider an example: At noon, you get a call from Chris, a businessperson who owns property you are interested in buying—for the right price. Chris tells you that your opening offer of $140,000 was too low and so has decided to reject your offer. Chris then mutters something about being anxious to sell the property because of a move out of state within the month.

An important implication of long-term memory is that our recall of information is not limited to actual events. Our recall of events is based upon inferences from what we already know and can plausibly assess. Therefore, when someone asks us about how the seller responded to our opening offer, we answer with information that goes beyond what actually happened.

We draw on two kinds of information to make inferences, derived from our two types of long-term memory repositories: semantic and episodic. On the basis of our semantic knowledge of people who own property, we might infer that the seller is a professional businessperson with a portfolio of assets. In addition, we also make inferences about the context and situation—the probable antecedents or reasons for the event, the probable consequences for it, and so on. In short, we fit the event into our "model of the world."

Consider the episode with the seller, Chris, above. We may infer any and all of the following:

- Chris' reservation point is not very attractive.
- Chris is bluffing.
- Chris has already bought another property in a different state.
- Chris will make a counteroffer.
- Chris does not have another offer from a buyer.
- Chris is overconfident about the value of the property.
- Chris is desperate.

This is only a brief list of the many inferences we may make about out interaction with Chris even though Chris didn't say any of these things.

Theory-based and Data-based Processing: The Eye of the Beholder and the Beholden

Most of us believe that we have a well-developed way of processing information that is invariant across persons, settings, and time. We further believe that this processing produces flawless judgment. However, we do not consistently process information. Rather, we *selectively* process information.

The example in Box 7–1 illustrates that information processing represents a duality between two types of processing: top-down (or theory-based) and bottom-up (or data-based). That is, to perceive any event we need to have some pre-existing knowledge (theory) but also be attentive to the information we receive (data).

Theory-based processing is guided by our expectations, pre-existing views, and beliefs. Taken to an extreme form, theory-based processing leads people to see the world exactly as they want or expect to see it—they are not at all attuned to the environment. **Data-based processing** is determined by features of the stimulus situation, not our pre-existing beliefs.

Is it better to be a theory-based or data-based processor? It depends on our perspective in a given situation. If we believe that we have been victimized by faulty race, gender, or ethnic stereotypes, we hope that the person evaluating us (e.g., our supervisor in our promotion decision) does not rely on faulty theories but, rather, evaluates us on the merits of our actions. In contrast, in other situations, we may desire to call up particular theories, if we see them working to our advantage. For example, if students from your school have a reputation for being "team players," you hope that a recruiter is aware of MBA stereotypes when assessing your qualifications.

Social perception requires a balance of theory-based and data-based processing. All social perception requires the existence of knowledge structures; otherwise, perception does not make sense. The purely data-based processor sees a sea of moving color around a sta-

---

BOX 7–1

Schematic Information Processing

Consider the following:

"The procedure is quite an art. First, it is necessary to manually transform thick pellets into thin skins. This may be achieved by angular momentum or centrifugal aerodynamic methods or by tools of engineering designed to produce the desired effect. The ingredients are critical and the receiver ultimately makes these decisions. Homogenous topological arrangement is a key to consistent experience. The ultimate selection may be simple or quite complex. The entire mass is subjected to heat convection for a predetermined period of time. Consumption is then imminent."

Most people read this passage and have no idea what is going on. But when the reader is told that the passage describes making a pizza, the information makes much more sense.

Source: Adapted from Bransford, J. D. and M. K. Johnson (1972). Contextual prerequisites for understanding: Some investigations of comprehension and recall. *Journal of Verbal Learning and Verbal Behavior* **11**: 717–726.

tionary, oblong object; the theory-based processor perceives a committee meeting in a conference room.

Theory-based processing guides our perceptions and tells us what features of the environment are important. It tells us what to look for and what to expect. Most of us take our theory-based processing mechanisms for granted. For example, all of us have a theory about how to behave in restaurants (Abelson, 1976): We wait to be seated, order from a menu, eat, and then pay a bill. However, few of us have a theory about how to behave at an American Indian ritual ceremony or a negotiation session in Tokyo. Many of our most important negotiations are novel, and therefore we do not have well-developed schemas for dealing with them. For example, think of your first salary negotiation or the first time you bought a house or a car. Most people lament that they "wish they had known then what they know now." In short, they needed a schema to make sense out of the situation—to tell them what to ask for and what to look for.

Heuristic and Systematic Processing: Automatic Pilot or Manual Steering?

Most people believe their attitudes and judgments form and change based on thoughtful consideration of relevant information. When we think deliberately and carefully about decisions, we exercise a controlled, or systematic mode of information processing—but we don't do this all the time. Heuristic information processing is done without much deliberation or control. People usually engage in thoughtful information processing when they are sufficiently motivated and have the capacity to do so (Chaiken, 1980; Chaiken, Liberman, and Eagly, 1989).

Consider a project meeting. When the topic or issue is important to us, we carefully attend to the arguments, note the inconsistencies, and raise relevant issues. Other times, we are distracted or are not sufficiently motivated to care. We are aware of the interaction going on, but we are not processing it deeply. The same thing can happen when we ask a friend or spouse about his or her day. Sometimes we think deliberately and deeply about the message conveyed; other times, we are on automatic pilot and mindlessly nod and say "That's nice."

Through experience, we learn certain heuristics and rules that help us process information and facilitate interaction. For example, we believe that printed material is to be trusted, and we reply that we are "fine" when someone asks how we are, even when we are sick, have lost our wallet, or had our car towed. Much of the time our heuristic information processing is efficient because it allows us to devote our efforts and energies to other problems. In this sense, we can multitask. Other times, heuristic information processing can lead to serious problems. For example, if we are distracted or in a hurry, we may not attend to the fine print in an argument, or we may erroneously assume that the other party's handshake is indicative of good faith bargaining when it is not.

Don't Think about White Bears

Sometimes we are plagued by unwanted thoughts when we negotiate. These thoughts may be silly, absurd, distracting, or just plain uncomfortable. For example, have you ever thought about how someone might look naked, imagined yourself dancing on a table in a serious meeting, worried about choking during an important speech, or been convinced that someone was trying to ruin your life? Unwanted, intrusive thoughts are conscious, in that we are acutely aware that they are there. However, they are largely **automatic** and not under our control—meaning that we can't really turn them off.

Consider Fred, an assistant account manager with a major hotel firm. Fred is in charge of arranging special pricing for conventions and special events. One of Fred's worst fears is that during a meeting with a major client, one of the giant chandeliers in the hotel will come crashing down on the prospective client's head, which, of course, will lose the client and create a public relations nightmare. Fred's dreaded event is an extremely unlikely scenario, but it nevertheless plagues his ability to concentrate in meetings with clients. Fred does his best to suppress his unwanted thoughts but occasionally finds that, to his horror and the client's dismay, he will glance nervously at the ceiling and steer clients in a peculiar fashion to avoid walking beneath one of the large chandeliers. What begins as a nonissue quickly becomes an uncomfortable point of discussion, as the client questions the structural integrity of the facilities. What would you advise Fred to do to control (and ideally eliminate) his unintentional thoughts? Most people tell Fred that he should say "Stop!" every time such a thought comes to mind.

Examinations of thought control and suppression have revealed some interesting insights into the workings of the human mind (Wegner, 1989; 1994). Unwanted thoughts tend to occur when people are experiencing excessive cognitive demands. For example, Fred's chandelier fear is more likely to occur when Fred is under pressure. When Fred consciously tries to suppress his unwanted thoughts, he is successful in the short term, but they come back to haunt him even more in the long term. Why? If we think back to the model of the mind presented earlier, we realize that when Fred attempts to suppress his thoughts about the chandelier, they are being associated with (linked to) otherwise neutral stimuli. This means that these neutral stimuli (e.g., the coat that Fred is wearing, the hotel lobby, the smell of coffee, etc.) will now elicit the very thoughts that Fred tried to suppress.

KNOWLEDGE STRUCTURES: OUR THEORIES OF REAL PEOPLE

The heuristic and systematic processing mechanisms we have discussed operate on our knowledge structures, or schemas. **Schemas** are cognitive structures which consist of our knowledge, beliefs, and expectations pertaining to some stimulus domain (Hamilton, 1981). A stimulus domain can be a person, a group of people, a type of event (such as a party)—almost anything we can conceive of. Consider the schema in Figure 7–2, which is a hypothetical mental category for different types of negotiators. We might have such a view of negotiators contained in our mental dictionary, or semantic long-term memory structure.

Hierarchical Organization

Schemas are organized from the top down in terms of their generality and abstractness. Notice, for example, that the schema in Figure 7–2 goes from a general category (negotiators in general) to more specific ones, types of negotiators, to even more specific categories (identities of actual negotiators). We organize information in our social world hierarchically in terms of similarities and generalities.

Individual Differences

To some extent, we all share similar schemas. There is remarkable, within-culture similarity for certain types of schemas—such as buying a used car or asking for a raise. However, there can be marked differences among people in their schemas as a consequence of their personal experience, background, culture, interests, and knowledge. Consider, for example, the standard Ameri-

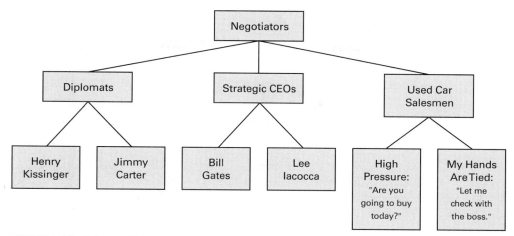

FIGURE 7–2. Schema of Negotiators

can business greeting: Two people shake hands firmly within seconds of being introduced. One of the parties will often touch or slap the other on the back. After this point, parties refer to one another by first name. In contrast, consider a typical Japanese business greeting: Parties exchange business cards, bow, and refer to one another by their formal title or surname. Schemas are so powerful that they are difficult for us to turn off even when we want to. A strange battle of wills occurs when two people of different cultural backgrounds meet: The American colleague feels that business cannot commence until a hearty handshake has been made; the Japanese colleague feels insulted by the failure to follow the decorum of exchanging cards.

Emotion

Most people like to believe that they are cool-headed information processors whose judgments are not colored by emotions. We often equate the absence of emotion with rationality. However, like it or not, we have affective reactions to almost every person, object, and idea in our social world. We make positive/negative evaluations of nearly everything, from our supervisor to particular stocks and product development ideas. Some of our affective reactions may be mild, pleasant states, but often they are strong or negative. Emotional reactions can be triggered just by thinking about a certain topic (Tesser, 1978). For example, most of us have had the experience of seeing someone we know become agitated by the mere mention of someone's name.

Types of Schemas

We have schemas for just about everything in our social and business world. Some common schemas include self-schemas, person schemas, role schemas, group schemas, and event schemas (Taylor and Crocker, 1981).

Self-schema

A **self-schema** is a mental representation of ourselves, including information about our appearance, personality, behavior, roles, and self-concept (Markus, 1977). What do we need to know about our self-schema? We attend to and remember information that is self-relevant.

For example, we remember that the other party in a negotiation went to the same university that we did and enjoys our hobbies. The danger is that we often forget information that is not relevant to our self-schema but is relevant for understanding the situation.

Person Schemas

We also have schemas for people we know, or **person schemas,** such as our colleagues, spouse, and friends. Person schemas contain factual, objective information (e.g., year of birth, country of origin), as well as subjective impressions (e.g., intelligent, compassionate, etc.). We are more likely to develop person schemas when

- the person is important to us
- we expect to have future interaction with him or her
- we have much knowledge of the person
- the person is familiar to us

Group Schemas

Group schemas contain our beliefs about social groups; group schemas are stereotypes. Many of us have stereotyped beliefs about members of social groups, and this may be especially true in negotiations (Kramer and Brewer, 1986; Thompson, 1993). Amazingly, stereotypes and discriminatory behavior can occur even when social groups are randomly determined. As an example, what do you think would happen if a large group of people was divided into two groups (e.g., alphas and betas) on the basis of a completely arbitrary distinction (random draws from a hat)? Further, imagine that members of each group were told that in a few minutes they would either negotiate with a member of their own group or a member of the other group. Would this affect people's evaluations of their opponent? Group membership dramatically affects people's anticipation and evaluations of others. Those who expect to negotiate with a member of the "out group" anticipate a much more competitive negotiation and expect the other person to be less thoughtful, sincere, and cooperative than those who expect to negotiate with a member of their own group (Thompson, 1993). Given that strong differences can emerge in groups created by completely meaningless distinctions, we should expect that negative evaluations of out groups when group memberships are meaningful (rather than arbitrary), will be even more extreme, such as between rival firms or organizational departments.

Role Schemas

Role schemas contain our beliefs about persons who occupy particular roles, such as bill collectors, insurance adjusters, chief executive officers, used car salesmen, attorneys, and middle-level managers. We expect certain people to engage in particular behaviors and express particular attitudes merely as a function of their social role.

Event Schemas

Event schemas, or scripts, represent stereotypical or routine sequences of events. For example, going to the grocery store and buying a new car are event schemas. Unlike self, person, group, and role schemas, event schemas do not have a hierarchical organization. Their organization is **temporal,** meaning that the schemas are organized in terms of time. Event schemas allow us to know what to expect in a given situation, and they tell us how to behave.

Negotiation Schemas

A negotiation schema is a particular kind of event schema. **Negotiation schemas** contain our knowledge and expectations regarding bargaining situations. The information in these knowledge structures is derived from our personal experience as well as observations of others and cultural folklore. For example, many of us have never bought a used car from a lot but have a schema for the used car negotiation. The sequence of activity, the appropriate display of emotion, and the behaviors and use of tactics may be information that we have gleaned from friends, movies, and popular culture. Sometimes, we do not have a well-developed knowledge structure for a negotiation. For example, many students often do not have a well-developed job negotiation schema. In contrast, employers often do because they have more experience.

Fixed-pie Perception   A dominant schema characterizes most untrained people's understanding of negotiation. The fixed-pie perception is the belief that the other party's interests are directly and completely opposed to one's own (Bazerman and Neale, 1983; Thompson and Hastie, 1990). The fixed-pie perception stems from theory-driven processing. Negotiators fail to pay attention to evidence inconsistent with the fixed-pie perception. Most untrained negotiators view negotiation as a purely distributive task: they assume that their interests are incompatible, that impasse is likely, and that issues are settled one by one rather than as packages (O'Connor and Adams, 1996). In one investigation, negotiators' perceptions of the other party's interests were assessed immediately before, during, and then following a negotiation (Thompson and Hastie, 1990). Most negotiators perceived the other's interests to be completely opposed to their own. In fact, negotiators shared interests which could be profitably logrolled and completely compatible. In short, negotiators with fixed-pie perceptions literally throw money away.

How many negotiators throw money away as a result of the fixed-pie perception? Two-thirds of all (untrained) negotiators is a conservative judgment. In an analysis of the behavior of highly motivated MBA students engaged in a two-party negotiation exercise, 90 percent needlessly threw money away. Unfortunately, banishing the fixed-pie perception is very difficult. It is not enough to warn negotiators of its existence (Thompson, 1991). Further, it is not enough for negotiators to have experience (Thompson, 1990a, 1990b). It is not even enough for negotiators to receive feedback about their opponents' interests to eliminate the fixed-pie perception (Thompson and DeHarpport, 1994). We'll talk more about how to successfully challenge the fixed-pie perception when we examine learning and experience (chapter 13).

Using Our Schemas in Negotiation

We use schemas to make sense of the world. Without schemas, we would not realize, for example, that the person wearing a blue suit with a badge is an officer of the law, or the person with the cigar and leisure suit is a used car salesman. Below, we discuss how schema use affects our impressions of others, others' impressions of us, our interpretation of events, our judgment, and, ultimately, our actual behavior in negotiations.

Impression Management

Negotiation involves sizing up others and making first impressions. We all know the importance of a first impression. **Impression management** is the art of controlling the way we present ourselves to others (Goffman, 1959).

How Do We View Others?

Our impressions of others (and others' impressions of us) can be summed up in four words: evaluation, consistency, immediacy, and inference. The judgments we make about others tend to be highly evaluative. That is, we tend to either like or dislike people (Osgood, Suci, and Tannenbaum, 1957). In fact, evaluation is the dominant way we act on our impressions: If we like someone, we do things for him or her; if we don't like someone, we are unsupportive and even antagonistic.

The judgments we make about others are highly **internally consistent.** Once we decide that a person is likable, other qualities about that person are perceived as consistent with our favorable impression of him or her. We do not perceive contradictions or inconsistencies. This tendency is so powerful that it is known as the **halo effect,** because once we decide that a person has a good quality on one dimension, we assume that they have other desirable qualities—whether we know anything about them or not. This extends even to judgments of physical beauty. As much as we don't like to believe that our liking of others is influenced by their physical attractiveness, we like attractive people more than unattractive people; furthermore, we think attractive people are smarter and produce better work (Dion, Berscheid, and Walster, 1972; Landy and Sigall, 1974). Of course, the complementary process operates as well: Once we have labeled someone as bad, we see them as having other undesirable characteristics in completely unrelated domains. Unfortunately, **forked-tail impressions** are quite resilient; it is very difficult to recover from making a bad impression. Negative information sets up a directional tendency with which we interpret subsequent information about that person (Asch, 1946).

The order in which we learn information about a person affects our judgments. As a negotiator, which type of information should you first present to the other side—positive information or negative information? We attempt to consolidate each successive piece of information we learn about someone with our previous impression of that person. The initial information we have about someone sets up a directional tendency with which we interpret subsequent information. This is the **primacy effect:** The first pieces of information are more influential. The effect is so powerful that even when people have identical traits, our impressions of them may differ dramatically depending upon which information we learn first about them (Jones et al., 1968). The practical implication is clear: Negotiators should present favorable information about themselves first.

Our impressions of others are immediate. The judgments we make about others and the judgments they make about us are often automatic (Bargh, Lombardi, and Higgins, 1988) and occur without our awareness. Whereas snap judgments allow us to categorize people quickly and efficiently, our observations can often be in error.

In addition, we form impressions of others on the basis of very **limited information,** such as name, appearance, workplace, and age. We tend to make a number of inferences given a single piece of information about someone.

Interpretation

Imagine that you and a business associate are beginning negotiations with a competitor firm to discuss a joint venture. You notice that the representative from the other firm attended a rival school's MBA program, whose graduates are known to be cut-throat, game-theoretic types. You brace yourself for a competitive stance. Your colleague notices that the other representative's firm was recently named one of the "Green" companies of the year. Your colleague attributes altruistic, cooperative motives to the firm, and decides to make a generous offer. In a brief conference with your colleague, it becomes apparent that you interpreted the same situation very differently as driven by what you noticed about the other party. This example illustrates how two people perceiving the same situation may come to very different conclusions.

Judgment

Often, when a controversial news story appears or a presidential debate is aired, partisans on different sides of the issue both claim victory. However, both sides can't win. So, what is going on? Are one or both parties living in a dream world? Partisan groups who view the same body of mixed and inconclusive evidence increase the strength and polarization of their respective beliefs (Lord, Lepper, and Ross, 1979; Nisbett and Ross, 1980; Ross and Lepper, 1980; Vallone, Ross, and Lepper, 1985). Moreover, partisans perceive the beliefs of the opposing party to be more extreme than they really are (Robinson, Keltner, Ward, and Ross, 1994; Robinson and Keltner, 1996); partisans polarize views of opposing groups (Robinson, et al., 1994). How is it that two people can look at the same body of evidence and come to very different conclusions about it?

Imagine that you are watching a videotape of a negotiation between a potential employee and an employer of a firm. Would you be able to accurately understand both parties' points of view? As it turns out, what you see in negotiation depends upon your point of view (Thompson, 1995b). If you are told to be as objective, unbiased, and nonpartisan as possible, you are much more likely to realize the existence of mutual interests among the employee and employer than if you are actually negotiating in the situation! This is a striking example of the power of point of view: Nonpartisan observers see the potential for integrative agreement that negotiators do not even realize. The message: Try to adopt as objective, unbiased a view as possible in negotiation.

Intuitive Scientists and Intuitive Lawyers

There are two roles that lend insight into the mind of the negotiator: lawyers and scientists. The **intuitive scientist** wants to find the correct or optimal conclusion. By contrast, the **intuitive lawyer** wants to make the best case for a particular, preselected conclusion. Who do you think would make a better negotiator?

Both lawyers and scientists are motivated people. It would seem that high involvement should increase careful, systematic processing of information and therefore make it more likely for people to realize when they share compatible interests in negotiation (Erber and Fiske, 1984; Darley, Fleming, Hilton, and Swann, 1988; Devine, Sedikides, and Furhman, 1989; Ruscher and Fiske, 1990).

Although involvement is typically thought to eliminate bias by increasing attention to information and instigating thoughtful information processing, involvement may actually increase bias depending upon the **motivations** of the perceiver (Thompson, 1995b). That is, people may be highly motivated (or not) to reach either a specific conclusion or whatever conclusion is appropriate and correct (Baumeister and Newman, 1994; Kunda, 1990; Kruglanski, 1989, 1990).

To the extent that someone has a partisan perspective (such as a lawyer), greater involvement or motivation should induce that person to find support for his or her conclusion (Baumeister and Newman, 1994; Kruglanski, 1989). But those with a nonpartisan perspective (such as scientists) should improve judgment accuracy through greater involvement or motivation. Imagine again that you are observing a negotiation between a potential employee and an employer. Imagine that, in one case, you are highly involved and you have a great stake in the outcome of the negotiation, because you are about to interview with the same firm next week. In contrast, imagine that, in another case, you are not really involved or that interested in what is going on. In which case are you more likely to accurately assess parties' true interests in a way that allows identification of compatible issues? It seems straightforward to conclude that involvement increases accuracy.

Now, let's consider what happens to the accuracy of our judgment when we are partisan or nonpartisan. As it turns out, partisans are less accurate when they are highly involved than when they are less involved. The opposite is true for nonpartisans. Once we start feeling and acting like a lawyer, we are less likely to make accurate judgments than when we act like scientists.

Behavior: How We Act upon Our Beliefs

Schemas dictate people's preferences about everything from buying behavior to foreign policy. Consider two small democratic countries, each threatened by an aggressive, totalitarian neighbor (see Gilovich, 1981). The situation in one country is described in a way that is reminiscent of World War II (e.g., references to Winston Churchill, boxcars, FDR, blitzkrieg). The situation in the other country is described much more like Vietnam (e.g., references to the Dean Rusk Hall, Chinook helicopters, LBJ). Otherwise, the situation in the two countries is exactly the same and clearly hypothetical. Your decision is to choose an appropriate foreign policy for each country. When people are given irrelevant allusions to World War II events, they are more likely to support intervention than when they are given Vietnam allusions. Identical facts may be interpreted in very different ways, depending upon which schemas are evoked.

Consider the following hypothetical scenario: You and a business associate are formulating strategy for the next round of negotiations with an important client. The two of you are discussing your strategy at a local bar, where a big-screen TV is broadcasting a particularly vicious boxing match. You and your associate are not really watching the fight but hear the referee's calls and description of the action in the background. You notice that your associate talks about "packing a punch" and "hitting below the belt" and you wonder whether the social context is affecting your associate's judgment about negotiation. You suggest that the two of you walk down the street to the Honey Bear Cafe; the local music that night is a folk group called "Brotherly Love." As the two of you are sipping coffee, your associate once again starts talking about the upcoming negotiations. You listen as he talks about "harmony" and "building a community" and wonder again whether features of your location are influencing your friend's judgment.

This scenario illustrates how people are often manipulated by social-contextual cues. Sometimes these cues are random or naturally occurring products of the environment (such as in the bar); sometimes they may be "planted" (by a savvy negotiator). Obviously, it is important to understand which schemas we use to make sense of negotiation situations and whether one behavior might differ if we were to use another schema.

Choosing the Right Mindset

What determines which schemas we use to evaluate events and people that we meet?

Salience: Hey You in Red   We use whatever dimension about a social situation is **salient,** or stands out, to interpret a given situation. For example, the young woman on an otherwise all-male corporate board is salient in terms of her gender. This means that we are likely to think about feminist issues and sex discrimination when perceiving this situation. Conversely, if the context surrounding this woman is changed, different schemas may be invoked to explain the same woman's behavior. For example, the same young woman on a corporate board of mixed-sex individuals all over the age of 55 is now salient in terms of her age. Ageism and seniority become important schemas to take into account in interpreting the situation.

Priming: Beware the Top of the Head   Schemas that have been recently activated, or **primed,** are often used to interpret new information (Higgins, Rholes, and Jones, 1977). Schemas that have recently been activated are more readily accessible for interpreting new information.

Primes are not always conscious. Our judgment and behaviors are affected by unconscious priming. This is often the case in stereotyping and discrimination. Suppose that you are a white person who took the bus to work one day. A gang of white youths on the bus made several racial epithets—"black people are lazy," "black people are musical," and so on. You were engrossed in reading the newspaper and did not even remember hearing these epithets shouted. At work, you are asked to interview two candidates for a new position. One of the candidates is black; the other is white. Is your hiring decision affected by your morning bus ride? Most people righteously claim it is not. However, there is disturbing evidence that it might be.

For example, in one investigation, people were presented with words on a computer screen that involved racial stereotypes associated with African Americans (e.g., poor, jazz, slavery, Harlem, and busing). The words were flashed extremely quickly—in fact, people were not even aware that anything was on the screen. White people, in an ostensibly unrelated second task, judged a race-unspecified target male to be more hostile than did people for whom only 20 percent of the words had a black stereotype association (Devine, 1989). A similar effect occurs for gender stereotyping, such as when people rate identical essays attributed to authors with male names more positively than ones with female names (Goldberg, 1968).

Individual Differences   Another principle of schema use is the fact that different people tend to be "schematic" for different things (Markus, 1977). Our colleague who is a sports buff sees every interaction as a "play" where someone "fumbles," "strikes out," or "scores." Others, schematic for theater, see events as "staged interactions" where persons enact "roles" and create "scenes." To be an effective negotiator, it is important to understand not only which schemas we use as a lens to view the world, but also how our opponents make sense out of the world.

Cultural differences are an important aspect of individual differences. For example, there are strong cultural differences in terms of how individuals explain the cause of social events. Typically, members of Asian cultures explain social events in terms of situational factors, whereas Western cultures explain the same social events in terms of the personal attributes and dispositions of the persons involved (Morris, Nisbett, and Peng, 1994).

Advantages and Disadvantages of Schematic Information Processing

Given all the unwarranted inferences created by our schemas, we might wonder what functions schematic information processing serves. Schematic processing facilitates information processing by helping us to recognize what is important in a given situation swiftly and effi-

---

BOX 7–2

Confirmatory Information Processing

Consider the following situation:

A colleague approaches you and says that she is interested in evaluating a particular software product. She wants your help in deciding what questions to pose to the software developer. What questions do you suggest that she ask? (Take a few minutes to make a list of questions.)

Many people suggest questions such as: How successful has the product been in marketing surveys? How successful has the company been in promoting other products in the past? What strategic advantages does the company have that would make success more likely?

---

ciently. Further, schematic information processing facilitates our memory for people and events; in general, we recall information consistent with our schema. Schemas provide the information processor with missing information, much in the same manner as a default option in a computer program. Even if we don't know something about someone, we can make assumptions based upon how we have categorized them.

As might be obvious, schematic information processing has a number of *disadvantages* for the negotiator. Information that is inconsistent with a schema tends to be forgotten or accorded less weight. In general, people tend to see what they want to see—information that confirms their beliefs and expectations. Consider the situation in Box 7–2.

All of these questions are designed to confirm the initial supposition about the software (Klayman and Ha, 1987). A much more diagnostic and useful set of questions is to consider the ways that the software could fail (e.g., "What are the major shortcomings of the application?"; "How are the competitors' products superior to this one?"; etc.) Simply stated, we do not learn much if we seek only information that confirms our previously held beliefs. A much more useful approach is to seek information that potentially disconfirms our beliefs.

Another potential disadvantage of schematic information processing is that people interpret ambiguous information as supporting their own views. In sum, schemas are extremely powerful; they guide our behavior and decision making.

CONCLUSION

We have reviewed the fundamental mechanisms and processes of the individual information-processing system. These processes influence the information we attend to, utilize, and remember during negotiation. We are influenced by our pre-existing knowledge and beliefs when we attempt to form an impression of someone or make a judgment in negotiation. Our judgment is characterized at different times by one of two processing mechanisms: systematic and heuristic.

TAKE-AWAYS

- Our information-processing system does not behave like a video camera; we are selectively attentive and strongly influenced by our presuppositions, even when we are not aware of them.

- The fixed-pie perception is the most common belief held by negotiators. It is also the most fatal belief in terms of optimal performance: Negotiators with fixed-pie perceptions frequently fail to reach integrative agreements.

- It is possible to influence people's thought, attitudes, and behavior by priming them.

- We generally size people up by deciding whether we like them, and then we interpret subsequent information to be consistent with our first impression.

CHAPTER 8

Biases and Illusions:
Stumbling Blocks on the Road to Successful Negotiation

In the movie Double Indemnity, *Fred McMurray plays an insurance salesman, Walter Neff, who gets entangled with femme fatale Phyllis Dedrickson, played by Barbara Stanwyck. The two plot the murder of Phyllis' husband so that Phyllis can collect accident insurance in the sum of $100,000 and ostensibly live happily ever after with Walter. Walter Neff carefully orchestrates each move in what looks to be a flawless plan to murder Mr. Dedrickson and make it look like an accident on a train.*

After the murder, an investigation opens up, headed by the insurance company's claim manager, Barton Keyes, played by Edward G. Robinson. Keyes is a bloodhound who, after 25 years in the business, claims to have never been wrong. Keyes says he has a "little man" in the pit of his stomach who tells him whether a claim is phony, and that he can smell murder and foul play a mile away. Hours after the murder, Keyes seems content with the police report of "accidental death." Relieved, Walter Neff goes home that night to relax and begin thinking about his new life with Phyllis.

Later that night, there is a knock on Walter's door. Keyes tells Walter that he has a terrible feeling in the pit of his stomach. Keyes suspects that the "accident" was not an accident at all but, rather, foul play of the most sinister kind—murder. Walter gently tries to steer Keyes away from this conclusion, but it is too late: the "little man" has spoken.

If each of us had a "little man" as accurate as Barton Keyes' in the pit of our stomach, we could accurately predict people's behavior. We could know, for example, whether someone was lying or bluffing. Unfortunately, most of us don't have a little man in our stomach: There is no such thing as a crystal ball when it comes to predicting the behavior of another person or how an event will unfold.

If we don't have a crystal ball, how then should we predict human behavior? One way is to leave things up to chance (i.e., roll a die or flip a coin). But this is not a very satisfying solution. A second way is to derive predictions from principles of normative models. As we have seen, however, normative models do not reliably predict behavior. In this chapter, we introduce another strategy: predicting behavior based upon social psychological principles.

The purpose of this chapter is to provide a "big picture" view of the ways in which negotiators reason about themselves and others. We first define rationality, irrationality, and nonrationality. We then introduce an encyclopedia of social psychological principles that characterize human behavior. We examine how we view ourselves, how we view others, and how we see the world.

RATIONALITY

In the everyday sense of the term, rationality means being of sound mind (Webster's dictionary). In a technical sense, rationality has a more precise meaning: the maximization of utility and the assumption that others behave rationally (i.e., others are utility maximizers also).

There are several different types of rationality which represent alternatives to classical economic rationality: limited rationality, contextual rationality, game rationality, process rationality, adaptive rationality, selective rationality, and posterior rationality (March, 1988).

Limited rationality emphasizes the extent to which people simplify a decision problem because of the difficulties of anticipating or considering all alternatives and all information (March and Simon, 1958).

Contextual rationality emphasizes the extent to which choice behavior is affected by the demands on the attention of the decision maker, such as an interrupting phone call or an unpredicted problem. Choice behavior in a particular situation is affected by the opportunity costs of attending to that situation and by the apparent tendency for people, problems, solutions, and choices to be joined by the relatively arbitrary accidence of their simultaneity rather than by their prima facie relevance to each other.

Game rationality emphasizes the extent to which organizations and other social institutions consist of individuals acting in relation to each other to pursue individual objectives by means of individual calculations of self-interest (Harsanyi and Selten, 1972). Game rationality is closest to the rationality spelled out in chapter 5.

Process rationality emphasizes the extent to which decisions find their sense in attributes of the decision process rather than in attributes of decision outcomes (Cohen and March, 1974). Explicit outcomes are viewed as secondary, and decision making becomes sensible through the intelligence of the way it is orchestrated. For example, people care about the *way* in which justice is administered so much that if any part of the process is not carried out (e.g., the victim is read Miranda rights, there is a judge-approved search warrant, etc.), this is grounds for dismissal of a case.

The above types of rationality make assumptions about how intelligent people calculate the consequences of actions for objectives and act so as to achieve those objectives. The following kinds of rationality are systemic, rather than calculated, evolving over time within a system.

Adaptive rationality emphasizes the experiential learning of individuals and collectives (Cyert and March, 1963). For example, consider a company in which there are no explicit rules concerning citizenship behavior. Nevertheless, employees who exhibit the greatest amount of citizenship behavior are offered greater organizational rewards. Consequently, managers adapt their behavior to perform more citizenship behaviors.

Selected rationality emphasizes the process of selection among individuals or organizations through survival or growth, with rules of behavior achieving the status of rationality by virtue of the survival and growth of social institutions in which such rules are followed.

Posterior rationality emphasizes the discovery of intentions as an interpretation of action rather than as a prior position (Weick, 1969; March, 1973). People make sense of their behavior *after* it occurs. Consider, for example, a negotiator who walks out in indignation on a potential major client. Later the negotiator realizes that the client was an extremely bad risk. Even though this information was not available at the time, the negotiator who walked out justifies her behavior as a rational response to an untrustworthy client.

In summary, rationality does not have one meaning (see Manktelow and Over, 1993). Behavior considered to be rational by one person may be regarded as nonrational by another. It is important for the negotiator to be aware of the logic guiding his or her behavior.

Nonrationality and Irrationality

We often regard the behavior of people whose choices do not conform to prescriptions of economic models as **irrational.** A better term would be **nonrational.** Irrational behavior is unpredictable. When we conclude that people are irrational, we are saying that we cannot predict their behavior or that their behavior is random; we don't know what they will do in a given situation. Often, people who express emotions are regarded to be irrational. However, emotional people are not unpredictable; they have systematic and predictable patterns of responding. Nonrational means that a person's behavior does not conform to economic notions of rationality, but their behavior is predictable. For example, if we notice that our friend always selects the item in her right hand when choosing among panty hose, breakfast cereal, or videotapes, her behavior is systematic, but not rational.

The distinction between nonrationality and irrationality is important for our goal of prediction. Whereas the behavior of an irrational person is unpredictable by definition, the behavior of a nonrational person is predictable, provided we understand the nature of his or her judgment processes. If we know our friend always chooses what is in her right hand, we can predict her choice.

Utility

Utility is derived or experienced satisfaction. For example, each of us has a utility for eating a hamburger, watching television, or playing golf. We saw in chapter 5 that everything has an associated utility, and this means that everything is comparable.

When we talk about **maximizing utility,** we don't just mean the maximization of monetary wealth. Consider Figure 8–1, which identifies six types of resources that people may exchange: love, money, services, goods, status, and information (Foa and Foa, 1975).

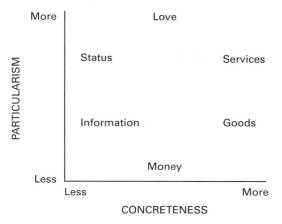

FIGURE 8–1. Resources that May Be Exchanged in an Independent Relationship

Source: Foa, U. and E. Foa (1975). *Resource theory of social exchange.* Morristown, NJ: General Learning Press.

Each of these six types of resources varies in terms of **particularism** (how much utility we derive depends on who is providing it) and concreteness (how tangible it is). Love and status are less concrete than services and goods. Love is more particular than money.

Experienced and Predicted Utility

Imagine that you are about to undergo a painful but necessary medical treatment—a colonoscopy procedure. The doctor presents you with two choices: treatment A or treatment B. Treatment A lasts for 20 minutes with the highest amount of pain at the very end stage; treatment B lasts for 25 minutes, and the highest amount of pain occurs during minute 20, with the last five minutes being progressively less painful. Both treatments are equally effective. Which treatment do you prefer? (Adapted from Kahneman, Fredrickson, Schreiber, and Redelmeier, 1993.) When faced with this choice, most people uniformly choose treatment A; it is shorter and less painful overall. However, when medical patients actually *undergo* the two procedures and rate the experience of each, they prefer treatment B and perceive it to be less painful. How can it be that patients prefer more pain to less?

This demonstration highlights the difference between **predicted utility,** our projections about what we like and don't like, and **experienced utility,** our actual experience of what we like and don't like. It would seem that the two would be highly related, but they aren't always. Why does this happen?

The answer has to do with how people sum up their overall experience—pleasure or displeasure—of an event. Apparently, people consider the *peak* moment and the *ending* moment to arrive at an overall evaluation of the experience (Kahneman, Fredrickson, Schreiber, and Redelmeier, 1993). A negative event is most negative when it ends badly and has an extreme, intense high point. The same pattern holds true for positive events.

The message is: Make sure your experiences do not end when displeasure is highest; otherwise the entire event will be regarded as more negative. Consider Keith, who was negotiating the sale of a travel company. As part of the negotiation, he took the prospective buyers on a tour. Unexpectedly, the last day of the tour went badly. The luggage was lost, the hotel was overbooked, the food was poor, and the weather foul. Keith skillfully extended the tour another two days, thus moving the peak negative experience away from the end of the trip, and closed the deal with the buyer.

A PRIMER ON SOCIAL BEHAVIOR: WHAT MAKES PEOPLE TICK?

For ages, people have asked the question, "What makes people tick?" We have made the point several times in this book that human behavior at the bargaining table does not follow the principles of rational behavior outlined in chapters 5 and 6. What exactly, then, should we expect people to do? The following is a short course in the key ways that people think, behave, and feel. Our review is a useful checklist for the judgments we make about ourselves and others (also see Marcus and Zajonc, 1986; Kahneman, Slovic, and Tversky, 1982; Fiske and Taylor, 1991; Ross and Nisbett, 1991). As a way of organizing our discussion, we focus on how we view ourselves, others, and events (see Table 8–1).

Sizing Up Ourselves: A Look in the Mirror

We are often required to take stock of ourselves and evaluate our abilities, intentions, and behavior. How do we see ourselves? Do our evaluations of ourselves reflect how we are viewed by others? Unfortunately, this is usually not the case.

TABLE 8–1. What Makes People Tick?

Type of Judgment	Social–Psychological Factors
Sizing up ourselves	• Self-enhancement • Self-serving bias • Positive illusions • Egocentric judgment • Overconfidence • False uniqueness
Sizing up other people	• Halo and forked-tail effects • Primacy • Positivity bias • Negativity effects • Correspondent inference • Actor–observer differences • Fixed-pie perception • False consensus
Looking at the world	• Hindsight bias • Anchoring and adjustment • Unwarranted causation • Perseverance • Rosy effect • Balance effects • Illusory correlation • Just world
Behavior and action	• Social desirability • Behavioral confirmation • Acquiescence

Self-enhancement: I'm the Greatest

Delores regards herself to be at the top of her profession and chosen field. She thinks she is more likely than her peers to land a good job, win the lottery, and be promoted within three years. Is she unusual? No. Most of us are like Delores when it comes to thinking about ourselves. The constellation of evaluations that we make about ourselves are usually **self-serving** or **self-enhancing.** The pervasive tendency to enhance ourselves stems from a need to maintain and develop positive self-regard.

There may be some benefit to having unrealistically positive self-views. Positive illusions about ourselves have beneficial consequences for our well being (Taylor and Brown, 1988). For example, people who see themselves in an unrealistically positive fashion are less likely to suffer from depression and mental illness.

Does this mean that people who are happy fool themselves? Do we live in a dream world, completely divorced from reality? Not at all. People are not at complete liberty to evaluate themselves. It would be absurd to think that after failing an achievement test we had been successful. How, then, do we manage to maintain and enhance our self-esteem in the face of obvious failures, shortcomings, and flaws? Consider the student who does not have any job offers. How could his or her self-views possibly be inflated? The answer is deceptively easy.

Most of the dimensions on which we evaluate ourselves (e.g., intelligence, kindness, sincerity, creativity, etc.) do not have absolute, universally shared meanings. The definitions of these qualities are sufficiently abstract to allow people to define them in ways that reflect their strongest assets (Dunning, Meyerowitz, and Holzberg, 1989). For example, the student who does poorly on an exam but excels on a written assignment may define "intelligence" in terms of "creativity" and "written expression," whereas the student who does poorly in courses but has very high board scores may define "intelligence" as "aptitude." Neither student can be accused of living in a dream world, but each has defined intelligence in terms most favorable to their own abilities. The entrepreneur who has not made any money but has given away ideas may define success in terms of generativity; the consultant may measure success in terms of hours billed.

In a negotiation situation, multiple interpretations can present problems for effective dispute resolution (Thompson and Loewenstein, 1992). For example, even if both parties are exposed to the same factual evidence, each may draw different interpretations of the evidence in a way that suits his or her interests. Paradoxically, more information can exacerbate conflict, allowing parties to further entrench themselves in their own positions. As we'll see, inflated perceptions about the viability and reasonableness of one's negotiation position lead normal people to expect that a completely neutral third party will favor their own view. If both parties to a conflict believe that they are right and that a third party will see their point of view, one person is going to be severely disappointed. Inflated perceptions escalate destructive conflict behavior.

Taking Credit for Success; Blaming Others for Failure

People attribute their successes to skills and personality but attribute their failures and shortcomings to factors beyond their control (Beckman, 1970; Schlenker, Weigold, and Hallam, 1990). When we do well on an examination, we attribute our high performance to our intelligence and motivation; when we do poorly, we point to factors in the situation as the cause of suboptimal performance—difficulty of the test, poor teaching style of the professor, and our level of stress. The problem with this self-serving attributional pattern is that it hinders our ability to learn from experience and adapt our behavior.

Positive Illusions: The Future Is So Bright I Have to Wear Shades

Three sets of beliefs form the cornerstone of illusory thinking: optimism, self-regard, and control (Taylor and Brown, 1988). In general, people are optimistic in terms of their own good fortune. For example, most people think they are more likely to have a good job, happy marriage, and gifted children than are their peers. Of course, this can't happen for everyone, but most people think fate will be kinder to them than to others. The same process works for negative events—people think bad fortune is more likely to come to others than to themselves.

It's All under (My) Control

People tend to view situations and events to be within their control when, in fact, they often are not. For example, people believe that a winning number is more likely to turn up if they roll the dice than if another person or a random device rolls the dice (Langer, 1975). This, of course, is absurd, as the device has no knowledge of the manipulator. Yet, people go to great lengths to maintain control over random events.

Egocentric Judgment: It's All because of Me

Egocentric judgment is the tendency to assume greater responsibility for joint activities than is actually warranted. For example, consider husbands' and wives' perceptions of responsibility for a variety of household and relationship activities such as cleaning dishes, shopping, and child care. Both partners assume themselves to be more responsible than the other (Ross and Sicoly, 1979). When both spouse's contributions are totaled for a "couple" score, the perceived contributions frequently amount to over 100 percent. Obviously, two people cannot both be 150 percent responsible for child care and household chores, so one or both spouses are overestimating their contributions. The same pattern can happen in product development teams. Such differences in perception can magnify conflict.

What explains why people have egocentric biases, or the belief that "the world revolves around me"? First, people seek almost any opportunity to enhance their self-esteem. But egocentric bias also affects judgments of responsibility for behaviors that are not necessarily self-enhancing, such as initiating arguments (Ross and Sicoly, 1979). Egocentric judgments are a natural consequence of the way we mentally encode information. As we saw in chapter 7, we have a well-developed, vast network of information about the self (in the form of "self-schemas") that allows us to readily encode and retrieve information about ourselves. Our behaviors are also more salient to us than are the behaviors of others. All three factors—self-esteem maintenance, encoding, and self-schemas—contribute to a general tendency for people to assume more responsibility for joint projects than is warranted.

Overconfidence: I'm 99 Percent Sure

People have unwarranted confidence in the accuracy of their own views and the likelihood of their success in competitive situations. For example, in final-offer arbitration, negotiators believe that neutral arbitrators will select their proposal over that of the other side (Neale and Bazerman, 1991). The harsh reality, of course, is that in final-offer arbitration, both parties cannot "win"; the arbitrator selects only one proposal. Overconfidence does not simply reflect wishful thinking; rather, people truly believe that their own position is more meritorious and reasonable than that of the other side (see Robinson et al., 1994).

False Uniqueness: Standing out in the Crowd

A basic human need is the desire to be accepted and approved of by others. One way to gain the acceptance and approval of others is to do what others do—in other words, conform. Whereas conformity often has negative connotations, particularly in a culture that values independence, we conform to others every day in our dress, behavior, and attitudes. Further, conformity is adaptive: We like others who agree with us (Deutsch and Gerrard, 1955). In addition, the consequences of nonconformity or deviance can be great; nonconformists are often disliked and rejected (Schachter, 1951). This is not to say that people conform to the point where they lose their identity. Rather, people desire to present themselves as distinct from others, especially on dimensions of most importance to them. The tendency to view oneself as different (in a positive direction) from others is known as **false uniqueness** (McFarland and Miller, 1990). The belief is false because we are not as unique as we believe ourselves to be.

Sizing up Other People: Is It All in Our Head?

There is a high degree of variability in our evaluations of other people. We may regard someone to be perfectly reasonable, intelligent, and helpful, whereas our colleague may view the same person as unimpressive, demanding, and unpleasant. Our evaluations of others are not simple reflections of their abilities and traits (Dornbusch et al., 1965). Instead, our views and beliefs affect how we view others.

As an illustration, consider four managers: Aaron, Bala, Chris, and Dee. Each manager is asked about his or her impressions of the other managers in a variant of a 360-degree feedback system; for example, Bala evaluates Aaron, Chris, and Dee, and so on (see Dornbusch et al., 1965). We would expect that there should be a reasonable amount of overlap in, say, Aaron's evaluation of Chris and Bala's evaluation of Chris because each manager is sizing up the same person. If, for example, Chris is arrogant and impulsive, Aaron and Bala should hold this perception. What should we expect in terms of the amount of overlap in Aaron's evaluation of Bala and Aaron's evaluation of Chris? Obviously, this is hard to determine without knowing how similar Bala and Chris are, but it seems clear that the amount of overlap should be less than in the case where Aaron and Bala evaluate Chris. That is, we should expect to see the most overlap or consistency in agreement when two people rate the same target person than when one person rates two different people. The surprising fact is: we don't! As can be seen in Figure 8–2, there is more consistency of evaluation within *raters* than among ratees. Our impressions of others are not based on objective reality as much as on our own schemas.

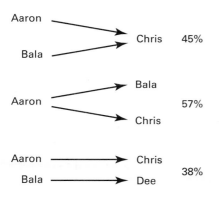

FIGURE 8–2. Percent of Overlap or Consistency in Impression

Source: Dornbusch, S. M., A. H. Hastorf, S. A. Richardson, R. E. Muzzy, and R. S. Vreeland (1965). The perceiver and perceived: Their relative influence on categories of interpersonal perception. *Journal of Personality and Social Psychology* **1**: 434–440.

Halo and Forked-tail Effects: Angels and Devils

The halo effect refers to the assumption that if people have one socially desirable characteristic (e.g., intelligence, sincerity, etc.), then they also possess other attractive traits. For example, physically attractive people are also regarded as more intelligent and warm than those who are not physically attractive (Romano and Bordieri, 1989; Feingold, 1992). In short, we generalize our favorable impressions of people on one dimension to a variety of other unrelated dimensions.

The halo effect also works in the opposite direction; that is, when we learn something negative about a person, we label him or her with other undesirable characteristics. This is the forked-tail effect.

Our evaluations of others tend to be more internally consistent than most people themselves really are. We view people whom we like and attractive people to be better in all ways than they really are; similarly, people in our disfavor are regarded to be unpleasant in all respects.

Primacy: The Power of First Impressions

The primacy effect occurs when information that is presented initially is accorded greater weight than is later evidence, even if the evidence is equally objectively valuable. For example, imagine that you learn that Sue is greedy, manipulative, and dishonest. A month later, you learn that she is intelligent, organized, and conscientious. What is your overall impression of Sue? Now imagine that you learn that Sandy is considerate, intelligent, and dependable. Later, you learn that Sandy is also pushy, demanding, and arrogant. What do you think of Sandy overall? If you are like most people, you like Sandy more than Sue even though the ratio of positive to negative information is identical. Why does this happen? Early information sets up a directional tendency with which we view subsequent information (Asch, 1946).

The implications of the primacy effect are serious. Suppose you are in a job interview and a recruiter asks you to candidly discuss your weaknesses and strengths in particular areas. What should you do to optimally influence the recruiter's impression of you? According to the primacy effect, the recruiter will reach a very different overall impression of you, depending on whether you present your positive features (creative, enterprising, and multilingual) before your negative features (little experience, quantitatively challenged, and not well organized). The message is clear: Present your positive features first, even if this means restructuring the flow of the interview.

Positivity Bias: Up with People

In general, we evaluate most people positively (Sears, 1983; Miller and Felicio, 1990). For example, we rate most people to be "above average." We do not accord nonperson entities with the same above-average evaluations, however. For example, when students evaluate a course, they rate "contributions of the instructor" higher than the "course as a whole," even though the two questions are almost conceptually identical (Sears, 1983).

Negativity Effect: A Worm in the Apple

When we learn something negative about a person, it has more influence on our impression of that person than does positive information. The **negativity effect** refers to the fact that negative information carries more weight in our impressions of others than does positive information. This explains why it is often difficult for people to recover from making a bad first impression.

At first glance, it would seem that the negativity bias is contradictory to the positivity bias. However, these principles are not contradictory at all; they are complementary. It is precisely because we view most people in favorable terms that if we encounter a clearly negative piece of information about a person, it is especially salient and accorded greater weight in our evaluation of them.

Correspondent Inference: Showing Your True Colors

If we know *why* a person does something or acts in a particular way, we are in a much better position to predict his or her behavior. Generally speaking, people's behavior may be explained by either situational factors or dispositional factors. Consider, for example, a negotiator who makes a threat and angrily storms out of the room. A **situational** explanation is that he is having a bad day, pressure from work is getting to him, or he was provoked. A dispositional explanation is that he is a volatile, angry person. Situational attributions explain the cause of a person's behavior in the environment, largely outside of their control. In contrast, dispositional attributions locate the cause of behavior in the personality traits of the person. Dispositional factors provide greater insight about a person's behavior than situational factors because dispositional factors are constant across situations, whereas situational factors are capricious. This leads people to infer the cause of a person's behavior in their disposition rather than in the situation. The **correspondent inference phenomenon** (see Gilbert and Malone, 1995) is the tendency of perceivers to overattribute the cause of a person's behavior to his or her disposition and underestimate the causal influence of situational factors (Ross, Greene, and House, 1977; Ross and Nisbett, 1991).

Actor–Observer Difference: I'm a Victim of the Situation

Paradoxically, the opposite phenomenon occurs when we explain our own behavior. Whereas we attribute the behavior of others to stable, dispositional factors, we attribute our own behavior to situational circumstances. The **actor–observer difference** (Jones and Nisbett, 1972) may be explained by principles of perceptual salience (Storms, 1973). When we explain the behavior of another person, the *person* is salient in our perceptual field; in contrast, when we explain the causes of our own behavior, the *situation* is salient.

Fixed-Pie Perception

Perhaps the most pervasive way we think about others in negotiation is the fixed-pie perception (Bazerman and Neale, 1983; Thompson and Hastie, 1990). The fixed-pie perception is the belief that the other party's interests are directly opposed to our own. Most people view negotiations in purely distributive terms (i.e., who gets how much) instead of integrative terms. This perception is often erroneous because in most cases, people's interests are not completely opposed, and there is potential for joint gain. Indeed, the most frequent cause of ineffective negotiation agreements is that people do not believe it is possible that their interests could be anything but completely opposed to others' in a direct, one-on-one fashion (Thompson and Hastie, 1990).

False Consensus: Jump on My Bandwagon

In many situations, we try to predict what another person will do and look to our own behavior as a guide. However, this leads to the belief that others are more similar to ourselves in attitudes and behaviors than is actually the case, a phenomenon known as **false consensus** (Ross, Greene, and House, 1977; Ross and Nisbett, 1991). We believe that if we engaged in a particular behavior—say, wearing a huge sandwich-board sign and walking all over campus—that the majority of our peers would do so as well (Ross, Greene, and House, 1977). However, we greatly overestimate people's similarity to us.

At first glance, it would seem that false consensus would pave the way toward more friendly relations and enhance negotiated agreements. However, if negotiators falsely assume that the opponent has the same priorities as they do, the strategy of logrolling is useless. Negotiators falsely project their priorities concerning negotiation issues onto others when the situation is more abstract and ambiguous and consequently are less likely to effectively logroll their interests (Bottom and Paese, 1996).

What Makes Me Tick Is Not What Makes You Tick

Craig, a colleague of yours, arrives at work before 7:00 A.M. He never leaves until after 7:00 at night. Further, it is obvious that he spends weekends and late nights working as well. Clearly, Craig is working hard. Why is he so motivated? When we answer this question, most of us think that Craig is trying to get an early promotion or win the favor of his supervisor. In short, we see Craig's behavior as **extrinsically motivated.**

Now, imagine that you are the one who is working hard, burning the midnight oil, and setting new standards. How do we explain our own motivation? Most of us assume that we are **intrinsically motivated;** that is, we like doing worthwhile things, taking on challenges, and learning. Thus, we see ourselves as more intrinsically motivated and our colleagues as doing things for extrinsic reasons. We see our own behavior in intrinsic terms, but others look at our behavior as extrinsically motivated (Heath, 1996).

Looking at the World

Hindsight Bias: I Told You So

We are frequently called upon to explain the causes of events, such as the demise of an organization or the success of a particular company. We often perceive events that have already occurred as inevitable. Stated another way, once we know the outcome of an event, we perceive the outcome to be an inevitable consequence of the factors leading up to the outcome. This **creeping determinism** (Fischhoff, 1975) accounts for the Monday-morning quarterback or the "I knew it all along" phenomenon. That is, once someone knows the outcome, the events leading up to it seem obvious. The hindsight bias also accounts for why negotiators often think integrative agreements are obvious after the fact, but fail to see them when encountering a novel negotiation.

Anchoring and Adjustment: Start Here and Tweak a Little

Job candidates are often asked by recruiters what their salary range is. The job candidate, wanting to maximize his or her salary but at the same time not remove him- or herself from consideration because of unrealistic demands, faces a quandary. Similarly, the prospective home buyer struggles with what to make as an opening offer. What factors determine how we make such assessments of value?

According to Tversky and Kahneman (1974), people use a reference point as an anchor and then adjust that value up or down as deemed appropriate. For example, the prospective job recruit may have a roommate who just landed a job with a salary of $60,000. The candidate decides to use $60,000 as a starting point. There are two fundamental concerns with the **anchoring-and-adjustment process.** The first is that the anchors we use to make such judgments are often arbitrary (Tversky and Kahneman, 1974). Oftentimes, anchors are selected on the basis of their temporal proximity, not their relevance to the judgment in question—remember the United Nations example. The second is that we tend to make insufficient adjustments away from the anchor. That is, we are weighted down by the anchor. The message for the negotiator is clear: carefully select anchors, and be wary if your opponent attempts to anchor you.

Unwarranted Causation: Which Came First, the Chicken or the Egg?

Consider the following facts:

- Women living in the San Francisco area have a higher rate of breast cancer.
- Women of lower socioeconomic status are less likely to breast feed their babies.
- People who marry at a later point in life are less likely to divorce.

Before reading further, attempt to explain each fact. When people are asked to do this, they frequently conclude the following:

- Living in San Francisco causes breast cancer.
- People of lower socioeconomic status are not given postnatal care.
- People become wiser as they grow older.

All of these are reasonable explanations, but they are all unwarranted based upon the information given. The tendency to infer a **causal relationship** between two events is unwarranted because we do not know the direction of causality (for example, it is possible that women with cancer are attracted to the Bay Area). Further, a third variable could be the cause of the event (people who marry later may be richer or more educated). Maybe older, more professional women are attracted to the Bay Area, and this group is statistically more susceptible to cancer. Maybe women of lower socioeconomic status are younger and less comfortable breast feeding, more likely to be targeted by formula companies, or less likely to get maternity leave. The point is that there are a myriad of possible explanations. The tendency to make unwarranted causal attributions is derived from similar principles as the correspondence bias: We want to infer cause because it provides us with greater prediction.

Perseverance Effects: I've Thought This Way for So Long

The perseverance effect is the tendency of perceivers to continue to believe that something is true even when it is revealed to be false or has been disproved (Ross and Lepper, 1980). A hilarious example comes from the movie *Some Like It Hot.* Tony Curtis and Jack Lemmon, anxious to leave Chicago because gangsters are after them, dress up like women so they can join an "all-girls" band, traveling on a Florida-bound train. The two must keep up the stunt for days. Perseverance effects start to set in when Jack Lemmon, who calls himself "Daphne," starts to date a man. Tony Curtis, or "Josephine," tells the confused Lemmon, "you're a boy!" when Daphne really begins to think of herself as a girl. Another example: Imagine that you have taken an aptitude test and have been told you scored poorly. Hours later it is revealed to you that the exam was mis-scored. Are you able to erase this experience? Not if you are like most college students, who continue to persevere in their beliefs. Why is this? Once a causal chain or coherent structure is constructed, it is difficult to eliminate it. If you or your negotiation opponent has an erroneous belief about the other, even when it is proven wrong, the belief may still prevail. The important implication is to carefully examine the beliefs you hold about your opponent and be cognizant of faulty beliefs they may have about you.

Rosy Effect: Sweet Anticipation and Memory

We anticipate personal experiences to be more enjoyable than we actually experience them at the time of their occurrence. Further, we remember personal events as more pleasant and rewarding than we actually felt about them at the time of their occurrence (Mitchell and Thompson, 1994). For example, think about your most recent trip to Europe. If you're like most people, you fondly anticipated the trip and have extremely favorable memories of it. However, during the trip itself, most people are not as overjoyed as they later recall (Mitchell, Thompson, Peterson, and Cronk, in press). Why? The negative aspects of events drop out over time and are not anticipated. We don't remember the fly in our soup at dinner in Paris or our migraine headache in London. The "rosy effect" suggests that we may more fondly recall certain negotiation experiences than we actually experienced them at the time of their occurrence.

Balance, Assimilation, and Contrast: It All Adds Up

We perceive balanced, logical relations in our world (Heider, 1958). For example, we believe that if we like someone, so will our best friend. We believe that if we hold a particular political opinion, the candidate that we don't vote for is against it. We are extremely reluctant to perceive incongruence. Often, our need to perceive balance is so strong that our evaluations of people, events, and relationships are affected by it. For example, partisans to an issue tend to perceive the other side as having more extreme views than is actually the case (Robinson et al., 1994). After learning that another person is of a different political, moral, or social group, we exaggerate the difference in opinion.

Assimilation and contrast are closely related to the balance principle. Stimuli close to the anchor tend to be assimilated (i.e., shifted toward the anchor), whereas those further away are contrasted. For example, if we hear an extremist view on a political issue, we are more likely to accept (assimilate) the view if our own opinions (the anchor) are also strongly on that side of the issue. The assimilation–contrast principle states that to the extent parties hold extreme views, they will regard the opinions of the other party to be more dissimilar to their own than is actually the case.

Illusory Correlation: Bad Things Go Together

People often perceive relationships between distinct pieces of information as a mere consequence of their being presented at the same time (Hamilton and Gifford, 1976). For example, suppose you learn during the course of a negotiation with a business representative from Lebanon that 60 percent of Lebanese men are uneducated. Suppose that the same day you learn that 60 percent of crimes committed in that country are violent. Although there is no logical relation between the two statistics, most people assume that there is a correlation; that is, they assume that uneducated Lebanese men are responsible for violent crimes. In fact, there is no relationship between the two—it is illusory. Such correlations between separate facts are illusory because there is no objective basis for the relationships. Rather, our implicit theories are constructed so that we interpret relations between temporally proximate events.

Just World: Serves 'em Right

Most of us believe that the world is a fair place: people get out of life what they deserve and deserve what happens to them (Lerner, 1980). This leads to positive evaluations of others who have good things happen to them; for example, "good" people are likely to win lotteries. Unwarranted negative impressions are produced when others suffer misfortune; for instance, we assume that bad people or ignorant people are victims of crimes (Saunders and Size, 1986). **Blaming-the-victim attributions** are **defensive attributions** because they enable observers to deal with the perceived inequities in others' lives and maintain the belief that the world is just (Thornton, 1992). In short, if we believe that bad things could easily happen to us (e.g., dying in an airplane crash or losing a limb), the world is scary and less predictable.

Behavior and Action

The processes and mechanisms of social perception affect not only how we judge others but also how we behave toward others.

Social Desirability: I Just Want to Be Loved

Most people want to be accepted by others and avoid disapproval or rejection. One way to gain the approval of others is to behave in normatively appropriate ways—that is, to follow the implicit rules of organizations and groups, be a "good" organizational citizen, or agree with others. Indeed, non-normative, deviant behavior is sharply criticized (Schachter, 1951). In a very real sense, it pays to be liked. It may seem strange to think that negotiators care what the opponent thinks, but consider the times you have hesitated to ask a merchant for a reduction in list price for fear of insulting him or her.

Behavioral Confirmation: Don't Make Me Act That Way

The most powerful way that our perceptions and beliefs influence our behavior is through the **self-fulfilling prophecy,** or behavioral confirmation effect (Snyder, Tanke, and Berscheid, 1977). A self-fulfilling prophecy occurs when the beliefs held by a perceiver elicit behavior from a target person in a manner that confirms the perceiver's expectations. The behavioral confirmation process is comprised of six steps (Snyder, 1984), illustrated by the following scenario: (1) Amy believes Mark to be socially anxious and uncomfortable when interacting with people; (2) in Amy's interactions with Mark, she behaves in a way consistent with her beliefs about Mark (i.e., she doesn't smile, has speech interruptions, etc.); (3) Mark senses that Amy holds this belief about him; (4) Mark responds by behaving in an awkward fashion in his interactions with Amy; (5) Amy regards Mark's responses as confirming her initial beliefs; (6) Mark internalizes this impression and regards himself as a socially anxious and awkward person.

Self-fulfilling prophecies have been documented in classroom performance (Rosenthal and Jacobson, 1968), dating behavior (Snyder, Tanke, and Berscheid, 1977), and job interviewing (Neuberg, 1989). However, it is not always the case that our behavior is shaped by another person's impression of us; in some instances, we seek to **self-verify** (Swann and Ely, 1984). That is, we want others to have the same impression of us that we have of ourselves. What determines which process will operate? When we are aware of the perceptions held of ourselves by others or when our self-views are very strong, self-verification is more likely than behavioral confirmation.

Acquiescence Bias: Say 'yes'!

Are you enterprising? Do you like challenges? Do you like to be the best you can be? Most people agree that the above description accurately characterizes them. The **acquiescence bias** refers to the tendency of perceivers to agree with assertions, particularly ones made about them. For example, when people read a character description, they tend to believe that it describes them (Schlenker, 1980). The acquiescence effect is due in part to the way that people impose meaning on their interpretation of traits and behaviors and in part by a desire to be agreeable. This is a common sales ploy. For example, salespeople ask consumers "Do you like to save money?" and "Do you like offering your family the best quality?" Most people answer "yes," and therefore have already agreed to something that the other wants.

Our encyclopedic review of social psychological phenomena specifies how judgment and behavior deviates from rational behavior. There are a lot of principles to keep in mind when negotiating. Four key themes summarize what the negotiator should know about human behavior: evaluation, self-enhancement, prediction, and social desirability.

- **Evaluation:** Our evaluations of *others* are highly evaluative (i.e., we think of people as good or bad) and our impressions are internally consistent.
- **Self-enhancement:** Our evaluations of *ourselves* are self-enhancing (we see ourselves through rose-colored glasses).
- **Prediction:** We evaluate others and events in a way so as to maximize prediction and understanding.
- **Social desirability:** We want to be liked by others and avoid disapproval.

A TRIPOD OF SKILLS

Negotiation involves a constellation of three skills:

- decision-making skills
- social perception skills
- negotiation skills

We've talked about these skills and now it is time to examine how people's behavior varies for each skill (see Table 8–2).

TABLE 8–2.   A Tripod of Skills and Modus Operandi for Each

Decision Making	Social Perception	Negotiation
• Corrigible rationalist	• Consistency seeker	• Economic rationalist
• Bounded rationalist	• Naïve scientist	• Descriptive rationalist
• Error-prone intuitive scientist	• Cognitive miser	• Post-rationalist
• Slave to motivational forces	• Motivated tactician	• Victim of circumstance
• Butt of faulty normative models		

Decision Making

Most people believe they are rational. However, every so often we make mistakes, and we are forced to come to grips with our own shortcomings. Our explanations of our shortcomings reveal fundamental beliefs about human decision making. (Abelson and Levi, 1985). Which one best describes how you make decisions?

Corrigible Rationalist

Andy is a corrigible rationalist. He uses the MAUT decision-making principle to make decisions that do not involve risk and the expected utility principle to make risky decisions, whether he is buying a house or a light bulb. In short, Andy is a human computer. However, like computers, Andy is not perfect. He occasionally slips up. As a corrigible rationalist, Andy embraces the basic axioms of decision theory and regards this as the best way to make decisions (Edwards, 1961). As a corrigible rationalist, Andy immediately corrects his behavior once errors are pointed out to him.

Bounded Rationalist

Gloria is a bounded rationalist. She understands the principles that Andy follows, but Gloria makes so many decisions in her busy life that she simply doesn't have time to follow the MAUT model every time she buys a sweater or goes on a business trip. Gloria takes some shortcuts that save her time and effort. As a bounded rationalist, she understands the tenets and principles of normative axioms but does not always engage in a fully rational analysis because of time constraints or information-processing limitations (Simon, 1955). Rather than optimizing decisions which take time and effort, she **satisfices.** In other words, she makes a tradeoff in decision making by doing just enough to make a reasonable solution. Such tradeoffs are the essence of cost-benefit analyses (Simon, 1955). Gloria claims that if she were given sufficient incentives and no time constraints, she would reach optimal outcomes.

Error-prone Intuitive Scientist

Henry is an error-prone intuitive scientist. Henry doesn't see the point of Andy or Gloria's computer-like models, and claims that "using numbers is no way to make important decisions." Henry regards himself to be a rational person, but creates his own theories about human behavior. For example, one of Henry's maxims is to "never trust lawyers." Frankly, Henry does not understand or appreciate some of the principles of normative theories. Rather, he relies on implicit theories to guide his behavior. Neither experience, time, nor incentives will prompt Henry to use rational models.

Slave to Motivational Forces

Sara is a slave to motivational forces. Sara makes her decisions "from the heart and not the head." For example, Sara got so mad at a vendor last week that she tore up a contract and threw it on the table and stormed out. Sara will be the first to admit that, objectively, the vendor's terms were better than anything else she currently had, but her principles were at stake. Some people on occasion fall into the grip of emotional and motivational forces that they cannot control in the course of decision making (Janis and Mann, 1977). Emotions, self-esteem needs, impression-management concerns, defensive avoidance, regret, and disappointment hinder effective decision making. The difference between "slave" and the error-prone intuitive scientist is that the slave is more emotional than the "intuitive scientist." The intuitive scientist errs because of cognitive limitations; the slave errs because of emotional and motivational factors.

Butt of Faulty Normative Models

John is often called the "butt" of logical reasoning by his associates. The way John explains it is that he "sets his own standards." For John, normative models are silly. Therefore, it is not appropriate to infer that people are not rational when they fail to follow the prescriptions of economic theory, because normative decision theory is no more compelling than some other model (Cohen, 1981; Lopes, 1994; Beach and Lipshitz, 1993).

Social Perception

There are a variety of ways that people look at the world and account for the behavior of others (Fiske and Taylor, 1991). Which one explains how you see the world?

Consistency Seeker

Sue is a consistency seeker. She doesn't understand it when people say one thing (such as, "smoking causes cancer") and then contradict themselves (e.g., smoke). When Sue finds herself behaving in a way that is inconsistent, she is uncomfortable—a state she finds aversive. According to cognitive dissonance theory, inconsistency between thoughts and behavior, or among behaviors or thoughts, produces an aversive tension state that people are motivated to reduce through various means, either changing behavior and attitudes or rationalization (Aronson, 1992; Festinger, 1957).

Consider behavior at the horse races (Knox and Inkster, 1968). When bettors are asked how confident they are that their horse will win, those asked *before* they place their bet are less confident than those asked *after* they place their bet. Further, bettors who already placed their bets express greater confidence than those who have not yet placed their bets, suggesting that once a person has engaged in an irrevocable act, they are motivated to bring their beliefs in line with their behavior.

Naïve Scientist

Brian is a naïve scientist. As a child of the information-processing age, he is logical and rational in thought and behavior. For example, consider how Brian explains an everyday event, like why his friend, Sandy, was late to meet him for lunch. Brian asked himself the following questions: "Is Sandy late to lunch with everyone or just late to lunch with me?" (distinctiveness information); "Is everyone who meets me for lunch late or just Sandy?" (consensus information); and, "Is Sandy always late when meeting me for lunch or is this a one-time occurrence?" (consistency information) (Kelley, 1972). By examining the pattern of answers, Brian can make either an internal attribution for Sandy's behavior (e.g., Sandy doesn't like him) or an external attribution (e.g., Sandy got caught in traffic).

Cognitive Miser

Marika is a cognitive miser. She thinks Brian wastes too much time thinking about trivial things. Marika operates on automatic pilot through many of her interactions (Langer, 1989). For example, she'll nod in agreement and sign off on reports without really reading them.

As an illustration of how people are on "automatic pilot" in everyday life, Langer, Blank, and Chanowitz (1978) examined behavior in a duplicating area of the library. Typically, there are long lines of students waiting to photocopy material. Langer et al. instructed someone to cut into one of the lines. In one situation, the person asked to cut in line because "he was in a terrible hurry" (legitimate excuse); in another situation, the person asked to cut in line because "he needed to make some copies" (illegitimate excuse); in yet another situation, the person cut in line without offering a reason (no excuse). Langer et al. then examined how often the person was allowed to cut. Whereas it would seem that rates of compliance would be highest in the legitimate excuse condition, those who offered an illegitimate excuse were also effective. Langer concluded that people do not deeply process information, which would require attending to the rationale of the excuse, but attend merely to superficial aspects of the situation.

Motivated Tactician

Max is a motivated tactician. His view of the world is guided by what he wants out of a particular situation. For example, if Max expects to interact with someone in the future, he is more likely to remember information about him or her and make more accurate judgments (Devine, Sedekides, and Fuhrman, 1989). Furthermore, Max is more likely to attend to someone if he anticipates being involved in a competitive interaction with him or her (Ruscher and Fiske, 1990).

Negotiator Rationality

Below, we consider the four profiles of rationality in negotiation: economic rationalist, descriptive rationalist, post-rationalist, and victim of circumstance. Which type characterizes how you explain your behavior?

Economic Rationalist

Vicky is an economic rationalist at the bargaining table. She is analytical, rational, and logical. She analyzes negotiation situations and the key elements. She seeks to maximize her utility (e.g., she refuses to settle for less than her reservation price and prefers options that offer more surplus than others). She derives conclusions from available evidence according to rules of logic. Vicky appreciates the normative principles and is able to enact them.

Descriptive Rationalist

Marc is a descriptive rationalist at the bargaining table. As a quasi-rationalist, Marc is not strictly rational and does not assume that his opponent is perfectly rational. Marc realizes that even if he is rational, he may face a negotiator who is not. Thus, the descriptive rationalist adopts strategies to best deal with a nonrational opponent. The **asymmetric descriptive–prescriptive approach** assumes that the focal negotiator is rational but may face a negotiator who is not, and therefore certain prescriptions may be altered when encountering someone who is not assumed to behave rationally in that situation (Raiffa, 1982).

The descriptive rationalist uses heuristics to guide his behavior. Some heuristics make sense and lead to efficient outcomes, but others are clearly erroneous, such as the fixed-pie perception.

Post-Rationalist

Jeanne is a post-rationalist. She argues that negotiation behavior is not necessarily guided by anticipated self-interest but is justified after the fact. Her behavior is determined to a large extent by social–contextual factors and goals outside the bounds of rational self-interest. She assesses her rationality after she engages in behavior rather than before.

Victim of Circumstance

Bill just completed an executive training course in negotiations. Before the program, Bill regarded himself as a highly skilled negotiator. After several sessions, in which Bill reached what the instructor labeled as "suboptimal" outcomes, Bill started to doubt the validity of the teaching materials and methods. In fact, Bill claimed he was an unwitting victim of circumstance. Stated simply, Bill argued that the negotiation course failed in some critical ways to capture the important features of his real negotiation situations, which, he argues, he excels at. Bill raised four important concerns in this regard: insufficient incentives, inappropriate sample, nonrepresentative task, and insufficient experience.

Insufficient Incentives   One of Bill's concerns is that the incentives for attaining profitable outcomes in the training course were insufficient (e.g., the participants were not paid and the stakes were trivial). In another variation on this argument, the incentive structure may be confounded with reputational concerns and familiarity. For example, if the participants are all members of a class which meets regularly, there may be an incentive to negotiate in a manner that does not anger or frustrate one's classmates. This behavior would be highly rational for a participant who does not want to risk his or her reputation by behaving in a self-interested manner. However, the evidence does not support Bill's argument: Participants who are paid based upon their performance do not significantly differ from unpaid participants (Grether and Plott, 1979) and, in some cases, perform worse (Thompson and Hrebec, 1996).

Inappropriate Sample   Another concern Bill raised is that the participants in the program were rookies with little previous experience in professional negotiations and therefore not representative of the population of persons who do have experience and expertise. However, again, there is no evidence to suggest that seasoned business executives behave differently from naïve students (Ball, Bazerman, and Carroll, 1991).

Nonrepresentative Task   A third concern Bill raised is that the classroom experience introduced other factors not representative of real-life situations. In particular, Bill argued that integrative agreements are quite rare in real life. At this point, the instructor reminded him of the hindsight bias.

Insufficient Experience   Finally, Bill used an economic argument: A key assumption of economic theory is that the market is self-correcting, meaning that if a person behaves in a nonrational manner, he or she will learn to adapt because of the real risk of being taken advantage of by others. An example is the **money pump,** in which an individual is induced to buy an object from one person for $10, then sell it for $11 (making $1 profit), and then buy it back for $11. Because individuals cannot ultimately survive by engaging in this behavior, they either learn to behave in an optimal fashion or are eliminated from the market. Unless classroom situations allow for such learning, one-shot investigations may be unrepresentative of common interaction. The self-correcting market assumption is not necessarily accurate. There are many examples of behaviors that are suboptimal in the marketplace but are not self-correcting; it is not always apparent to people that their behavior is flawed.

CONCLUSION

We introduced the concepts of rationality, irrationality, and nonrationality and concluded that rationality is multiply defined and that there are many forms of rationality. We then introduced an encyclopedia of behaviors that guide our self-evaluations, impressions of others, and impressions of the situation. The themes may be summarized by the principles of evaluation, self-enhancement, prediction, and social desirability. We concluded with an analysis of the profiles of decision making, social perception, and negotiation. We are now ready to turn our attention to specific negotiation situations. In chapter 9, we examine negotiation in groups and multiple parties.

TAKE-AWAYS

- Most negotiators make biased judgments about themselves, their opponents, and the world in general. These biases can seriously hinder the effectiveness of negotiators at the bargaining table.

- Negotiators are not solely concerned with maximizing monetary gain. Information, goods, services, approval, acceptance, and status are all important resources that may be negotiated.

- In general, people view themselves to be superior to others and are motivated to win the approval of others.

- There are several different kinds of rationality, or ways that we use to make sense of our behavior. It is important to know what the basis of rationality is for ourselves and the people with whom we negotiate.

CHAPTER 9

Groups and Teams:
Multiple Parties
at the Bargaining Table

Film Gate (FG), a new television production company, pitched a number of ideas for one-hour television specials to the three major networks. The executives at ABC liked one of the ideas and began negotiations with FG to develop the series. Because FG had never produced a network special, ABC insisted that FG co-produce the special with Tri-Color (TC), an experienced television production company. As it turns out, both FG and TC were represented by the same Hollywood agent (HA); in fact, TC was one of HA's largest and most established clients.

The FG negotiating team was composed of the president, chief financial officer, and head of production. Each member of the team found the prospect of working with TC modestly aversive, and after some discussion, the team was staunchly opposed to the plan. However, because there was no obvious alternative they proceeded to negotiate. The key issues to be addressed were: (1) credit for the program as listed in the titles; (2) monetary compensation; and (3) the option of follow-up programming with ABC. FG was most concerned with credit and the option of future programming so that they could establish a reputation within the industry. However, FG felt pressure to please its major shareholder (SH) in the negotiations. SH was most concerned with the short-term profitability of FG and was unwilling to continue staking FG unless it would show a profit in the near future. FG decided therefore that money would be as important as credit in the negotiation with ABC and TC.

Working through HA, the three principals (ABC, FG, and TC) arrived at a deal that gave top billing and generous compensation to FG. However, HA later sent a memo to ABC stating that the production would be credited to "TC in association with FG," and that ABC's future options would be exercised, if at all, solely through TC. FG was infuriated by HA's apparent betrayal and found a new agent. Furthermore, FG threatened to sue HA; this threat proved ineffective, as both FG and HA were convinced that a jury would side with them. Finally, FG explored the possibility with ABC of collaborating with Unicorn Productions (UP), another established production company. In light of this development, HA and TC relented and the deal went through under the original terms.[1]

How might we begin to analyze this complex negotiation situation? Thus far, our analyses of the processes and decisions in negotiation have involved only two parties. In the Film Gate situation, we have a complex assortment of players—some are parties, others are agents and still others are constituents. In this chapter, we analyze negotiation situations that involve more than two parties.

When we consider the fact that most of our waking hours are spent interacting and working with other people, it is clear that an understanding of group processes is important: 48 percent of social interactions are in dyads, 19 percent in triads, 11 percent in groups of four, and 22 percent in groups of five or more (Wheeler and Nezlek, 1977). Clearly, group membership is a necessary part of social life, and groups are the fundamental building block of organizational life.

Our experience in social and organizational groups ranges widely. Some groups are highly productive, motivated, and rewarding, whereas other groups are ineffective, inefficient, and highly frustrating. Although it might seem that the difference between effective and dysfunctional groups is determined by the compatibility of group members' interests, groups whose members have compatible interests are not always productive and groups whose members have incompatible goals are not always doomed. Understanding the nature of groups and what makes for effective group interaction is important for the individual who wants to negotiate successfully with others. This chapter provides the negotiator with a foundation for understanding and optimally managing group interaction. We first begin by defining groups, teams, and social aggregates.

GROUPS, TEAMS, AND SOCIAL AGGREGATES

The important criterion that distinguishes groups from other social aggregates is interdependence among members. A group is a collection of two or more persons who have the potential to affect each other's outcomes by their own actions. This definition includes formal groups such as project groups, work teams, hiring committees, and executive committees, as well as informal groups such as a Monday night bar group, a lunch group, and so on.

A team is a type of group, but not all groups are teams. A **team** is a group of people who are interdependent and working toward a common goal. Teams have the following five hallmark characteristics (Hackman, 1996):

---

[1]We are grateful to Alan Fox for this example, which also appears in Thompson and Fox (in press).

- Members are interdependent.
- Members manage themselves.
- The team is embedded in a social system.
- The team has a task to perform.
- The members of the team share a common goal.

ARE TWO (OR MORE) HEADS BETTER THAN ONE?

Intuition suggests that two heads, or three or four, are better than one. For example, the jury system in the United States is built on the principle that collective judgment is more fair and accurate than individual judgment. One of the earliest examinations of individuals versus groups occurred in 1932 when groups of people and people working alone were given intellectual puzzles which required Eureka solutions to solve (Shaw, 1932). (These puzzles are known as Eureka tasks because the correct answer is immediately obvious once it is known.) Groups performed better than individuals on these tasks because they caught errors made by members of the groups. The **group superiority effect** was also replicated by Davis (1969) and Laughlin (1980), who found that groups learned faster and made fewer errors than did individuals. But groups were less productive than individuals per person, leading Shaw (1981) to conclude that groups are more *effective* than individuals, but individuals are more *efficient.*

It Depends on the Task

The answer to the question of whether groups or individuals are more productive in terms of behavior or correct in terms of judgment depends upon the type of task the group faces (McGrath, 1984; Hastie, 1986; Hill, 1982; Steiner, 1972). Most group tasks may be categorized as either additive, conjunctive, disjunctive, or discretionary (Steiner, 1972).

- In an **additive task,** performance depends on the sum of each individual's effort. For example, in a radio station fund-raising drive, the total amount of money raised represents the input of all staff members' efforts. In additive tasks, group performance is usually better than individual effort. As we will see, however, the effort expended by each individual staff member may be less than what he or she would contribute if working alone. Individuals often do not live up to their potential in group situations.

- In **conjunctive tasks,** performance depends on how well the least talented member performs. For example, consider a team of software engineers working on a modular computer program, wherein the success of the program depends upon each part of the system. The program is only as good as its weakest link. For this reason, groups typically do worse on conjunctive tasks than do individuals.

- In **disjunctive tasks,** performance depends on how well the most talented member performs. For example, consider a team of people playing "trivial pursuit." If one member of the team has the answer, then the team wins the point. On these types of tasks, groups usually perform better than individuals.

  But there is an important caveat: On a disjunctive task, the person with the right answer needs to be able to convince other members that he or she is right (Steiner, 1972). A person's ability to convince others depends on two key factors: task demonstrability and the distribution of information. **Demonstrable tasks,** such as Eureka tasks, have an obvious, correct answer. Low demonstrability tasks, such as matters of opinion or taste, do not have an obvious, correct answer. It is easier for members to convince others when the task is highly demonstrable.

Another reason that groups often don't perform as well as individuals is that group members fail to share unique information—information they know but others don't. Typically, members of groups are not generalists, having complete knowledge of many areas. Many groups in organizations such as cross-functional teams are composed of members with highly specialized knowledge. Successful task performance on cross-functional teams requires members to pool or share information. Surprising as it may seem, groups often fail to share critical information. What goes wrong? People in groups focus on information that all members have in common, rather than on unique information (Gigone and Hastie, 1993). For example, consider a group of individuals attempting to solve a murder mystery (Stasser and Stewart, 1992). All of the clues necessary to solve the mystery are held by group members. However, the information is dispersed among group members such that, to solve the mystery, members need to offer information about the clues that they have. When information needs to be pooled, groups are less likely to solve murder mysteries than when clues are shared by members of the group.

The same phenomenon happens when groups of experts, such as medical doctors, make decisions. For example, when physicians are asked to make diagnoses of patients, "shared" information is discussed more than "unshared" information. When accurate diagnosis depends on discussion of unshared information, misdiagnosis is more likely (Larson, Christensen, Abbott, and Franz, 1996).

- **Discretionary tasks** permit some members of groups to combine their individual contributions in any way that they wish. Presumably, the group could make the task disjunctive (by assigning total weight to the contributions of the most capable group member), conjunctive (by requiring that everyone complete the task), additive (by assigning equal weight to each group member), or some unique type. Thus, when the task is discretionary, the nature of the task can be determined only by analyzing the group's behavior.

What is the effect of increasing the size of a group? Increasing group size improves performance on disjunctive tasks at a decelerating rate, and decreases performance in conjunctive tasks at a decelerating rate (Steiner, 1972). Group composition may be heterogeneous or homogeneous with respect to human resources. Heterogeneity increases potential productivity in disjunctive tasks, decreases productivity in conjunctive tasks, and is irrelevant when the task is additive.

THE GROUP PERFORMANCE EQUATION

How productive are groups? An analysis of group productivity tells us how effective a group or team can be under the best of circumstances. Furthermore, it provides a means to locate the source of potential ineffectiveness. People often blame poor group performance on the low motivation of other members. However, group ineffectiveness can often be traced to simple coordination problems that may often be easily corrected. For the manager interested in improving efficiency of group negotiation, it is essential to understand the major threats to group productivity.

The productivity of groups may be expressed in terms of a simple formula (Steiner, 1972):

$$AP = PP + IG - IL,$$

where

$$AP = \text{Actual Productivity}$$
$$PP = \text{Potential Productivity}$$
$$IG = \text{Interaction Gain}$$
$$IL = \text{Interaction Loss}$$

We will now examine each of the variables affecting actual performance.

Potential Productivity

The **potential productivity** of a group depends upon three factors: the task demands, the resources available to the group, and the group process:

- **Task demands** are the requirements imposed upon the group by the task itself and the rules governing task performance. Task demands determine the resources needed for optimal performance and how to combine resources. The task of a union is to meet its constituents' interests and maintain union solidarity.

- **Resources** are the relevant abilities, skills, and tools possessed by people attempting to perform the task. The union negotiating team may be a six-member group that has legal and political expertise.

- Process concerns the way groups use resources to meet task demands. Group process describes the steps taken by the group when attempting the task and includes nonproductive as well as productive actions. The union team may hold its key meetings via telephone because of travel constraints. All information may be funneled through a single leader.

In summary, the task demands reveal the kinds of resources needed; the resources determine the group's potential productivity; and the process determines the degree of potential realized. Next, we focus on the things that can go right, or **interaction gains,** and on the things that can go wrong, or **interaction losses.**

Interaction Gains

It is rare for groups to perform better than their best member. There is one general exception to this disappointing conclusion: **group potency.**

Group Potency

Group potency refers to the collective perception held by members of a group that their efforts, decisions, and products are superior, valued, and worthwhile (Guzzo, Yost, Campbell, and Shea, 1993). Group potency is a shared belief within a group that it can be effective. Many groups exhibit high levels of potency—usually in excess of objective measures of performance and in excess of the average of that of individual members. Why is this? Why do groups feel that they are collectively powerful and accurate?

Consider a group of people developing a new product. They come up with a number of designs. Group members each may advocate a particular design but have different reasons for their choice. When group members hear different, but supportive, reasons for choosing the same design, their initial feelings are intensified. Thus, one reason why groups have inflated efficacy is that they hear more reasons favoring their own opinion. A second reason that explains efficacy has to do with the fact that people in groups want others to like them. A sure-fire way of getting people to like you is to agree with what they say. These two processes lead individuals in groups to feel overly confident about the decisions that the group makes.

Interaction Loss

The depressing fact is that groups are more often plagued by interaction losses than interaction gains. Actual productivity usually falls short of potential productivity. Interaction loss reflects a group's failure to act in the most productive way possible.

The following are three general sources of interaction loss:

- **Coordination loss** occurs when group members do not optimally organize their efforts. For example, consider a dance troupe in which dancers are not moving in synchrony; each member is a skilled professional, but as a group they are not as effective because their efforts are not coordinated. Often, groups fall short of realizing their potential because they have not developed a system for communicating and working smoothly together (see Shaw, 1981).

- **Motivation loss** occurs when members do not try as hard as they could when working together as when working alone. When people feel that their contributions are not valued or that they are not positively rewarded for their efforts, they are less motivated. Consider a group of students writing a term paper together. They will each receive the same grade. Each member is reluctant to work really hard because each doesn't want to do all the work if the others will free ride.

- **Conceptual loss** occurs when group interaction hinders the ability of group members to think. This can occur because individuals are cognitively taxed in groups, meaning that it is hard to think, listen, and contribute all at one time, and because time spent interacting with others diverts attention from the overall goal of creating additional resources.

Each form of interaction loss detracts from the quality of negotiated agreements.

Social Loafing

One form of motivation loss is **social loafing,** in which people in a group fail to contribute as much as they would if they worked independently.

Why does social loafing occur? People know that others do not work as hard as they can in groups. Because people are concerned with equitable outcomes, they are reluctant to do more than their fair share (i.e., they don't want to be a sucker). In short, people would rather reduce their own outcomes than "carry" free riders.

Another cause of social loafing is diffused responsibility within the group (Darley and Latane, 1968). In a collective activity, like the group project assignment, individuals' contributions are less recognizable. In a sense, the group provides anonymity. This is common in **information-reducing tasks** such as a group report or sales presentation, which combine members' inputs, versus **information-conserving tasks** such as a variety show where each member performs an act, thus preserving members' inputs. In contrast, in collective activities, one's own contributions are less recognizable. One method of decreasing social loafing is to identify and monitor individual performance. Increasing an individual's personal involvement in the task, responsibility, and unique contributions may also decrease loafing. For example, when people perceive the task to be challenging or difficult, loafing decreases (Weldon and Mustari, 1988).

Group Creativity

An advertising executive developed a technique called **brainstorming** to unleash process gain in groups (Osborn, 1957). The goal of brainstorming is to increase the quality and quantity of group ideas by encouraging free exchange and by removing criticism. The guidelines of brainstorming are simple: The group should generate as many ideas as possible; the wilder and more creative the ideas, the better; members should express ideas without concern for quality or fear of others' reactions; others should not evaluate people's ideas until all possible solutions have been advanced; and members should feel free to elaborate and improve on ideas already suggested.

The brainstorming process would seem to be an effective technique for enhancing creativity in groups. However, despite its strong intuitive appeal, there is no evidence that brainstorming enhances creativity; in fact, brainstorming often leads to worse performance in terms of both quality and quantity (Diehl and Stroebe, 1987). How can the creativity of a brainstorming group be measured? One way is to compare **real groups** to **nominal groups,** composed of individuals who work alone. For example, a real group may be a six-person team of advertising executives; a nominal group would be six executives working alone in their offices. Nominal groups generate more ideas and better ideas. Why is this? Real groups suffer from **production blocking**—when one person has the floor, others cannot make contributions; they must wait until the other has relinquished the floor. People find it difficult to think and listen at the same time. When production blocking is removed, through interactive communication devices, group creativity improves (Connolly, Jessup, and Valacich, 1989).

Despite the lack of evidence for brainstorming as an effective technique, people still believe that it works. Why? The illusion of **group efficacy** is the belief held by groups that the solutions they reach are better than the solutions reached by individuals (Sniezek and Henry, 1989).

LEVELS OF ANALYSIS: A FRAMEWORK

How might we analyze the Film Gate negotiation situation introduced at the beginning of the chapter? The negotiation involves a myriad of players, relationships, and issues (see Figure 9–1).

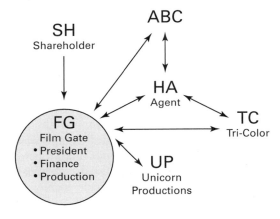

FIGURE 9–1. Film Gate Negotiation Structure

Negotiations within and between organizations are embedded in an intricate web of interdependent relationships and interests. Just as a complete understanding of human anatomy requires analysis at the levels of cell chemistry, tissues, organs, and organ systems, a complete understanding of negotiation within and between organizations requires analysis at several levels (Thompson and Fox, in press). In this chapter we identify and describe seven levels of analysis, as depicted in Figure 9–2: the individual, the dyad, the **polyad,** the third-party **intermediary, collateral relationships,** the **intragroup,** and the **intergroup.** We set the stage by defining each level and then explore the dynamics that operate at each level.

FIGURE 9–2. Levels of Analysis in Negotiation

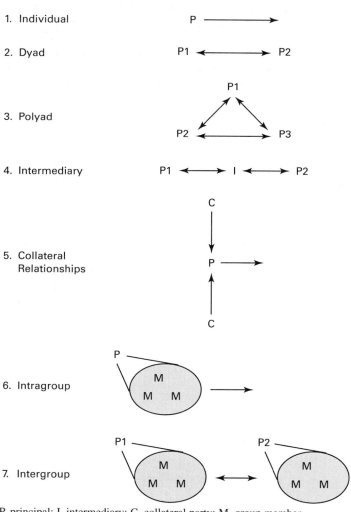

1. Individual

2. Dyad

3. Polyad

4. Intermediary

5. Collateral
   Relationships

6. Intragroup

7. Intergroup

P, principal; I, intermediary; C, collateral party; M, group member.

Step 1: Setting the Stage

The first step in the analysis is to identify the parties, the roles they play, and the structure of their relationships to one another, as illustrated in Figure 9–2. We identify four kinds of parties: principals, intermediaries, collaterals, and groups. Each party may be an individual or a **monolithic** group of individuals that acts as a single unit, as if they have identical values and beliefs (cf. Raiffa, 1982). Although individuals comprising a group seldom act as one, it will be convenient at some levels of analysis to treat them as if they do and postpone an exploration of the within-group heterogeneity and interactions for other levels of analysis.

Principals

A principal (P in Figure 9–2) has a direct stake in the outcome of a negotiation and some influence in its process. In the Film Gate example there are three principals: Film Gate, ABC, and Tri-Color. Unicorn Productions is a potential principal.

Intermediaries

An intermediary (I in Figure 9–2) serves as agent or intervenes between two or more principals. An intermediary has a stake in the outcome (e.g., a real estate agent earns a commission on the sale of a home; a mediator may experience a feeling of pride when successfully facilitating an end to a dispute); however, it is the principals that initially motivate negotiation. In the present example, the Hollywood agent is an intermediary between Film Gate and ABC, and also between Tri-Color and ABC.

Collaterals

A collateral is ostensibly on the "same side" as a principal but exerts an independent influence on the outcome through the principal. We distinguish three types of collateral parties: a **superior** has authority over a principal; a **subordinate** is under the authority of a principal; and a **constituent** is the party whom the principal represents—that is, for whom the principle is responsible and to whom the principal is accountable (collateral parties are represented by C in Figure 9–2). In our example, Film Gate has a collateral relationship with its major shareholder, who acts in some ways as a superior.

Multilithic Groups

A group member (M in Figure 9–2) is a party within a **multilithic group.** Each member of the group might have different values and beliefs, but ultimately they must act in concert with other members as a decision-making unit. In the example, Film Gate is represented by a three-member negotiating team consisting of the president, the chief financial officer, and the head of production.

Step 2: Exploring Each Level

The second step in our approach is to undertake a normative, descriptive, and/or prescriptive analysis at each of the seven levels in Figure 9–2. Using the levels of analysis framework, we present the key challenges and obstacles that negotiators face when attempting to resolve disagreements efficiently. We build upon our analysis of the individual and dyad covered thus far in the book.

Multiparty Negotiation: Polyads

A multiparty negotiation is a group of three or more individuals, each representing their own interests, who attempt to resolve perceived differences of interest (Bazerman, Mannix, and Thompson, 1988; Kramer, 1991). For example, a group of individuals who must collectively prepare and present a group project for a course grade is a multiparty negotiation, as is a group of specialists in an architectural firm who must design a house for a client (see Palmer and Thompson, 1995). The parties in a polyad may be individuals, teams, or groups. The involvement of more than two principals at the negotiation table complicates the situation enormously: Social interactions become more complex, information processing demands increase exponentially, and coalitions can form. In the dyadic case, parties cannot reach settlement without the consent of the opponent; however, in the case of the polyad, parties can exclude individuals from an agreement.

In our example, a coalition may include Film Gate, ABC, and either Tri-Color or Unicorn Productions. Film Gate may pressure Tri-Color to concede on the terms of the agreement by threatening to collaborate with Unicorn Productions.

Complex Tradeoffs

Integrative agreements are more difficult to fashion in multiparty negotiations because the tradeoffs are more complex. In a multiparty negotiation, integrative tradeoffs may be achieved either through circular or reciprocal logrolling (Palmer and Thompson, 1995). **Circular logrolling** involves tradeoffs that require each group member to offer another member a concession on one issue, while receiving a concession from yet another group member on a different issue. A circular tradeoff is typified by the tradition of drawing names from a hat to give holiday gifts to people. People receive a gift from one person and give a gift to yet another person. In contrast, **reciprocal tradeoffs** are fashioned between two members of a larger group. Reciprocal tradeoffs are the more traditional form of exchanging presents. Circular tradeoffs are more risky than reciprocal because they involve the cooperation of more than two group members.

Coalitions

The key difference between two-party and group negotiations is the potential for two or more parties within a group to form a coalition to pool their resources and have a greater influence on outcomes (for a review, see Komorita and Parks, 1995). A **coalition** is a (sub)group of two of more individuals who join together in using their resources to affect the outcome of a decision in a mixed-motive situation (see Murnighan, 1978; Komorita and Parks, 1995, for a review) involving at least three parties (Gamson, 1964). For example, parties may seek to maximize control over other members, maximize their status in the group, maximize similarity of attitudes and values, or minimize conflict among members. Coalition formation is one way that otherwise weak group members may marshal a greater share of resources. Coalitions involve both cooperation and competition: Members of coalitions cooperate with one another in competition against other coalitions but compete against one another regarding the allocation of rewards the coalition obtains.

Coalitions face three sets of challenges: (1) the formation of the coalition, (2) coalition maintenance, and (3) the distribution of resources among coalition members. What is the ideal size for a winning coalition? Ideally, coalitions should contain the minimum number of people sufficient to achieve a desired goal. Coalitions are difficult to maintain because members are tempted by other members to join other coalitions and agreements are not enforceable (Mannix and Loewenstein, 1993).

Dividing the Pie Three Ways?   The distribution of resources among members of coalitions is complex because a normative method of fair allocation does not exist (Raiffa, 1982). Consider the following example. Lindholm, Tepe, and Clauson are three small firms producing specialized products, equipment, and research for the rehabilitation medicine community.[2] This area has become a critical, high-growth industry, and each firm is exploring ways to expand and improve its technologies through innovations in the research and development (R&D) divisions. Each firm has recently applied for R&D funding from the National Rehabilitation Medicine Research Council (NRMR).

The NRMR is a government agency dedicated to funding research in rehabilitation medicine and treatment. The NRMR is willing to provide funds for the proposed research, but because the firms' requests are so similar, they will fund only a **consortium** of two or three firms. The NRMR will not grant funding to Lindholm, Tepe, or Clauson alone.

The largest of the three firms is Lindholm, followed by Tepe, and Clauson is the smallest. The NRMR took a variety of factors into consideration when they set the following caps on funding (see Table 9–1).

The NRMR has strictly stipulated that for a consortium of firms to receive funding, the parties in the consortium (either two or three firms) must be in complete agreement concerning the allocation of resources among firms.

If you are Lindholm, what consortium would you consider to be the best for you? Obviously, you want to be in on some consortium, with either Tepe or Clauson or both, to avoid being left out in the cold. But what is the best division of resources within each of those consortiums? Suppose that you approach Tepe about a two-way venture, and Tepe proposes that she receive half of the $220,000 or $110,000 for herself. You argue that because you are bigger, and bring more synergy to the agreement, that you should earn more. You demand $200,000 for yourself, leaving $20,000 for Tepe. At this point, Tepe threatens to leave you and approach Clauson. Tepe argues that she and Clauson can command $150,000 as a consortium without you, and each can receive $75,000. At this point, you argue that you can outbid her offer to

TABLE 9–1.   Maximum Funding Caps as a Function of Parties in Consortium

Organizations in Consortium	Cap for R&D Funding
Lindholm alone	0
Tepe alone	0
Clauson alone	0
Lindholm and Tepe	$220,000
Lindholm and Clauson	$190,000
Tepe and Clauson	$150,000
Lindholm, Tepe, and Clauson	$240,000

[2] This example is based on a case, Federated Science Fund, written by Elizabeth Mannix, Columbia University.

Clauson with $80,000 and keep $110,000 for yourself. Just as Tepe is threatening to overbid you for Clauson, Clauson steps in and tells Tepe that she would want at least $100,000 of the $150,000 pie that she and Tepe could command. Tepe is frustrated, but relents.

You get nervous in your role as Lindholm. You certainly don't want to be left out. You could attempt to get Clauson or Tepe in a consortium. But, then, a thought occurs to you: Maybe all three of you can be in a consortium. After all, all three firms command the greatest amount of funding ($240,000). But how should the $240,000 be divided between the three of you? You are the biggest firm, so you propose that you keep half of the $240,000, or $120,000, that Tepe get $80,000, and that Clauson get $40,000. This strikes you as fair. At this point Clauson gets upset and tells you that she and Tepe can go it alone and get $150,000. She thinks that your share is unfair and should be reduced to something less than $90,000. You then remind Clauson that you and Tepe can get $190,000 together, of which you certainly deserve at least half, which is better than the $90,000 offer. Then the three of you are at it again in a vicious circle of coalition formation and demolition.

The negotiation between Lindholm, Tepe, and Clauson illustrates the unstable nature of coalitions. In this example, the left-out party is always able to approach one of the two parties in the coalition and offer him or her a better deal, which can then be beaten by the remaining party, ad infinitum. Furthermore, splitting the pie three ways seems to offer no obvious solution. So, what should the three parties do? Is there a solution? Or are the three destined to go around in circles forever?

Getting Out of the Vicious Circle   As a way out of the vicious circle, let's conceptualize the problem as a system of simultaneous equations to solve. Namely,

$$L + T = \$220,000$$
$$L + C = \$190,000$$
$$T + C = \$150,000$$
$$L + T + C = \$240,000$$

$$L + T + C = (\$220,000 + \$190,000 + \$150,000)/2$$
$$= \$560,000/2$$
$$= \$280,000 \text{ total funds needed}$$

However, it is impossible to solve all simultaneous equations. We are $40,000 short of satisfying each partiy's minimum needs. What should we do? Consider the following three solutions: the core solution, the Shapley solution, and a hybrid model (Raiffa, 1982).

The core solution. The core solution is a set of alternatives that are undominated (McKelvey and Ordeshook, 1980). An alternative is in the core if no coalition has both the power and desire to overthrow it.

The first step in computing the core solution is to determine what would be each party's share if there were no shortage of funds. Thus, we solve for L,T, and C shares as follows:

$$(L + T) - (L + C) = \$220,000 - \$190,000$$
$$= (T - C) = \$30,000$$
$$(L + T) - (T + C) = \$220,000 - \$150,000$$
$$= (L - C) = \$70,000$$

$$(T + C) + (T - C) = \$150,000 + \$30,000$$
$$2T = \$180,000$$
$$T = \$90,000$$
$$L + T = \$220,000$$
$$L + \$90,000 = \$220,000$$
$$L = \$220,000 - \$90,000$$
$$L = \$130,000$$
$$L + C = \$190,000$$
$$\$130,000 + C = \$190,000$$
$$C = \$190,000 - \$130,000$$
$$C = \$60,000$$

check:
$$L = \$130,000$$
$$T = \$90,000$$
$$C = \$60,000$$
$$\text{Total} = \$280,000$$

Thus, if we had a total of $280,000, we could solve each equation. But, the harsh reality is that we don't. So, the second step is to get the total down to $240,000 by deducting $40,000 from somewhere. In the absence of any particular argument as to why one party's share should be cut, we deduct an equal amount, $13,333, from each party's share. In the final step, we compute the "core" shares as follows:

Lindholm:	$116,670
Tepe:	$76,670
Clauson:	$46,670

As Lindholm, you are delighted. Tepe agrees, but Clauson is not happy. She thinks that $46,670 is too little. She hires an outside consultant to evaluate the situation. The consultant proposes a different method, called the Shapley model.

The Shapley model. Consider a coalition formation in which one player starts out alone and then is joined by a second and third player. The Shapley model determines the overall payoff a player can expect on the basis of his or her **pivotal power,** or the ability to change a losing coalition into a winning coalition. The consultant considers all possible permutations of players joining coalitions one at a time. The marginal value added to each coalition's outcome is attributed to the pivotal player. The Shapley value is the mean of a player's added value (see Table 9-2). When all players bring equal resources, the Shapley value is the total amount of resources divided by the total number of people. This, of course, is the "equal division" principle, as well as the "equity principle."

When Clauson's consultant presents this report, Clauson is delighted—her share has increased by almost $20,000. Lindholm is nonplussed because her share has decreased. Tepe is tired of all the bickering and proposes that they settle for something in between the two proposed solutions.

Raiffa's hybrid model. We have presented two models to solve for shares in coalition situations. The medium-power player's share in both models is identical, but the high- and low-power player's shares fluctuate quite dramatically. It is possible that an egocentric argument could ensue between Lindholm and Clauson as to which model to employ. One solution is a hybrid model in which the mean of the Shapley and core values is computed (Raiffa, 1982). This model yields the following shares:

Lindholm: $107,500
Tepe: $77,500
Clauson: $55,000

Tips for Low-power Players   We presented three different models of fair solutions. Each is compelling and defensible because each makes explicit the logic underlying the division of resources. It is easy to be a high-power player in coalition situations. However, the real trick is to know how to be an effective low-power player. Weakness can be power if you can recognize and disrupt unstable coalitions.

Power is intimately involved in the formation of coalitions and the allocation of resources among coalition members. Power imbalance among coalition members can be detrimental for the group. Compared to egalitarian power relationships, unbalanced power relationships produce more coalitions defecting from the larger group (Mannix, 1993), fewer integrative agreements (Mannix, 1993; McAlister, Bazerman, and Fader, 1986), greater likelihood of bargaining impasse (Mannix, 1993), and more competitive behavior (McClintock, Messick, Kuhlman, and Campos, 1973). Power imbalance makes power issues salient to group members, whose primary concern is to protect their own interests. What is best for the coalition is often not what is best for the organization.

Is there an optimal way for multiple parties to allocate resources so that group members are not tempted to form coalitions that may hinder group welfare? Usually not. Whereas there are several defensible ways to allocate resources among coalition members, there is no single best way (for an extensive treatment, see Raiffa, 1982).

Coalitions: Who Joins and Who Stays?   The logic of the core solution and the Shapley model argues that coalitions form on the basis of expected utility and stability. Yet, there is a strong pull for members of coalitions to remain intact even when it is not rational to do so (Bottom, Eavey, and Miller, 1996). According to the **status quo bias,** even when a new coalition structure that offers greater gain is possible, members are influenced by a norm of **coalitional integrity,** such that they stick with their current coalition (Bottom, Eavey, and Miller,

TABLE 9–2. Analysis of Pivotal Power in Shapley Model

Order of Joining	Lindholm Added Value	Tepe Added Value	Clauson Added Value
LTC	0	$220,000	$20,000
LCT	0	50,000	190,000
TLC	$220,000	0	20,000
TCL	90,000	0	150,000
CLT	190,000	50,000	0
CTL	90,000	150,000	0
Shapley (average)[2]	**98,333**	**78,333**	**63,333**

---

[2] These figures are rounded slightly.

1996). The implication is that negotiators should form coalitions early in a polyad negotiation so as to not be left without coalitional partners.

Decision Rules

Groups often simplify negotiation of multiple issues among multiple parties through voting and decision rules.

Voting and Majority Rule   You are a member of a new product development team. After your first week working with the cross-functional team, three designs have emerged: design A, design B, and design C. However, there is a lot of difference of opinion. Everyone is frustrated, and the group has argued for hours. Finally, Raines, a member of the team, suggests that the group vote on the two top designs under consideration. Before reading further, consider whether you think this is a good idea.

The most common procedure used to aggregate preferences of team members is majority rule. Voting is the procedure of collecting individuals' preferences for alternatives on issues and selecting the most popular alternative as the group choice. However, majority rule presents several problems in the attainment of efficient negotiation settlements. Despite its democratic appeal, majority rule fails to recognize the strength of individual preferences. One person in a group may feel very strongly about an issue, but his or her vote counts the same as the vote of someone who doesn't have a strong opinion about the issue. Consequently, majority rule does not promote integrative tradeoffs among issues. In fact, groups negotiating under unanimous rule reach more efficient outcomes than groups operating under majority rule (Thompson, Mannix, and Bazerman, 1988; Mannix, Thompson, and Bazerman, 1989).

Although unanimity rule is time consuming, it encourages group members to consider creative alternatives to expand the size of the pie and satisfy the interests of all group members. Because strength of preference is a key component in the fashioning of integrative agreements, majority rule hinders the development of mutually beneficial tradeoffs. Voting in combination with other decision aids, such as agendas, may be especially detrimental to the attainment of efficient outcomes because it prevents logrolling (Thompson, Mannix, and Bazerman, 1988; Mannix, Thompson, and Bazerman, 1989).

There are other problems with voting. Group members may not agree upon a method for voting; for example, some members may insist upon unanimity, others may argue for a simple majority rule, and still others may advocate a weighted majority rule. Even if a voting method is agreed upon, it may not yield a choice. For example, a group may not find a majority if there is an even split in the group. Voting does not eliminate conflicts of interest, but instead, provides a way for group members to live with conflicts of interest; for this reason, majority rule decisions may not be stable. In this sense, voting hides disagreement within groups, which threatens long-term group and organizational effectiveness.

As an example, let's return to the product development team. You are a member of a three-person PD team (Raines, Warner, and Lassiter). The three of you are in conflict over which design to use—A, B, or C. The preference ordering is depicted in Table 9–3. As a way of resolving the conflict, Warner suggests voting between designs A and B. In that vote, A wins and B is tossed in the trash. Warner then proposes that the group vote between A and C. In that vote, C wins. Warner then declares that design C be implemented. Lassiter concludes that the group vote was fair and agrees to develop design C. However, Raines is perplexed and suggests taking another vote. Warner laughs and says, "We just took a vote and you lost—so just accept the outcome!" Raines glares at Warner and says, "Let's do the vote again

TABLE 9–3. Managers' Preferences for Product Designs

Manager	Design A	Design B	Design C
Raines	1	2	3
Warner	2	3	1
Lassiter	3	1	2

and I will agree to accept the outcome. However, this time I want us to vote between *B* and *C* first." Warner has no choice but to go along. In this vote, *B* is the clear winner and *C* is eliminated. Next, the vote is between *A* and *B*, and *A* beats *B*. Raines happily declares *A* the winner. Lassiter then jumps up and declares that the whole voting process was fraudulent, but cannot explain why.

Raines, Warner, and Lassiter are victims of the **condorcet paradox.** The condorcet paradox demonstrates that the winners of majority rule elections will change as a function of the order in which alternatives are proposed. Alternatives that are proposed later, as opposed to earlier, are more likely to survive sequential voting (May, 1982). Thus, clever negotiators arrange to have their preferred alternatives entered at later stages of a sequential voting process.

The unstable voting outcomes of the product development team illustrate the **impossibility theorem** (Arrow, 1963), which states that the derivation of group preference from individual preference is indeterminate. Simply put, there is no method of combining group members' preferences that guarantees that group preference has been maximized when groups have three or more members and there are three or more options. That is, even though each manager's preferences were transitive, the group-level preference is intransitive.

Strategic Voting   The problem of indeterminate group choice is further compounded by the temptation for members to **strategically misrepresent** their true preferences so that a preferred option is more likely to be favored by the group (Chechile, 1984; Plott, 1976; Ordeshook, 1986; Plott and Levine, 1978). For example, a group member may vote for his least-preferred option to ensure that the second choice option is killed. Raines could have voted strategically in the first election to ensure that his preferred strategy did not lose out in the first round.

Agendas   Groups often use agendas to organize the discussion of negotiation issues. This is true in complex discussions that involve several issues. By determining the order in which negotiation issues will be raised, discussed, and voted on, agendas are essential to efficient decision making. Agendas lead to less integrative agreements, however, than when issues are discussed simultaneously; they hinder the simultaneous discussion of issues (Mannix, Thompson, and Bazerman, 1989; Thompson, Mannix, and Bazerman, 1988).

Consensus Decisions   Consensus agreements require the consent of all parties to the negotiation before an agreement is binding. However, consensus agreements do not imply unanimity. For an agreement to be unanimous, parties must agree inwardly as well as outwardly. Consensus agreements imply that parties agree *publicly* to a particular settlement, even though their *private* views about the situation may be in conflict.

Although consensus agreements are desirable, there are several problems with them. They are time consuming because they require the consent of all members, who are often not in agreement. Second, they often lead to compromise in which parties identify a lowest common denominator acceptable to all. The "dumb" look of many automobiles manufactured in the 1980s is a consequence of compromise decision making. Compromise agreements are an extremely easy method of reaching agreement and are compelling because they appear to be fair, but they are usually inefficient because they fail to exploit potential pareto-improving tradeoffs.

Group Influence Tactics

As organizational actors attempt to build consensus, they may employ group influence tactics to persuade others to change their views or interests. There are several group influence tactics that organizational actors may use to persuade others, including ostracism, logic, and morality.

Ostracism   People desire to be liked and respected by members of their referent group. A group may exert influence on a member by threatening to dismiss him or her from the group either physically or emotionally (Williams, 1994). When members don't agree with the views of the group, the group will first try to persuade the member to change his or her mind, but, if unsuccessful, will ultimately reject the member (Schachter, 1951). Ostracism is perhaps the worst form of social punishment.

Logic   People desire to have accurate views of reality. One way of assessing the accuracy of one's views is by comparing oneself with others (Festinger, 1954); if others' views are discrepant, we may question the veracity of our own views. Group members often use logic and facts to influence others. A group member may persuade others of the virtue of his or her position by supporting it with objective data, factual knowledge, and financial reports.

Morality   People want to hold the "right" values. For example, it is often not acceptable for organizational members to advocate a position of self-interest. Rather, members use organizational values and goals to justify self-serving needs.

Consider a group member who is reluctant to support hiring a person that all other group members prefer to hire. The group previously decided that consensus is needed before making a new hire. The group could threaten to ostracize the dissenting member (e.g., not invite him or her to social outings); they could provide additional, corroborating information about the attractiveness and skills of the candidate (e.g., letters of recommendation); or they could exert values influence by suggesting that not hiring this person threatens the value of the organization.

Communication

When groups grow large, communication among all parties is difficult. One way of simplifying negotiations is for group members to communicate in smaller groups, thereby avoiding full-group communication. What are the effects of limiting communication opportunities in multiparty negotiation? Full-group communication is more time consuming but enhances equality of group members' outcomes, increases joint profitability, and minimizes perceptions of competition (Palmer and Thompson, 1995). However, there is a caveat to the benefits of full communication. When the task structure requires group members to logroll in a reciprocal fashion (as opposed to a circular fashion), restricted communication leads to higher joint outcomes than full communication.

Intermediary

Consider the conflict of interest that the Hollywood agent experiences by simultaneously representing two production companies in the negotiations with ABC. The longer-standing and more lucrative relationship with Tri-Color leads the agent to place the interests of that company ahead of the interests of Film Gate.

There are a number of ways in which a third party may intervene in a dispute. The intermediary can act as an **agent** by representing the interests of one or more parties. Alternatively, the intermediary may facilitate negotiation through mediation or impose a solution through arbitration, adjudication, or autocratic decision making (see Pruitt and Carnevale, 1993, chapter 12). In **mediation,** the third party aids disputants in resolving the dispute but does not have the power to impose a settlement. In **arbitration,** principals present their case or final offer to a third party who has the power to impose a solution. Arbitration may be passive or inquisitive, and the arbiter can have full discretion to impose any kind of settlement or have constraints such as the requirement to choose one side's final offer.

Agency

There are many advantages to using agents to represent one's interests. Agents provide substantive knowledge (e.g., a tax attorney), expertise in the negotiation process (e.g., a real estate agent), or special influence (e.g., a Washington lobbyist) (Rubin and Sander, 1988). Moreover, they provide emotional detachment (e.g., a divorce attorney) and tactical flexibility. However, there are costs to agency. Because they are usually compensated for their services, agents diminish the resources to be divided among the principals. Second, ineffective agents complicate the negotiation dynamic and thereby inhibit settlement. Most problematic, the agent's interests may be at odds with those of the principals (for an overview of principal-agent issues in economics, see Jensen and Meckling, 1976).

For example, consider a typical home sale involving two principals and two agents. Is it wise for a home buyer to tell her agent how much she is willing to spend for a particular house? Similarly, should a seller tell his agent the least amount of money he would accept for his home? Agents for home buyers desire higher selling prices because their fees are based on selling price. For this reason, it may not be in a buyer's interest to reveal his or her reservation price (i.e., the maximum he or she is willing to pay) to the agent. In fact, there is a distinct disadvantage for parties with agents: Selling prices are lowest when the agent knows only the seller's reservation price and highest when the agent knows only the buyer's reservation price (Valley, White, Neale, and Bazerman, 1992). Agents increase the likelihood of impasse (Bazerman, Neale, Valley, Zajac, and Kim, 1992). The message is that agents may be maximally effective only when their interests are aligned with those of the principal.

Arbitration and Mediation

There are a number of criteria to judge the success of third-party dispute resolution. An ideal procedure should: (1) increase the likelihood that the parties reach an agreement if a positive bargaining zone exists; (2) promote a pareto-efficient outcome; (3) promote outcomes that are perceived as fair in the eyes of disputants; and (4) improve the relationship between the parties.

However, there are a number of obstacles that threaten the success of third-party intervention. First, there is no guarantee that third parties are neutral (Gibson, Thompson, and

Bazerman, 1994). In fact, third parties evince many of the biases that plague principals, such as framing effects (Carnevale, 1995). Even a neutral mediator may be mistakenly viewed as partial to one's adversary (Morris and Su, 1995). Second, third parties may have a bias to broker an agreement at any cost, which may be disadvantageous to the principals—if there is no positive bargaining zone. Finally, the threat of third-party intervention may inhibit settlement if principals believe that an arbitrator is inclined to impose a compromise settlement. For this reason, final-offer arbitration may be more effective than traditional arbitration (Farber, 1981; see also Chelius and Dworkin, 1980; cited in Raiffa, 1982, Table 4).

Managers are often called on to resolve disputes in organizations (Tornow and Pinto, 1976). In contrast to traditional arbitrators and mediators, managers may have a direct stake in the outcome and an ongoing relationship with the disputants. In addition, managers are more likely to have technical expertise and background knowledge about the dispute. Although several intervention techniques are available to managers, they often choose techniques that maximize their own control over the outcome (Sheppard, 1984; Karambayya and Brett, 1989).

Collateral Relationships

When a negotiating party is embedded within an organization, several peripheral players ostensibly on the same side may have an indirect stake in the outcome and influence the negotiation process. Collateral relationships refer to negotiations within organizations in which the negotiator is linked to other organizational actors, such as superiors, subordinates, or constituents. In our example, Film Gate is accountable to the major shareholder, who is ostensibly on their side, but has interests of his own. The shareholder's strong interest in short-term profitability leads Film Gate to weight the issue of financial compensation more heavily than it otherwise would in the negotiation.

Consider the organizational actor who is accountable to a constituency. There are two extremes of the organizational actor who represents a constituency: (1) the organizational puppet and (2) the organizational autocrat. The **organizational puppet** is elected to serve the interests of the larger constituency and negotiates on behalf of his or her constituents. The organizational puppet does not have decision control but depends upon approval of the constituency. The puppet's hands are tied. In contrast, the **organizational autocrat** has complete decision control. The negotiator does not seek the approval of his or her constituency before enacting an agreement. Negotiators should determine in advance whether or not their opponent has the power to ratify agreements. Is the opponent a puppet or an autocrat?

Accountability

Negotiators at the bargaining table comprise the primary relationship in negotiation. The relationship that parties share with their constituents is the **second table** (Ancona, Friedman, and Kolb, 1991). Constituents don't have to be physically present at the negotiation table for their presence to be strongly felt (Pruitt and Carnevale, 1993; Tetlock, 1985; Kramer, Pommerenke, and Newton, 1993). Negotiators who are accountable to their constituents make higher demands and are less willing to compromise in negotiation than those not accountable to constituents (Ben-Yoav and Pruitt, 1984; Carnevale, Pruitt, and Britton, 1979; O'Connor, 1994).

The second table has a paradoxical effect on the primary table: Representatives of constituents often are not given power to enact agreements; that is, the representative is not monolithic (Raiffa, 1982). Whereas this would seem to reduce his or her power at the bargaining table, the opposite can be true. The negotiator whose "hands are tied" is often more effective than is the negotiator who has the power to ratify agreements. Anyone who has ever negotiated a deal on a new car has probably experienced the "my hands are tied" or "let me take it to the boss" ploy, in which the salesperson induces the customer to commit to a price which requires approval before a deal is finalized.

Accountability to collateral actors is an inevitable aspect of organizational life (Tetlock, 1985, 1992). There are at least two motivational processes that are triggered by accountability: decision-making vigilance and evaluation apprehension.

Decision-making Vigilance   Decision makers who are accountable for their actions consider relevant information and alternatives more carefully (Tetlock, 1985, 1992). Accountability increases thoughtful, deliberate processing of information and decreases automatic, heuristic processing (see also Chaiken, 1980; Fiske and Neuberg, 1990). Accountability would seem to uniformly improve the quality of decisions made by negotiators and increase the likelihood of integrative agreements.

However, decision accountability may not always promote more thorough and unbiased processing of information if organizational actors are partisan to a particular view (Thompson, 1995b). Imagine a situation in which an observer watches a videotape of people negotiating. Some observers are told to take an objective and impartial view of the situation; other observers are instructed to take the perspective of one of the parties. Further, some observers are told that they will be accountable for their actions and behaviors (e.g., they must justify their decisions to others who will question them), whereas others are not accountable. After watching the tape, observers indicate what they think each negotiator wanted. Accountable partisans fall prey to the fixed-pie assumption because they are motivated to reach a particular conclusion. However, nonpartisan observers are willing to reach whatever conclusion the data will allow, and their judgments are therefore driven by the evidence, not their desires.

Evaluation Apprehension and Face Saving   Negotiators who are accountable for their behaviors are concerned with how they are viewed by others. When people are concerned what others will think, they use face-saving strategies and make their actions appear more favorable to relevant others. Negotiators who want to save face will be more aggressive and uncompromising so that they will not be viewed as suckers or pushovers. Negotiators who are accountable to constituents are more likely to maintain a tough bargaining stance, make fewer concessions, and hold out for more favorable agreements compared to those who are not accountable (see Carnevale and Pruitt, 1992).

However, an interesting twist happens when teams are accountable for their actions at the bargaining table. A **diffusion of responsibility** occurs across members of the team (O'Connor, 1997). Teams respond differently than solo negotiators to accountability pressure.

Constituent Goals

Negotiators often face a conflict between their goals and those of their constituency. For the manager interested in effective dispute resolution, it is not only important to understand the relationships negotiators share *across* the bargaining table, it is important to understand the hidden table of collateral relationships (see Kolb, 1983). Consider a negotiation involving teams of two people who are either personally acquainted or strangers to one another. Each team reports to a manager. Some teams report to a "profit-oriented" manager who instructs the team to "serve the interests of the group at all costs." Some teams report to a "people-oriented" manager who instructs the team to maximize interests while maintaining harmonious intergroup relations. Teams who report to the "profit" supervisor claim a greater share of the resources than do teams who report to the "people" supervisor and teams not accountable to a manager (Peterson and Thompson, 1997). When team members are acquainted, there are no differences in relative profitability. Why? Negotiators are better able to maximize profit when the goal is clear and they do not share a previous relationship.

Teams and Intragroup Dynamics

Consider the following situations:

- a husband and wife negotiating with a salesman on the price of a new car
- a group of disgruntled employees who approach management about wages and working conditions
- a small software company approaching the largest software company in the world concerning a joint venture

In all of these examples, people join together on one side of the bargaining table as a team. Presumably, in each of these cases, one member could do all the negotiating for the team; but teams believe that they will be more effective if they are both at the bargaining table. Are teams effective at exploiting integrative potential at the bargaining table? To answer the question of whether two heads are better than one, Thompson, Peterson, and Brodt (1996) compared three types of negotiation configurations—team vs. team, team vs. solo, and solo vs. solo negotiations. The presence of at least one team at the bargaining table dramatically increased the incidence of integrative agreement. Why are teams so effective? Negotiators exchange much more information about their interests and priorities when at least one team is at the bargaining table than when two individuals negotiate (Thompson et al., 1996; Rand and Carnevale, 1994; O'Connor, 1994). Information exchange leads to greater judgment accuracy about parties' interests (Thompson et al., 1996; Rand and Carnevale, 1994; O'Connor, 1994), which promotes integrative agreement (Thompson, 1991). The **team effect** is quite robust: It is not even necessary that members of teams privately caucus with one another to be effective (Thompson et al., 1996).

The presence of a team at the bargaining table increases the integrativeness of joint agreements (Rand and Carnevale, 1994; O'Connor, 1994), but what about the distributive component? Do teams outperform their solo counterparts? Not necessarily. Nevertheless, both teams and solo players *believe* that teams have an advantage—a team efficacy effect (O'Connor, 1994; Rand and Carnevale, 1994; Thompson, 1995). Even in situations in which teams reap greater shares of profit than their solo counterparts, solos are still better off negotiating with a team than with another solo player. The solo negotiator earns less than the team, but the amount of jointly available resources is greater in the team–solo negotiation than in the solo–solo negotiation.

An intragroup analysis examines the benefits and shortcomings of teamwork. In the opening example, Film Gate is represented by a negotiating team of three individuals. Although these individuals must make decisions together, they each have disparate interests. What do we need to know to be effective team players?

Size

Most of our interactions with others occur in small groups of fewer than five persons. But important differences emerge even in groups of two to three people (see Bazerman,

Mannix, and Thompson, 1988). For example, decision rules become more complex and indeterminate; conformity pressures increase with group size, peaking at around five and then leveling off (Latane, 1981); and, as groups grow in size, coordination problems increase. Although optimal size depends upon the task the group faces, as a general rule, groups should not be larger than nine members.

Structure

Each member of a group occupies a position, and the pattern of relationships among the positions constitutes the **group structure.** Each position is evaluated by the members of the group, including the occupant, in terms of prestige, importance, and value to the group, or **social status.** In many cases, status differences exist and the group structure is hierarchical. The structure of a group, once established, is largely independent of the particular individuals who comprise the group, even when group members change (Jacobs and Campbell, 1961).

Norms

A **norm** is a behavioral rule adhered to by members of a group; it is a felt obligation, behavior, or attitude that is approved and expected by a group (Thibaut and Kelley, 1959). Norms involve three components: (1) statement of a rule, (2) surveillance, and (3) sanctions (Thibaut and Kelley, 1959). Norms develop to ensure that members will behave in ways they would not in the absence of enforcement, thus introducing regularity and predictability to group interaction. They are functional because they reduce the necessity of direct influence. However, they are dysfunctional when they inhibit novel behavior and increase pressure to conform.

Good communication is essential for norm sending, especially as a group gets bigger. The maintenance of normative behavior is achieved through the process of sending and receiving norms. Those activities are not necessarily evenly distributed among members. Some people may be norm senders; others, norm receivers.

Roles

Roles are expected behaviors associated with a given position in a group. A person in a group occupies a role when the norms applicable to his or her behavior are different from those of others in the group. For example, Sarah finds that people expect her to be the secretary of the group; they give her notes and ask her for memos. They don't ask Bob to do these tasks. Roles are "clusters of norms providing a function for the division of labor and specialization of functions among members of a group" (Thibaut and Kelley, 1959).

Group Goals

Group goals are objectives that group members consensually agree upon or impose (Cartwright and Zander, 1968). Goals depend on consensus among members. Goals develop for specific, nonrecurring purposes and involve deliberate, planned decisions. Goal acceptance requires that members believe their outcomes will be improved by adherence to the goal.

Three types of goals are important for understanding groups: utilitarian, knowledge, and identity goals (Mackie and Goethals, 1987). **Utilitarian goals** result in tangible outcomes; people join groups so as to obtain outcomes (Jones and Gerard, 1967). With **knowledge goals,** individuals are dependent on others for information (Jones and Gerard, 1967; Festinger, 1950). People with **identity goals** have a desire to understand themselves.

Status

Subjective status is a person's evaluation of how his or her own outcomes compare with those attained by other members of a group. Others' outcomes define a special comparison level to appraise one's own outcomes. If the outcome is favorable, a person will evaluate him- or herself as having high subjective status.

Social status is comprised of commonly held opinions about how one's own outcomes compare with those of other group members. A **status system** exists when there is a general consensus regarding a person's status in the group. Consensus is likely when status differences reflect initial power differences or when the status system provides a common currency with which members are compensated in proportion to their importance in the group (i.e., salary).

Cohesion

Cohesion is the strength of positive relations in a group (Evans and Dion, 1991), the sum of pressures acting to keep individuals in a group (Back, 1951), and the result of all forces acting on members to remain in a group (Festinger, 1950). Cohesive groups perform better than less cohesive groups (Evans and Dion, 1991). There are three sources of cohesion: (1) attraction to group or resistance to leaving the group, (2) morale and motivation, and (3) coordination of efforts.

There are different kinds of bonds that keep groups together. **Common-identity groups** are composed of members who are attracted to the group; the individual members may come and go. For example, Joe is a member of a gay student's organization. He has several friends in the group, but the basis of his attraction to the group is its mission and purpose. **Common-bond groups** are composed of members who are attracted to particular members in the group (Prentice, Miller, and Lightdale, 1994). Anne belongs to a bowling league. She has known some of the other players for over 20 years. If they were to move away, Anne would want to move as well since the basis of her attraction is the particular people in the group.

Power

Power is a function of group members' dependence on one another (Thibaut and Kelley, 1959). A group member has power to the extent that other group members are dependent upon him or her; a person is more powerful if by varying their behavior they affect the outcomes obtained by others.

Subgroups

Within a given group, there may be different subgroups—groups of members who have differing identities, interests, or beliefs than others. Subgroups may be coalitions in the case of scarce resource conflict or factions in the case of conflict about beliefs.

Communication Networks

Communication networks describe who talks to whom within a group (Leavitt, 1951). No single type of communication network is effective for all groups; it depends on the type of task. Communication is intimately linked with power; those who control communication are more influential than others. Communication affects the ability of groups to solve problems. Complex problems are solved more readily in groups with open communication structures, and simple problems are solved more readily with a central source (Shaw, 1981).

Stages

Groups come in and out of existence; group memberships continually change as members come and go (Levine and Moreland, 1994) and as groups form and dissolve. There are systematic stages of group development, as may be seen in Figure 9–3 (Moreland and Levine, 1988).

Distributed Cognition

Often organizational members negotiate as a team or a group because no single person has the requisite knowledge and expertise required to negotiate effectively. Thus, knowledge is distributed among team members. How effective are teams at utilizing knowledge that is distributed among members? There are three central issues involved in distributed cognition: (1) information processing, (2) communication, and (3) responsibility.

Information Processing   The fundamental building block of distributed cognition in teams is the individual information processing system that we presented in chapter 7. When an individual attempts to retrieve information, a search through long-term memory is instigated. In the

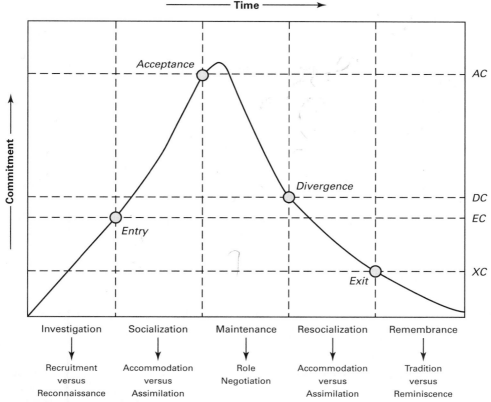

FIGURE 9–3. Stages of Group Development

Source: Moreland, R. L. and J. M. Levine (1982). Socialization in small groups. Temporal changes in individual–group relation. In *Advances in Experimental Social Psychology*. Vol. 15. L. Berkowitz, ed. New York: Academic Press: 137–192.

group context, the search for a piece of information occurs at the level of the group, with individuals treating other members of the group as storage locations to be searched (e.g., "Hey Joe, do you remember what the IBM sales guy's name was?") (Wegner, 1986). Similar processes operate for encoding: "You're the numbers person on this project," one member might say to another, "I am counting on you to know the financial end of this deal."

Communication   In a group or team situation, each member serves as a storage receptacle for certain information. For a team to retrieve a given piece of information, the location of the information must be known and the person who stores the information must have given it the same label as that used by other members of the group. Consider a research and development group in a company preparing for a negotiation with upper management concerning the development and sale of a new product. Key issues include the history of the product, the initial agreement settled upon, the market viability of the product, and potential sales. The R&D group includes a member of the marketing group on their team to provide expertise about the market.

Communication, or **information pooling,** is facilitated if members are acquaintances or share a relationship. For example, when the clues for solving a murder mystery task are distributed among group members, groups of friends are more likely to pool their diverse information than are groups of strangers (Gruenfeld, Mannix, Williams, and Neale, 1996).

Responsibility   The issue of how teams decide who is responsible for storing and retaining information is crucial to the effectiveness of the team. There are tradeoffs involved in the storage of information. It is more efficient for each team member to be responsible for a particular piece of information so that each member is not overwhelmed by too much data. However, as the redundancy of storage is minimized, so are the chances of successfully retrieving the desired information. Furthermore, groups are less likely to consider and discuss information that is shared only by a subset of its members. They suffer from the **common information bias** (Stasser, 1992; Gigone and Hastie, 1993).

It cannot and should not be assumed that members of a group are privy to the same facts and information. People rely on others for information. In fact, members of product development teams rely on informal social exchanges more than technical reports for information. Teams of individuals can be more efficient by dividing the labor. However, distributed cognition is risky because if a team loses one of its members, information may be lost to the entire group. Thus, groups face a dilemma: divide responsibility, which increases their dependence upon each individual member, or share information, which is clumsy and redundant.

Intergroup Negotiation

Individuals who represent different social groups often negotiate with members of other groups (see Deutsch, 1973; Sherif, 1936; Klar, Bar-Tal, and Kruglanski, 1988). For example, members of a student council and university administrators, union and management negotiators, and groups of students from rival universities are all examples of intergroup negotiators.

In **intergroup negotiations,** parties identify with their organization and often hold negative impressions about members of the other organizations (Kramer, 1991; for reviews, see Stroebe, Kruglanski, Bar-Tal, and Hewstone, 1988; Worchel and Austin, 1986). For example, Tri-Color is considered by Film Gate to be rather traditional, whereas actors within Tri-Color consider their company to be pragmatic and reliable. Meanwhile, Film Gate is considered by Tri-Color to be quixotic and naïve about the industry; actors within Film Gate consider the company to be daring and innovative. These disparate and possibly exaggerated perceptions influence both companies' willingness to collaborate.

People identify with many different social groups (Kramer, 1991). For example, a student might consider a relevant group to be the other students in his or her study group, the class as a whole, marketing majors in general, or the entire student body. At any given time, one group might be more or less salient to the student: At a football game, students might identify most strongly with the entire student body; in a dining hall, students might identify most strongly with a particular dorm or floor.

Imagine that you are in an organization in which marketing and finance are distinct subgroups located on different floors of a building. Contrast that to a situation in which marketing and finance are not separated by physical distance. Further, members of these groups comprise cross-functional teams. What happens in the case in which a marketing manager negotiates with a financial manager? Negotiations among individuals representing different social groups are less mutually beneficial than negotiations among individuals who perceive themselves as belonging to a larger social organization—one that encompasses all those present at the bargaining table (Kramer, 1991).

Group distinctions and social boundaries may be created on the basis of completely arbitrary distinctions (Tajfel, 1970). For example, Thompson (1993) divided participants into two groups on the basis of an arbitrary procedure (random draws from a box). Then, individuals negotiated with either a member of their "own group" or the "other group." Even though the information concerning the negotiation situation was identical in both respects, negotiations with members of out-groups were anticipated to be more contentious than negotiations with members of in-groups; further, the mere anticipation of negotiation with an out-group member led to increased **in-group bias,** or positive evaluations of one's own group relative to the out-group.

Realistic and Identity Conflict

Sometimes conflict between groups is based upon scarce resources, such that if one group gets something (e.g., office space, raises, etc.), other groups don't. When resources are in conflict, rivalry and hostility are likely; where they coincide, peace and harmony are likely.

However, sometimes conflicts between groups are not based on resource scarcity. The mere categorization of people into in-groups and out-groups will lead to conflict (Tajfel and Turner, 1979, 1981; Turner, 1982). For example, when people are divided into groups on the basis of an arbitrary distinction (random draws from a hat), they evaluate the members of their own group more favorably than members of the other group (Tajfel, 1970). Furthermore, people expect negotiations with members of out-groups to be more contentious than negotiations with members of their own group (Thompson, 1993).

People of high status, those of low status who have few alternatives, and members of groups who have an opportunity to improve their group are most likely to identify with their group. Members of groups with lower perceived status display more in-group bias than members of groups with higher perceived status (Ellemers, Van Rijswijk, Roefs, and Simons, 1997). However, high-status group members show more in-group bias on group status-related dimensions, whereas low-status group members consider the in-group superior on alternative dimensions (Ellemers and Van Rijswijk, 1996).

Social Identity

People derive self-esteem and identity through their memberships in groups (Tajfel and Turner, 1981), and group membership is a source of esteem and identity for organizational actors (Kramer, 1990). Group membership, however, may be defined in several different ways, depending upon what features are salient in a particular situation. Within an organization, people may identify their existence at any of three levels—the individual level, the group level, and the organizational level (Kramer, 1991). Not surprisingly, level of identification has serious implications for how people negotiate. Imagine you are a manager of two historically rival groups. Your goal is to build greater harmony. What do you do? When people define their social identity at the level of the organization, they are more likely to make more organizationally beneficial choices than when social identity is defined at an individual or subgroup level. For example, when group members are instructed to consider features they have in common with another group, behavior toward out-groups is much more generous than when they consider features that are distinct (Kramer and Brewer, 1984).

In-group and Out-group Negotiations

Suppose that you are a manager of a small firm that produces audio products. Most of your negotiations are internal (i.e., between divisions within your firm). You have been asked to meet with a member of a competitor firm to discuss a joint venture. How are negotiations with out-group members different from those with members of your firm? When we anticipate negotiations with out-group members, we are more likely to engage in **downward social comparison** (Wills, 1981). We evaluate the competitor to be less attractive on a number of organizationally relevant dimensions (such as intelligence, competence, and trustworthiness) than our group. However, after successful negotiation with out-groups, intergroup relations improve and downward social comparison virtually disappears (Thompson, 1993). Negotiation with out-group members is threatening to organizational actors, but to the extent that integrative agreements are feasible, negotiation has remarkable potential for improving intergroup relations.

Although our initial expectations may be quite pessimistic, interactions with members of opposing groups often have a beneficial impact on intergroup relations if several key conditions are met, such as mutual dependence goal attainment (see Aronson and Bridgeman, 1979). The best methods to smooth and enhance intergroup relations are to allow members of groups to have voice or express views (Lind and Tyler, 1988), to develop a single document or text that attempts to integrate parties' interests (Raiffa, 1982), and to have parties interact with individual members of out-groups rather than with collectives.

Perceptions of Out-groups

Groups in conflict often misperceive each other's beliefs. Parties in conflict do not have an accurate understanding of the views of the other party and exaggerate the position of the other side in a way that promotes the perception of conflict (Ross and Ward, in press; Robinson, Keltner, Ward, and Ross, 1994). Each side views the other as holding more extreme and opposing views than is really the case. Consider the Howard Beach incident, a racial dispute. Each side to the conflict held exaggerated perceptions of the views of the other party, thereby exacerbating the perception of a difference in opinion.

Why is this? According to the **naïve realism** principle (Ross and Ward, in press), people expect others to hold views of the world similar to their own. When conflict erupts, people are initially inclined to sway the other party with evidence. When this fails to bridge interests, people regard dissenters as extremists who are out of touch with reality.

CONCLUSION

Having explored a few features of the Film Gate negotiation at each level of analysis, it is clear that all levels are necessary to fully understand the dynamics of this dispute. For example, had we restricted our analysis merely to the level of the interaction between the principals, we would have failed to detect the conflict of interests of the Hollywood agent and would have failed to appreciate the role of group polarization and out-group stereotyping in Film Gate's reluctance to work with Tri-Color. Had we focused instead on the intergroup processes, we would have failed to understand the role of framing in Film Gate's aggressive bargaining position and would have failed to see how egocentric bias could render the threat of a lawsuit ineffective.

TAKE-AWAYS

- Teams of people have the potential to perform and produce more than individuals. However, team and group effort is often hampered by the tendency of group members to work less hard, communicate less effectively, and think less clearly in groups than when alone.

- It is a good idea to form a coalition if you suspect you could be outvoted by a coalition of persons. Negotiators need to stabilize their coalitions by forming them early, and by giving other members enough resources so that they are not tempted to defect.

- When involved in a negotiation situation, the negotiator must consider seven different levels of analysis: the dyad, multiple parties, relations with other groups, teams, constituents, agents, and intermediaries.

- People can (and often do) vote strategically.

CHAPTER 10

Relationships and Emotion: *Building Rapport*

Laurel and Donna had been friends and business associates for over 30 years and had developed a number of joint business ventures together. They bought and sold property, drilled for oil, and rented property as a partnership. Then Laurel got very sick with a life-threatening illness. Her son, Gerhart, took over Laurel's affairs, as he was the eldest child in the family. Donna and her husband, Ray, had known Gerhart as a child but had not seen him for over 20 years.

Five years ago, Donna had an option to buy two twin buildings that were worth over $1 million each on a downtown lot. Donna convinced three other friends to go in on the deal and loaned Laurel the money to become an investor. Three years later, Laurel bought the three other friends out. It was about that time that Donna was going through a divorce from her husband. As part of the divorce settlement, Donna gave her husband her share of the building investment. Ray was not terribly excited about jointly owning two downtown buildings, so he called Gerhart to see whether Gerhart would consider buying him out. Gerhart curtly informed Ray that he did not have the money to buy him out.

When Laurel had owned the building, she had given the other owners an annual distribution payment because the building was rented. When Gerhart took over his mother's affairs, the distribution payments stopped. Apparently Gerhart knew nothing about the distribution payments, which had never been formalized.

The conflict between Gerhart and Ray mounted for over nine months. Ray insisted upon getting paid $136,000 to be bought out. Gerhart reluctantly offered Ray $112,000 as a buyout. Ray then offered to accept $100,000, in addition to a condo in the unit. Gerhart countered with an offer of $50,000 plus a condo. The battle continued. To make matters worse, Laurel passed away and there was a nasty scene at the funeral service.

This negotiation situation involves relationships between people that go back several decades. Furthermore, there are very strong emotions and feelings involved between the parties. These features—the relationship between parties and the emotions at the bargaining table—make up the **social context** of negotiation. Social context is more than just a backdrop, random noise, or a nuisance factor in a negotiation. The social context dramatically affects the processes and outcomes of negotiation (Thompson, Peterson, and Kray, 1995). The purpose of this chapter is to examine how social context affects negotiations.

RELATIONSHIPS

Relationship can refer both to the structural relationships among parties (i.e., employee and employer, two-party, or team negotiation) and to personal relationships (i.e., friends, strangers, enemies). In this chapter, we focus on the interpersonal aspects of relationships. We answer the question of how negotiation is different with friends than with nonacquaintances.

Close Relationships: Defined

Negotiations with close friends and colleagues are among our most important forms of social interaction—because of their enduring nature and because they involve our most valued and treasured resources (Kelley, 1979; Valley, Neale, and Mannix, 1995). The following are four key characteristics of close relationships (Kelley, 1979):

- *Frequent interaction over a long period of time.* People in close relationships interact on a regular basis and have a long history of shared experiences with one another.
- *Variety of activities or events.* In close relationships, people touch on all aspects of each other's lives. Laurel and Donna shared business deals as well as leisure time. Two people who talk to one another at the office but do not share in each other's personal lives are not as close as people who enjoy recreational outings together outside of the workplace.
- *Strong influence between people.* Close relationships are characterized by strong mutual influence between people. Whereas all negotiation situations are characterized by interdependence, the degree of interdependence is much greater in close relationships: Our relationships with some people have a profound impact on our lives; in contrast, interactions with others may only momentarily affect us. Consider a manager's relationship with a subordinate who has been on the job for two weeks. The two are interdependent, but the degree of potential influence is not as strong as between a manager and a subordinate who has been with the division for 10 years.
- *Potential for arousing strong emotions.* Close relationships are characterized by their potential to arouse strong emotions. Most of the time we do not experience strongly felt emotions in our close interactions with others, but the potential for either positive or negative emotion is very strong. It is the potential for strong emotion, not strong emotion itself, that guides our behavior and actions.

Close Relationships: Across the Bargaining Table

In a given day we may negotiate with a friend about a social outing, with our spouse to allocate chores, with a colleague to determine project responsibilities, and with a customer about a service (for a review, see Valley, Neale, and Mannix, 1995). In all of these situations, we have a close relationship with our friend, spouse, colleague, and customer. How do our relationships affect the processes and outcomes of negotiation?

According to the **crude law of social relations,** the characteristic processes and effects elicited by a given type of social relationship (cooperative or competitive) tend also to elicit that type of social relationship (Deutsch, 1973). This law suggests that close, positive social relationships should engender mutually beneficial processes; and distant negative relationships should lead to competitive strategies.

Not surprisingly, in our negotiations with close others we are less competitive (Schoeninger and Wood, 1969; Halpern, 1992); exchange more information (Greenhalgh and Chapman, 1995; Schoeninger and Wood, 1969; Thompson and DeHarpport, in press); and make more concessions (Halpern, 1992; Schoeninger and Wood, 1969) and fewer demands (Halpern, 1992; Schoeninger and Wood, 1969).

However, there is a serious drawback to negotiations with friends: Joint outcomes are often less mutually beneficial or integrative (Fry, Firestone, and Williams, 1983), or at least are no more integrative than are negotiations with others with whom we do not share a close relationship (Valley, Moag and Bazerman, under review; Schoeninger and Wood, 1969; Thompson and DeHarpport, in press; Greenhalgh and Chapman, 1995; Valley and Neale, 1993).

It seems particularly ironic that our negotiations with close others should fall short of level 2 and level 3 integrative agreements. What explains why people in interpersonal relationships are less able to craft mutually beneficial agreements?

Conflict Avoidance

Conflict in close relationships is disturbing and disruptive to smooth interaction (Fry, Firestone, and Williams, 1983). People in close relationships do not always avoid conflict. In fact, friends are often more critical of one another than are nonacquaintances (Oskamp and Perlman, 1965, 1966; Barker and Lemle, 1987; Shah and Jehn, 1993; Nelson and Aboud, 1985). This suggests a critical distinction between two types of close relationships: task-oriented versus **expressive/emotional** relationships (Bales, 1958). It may be less threatening for people to discuss differences and engage in criticism in task-oriented or instrumental relationships than in relationships based upon social support.

Two key features of close relationships are commitment and satisfaction (Thibaut and Kelley, 1959). A person's **commitment** to a relationship is determined by her alternatives to a relationship, or comparison level for alternatives. People who have other potential relationships feel less committed to a particular relationship (Rusbult, 1983) and consequently may be more likely to discuss differences of interest. For example, a manager may be more likely to discuss a possible raise and promotion with senior management if she has just gotten a call from a headhunter. Commitment is determined by a person's BATNA. Satisfaction in a relationship is determined by a person's belief about what she deserves, independent of the alternatives that are currently available. People who are less satisfied with their relationships may be more likely to bring up issues of conflict.

Convergence of Interests

People who have differing interests in close relationships may, in the course of negotiation, converge upon a mutually shared set of interests. For example, husbands' and wives' decisions about consumer products tend to converge upon a middle ground (Menasco and Curry, 1989). When one product represents a particular spouse's domain of interests or expertise, however, joint decisions shift toward the dominant spouse (Menasco and Curry, 1989).

Mutual Obligation

The behavior of people in relationships is guided by shared sets of rules (see Argyle and Henderson, 1984; Clark and Mills, 1979). Individuals in relationships seek to abide by the rules of relationships and not violate the expectations of others. For example, most people in relationships prefer to divide resources equally, rather than in terms of equity (Austin, 1980). Unfortunately, equality norms may promote compromise agreements, thereby inhibiting the discovery of integrative tradeoffs. However, norms of equality are not blindly applied by people in close relationships. For example, friends who differ in their ability and effort in a joint task will favor the less able, but more diligent, partner in the allocation of resources (Lamm and Kayser, 1978). Similarly, individuals in communal relationships will meet the other's needs, with no expectation of remuneration (Clark and Mills, 1979).

Future Interaction: Will We Meet Again?

Sometimes we do not share a close relationship with someone, but we expect to have future interactions with him or her. Even when we buy a car, we expect (or the dealer often expects) to engage in repeat business, provided things go well. The job candidate who negotiates with an employer expects to have a long-term relationship. In other instances, we may not expect to interact with a particular person again, but we expect to interact with someone who is aware of our previous interactions. In such situations, we are concerned with our **reputation.**

Discrete transactions are of limited time duration, whereas **relational exchanges** (Arndt, 1979; Macneil, 1978, 1980) occur when parties anticipate a shared future together (Dwyer, Schurr, and Oh, 1987). How does the shadow of the future affect our negotiations?

Trust

Whenever there is informational uncertainty or asymmetry in a relationship, there is opportunity for deceit, and one or both parties risk exploitation. Paradoxically, if there is no risk in an exchange situation, exploitation cannot occur, but high levels of trust will not develop (Thibaut and Kelley, 1959). Thus, trust is a consequence or response to uncertainty (Kollock, 1994; Granovetter, 1973).

An intriguing example of the development of trust among negotiators concerns the sale of rubber and rice in Thailand (Siamwalla, 1978; Popkin, 1981). For various reasons, rubber is a product in which quality cannot be determined at the time of sale but only months later. Thus, when rubber is sold, the seller knows the quality of the rubber, but the buyer does not. This is a classic case of one-sided informational asymmetry. In contrast, in the rice market, the quality of rice can be readily determined at the time of sale (no informational uncertainty). It would seem that the rubber market, because of its informational asymmetries, would be characterized by exploitation on the part of sellers who would only sell cheap rubber at high prices, creating a market of lemons (Akerlof, 1970). However, buyers and sellers in the rubber market have abandoned anonymous exchange for long-term exchange relationships between particular buyers and sellers. Within this exchange framework, growers establish reputations for trustworthiness, and rubber of high quality is sold.

Dependence

Relational exchanges increase dependence and commitment among parties (Dwyer, Schurr, and Oh, 1987; Kollock, 1994). For example, suppliers who regularly negotiate with certain customers develop highly specialized products for their customers. Such product differentiation can create barriers to switching suppliers. In addition to economic dependence, people become emotionally committed to relational exchanges. For example, in markets characterized by information asymmetries, once negotiators develop a relationship with someone they find to be trustworthy, they remain committed to the relationship, even when it would be profitable to trade with others (Kollock, 1994). When switching does occur, the party who is "left" feels indignant and violated. For example, the decision of major car manufacturers to switch to lower-cost suppliers has left their higher-cost long-time suppliers feeling betrayed.

Cooperation

The expectation of future interaction enhances honesty and cooperation (Ben-Yoav and Pruitt, 1984). People who expect to interact with others in the future are less likely to exploit them even when given an opportunity (Marlowe, Gergen, and Doob, 1966). When negotiators anticipate extended relationships, they are more likely to cooperate with customers, colleagues, and suppliers, but not with competitors (Sondak and Moore, 1994). These relationships and the perception of low mobility among individuals promote development of integrative agreements across interactions, rather than only within given transactions (Mannix, Tinsley, and Bazerman, 1995).

Similarity: Birds of a Feather . . .

People who are similar to each other like one another (Griffin and Sparks, 1990). The **similarity–attraction effect** occurs on the basis of very little or even trivial information. For example, consider a situation in which people write down all of the ways in which they are similar to an opponent. A different group writes down all of the ways in which they are different or unique from their opponent. In fact, members of all groups are randomly composed. Those who perceive themselves to be similar to others are more concerned with equality, express more satisfaction with the outcome, and rate the entire experience to be more cooperative than do those who focus on their differences, even though they are in no objective sense more similar to others—they only think they are (Kramer, Pommerenke, and Newton, 1993).

Another basis of similarity is group membership. Members of the same group perceive themselves to be more similar to one another than to members of out-groups. Negotiators treat members of out-groups differently than members of in-groups. Perceived similarity—perhaps even guilt—stirs up feelings of obligation to help similar others. Negotiators who perceive the other party to be disappointed feel successful but guilty (Thompson, Valley, and Kramer, 1995). These bittersweet feelings of success are magnified when the other party is a fellow group member. Negotiators are more likely to voluntarily allocate resources to members of their own group than members of other groups, but only if they perceive the opponent to be disappointed with the outcome received in a previous negotiation (Thompson, Valley, and Kramer, 1995). If the opponent seems happy, whether he or she is a member of one's own group or a rival group, there is no difference in allocation behavior.

For example, imagine that you have negotiated with a member of your own division in your company. After the negotiation, your partner says that he feels disappointed about how things went. Sometime later, you have the opportunity to allocate 100 stock options between yourself and your partner. You can choose to allocate 0, 100, or any number in between. How many do you allocate? Now, imagine that your partner said that he felt happy about the negotiation. As it turns out, people allocate a much greater number of stock options to their partner

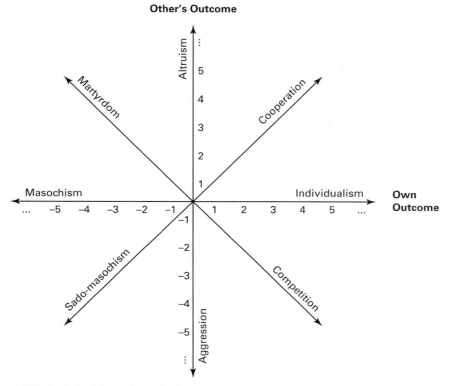

FIGURE 10–1. Subset of Social Values

Source: McClintock, C. G. and E. van Avermaet (1982). Social values and rules of fairness: A theoretical perspective. In *Cooperation and helping behavior.* V. J. Derlega and J. Grezlak (eds). New York: Academic Press, 43–71.

when they think he is disappointed than when they think he is happy, no matter how well they did in the negotiation. The point is that our own behavior is substantially affected by the emotional state of others. Later in the chapter, we will talk about the management of emotion.

Relationship Goals

Relationship goals are our intentions toward others with whom we are interdependent. Relationship goals are more complex than simple cooperation versus competition. Consider the typology of goals in Figure 10–1 (Messick and McClintock, 1968; MacCrimmon and Messick, 1976).

SOCIAL NORMS

Social norms are the beliefs that the members of a particular culture, organization, group, or institution define as acceptable behavior (Bettenhausen and Murnighan, 1985). Social norms are the "oughts" in an organization. They are not printed or passed along in employee handbooks, yet they are enacted the first day a new hire walks in the door of the organization. Our social context framework considers four types of norms: social interaction norms, relationship norms, decision-making norms, and negotiation norms.

Social Interaction Norms

Social interaction norms prescribe appropriate behavior in social interactions. There are many norms that guide our behavior, from the moment we take the bus to work to when we get a telephone call at 11 P.M. Two key norms are politeness and reciprocity.

Politeness Ritual

Most of us want our interactions with others to be pleasant. This serves our own interests and makes our interactions efficient. The politeness ritual is the series of scripted interchanges that we engage in when interacting with others (Goffman, 1967; Lim and Bowers, 1991). We are reluctant to disrupt the politeness ritual by raising a difference of interest.

Reciprocity

The norm of reciprocity dictates that individuals should give and take in kind (Gouldner, 1960), and also dictates the disclosure of information between people (Jourard, 1959; Worthy, Gary, and Kahn, 1969). When negotiators disclose information about their preferences and priorities to opponents, opponents tend to reciprocate by disclosing their interests (Thompson, 1991; Valley, Thompson, Gibbons, and Bazerman, 1997). The method of gradual and reciprocated reduction in tension relations (GRIT strategy) is based on the norm of reciprocity that calls upon individuals to match concessions (Osgood, 1962).

Relationship Norms

There are two basic kinds of relationships: communal and exchange relationships (Clark and Mills, 1979). **Communal relationships** are those in which the parties do not keep track of benefits received and costs incurred but, rather, respond to each other's needs. In communal relationships, parties do not try to establish or maintain equity, at least in short-term interactions. In contrast, in **exchange relationships,** people keep track of benefits received and costs incurred, and maintain and restore equity when it is necessary. For example, think about lunch dates you've had with a business colleague. There is often an explicit discussion about who paid the last time. Contrast this situation to a spousal interaction involving a favor, where there is little talk about the balance of accounts, or who is one-up and one-down.

Communal and exchange relationships are defined by the social roles held by parties and role relations between parties. For example, most spouses have a communal relationship, as do most parents with their children, and close friends. In contrast, many collegial relationships are characterized more by the rules of exchange relationships. This is most typical in the case of short-term exchange but can be the case even in long-term relations.

Whether a person adopts a communal or exchange orientation may also be determined by the parties' goals in the relationship (Clark, 1984). For example, if we desire to have a long-term, communal relationship with another person, we may act in a way that reflects our long-term goals. The mere expectation of future interaction fosters the development of communal norms of exchange (Clark and Mills, 1979). Similarly, the expectation of limited or short-term interaction may foster an exchange relationship.

When both parties share similar perceptions of their relationship, the nature of interaction, whether communal or exchange, is smoother than in the case in which parties hold divergent perceptions of the nature of their relationship (Thompson and DeHarpport, 1998). For example, we have all experienced the dilemma of not knowing whether to offer to pay someone for a favor they did for us or to graciously accept their kindness.

Decision-making Norms

Decision-making norms prescribe how decisions should be reached by groups. Decision-making norms are popular because they appeal to our intuitive sense of justice and fairness but are potentially detrimental because there are many different ways to implement such norms, which may often be self-serving (Messick and Sentis, 1985; van Avermaet, 1974). For example, the use of majority rule combined with agendas in group negotiation actually produces worse outcomes than when groups follow a unanimity rule (Thompson, Mannix, and Bazerman, 1988; Mannix, Thompson, and Bazerman, 1989).

Negotiation Norms

Negotiation norms prescribe the appropriate behavior and conduct of bargaining and include reciprocity, good-faith bargaining, and symmetric concessions (Schelling, 1960; Lindskold, 1978). Negotiation norms also prescribe criteria of negotiation outcomes. For example, negotiators may settle upon focal points or obvious solutions on the basis of relatively arbitrary criteria (Schelling, 1960). Negotiators settle upon previously reached solutions that are not as focal a disproportionate amount of the time, even though the solutions are not objectively better than others (White and Neale, 1994).

EMOTION

Some people believe that they are not emotional. The truth is, we are always in an emotional state. At any given time, we feel calm, relaxed, disgusted, angered, frightened, embarrassed, or joyous. If we are frustrated, we may lose our temper in negotiation and make a threat; if someone insults us with a very low offer for our house, we feel discouraged and resentful; if someone offers us a concession, we feel grateful and may reciprocate. Emotions guide our behavior; our reactions to events are part of the process of negotiation. Emotions are essential for negotiation; they enable people to understand their opponent and achieve their goals (Thompson, Nadler, and Kim, 1996).

The assertion that negotiation is an emotional interaction seems to contradict the basic assumption that negotiators are rational actors. However, "getting emotional" is not a personal reaction but, rather, is a claim about one's identity or definition of the social situation (Parkinson, 1995; Gallois, 1994). Because negotiation is a highly rule-governed interaction, negotiators may feel a tension between maintaining a relationship, expressing their feelings, and saving face.

There are three sources of emotional information in negotiation: our own emotional reactions, the emotional reactions of others to us, and the emotional reactions between other people. The task of negotiators is to understand how their emotional reactions are shaped by others and how their emotions influence the behavior of others. Indeed, interpersonal relationships are more successful when people are sensitive to nonverbal cues, such as emotions (DePaulo, 1992).

Emotional packages are a complex of facial, vocal, and postural cues (Ekman, 1984). Because emotion is largely automatic, it is difficult to consciously control all of these mechanisms (Ekman, 1984). We react to others on an emotional level that we are often unaware of; emotional information processing is not always accessible to conversational awareness.

Emotions: Some Distinctions

The terms emotion, affect, feeling, mood, evaluation, and preference are often used interchangeably, but there are important differences between these constructs (Fiske and Taylor, 1991).

- **Affect** refers to the whole range of preferences, evaluations, moods, and emotions. Affect is assessed in terms of arousal and pleasantness (Watson and Tellegen, 1985).
- **Preferences** include relatively mild subjective reactions that are essentially either pleasant or unpleasant. The preferences we make most frequently are interpersonal evaluations.
- **Evaluations** are simple positive and negative reactions to others, such as attraction, liking, prejudice, and so on. Positive and negative evaluations have obvious importance in social interaction, telling us who to approach and who to avoid.
- **Moods** are low-intensity, diffuse, and relatively enduring affective states. Moods are different from preferences and evaluations in that they have a less specific target. For example, a person can have an evaluative reaction toward a person, but one does not typically have a mood directed toward someone. Moods affect a wide range of social cognitions and behaviors. Like preferences and evaluations, moods are primarily considered to be simply positive or negative. Preferences, evaluations, and moods are not normally fleeting experiences but typically have some duration.
- **Emotion** refers to the complex assortment of affects, beyond merely good feelings and bad, that include several feeling states. Emotion also can imply intense feelings with physical manifestations, including physiological arousal. Emotions may be of short or long duration, but they do not usually last over periods as long as preferences and evaluations.

As seen in Figure 10–2, two common dimensions of affect are pleasantness/unpleasantness and high/low arousal or engagement (Russell, 1978, 1983). Whereas it is possible to feel happy and aroused or happy and calm, it is unlikely that we feel both happy and discontent at the same time. When examined separately, negative emotions have a more complex dimensional structure than do positive emotions (Averill, 1980; Ellsworth and Smith, 1988). A hierarchy of emotions is illustrated in Figure 10–3.

Social Rules

Emotions are intimately related to the rules, conventions, and moral codes that structure relationships (Keltner, 1994; Goffman, 1959; Frank, 1988; Solomon, 1990). People feel angry when violations of rights, property, and justice occur (Smith and Ellsworth, 1985; Solomon, 1990). Disgust is related to the rejection of social groups and ideologies that threaten the individual's self-definition (Rozin, Haidt, and McCauley, 1992). Contempt is expressed at the transgression of social hierarchies (Lazarus, 1991). Embarrassment is felt when social conventions are violated (Goffman, 1959; 1967; Keltner and Busswell, 1994; Miller, 1992). Shame is experienced when an individual's reputation has been tarnished (Keltner and Busswell, 1994; Tangney, 1992). Finally, guilt is felt when obligatory moral codes, such as not physically harming or lying to others, have been violated (Keltner and Busswell, 1994; Tangney, 1992).

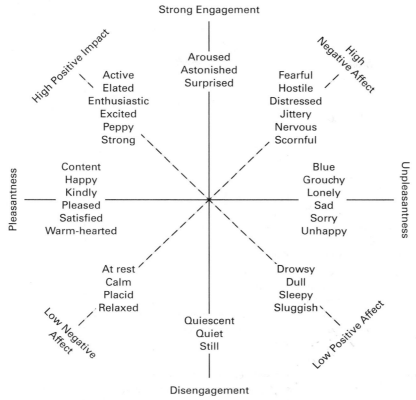

FIGURE 10–2. Two-factor Solution to the Structure of Affect

Source: Watson, D. and A. Tellegen (1985). Toward a consensual structure of mood. *Psychological Bulletin* **98**: 219–235. Copyright © 1985 by the American Psychological Association. Reprinted with permission.

Goals

Emotions motivate negotiators to alter the circumstances eliciting the emotion. This motivational function of emotions is critical to the adherence to social–moral rules (Frank, 1988; Solomon, 1990). For example, when people anticipate aversive emotions, such as guilt, shame, or embarrassment, they are motivated to conform to morals and conventions (Miller and Leary, 1992). Furthermore, when faced with self-serving choices that contradict moral guidelines and conventions, emotions alter the cost–benefit analysis of such actions, enabling people to adhere to the relevant rule. For example, feelings of collegiality, loyalty, and commitment enable people to negotiate certain terms, when simple self-interest would suggest a different course of action.

Emotions enable people to negotiate reciprocity issues that define interdependent relations. When both parties cooperate, friendship, love, and feelings of obligation characterize their relationship. These emotions motivate subsequent cooperation. When one party cooperates and the other competes, the cooperator is likely to feel anger at the injustice, whereas the competitor feels guilt and anxiety about having received too much at the other's expense. When both parties compete, rejection and hatred ensue.

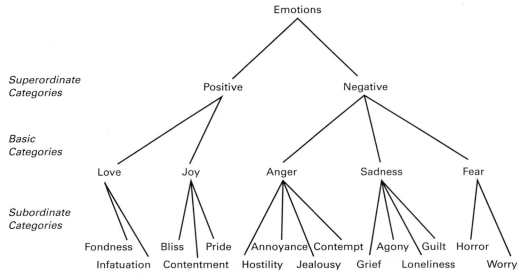

FIGURE 10–3. An Emotion Hierarchy

Source: Fischer, K. W., P. R. Shaver, and P. Carnochan (1990). How emotions develop and how they organize development. *Cognition and Emotion, 4:* 81–127.

To Be Emotional or Not?

A common belief is that negotiations should be resolved without a lot of emotion. A quite different perspective is that emotions are not harmful, but in fact are essential for effective negotiation. Emotion regulates the process of dispute resolution and therefore serves an important adaptive function.

The Rose-colored Glasses Effect

Positive mood in negotiation is a little like looking at the world through rose-colored glasses. Compared to negotiators in neutral moods, people in positive moods

- rate themselves as getting more of the pie than their opponent (Kramer, Pommerenke, and Newton, 1993)
- rate themselves as having performed well
- are more satisfied with their outcomes
- prefer using less competitive strategies to resolve future conflicts (Baron, 1990)
- rate their teams as more cohesive (Forgas and Moylan, 1996)

In short, regardless of what actually happens, happy negotiators display a rosy glow after the negotiation experience. But does positive emotion result in better *objective* outcomes for the negotiator?

You Can Catch More Flies with Honey

Negotiators in a positive mood are more effective in integrative and distributive bargaining than negotiators in neutral or bad moods. For example, on bargaining tasks with integrative potential, happy negotiators who negotiate with happy opponents achieve better individual outcomes (Kramer et al., 1993) and better joint outcomes (Carnevale and Isen, 1986) than neutral-mood negotiators who negotiate with neutral-mood opponents. If both parties are in a good mood during the negotiation, they increase the total available resources as well as their own share of that total more than negotiators who are both in a neutral mood.

In addition to outperforming neutral-mood negotiators, happy negotiators are also more successful than sad negotiators at distributive negotiation. On fixed-sum bargaining tasks, for example, happy negotiators who negotiate with sad opponents achieve a larger share of the resources than the sad negotiators (Forgas and Moylan, 1996).

Why are happy negotiators more successful? When planning their negotiation strategy, happy negotiators plan to be more cooperative (e.g., "I'll support my opponent's choices so they will support mine"), whereas unhappy negotiators plan to be more competitive (e.g., "I won't support the opponent's choices so that mine have a better chance") (Forgas and Moylan, 1996). Happy negotiators may overestimate the likelihood that their opponents will be cooperative, and negotiators in a good mood are more trusting of the opponent than are negotiators in a neutral mood (Kramer et al., 1993). Negotiators in a bad mood, on the other hand, expect their opponent to be uncooperative. Negotiators in a good mood use fewer contentious tactics (such as threats, positional commitments, contrived arguments designed to pressure the opponent to concede, and efforts to raise one's status in the eyes of the opponent), compared to negotiators who are in a neutral mood (Carnevale and Isen, 1986).

Happy negotiators propose more alternatives, make more requests for their opponent's reaction to offers, and propose more trade-offs (concessions on certain items to gain on others) than their neutral-mood counterparts in face-to-face negotiations (Carnevale and Isen, 1986). Furthermore, negotiators in a good mood engage in more information exchange and are more likely to recognize integrative solutions than those in a negative mood.

Positive mood is linked to creative thinking (Isen, Daubman, and Nowicki, 1987), flexible thinking (Murray et al., 1990) and motivated thinking (Pretty and Seligman, 1984). For example, on the Remote Associates Test, which is based on the associative memory structure thought to be related to creative thinking (e.g., what do the words blue, cottage, and Swiss have in common?), happy participants perform better than neutral or sad participants (the answer: cheese) (Isen, Daubman, and Nowicki, 1987). In addition, when asked to generate a list of unique features of different television programs, happy participants perform better than neutral-mood participants (Murray et al., 1990).

Happy negotiators are more confident about achieving their goals prior to the negotiation than negotiators in a neutral mood (Kramer et al., 1993). Negotiators in a good mood make more concessions than negotiators in a neutral mood (Baron, 1990). This result has mixed implications for the happy negotiator. In a bargaining task with integrative potential, more concessions could lead to better outcomes if negotiators recognize opportunities for trade-offs, or if the bargaining zone is so small that concessions are needed to prevent impasse. A negotiator in a good mood could make concessions to induce concessions from the opponent. On fixed-sum tasks, however, concessions may lead to worse outcomes—each unmatched concession relinquishes more of the resource pie to the opponent.

In sum, negotiators in a good mood achieve better individual outcomes and better joint outcomes than their neutral- and bad-mood counterparts. Happy negotiators are more cooperative and use fewer contentious tactics than negotiators in a neutral or bad mood. Negotiators in a good mood propose more alternatives, make more requests for information, and are more confident about achieving their goals than sad or neutral-mood negotiators. Positive mood is linked to creative thinking: happy negotiators are more imaginative about proposing solutions that maximize joint payoffs.

Dr. Jekyll and Mr. Hyde at the Negotiation Table

We have talked about the beneficial consequences of a good mood and positive disposition at the bargaining table, but what happens when negotiators are in a bad mood or are downright hostile? Negative emotion can ruin the chance of reaching integrative agreement. For example, when a negotiator is made to look foolish by his opponent in the presence of an audience—that is, when he feels embarrassment or humiliation—he is likely to retaliate despite knowing that he will worsen his own outcome (Brown, 1968). Negotiators who feel high anger and low compassion toward the other party are less accurate in judging their opponents' interests, and achieve lower joint gains than negotiators low in anger and high in compassion (Allred et al., 1996).

Negative emotions arising from an acrimonious relationship between parties hinder effective negotiation. Negotiators with an acrimonious history are more concerned with their own outcome than are negotiators who have a harmonious or neutral relationship (Loewenstein, Thompson, and Bazerman, 1989). Whereas negotiators with a harmonious or neutral history dislike advantageous unequal outcomes (i.e., where they come out ahead of the other party), negotiators with an acrimonious history prefer advantageous but unequal outcomes—equity concerns diminish with acrimony.

The norm of reciprocity governs the mutual expression of emotion. The propensity for people to reciprocate the emotional response of others is a basic tendency (Lazarus, 1991), often occurring outside of conscious awareness (Ohman, Dimburg, and Esteves, 1989). Once negative affect is expressed, it opens the door to greater expression of negative affect, leading to an escalating, destructive conflict spiral (Deutsch, 1973; Rubin, Pruitt, and Kim, 1994).

Reciprocating others' negative emotions also inhibits altruistic, prosocial behavior (Eisenberg et al., 1989). The perils of emotional contagion are striking and likely to produce hostility, avoidance behavior, and conflict escalation during negotiations (Keltner, 1994).

Emotional stress impairs decision making, which can lead to fixed-pie perceptions. Emotional stress is linked to international conflicts that escalate into full-blown crises (Holsti, 1989; Janis, 1972). Emotions influence judgments of objectives entirely unrelated to the cause of the emotion (Schwartz, 1990). Thus, emotions associated with circumstances unrelated to a negotiation may generalize into judgments of negotiation-related issues.

People who are angry accentuate the blameworthiness of other's actions (Keltner, Ellsworth, and Edwards, 1993) and misperceive hostile intentions in others' actions. Fear increases stereotyping of out-group members and exaggerated responses to the actions of others (Stephan and Stephan, 1985).

The escalation of conflict stems from misperception and biased perceptions of others (Deutsch, 1973). The intensification of conflict follows the **Gresham law of conflict:** the harmful and dangerous elements drive out those which would keep conflict within bounds (Coleman, 1961).

Opposing partisans may explain their own emotions, such as fear, contempt, and anger, by delegitimizing their opposition (Bar-Tal and Geva, 1986), or by dehumanizing, stigmatizing, and stereotyping others. Further, opposing partisans are prone to impute bias to the other side. As a consequence, people believe that others' emotions are more influenced by irrational bias than are their own (Ross and Ward, 1994; Shaver, Schwartz, Kirson, and O'Connor, 1987).

People differ in the extent to which they treat negotiation as an emotional or a rational interaction. Some negotiators focus on the affective components of a conflict (e.g., jealousy, hatred, anger, frustration); other negotiators focus on purely intellectual dimensions (Pinkley and Northcraft, 1994). Negotiators with an emotional conflict frame focus on emotional characteristics of a conflict situation while avoiding focus on the actions and behaviors that occur in the negotiation (Pinkley and Northcraft, 1994). Negotiators with an emotional conflict frame are less satisfied with the outcome of the negotiation compared to negotiators with an intellectual frame. In addition, negotiators with an intellectual frame feel that the negotiation was good for their relationship with their opponent, more than do negotiators with an emotional frame (Pinkley and Northcraft, 1994).

Should Negotiators Get in Touch with Their Emotions?

Emotion influences the likelihood that negotiators will

- discover and create new resources or simply split the existing resources
- use cooperative or competitive strategies
- consider a number of alternatives and requests for information that negotiators make
- accurately judge one another's interests
- feel positively or negatively about the negotiation outcome as well as their own performance

Rather than ignore or suppress the emotion implicit in the negotiation process, negotiators should acknowledge their emotions and tap into those emotions that aid discovery and development of resources that can be allocated to both parties.

The Bipolar Negotiator

To be effective, it appears that negotiators should attempt to get themselves in a good mood prior to the negotiation. Yet, this recommendation does not square with intuition. If positive mood consistently leads to more favorable negotiation outcomes, then why do negotiators get angry or upset so frequently in bargaining situations? Whether we are buying a car, trying to get a refund, allocating household chores, discussing which job candidate should be hired, or bidding on a house, it is not unusual to experience and/or display negative emotions.

Negative emotions may serve a useful purpose in negotiation. For example, negotiators may demonstrate resolve and firmness by acting tough, angry, irritated, and upset. The absence of negative affect may be viewed by an opponent as an indication that the negotiator does not care much about the issue, or is willing to acquiesce. For example, just prior to the Gulf War in 1991, the U.S. Secretary of State, James Baker, met with the foreign minister of Iraq, Tariq Aziz, and Saddam Hussein's half brother, Barzan al-Tikriti (Triandis, 1994). Baker stated his position very clearly to his opponents: If Iraq did not move out of Kuwait, the United States would attack. Barzan al-Tikriti telephoned Hussein and told him, "The Americans will not attack. They are weak. They are calm. They are not angry. They are only talking" (Triandis, 1994). Six days later, the United States went to war against Iraq, resulting in the death of about 175,000 Iraqi citizens, and property damage in the amount of about $200 billion.

This example suggests that negotiators should act tough to make their opponent understand their priorities. Acting tough sometimes requires displaying anger, irritation, and exasperation. Ironically, James Baker's failure to display anger and irritation during the negotiations with Iraq was probably a result of extensive training in which diplomats are taught to suppress instinctive displays of anger and other negative emotions. Negative emotions, which seem to occur quite automatically in some situations, may actually serve us well. The paradox, then, is that effective negotiation outcomes are best achieved by maintaining positive mood during the negotiation, but we must act tough and get angry and upset to show we are serious. So what gives?

In high-stakes negotiations, negotiators *expect* their opponents to display negative emotions, such as anger, to demonstrate the importance of those issues. This presumably was the expectation of Hussein's half brother, Barzan al-Tikriti, during the negotiations with the United States prior to the Gulf War. The anxiety and tension that negotiators experience during a high-stakes negotiation results from "leakage"—negative emotion is not a tactic but is genuinely felt. The display of negative emotion in circumstances where the stakes are high, therefore, might promote effective negotiation outcomes by allowing negotiators to communicate their priorities, while motivating them to avoid suboptimal outcomes on the issues that are most important.[1] In this sense the effective negotiator is a **bipolar negotiator,** fluctuating between good moods to instigate creative thinking and occasional anger to communicate resolve.

A TRAINING COURSE IN RAPPORT BUILDING FOR THE NEGOTIATOR

You've sharpened your distributive and integrative negotiation skills. You are well versed in logrolling, trading off differences, and reservation points. You've thought about your opponent's interests. You are ready to negotiate. Or are you? How are you going to build rapport with the other party? Rapport and the establishment of an interpersonal relationship is essential for effective negotiation (Tickle-Degner and Rosenthal, 1990; Drolet and Morris, 1995), yet many people don't have the first idea of how to build rapport in an interpersonal interaction. All too often, we leave this up to chance and hope the "chemistry" is right. In this section, we offer a mini-course on rapport building for the negotiator.

Social Facilitation

Joggers on paths speed up when an observer is facing them (Worringham and Messick, 1983); experienced pool players improve their game when others are watching (Michaels, et al., 1982); and cyclists ride faster in races with others than when racing alone (Triplett, 1888). According to the **social facilitation effect** (Zajonc, 1960), behaviors performed in the presence of others are facilitated, augmented, or exaggerated to the extent that they are well learned and debilitated to the extent that they are not well learned (Zajonc, 1960). Social facilitation occurs for emotional experiences as well. For example, people laugh longer and think comedy shows are more humorous when someone else is present than when they are alone. The social facilitation of emotion is largely nonconscious; people are not aware that their emotions are more intense when experienced in the presence of others. Negotiations may be more emotionally exaggerated when parties are in the presence of others than when they are alone; multiparty negotiation may be more emotional than dyadic negotiation. Con-

---

[1] It should be kept in mind that the term "high stakes" is relative to the participants and the situation. Thus, while a negotiation over whether to go to war is considered high stakes to a diplomat, a negotiation over the price of a house or an annual raise in salary is high stakes to an average citizen.

sider a negotiation concerning a joint venture between two business firms that takes place in a private meeting room versus a public place. The presence of others in the public place may augment the emotions felt by the negotiators.

Emotional Contagion

Have you ever talked to a depressed person and then felt depressed yourself? **Emotional contagion** is a process whereby the emotions experienced by one person are transmitted to another person (Howes, Hokanson, and Loewenstein, 1985; Hatfield, Caccioppo, and Rapson, 1992). The process of emotional contagion consists of three mechanisms. The first process is **mimicry,** wherein people nonconsciously mimic the facial expressions, voice tone, posture, and movement of others. The second process is the **feedback** about our emotions that our facial, vocal, and postural behaviors provide to us. The third is the actual **contagion** process. We discuss each below.

Mimicry

People imitate the facial, vocal, and postural movements of others. However, we aren't aware that we do this. Probably the most common experience of mimicry is yawning, which is infectious and largely out of our control. Laughter is equally contagious. Yawning, laughter, and other behavioral expressions like smiles, head nods, and shoulder shrugs, are not controlled, deliberate processes; they are automatic and, often, irrepressible. It is difficult or impossible for people to consciously and deliberately mimic others because the process of mimicry is too complex and too fast. In fact, when people deliberately attempt to mimic others, they are regarded as phonies (Davis, 1982). Mimicry is so natural in social interactions that people feel uncomfortable in the absence of behavioral synchrony.

The basic processes of mimicry involve the adaptation of one's face, voice, movements, and postures to others (see Dimberg, 1982; Vaughn and Lanzetta, 1980; Ekman, 1984; Hatfield, Caccioppo, and Rapson, 1994). Facial mimicry is almost instantaneous, and people are remarkably adept at tracking the most subtle, moment-to-moment changes. However, mimicry occurs even in the absence of face-to-face interaction. For example, when people watched a videotape of an interview in which a man recounted one of the happiest or saddest events in his life, facial expressions of audience members matched those of the man in the tape (Hsee, Hatfield, and Chemtob, 1991).

We do not mimic others equally, however. We are especially likely to mimic others for whom we care and like. The degree to which people's movements seem orchestrated determines how much emotional rapport they feel (Bernieri, et al., 1991). If we dislike someone, the strong negative feelings we have for that person dampen our tendency to mimic him or her. The result is a more strained and awkward interaction.

We don't always mimic others; sometimes we countermimic. For example, people who are competing in fixed-sum games show counterempathic facial responses to the opponent's facial expression (e.g., they smile when the other is upset). However, when individuals share the same fate, such as when their outcomes are jointly shared, they show empathic facial responses (e.g., they smile when the other is pleased or is winning) (Englis, Vaughan, and Lanzetta, 1981). Thus, people who fall prey to the fixed-pie perception should be less likely to mimic their opponent than people who see joint interests. Negotiators who perceive the possibility for joint gain may be more inclined to synchronize their behavior with that of the opponent.

Whereas vocal mimicry and synchrony is crucial for smooth interaction between individuals, there is an important exception. Mimicry of positive facial expressions and emotions is conducive for pleasant social interaction, but in the case of negative expression and emotion, mimicking others is often not desirable. Indeed, when people are forced to interact with strangers or with people whose attitudes differ markedly from their own, they try to keep their voices and bodies from betraying their antipathy (Cappella and Palmer, 1990) presumably so as to salvage the interaction. For example, well-adjusted couples resist quid pro quo behavior in angry exchanges, whereas unhappy couples seem trapped in destructive tit-for-tat exchanges; anger sparks an angry response (Gottman, 1979). The same principle is true in negotiated interactions.

Emotional Feedback Systems

If I smile at you, the activation of the smile on my face will increase my emotional feelings of happiness and joy. On the other hand, if I clench my fists and grind my teeth, I am more likely to feel aggressive and hostile. The second mechanism involved in emotional contagion concerns our emotional experience as a result of feedback from our own vocal, facial, and postural expressions (James, 1890/1984). Feedback about emotional states is not limited to facial expression. Vocal feedback, such as pitch and tone, influences emotional experience. Basic emotions are linked with specific patterns of intonation, vocal quality, rhythm, and pausing (Clynes, 1980; Scherer, 1982). Further, postural position and movement mimicry also affect our emotional experience. Even if we attempt to use emotions in a strategic manner in negotiations, emotional feedback may induce us to ultimately experience these emotions to some degree. Thus, calculated or feigned emotion may often instigate real emotion.

Catching the Emotion of Others

You are in the waiting room of a major consulting company. You've arrived 20 minutes early for your "dream" interview. There is another person in the waiting room, seated across from you, and he is acting in a bizarre manner. You watch as he laughs uncontrollably, makes jokes, tosses magazines in the air, and leapfrogs over the water cooler. After a few minutes, you find yourself laughing and feeling good, too. What is going on? To examine this contagion phenomenon, people were put in the presence of a person who adopted a particular mood (e.g., angry, delighted) (Schacter and Singer, 1962). Some participants were aroused (with a drug); some were told what effect the drug would have on them; others were kept in the dark. Participants who were given the drug, but had no explanation for their arousal, adopted the mood of the person in the waiting room. In contrast, participants who were not aroused did not show emotional contagion; nor did participants who were aroused but provided with a physiological reason for their arousal. When people become aroused, they look for an appropriate label for their feelings; if a label is absent or ambiguous, they look to the behavior of others to interpret their own arousal. In this sense, people "catch" the emotions of others.

Members of work groups display consistency in their emotional expressions, which suggests that they regulate each other's emotional experience through a process of contagion. Further, the affect displayed among members of work groups is chronic, suggesting that emotional displays are a personality characteristic of groups (George, 1990). Even more important, emotion predicts behavior: Positive-affect groups have fewer sick days than negative-affect groups.

Emotional Leaders and Followers

The ability to infect others with emotion is a powerful strategy and skill for the negotiator. If we could induce a good mood in our angry landlord or delight the personnel director, we would be more successful in achieving our negotiation goals. In negotiated interaction, whose emotion prevails? That is, do we mimic others, or do others mimic us? In short, what determines who follows whom? Personality and situational factors determine who is most likely to be contagious (i.e., infect others) and who is most likely to be susceptible to contagion (i.e., catch others' emotions) in social interaction. Personality factors deal with stable, enduring characteristics of people; situational factors deal with more transient, but more controllable, mechanisms. We explore these next.

Characteristics of People High in Emotional Influence

There are three characteristics of people who are likely to be extremely influential in infecting others with their own emotions:

- people who *feel* strong emotions
- people who *express* strong emotions (via facial, vocal, postural cues)
- people who are relatively *insensitive* or unresponsive to the feelings of those experiencing emotions that are incompatible with their own (Hatfield, Caccioppo, and Rapson, 1992)

In contrast, people who are most susceptible to "catching" emotions of others are those who feel strong emotions but do not express them.

People who are expressive, charismatic, and who captivate others are the most powerful senders of emotion. These people are moving speechmakers and inspiring conversationalists; they are highly expressive and have the ability to hold the attention of others. Unfortunately, most of us don't have the God-given talents of charisma. Is emotional influence solely determined by personality? Are there any contextual elements that may predispose people to be especially emotionally influential in a particular situation? Emotional influence, like other forms of social influence, can be manipulated by situational cues. Below, we identify six factors that may increase emotional influence.

Power   Power is often treated as a personality characteristic, but as we've seen, the basis of power in negotiation is determined by who has the best alternative to a negotiated agreement (Fisher, Ury, and Patton, 1991), more information, and expertise (e.g., French and Raven, 1959). High-power persons can afford to be relatively oblivious to those of lesser power (Fiske and Deprét, 1996; Deprét and Fiske, 1993). In contrast, low-power people are often hypervigilant (Kramer, 1995). Thus, people with low power (i.e., weak reservation points) may be more susceptible to emotional contagion.

Mood   The degree and extent of emotional contagion also depends on the mood itself. Happy moods are easier to pass than are negative moods (Hatfield, Caccioppo, and Rapson, 1992). For this reason, emotionally expressive people are most likely to infect others with positive rather than negative emotion.

Medium of Communication   Because the processes of emotional contagion involve facial, vocal, postural, and body cues, the more channels of communication that are available, the greater the opportunity for emotional contagion. Face-to-face interactions should be more conducive to contagion than videoconferencing, which is more conducive than written or electronic mail interaction. It behooves low-power negotiators to interact on the phone or by e-mail, because these modalities equalize power differences (Keisler and Sproull, 1992).

Long-term Relationships   Negotiators who are involved in long-term relationships or who expect to have future interaction with one another may be more likely to experience and express emotions because of their greater involvement and investment in the interaction. People in long-term relationships have well-developed, synchronized empathic systems for responding to one another. People in close and long-term relationships are more attuned to one another and, therefore, more likely to experience contagion than those persons in short, exchange relationships.

Freedom to Express Emotion   There is dramatic variation across situations in the extent to which people are socially permitted to express emotion. Movie theaters, train stations, hospitals, and airports are more permitting than restaurants and shopping malls, which are more permitting than business organizations. Mimicry and contagion will occur in contexts more permitting of emotional expression. Depending upon the context, the negotiator might perceive him- or herself to be at greater emotional liberty; the emotionally competent negotiator will take this into consideration when planning his or her negotiation.

Ambiguity and Uncertainty   To the extent that the situation is ambiguous, novel, and uncertain, the expression of emotion may be more likely. In the absence of strong internal cues, people look to other people to determine which emotions are appropriate to feel and which emotions are appropriate to display.

When Are Others Likely to Influence Our Emotions?

People are highly capable of mirroring and mimicking the emotions of others, but they don't realize they do this, much less understand its importance. Thus, a first step in understanding how others are likely to influence our emotions in negotiation is to understand the automatic processes of mimicry and emotional feedback that results from mimicry. Our susceptibility to emotional contagion is determined by six primary factors (Hatfield, Cacioppo, and Rapson, 1992).

Focus of Attention   We are most susceptible to emotional influence if our attention is focused on others, as opposed to when we are self-absorbed or oblivious to them. We may be oblivious to the emotions of others because we don't care about them or because we worry we will care too much. Happy people are more outward focused and are, therefore, more likely to catch the moods of others. In contrast, sad and depressed people are inward focused and are relatively immune to influence.

Social Identity   If we focus on our interrelatedness to others rather than on our independence and uniqueness, we are more likely to catch the emotions of others. For example, when we interact with a member of our own group or organization, or with a person from a group in which we desire membership, we are more susceptible to emotional contagion. When an opponent makes appeals to shared social identity, we are more likely to succumb to emotional contagion.

Perception   Ironically, people who are good at reading others' emotional expressions, voices, gestures, and postures should be especially vulnerable to contagion. There are individual differences in ability to accurately detect nonverbal emotional cues (Ekman, 1992): Women are better at reading (deciphering nonverbal cues) and sending (behaving nonverbally in ways that are easy for people to understand) (Hall, 1984). However, although women are superior when it comes to deciphering truthful statements, men are more likely to pick up on nonverbal cues that someone is lying (Rosenthal and DePaulo, 1979).

Mimicry   Some people naturally mimic facial, vocal, and postural expressions of others. They are especially vulnerable to contagion. For example, when people are instructed to consciously mimic the facial expressions of others, they are more likely to accurately perceive and feel the emotion expressed by others (Osgood, 1980).

Awareness   If we are aware of our own emotional responses, we should be more vulnerable to contagion.

Emotional Reaction   If we are emotionally reactive, we are more vulnerable to contagion. Conversely, people who do not attend to others, view themselves to be distinct and unique persons, are unable to read emotions, fail to mimic emotions, or whose subjective emotional experience is not affected by feedback should be the most resistant to emotional contagion.

Is emotional contagion an advantage or disadvantage at the negotiation table? It would seem disadvantageous to be an emotional mimic of our opponent, yet, it would seem equally disadvantageous to always set the emotional tone of the negotiation. In some cases, we might want someone to regulate our mood. For example, if we are feeling frustrated and angry, it might serve our interests to catch the emotions of our relaxed opponent. Setting ourselves up to catch the emotions of others (rather than push our own emotions) has utilitarian advantages. Indeed, the popular press argues that you can "mimic your way to the top" (Reibstein and Joseph, 1988). Whether done consciously or not, subordinates show a relentless tendency to mimic their superiors' mannerisms, gestures, way of speaking, dress, and choice of cars and wine. The danger is when such behavior becomes obvious or encroaches on peoples' sense of uniqueness. Letitia Baldridge, an adviser on executive manners, recounts the story of a young assistant who wore a plaid suit to please the boss, who always wore plaid. The angered supervisor ordered the assistant to go home and change his clothes, as he felt his identity being stolen (Reibstein and Joseph, 1988).

Emotional Tuning

Emotion management involves adapting, regulating, and managing the emotions of others. We discussed mimicry as a basic process of social interaction that is largely automatic. Although certain conditions may facilitate or hinder emotional mimicry and contagion, they are often beyond a person's control. In this section, we consider controlled and deliberate mechanisms used by individuals in social interaction.

You've been asked by your supervisor to make a speech to a group of investors. The investors are keenly interested in product X; your own assessment tells you that product Y is more viable. What do you say in your statement to the investors? When people formulate a message for an intended recipient, they take their recipient's background, knowledge, attitudes, and opinions into consideration (Zajonc, 1960; Higgins, 1992; Hardin and Higgins, 1995). For example, when a communicator perceives that his or her audience dislikes a particular person or idea, they present that person or idea more negatively. Thus, people tune their message to their audience. **Tuning** is a form of management in that to the extent that we tune to our audience, we can be more persuasive and achieve our social interaction goals (Higgins, 1992).

Several rules or principles guide the manner in which people tune to one another in social interaction. One principle is the **maxim of relevance,** which states that people should communicate information of maximum relevance to their audience (Grice, 1975). Usually, this means saying something worthwhile or new to the audience. Another principle is the **maxim of pleasantness,** which states that communicators should maintain pleasant relations.

People also **emotionally tune** to their audience by considering their emotional state and disposition. We propose a **maxim of regulation** whereby people tailor their messages to an audience so as to regulate the other person's emotional reactions. People attempt to maintain happy moods in others and alleviate negative moods. Consider, for example, an employee approaching his supervisor about a raise. If the supervisor is extremely temperamental and moody, the employee will approach him in a more positive mood than if the supervisor is considered to be generally relaxed and calm.

However, tuning may have unintended effects. To return to the earlier example, communicators instructed to transmit a message to an audience that is believed to dislike a certain target person present a more negative message to the audience; communicators who believe their audience likes the target are more positive. However, the communicated message unintentionally changes the communicator's views: Those who communicate the negative message have less positive evaluations than those who communicate the positive message. To the extent that a communicator tailors his or her message to suit an intended audience, this influences the communicator's own mood and emotional reaction. Thus, emotional tuning can backfire by unintentionally changing our own attitudes!

Communicators are not always equally intent upon emotionally tuning with their opponent or teammate in negotiation situations. Four qualitatively different types of tuning may be employed by communicators: basic tuning, supertuning, antituning, and nontuning (Higgins, 1992; Hardin and Higgins, 1995). Thus far, we have discussed the principles of basic tuning.

Supertuning

Supertuning is used when people desire high rapport with their audience. For example, a person attempting to negotiate a raise from his or her superior is likely to supertune.

Antituning

Antituning occurs when people desire to block out the other person or dissociate themselves from interaction. When a salesperson telephones during the dinner hour, we may cut him or her off in midsentence stating that we are not interested and hang up.

Nontuning

Nontuning occurs when people are indifferent toward others or are preoccupied. Consider a negotiation we might have with someone who is interested in buying our home. The prospective buyer brings along a friend when he looks at our house a third time. We are likely to not tune to the friend—as she is not the person who might buy our house.

Emotional Labor

There is a potentially unfortunate consequence of emotional management in negotiation. People (especially those in the service industries) who manage their emotions may experience lower job satisfaction (Morris and Feldman, 1996). **Emotional labor** is the work that a person does to regulate the frequency of her emotional expression (e.g., smiling at every customer) and attentiveness to display rules (e.g., smiling at customers who make her mad), or to show a variety of emotions (e.g., concern, surprise) that are inconsistent with her true feelings.

Consider Michael, a salesperson for a travel agency, whose job is to help customers who have concerns about their travel plans. Michael quickly learned that most travel customers come to him when they are angry to the point of being irate, demanding full refunds, free trips, and threatening to sue the company. Michael's job is to handle the customers' concerns and defuse their emotion. Michael often feels that the customers are incorrect for taking their anger out on him—after all, it's not *his* fault that it rained, the plane was late, and their luggage was lost. Yet, Michael is the customer's window to the organization. His job involves emotional labor.

Detecting Emotions

The management of emotion depends upon negotiators' ability to accurately detect emotions in others. After all, if we cannot accurately detect emotion, we cannot manage it. Whereas most people are not able to voluntarily produce the reliable markers of emotion (Ekman, Roper, and Hager, 1980), they accurately identify expressions of anger, contempt, disgust, fear, sadness, and surprise (Ekman, Sorenson, and Friesen, 1969; Ekman, Friesen, and Scherer, 1976), as well as amusement, embarrassment, shame, and sympathy/compassion (Keltner, 1995). People can accurately recognize emotional states in others and reliably discern when emotions are truly felt or feigned (Ekman, 1972). The stronger the emotional state of another person, the better we are at detecting emotions. This is because people cannot reliably hide their inner feelings and emotional reactions (Ekman, Freisen, and Scherer, 1976). Strong emotions are likely to leak out and thus become possible to detect. This is especially true when negotiators try to cover up strong feelings.

Lie Detection

The emotionally skilled negotiator can detect lies, or deceptions. However, most people are not particularly adept at detecting lies. On average, we detect deceptive behavior 55 percent of the time when 50 percent is chance performance (Ekman, 1984). Why are we so inaccurate? One reason is that people pay attention to the least trustworthy sources when they attempt to detect lies: words and facial expressions. Liars usually do not monitor, control, and disguise all of their behavior. These are the easiest channels for a liar to control; thus, a negotiator may be easily misled. More reliable signs to look for when detecting lies are body movements, such as increase in **emblems** (cultural signs such as "OK" with the hand, or shrugging to indicate one doesn't care) and decrease in **illustrators** (e.g., placing emphasis on words or phrases, drawing a picture in space with one's hands, brow and eyelid movements, or "talking" with one's hands).

However, negotiators can accurately judge whether others will cooperate or compete in a game situation based upon brief (30-minute) interactions (Frank, 1988). This ability enables negotiators to selectively negotiate with those individuals with whom they will reach the most favorable outcomes.

When people do detect lies, it is emotional ones that often give the liar away (Ekman, 1992). "Most often, lies fail because some sign of an emotion being concealed leaks. The stronger the emotions involved in the lie, and the greater the number of different emotions, the more likely it is that the lie will be betrayed by some form of behavioral leakage" (Ekman, 1992, p. 21).

Emotional Systems in Groups

Dyads, teams, and groups have a group-level affective tone (George, 1990; Sessa, 1996; Smith and Crandell, 1984). Groups with negative affect feel nervous, worried, anxious, upset, and distressed; in contrast, groups with positive affect feel enthusiastic, energetic, and assured. To characterize a group as having an affective tone, the affective reactions of the members of the group must be consistent (George, 1990). Consider two groups, each composed of four persons. In one group, all members are moderately positive in affective tone; in the other group, two members are high in positive affect and the other two are low in positive affect. The first group would be characterized as having its own affective tone; the second group would not.

Transactive memory is a shared system within a group for the encoding, processing, storage, and retrieval of information (Wegner, 1986). Groups develop roles for members concerning the reception, storage, and retrieval of group-relevant information. Roles are assigned on the basis of two primary criteria: expertise and circumstance. For example, a team of negotiators may expect their legal counsel to collect and retrieve the legal aspects of their negotiation deal; this relieves the rest of the team from encoding such information. In other cases, responsibility for information is more circumstantial and depends on a person's temporary location, etc.

Similar systems develop within dyads and groups for perceiving, signaling, feeling, and expressing emotion. We call such systems **transactive emotion.** Consider a two-person negotiating team in which one partner consistently loses his or her temper. Initially, this loss of control may upset the other member of the team and hinder their effectiveness as a team. Over time, however, the other partner may depend on her partner to throw a fit as part of a bargaining strategy.

Good Cops and Bad Cops

In the good-cop, bad-cop routine, a suspect is held for questioning about a crime. However, the investigators do not have sufficient evidence to convict the suspect. Therefore, they must rely on a confession. The bad cop "works over" the suspect, treating him or her without respect or sympathy. Then, the bad cop disappears for a few minutes and the good cop enters. The good cop offers the suspect coffee and cigarettes and claims to be on the side of the suspect. The good cop suggests a plan of how the two of them can ward off getting more heat from the bad cop. The plan involves a confession on the part of the suspect. The badgered suspect, thankful for the good cop's kindness, confesses.

In this example, an emotional system is created by one party (consisting of two investigators) that engenders emotions in the opponent (the suspect). However, this is not the only way that transactive emotion may develop. Transactive emotional systems develop on the same side of the negotiation table as well as across the bargaining table, as opponents develop expectations for one another's behaviors and roles.

SOME LIKE IT HOT: THE CASE FOR THE EMOTIONAL NEGOTIATOR

Emotion is not only a natural part of a negotiated interaction (i.e., not just an intraindividual experience), it is essential for effective negotiation. Traditional views of negotiation prescribe rational behavior and eschew emotion. Here, we take up two issues related to this point. The first is whether rationality really precludes emotion and affect. The second is whether a negotiator who is truly devoid of emotion, but highly rational, is effective.

Is the Rational Negotiator a "Spock"?

In the classic TV show *Star Trek*, Mr. Spock is a character who is ultrarational, super-smart, and completely devoid of emotion and feeling. Is it necessary for a negotiator to choose between rationality and emotion as a bargaining strategy? Rationality and emotion are not contradictory; in fact, it can be rational for a person to behave in an emotional fashion (Frank, 1988). Consider, for example, an exit negotiation between an employee of a firm and his supervisor. The supervisor has determined that the firm should let the employee go, but realizes that it is wise to offer the employee attractive compensation and benefits to avoid possible recrimination by a potentially vengeful employee. From a purely objective standpoint, it is not in the employee's interests to seek revenge or initiate a lawsuit. However, if the employee becomes enraged because he feels that he has been dealt with unjustly, he may decide to seek revenge even when, in purely material terms, it does not pay. To the extent the supervisor believes the employee will seek revenge, she may offer the employee more benefits. By acting emotionally and irrationally, the employee maximizes his interests. The supervisor, by believing the employee, has acted rationally. It is in this sense that emotion and rationality are not contradictory. The key, of course, is that the negotiator's behavior and expression of emotion must be credible. A rational analysis of the above situation suggests that the employee's threat to retaliate with a lawsuit is not credible because it is not economically worthwhile for him. However, if the supervisor believes that his emotions will get the better of him, she will treat his emotions credibly. One implication, therefore, of the use of emotion in negotiation is the extent to which negotiators are able to signal emotions that are credible. Obviously, if a negotiator can convince the opponent that he is crazy, this can be an effective strategy.

The Head Versus the Heart

To the extent that a negotiator is devoid of emotion and behaves in a fully rational fashion, will he or she be as effective (or more effective) than the negotiator who is emotional, as we have described? Prescriptive treatment of negotiation cautions the negotiator not to allow emotions to rule behavior. The negotiator who is unable or unwilling to engage in behavioral synchrony of emotional expression, neither mimicking nor conveying emotion, will not be as effective as the negotiator who is emotionally responsive in negotiation.

CONCLUSION

The emotionally skilled negotiator is more likely to have an accurate perception of the other party based upon his or her ability to detect emotions in an opponent. People who mimic emotions and experience emotional contagion are more accurate in judging the true emotions of the target than those who do not mimic others' emotions. The emotional negotiator is more likely to infect his or her opponent with emotion. The emotional negotiator is also more likely to develop and effectively utilize emotional systems on both sides of the negotiating table.

TAKE-AWAYS

- To only consider the cognitive aspects of negotiation is to ignore an important feature of virtually any negotiation situation—the emotions felt by negotiators, motivational orientations triggered by emotion, and other social-contextual factors.
- Being in a close relationship with someone does not guarantee that a successful outcome will result; negotiators in relationships must work harder to identify and exploit differences in interest and avoid the temptation to compromise.
- A good mood is likely to stimulate creative thinking in negotiation.
- Good moods are "catching."
- Mimicking others can lead to greater feelings of rapport.
- People "tune" to others to achieve certain goals. However, when people "supertune" they are more vulnerable to catching the views and emotions of others.

CHAPTER 11

Social Justice, Fairness, and Social Utility: *All's Fair*

The law firm was unique in a number of respects. Most of the people, including the staff, had been with the office since the late sixties, when the office was opened during the height of the race riots and civil liberties movement. Seven young lawyers got together and took on civil rights cases for extremely low fees. The group decided during this time that all of the money that came into the office via attorneys' fees and settlement moneys should be placed in a group pool. After a settlement, the group would allocate the money among the partners. With the exception of the staff, who were always paid a fixed amount on a weekly basis, the attorneys in the office would be paid according to their needs, and it was understood that people would exercise self-restraint.

As a consequence, the take-home pay of the attorneys constantly fluctuated. The office nearly had to be closed twice because of a lean season. However, the group always managed to bounce back. On several occasions, the entire group survived on the earnings of one or two of the lawyers. Consequently, when these lawyers considered leaving the firm, there was tremendous social pressure to stay. Most of the lawyers in the office described the salary system as "completely communal." Despite its egalitarian-appearing nature, however, conflicts frequently erupted.

In a recent meeting, one of the partners explained to the group that he would like to have a little more money this month because he and his wife were expecting their second baby. The young, single female partner was opposed, arguing that she too had personal needs that were just as pressing as those related to the birth of a new child. A bitter argument ensued. One partner had a large family and had decided years ago never to ask for anything. As a result, he and his family barely subsisted on his meager salary. During the past month, the firm had hired a new attorney in the office—the first hire in over 15 years. Jerry, the new hire, was confused about the salary structure, "You mean that each month, we decide as a group what is fair? Shouldn't we be paid according to how much work we do?" The attorneys tried to explain the need-based system to Jerry.

I ssues of justice and fairness are central to negotiation, as well as social interaction. The importance of justice in small and large organizational groups stems from its relevance to situations in which benefits or burdens must be distributed. In this chapter, we first discuss four major conceptualizations of social justice, and then consider the impact of self-interest and fairness on negotiations.

SOCIAL JUSTICE

There are four distinct types of social justice that govern our existence (Tyler and Smith, 1995):

- **Distributive justice** concerns the fair allocation of resources to a circle of recipients (e.g., a group of attorneys allocating wages).
- **Retributive justice** concerns the distribution of "bads" or the allocation of punishments (e.g., a judge sentencing a criminal).
- **Relative deprivation** concerns how people evaluate outcomes in comparison to those they expect, have received in the past, or see others get (e.g., women forced to wear veils and stay at home after their once independent country is taken over by a Muslim dictatorship).
- **Procedural justice** concerns the process of justice procedures rather than the outcomes (e.g., a vote that is not "blind" is questioned by a group member who is concerned that social pressure may inhibit the expression of true preferences in the election of a chairperson).

Distributive Justice

Distributive justice pervades all aspects of social life from corporate policy to intimate social relations (Deutsch, 1985). Distributive justice centers on the fairness of the distribution of the conditions and goods that affect individual well-being (Adams, 1965; Hook and Cook, 1979; Messick, 1991; Rawls, 1971) and social welfare (Deutsch, 1985).

The Big Three

A company is expanding. Consequently, several new, attractive management positions must be created and filled. Who should get these jobs? How do people allocate rewards such as new jobs and other opportunities? Typically, people use one of three social justice principles: equality, equity, or need (Deutsch, 1985). Each of these principles evolves out of and results in different types of interdependence and represents a distinct value system that has different implications for negotiated interactions.

- The **equality rule,** or **blind justice,** prescribes equal shares for all. Outcomes are distributed without regard to inputs, and everyone benefits (or suffers) equally. The education system and the legal system in the United States are examples of equality justice: Everyone receives equal entitlement. In a university, all students have equal entitlement to the services of career placement.
- The **equity rule,** or proportionality of contributions principle, prescribes that distribution should be proportional to a person's contribution. The free market system in the United States is an example of the equity principle. In many universities, students bid for classes; those who bid more points have greater entitlement to a seat in the course.
- The **needs-based rule,** or welfare-based allocation, states that benefits should be proportional to need. The social welfare system in the United States is based on need. In a university, financial aid is based on need.

In addition to these three primary justice principles, other justice rules also exist including precedent or status quo (Bazerman, 1993), entitlement, Darwinian or competitive justice (Lerner, 1977), and ownership (Leventhal, 1979).

Social justice rules are highly context dependent. There is high consensual agreement about which social justice principle is appropriate, depending on the situation (Schwinger, 1980). For example, most of us believe that our court/penal justice system should be equality based: Everyone should have the right to an equal and fair trial regardless of income or need. In contrast, most of us believe that academic grades should be assigned on the basis of an equity-based rule: Students who contribute more should be rewarded with higher marks. Similarly, most people agree that disabled persons are entitled to parking spaces and easy access to buildings. The multiple orientations are a potential source of conflict, however (Deutsch, 1985). For example, consider a firm hiring for a management position. There is a notable lack of diversity in the firm—clearly a blemish on the firm's report card. The most qualified applicant is a white male in his mid-30s. However, the firm's only black manager, a female, is clearly capable of filling the position. Who should get the job? By what rationale? As we'll see, the answer depends on the goals we have in our interactions with others, our relationships with others, as well as cognitive factors.

Interaction Goals   People have different objectives, depending upon the nature of their interactions, that determine which social justice principle they employ (Mikula, 1980). For example, if our goal is to minimize waste, then a needs-based or social welfare policy may be most appropriate (Berkowitz, 1972). If our goal is to maintain or enhance harmony and group solidarity, equality-based rules are most effective (Leventhal, 1976). If our goal is to enhance productivity and performance, equity-based allocation is most effective (Deutsch, 1953).

Relationship to Others   A negotiator's relationship to the other party strongly influences the choice of social justice rules. When negotiators share similar attitudes and beliefs, when they are physically close to one another, or when it is likely that they will engage in future interaction, they prefer equality rule. When the allocation is public (others know what choices are made), equality is used; when allocation is private, equity is preferred. Friends tend to use equality, whereas nonfriends or acquaintances use equity (Austin, 1980).

People in relationships with others do not consistently employ one rule of justice but, rather, use different justice rules for specific incidences that occur within relationships. For example, when people in relationships are asked to describe a recent incident from their own relationships illustrating a particular justice principle (equity, equality, or need), need-based justice is related to incidents involving nurturing and personal development, whereas equity and equality-based justice are related to situations involving the allocation of responsibilities (Steil and Makowski, 1989). In general, equality principles are more desirable for making decisions than either equity or need-based principles. Regardless of the relationship, equality-based justice principles are associated with more positive feelings about the decision, the situation, and one's partner.

Managers often find themselves in the following positions: (1) allocators of rewards and costs, and (2) recipients of rewards and costs. For example, consider Constantine, a manager in a company that makes circuit boards. Constantine distributes scarce resources amongst her three project teams. At the same time, Constantine's superiors allocate rewards to her division based upon performance of the teams. In such situations, what rules govern our allocation behavior and our reactions as recipients? Allocators often distribute resources equally, even if they have different preferences. In contrast, recipients who have been inequitably, but advantageously, treated, justify their shares—even when they would not have awarded themselves the resources they received (Diekmann, Samuels, Ross, and Bazerman, 1997).

What's Being Allocated   Your product development team receives an unexpected gift from a pleased customer. How do you divide the money? The same team is asked to pay for damages accrued when some members of the team installed the new product. How do you allocate this burden? If you are like most people, you will divide the reward equally among all team members, but only fine those responsible for the faulty installation with damages. Whereas equality is often used to allocate benefits, equity is more commonly used to allocate burdens (Sondak, Neale, and Pinkley, 1995).

Cognitive Influences   The selection of social justice rules is also influenced by social cognition and judgment: Consider, for example, a physically handicapped person who attains an advanced degree. A person who overcomes external constraints is more highly valued than a person who does not face constraints but contributes the same amount.

When a situation is complex, involving multiple inputs in different dimensions, people are more likely to use the equality rule. Thus, groups often split dinner bills equally rather than compute each person's share. This can lead to a problem, however. Group members aware of the pervasive use of equality may actually spend more individually. No group member wants to pay for more than he or she gets; if people can't control the consumption of others, they consume more. Of course, when everyone thinks this way, the costs escalate, leading to irrational group behavior—a topic we discuss in chapter 12.

Equity Theory

At a major telecommunications company where salaries are strictly confidential, employees developed an elaborate system for comparing their own salary to that of others. Senior management, who makes salary decisions, did not like this practice at all. Are the employees of this company unique? No. Equity theory (Adams, 1965; Deutsch, 1985; Homans, 1961; Blau, 1964; Walster, Berscheid, and Walster, 1973) was originally developed in the context of organizations to explain workers' reactions to their wages (Walster, Walster, and Berscheid, 1978). According to equity theory, satisfaction and behavior are not linked to objective outcomes but to outcomes received *relative* to those judged to be equitable.

Equity theory is built upon principles of reinforcement (learning theory) and basic economic theory: individuals exchange resources with one another so as to maximize their outcomes. According to equity theory, people try to maximize their outcomes (where outcomes = rewards minus costs). So long as people believe that they can maximize their outcomes by behaving equitably, they will do so. If they perceive that they can maximize outcomes by behaving inequitably, they will do so. Equity exists when one's outcomes are proportional to one's inputs in an exchange relationship. Equity does not exist objectively; equity is subjective. This means that people in a relationship may have very different perceptions about the degree of equity in their relationship. Equity theory assumes that people attempt to secure rewards from their relationships and will maintain rewarding relationships and discontinue unrewarding ones.

Key Elements: Actors, Inputs, and Outputs   The key elements of equity theory are the **actors,** or the people involved in an exchange relationship, and their inputs and outputs. An **input** is an investment in a relationship which usually entails costs. For example, the person who manages the finances and pays the bills in a relationship incurs time and energy costs. An **output** is something that a person receives from a relationship. The person who doesn't pay the bills enjoys the benefits of a financial service. Outputs, or outcomes, may be positive or negative. In many cases, A's input is B's outcome, and B's input is A's outcome. For example, a company pays (input) an employee (outcome) who gives her time and expertise (input) to further the company's goals (outcome).

The Ratio Concept   At the heart of equity theory is the **ratio concept.** Equity is an interactive equilibrium: Participants in an interaction are allocated outcomes proportional to their inputs. Equity exists in a relationship if each person's outcomes are proportional to his or her inputs. Equity, therefore, refers to equivalence of the outcome/input ratio of parties; inequity exists when the ratio of outcomes to inputs is unequal. Equity exists when the profits (rewards minus costs) of two actors are equal (Homans, 1961). Complications arise if two people have different views of what constitutes a legitimate investment, cost, or reward, and how they rank on each.

Groups try to maximize their rewards by developing systems of equitable apportionment and inducing members to adhere to the system by rewarding those who act equitably and punishing those who do not (Walster et al., 1978). Thus, groups and other organizations function as socially mediated remedies for hedonism in exchange relationships. Because equity operates in the absence of control, equity norms must be internalized.

Equity exists when a person perceives equality between the ratio of his or her own outcomes (O) to inputs (I) and the ratio of the other person's outcomes to inputs, where a and b represent two people (Adams, 1965):

$$\frac{Oa}{Ia} = \frac{Ob}{Ib}$$

However, this equity formula is less applicable to situations in which inputs and outcomes might be either positive or negative. The basic equity formula may be reconstructed as:

$$\frac{Oa - Ia}{|Ia|^{ka}} = \frac{Ob - Ib}{|Ib|^{kb}}$$

This formula proposes that equity prevails when the disparity between person A's outcomes and inputs and person B's outcomes and inputs are equivalently proportional to the absolute value of each of their inputs. The numerator is "profit," and the denominator adjusts for positive or negative signs of input. Each k takes on the value of either +1 or −1, depending on the valence of participants' inputs and gains (outcomes − inputs).

Reactions to Inequity   Suppose that you were hired by your firm last year with an annual salary of $85,000. You felt happy about your salary, until you learned that your colleague, whom you regard to be of equivalent skill and background, is paid $5,000 more per year than you. How do you deal with this inequity? When people find themselves participating in an inequitable relationship, they become distressed. The greater the perceived inequity, the more distressed people feel. Distress is an aversive state of tension that drives people to attempt to restore equity to the relationship.

According to the equity principle, people who believe they are underpaid should be dissatisfied and seek to restore equity (Walster, Berscheid, and Walster, 1973). For example, underpaid workers lower their level of effort and productivity to restore equity (Greenberg, 1988) and, in some cases, leave organizations characterized by inequity to join an organization where wages are more fairly distributed, even if they are less highly paid in absolute terms (Schmitt and Marwell, 1972). Furthermore, according to equity theory, people who are overpaid should also be dissatisfied.

Restoring Equity   Consider the case of Sarah, who believes she is underpaid in her organization. She came to this conclusion when she had a "telling" conversation with Jay, an employee in the same department at her level. Jay was hired one year after Sarah; he is considerably older and has more experience. Now that Sarah knows that Jay is paid substantially more than her, she is distressed by the apparent inequity. How can Sarah deal with this situation? There are six means by which people may eliminate the tension arising from inequity (Adams, 1965):

- alter one's inputs (Sarah can work less hard, take on fewer projects, take days off, etc.)
- alter one's outcomes (Sarah can ask for a raise or bonus.)
- cognitively distort one's inputs or outcomes (Sarah can minimize the importance of her contributions and maximize the perceived value of her outcomes; e.g., by deciding that work satisfaction is more important than a high salary.)
- leave the situation (Sarah can quit her job.)
- cognitively distort either the inputs or the outcomes of one's exchange partner (Sarah may view Jay as contributing more and earning less than he actually does.)
- change the object of comparison (Sarah may stop comparing herself to Jay and start comparing herself to someone with a similar amount of experience.)

The use of the first two strategies depends on whether the person has been over- or underrewarded. Overrewarded individuals can increase their inputs or decrease their outcomes to restore equal ratios, whereas underrewarded people must decrease their inputs or increase their outcomes. For example, people work harder if they think they are overpaid. Conversely, people may cheat or steal if they are underpaid (Greenberg, 1990).

Given the various methods of restoring equity, what determines which method will be used? According to the economic model, people engage in a cost-benefit analysis and choose the method that maximizes positive outcomes. Usually, this minimizes the necessity of increasing any of one's own inputs that are difficult or costly to change and also minimizes the necessity of real changes or cognitive changes in inputs/outcomes that are central to self-concept. Simply put, it is easier to change our cognitions than our behaviors. Further, this type of change minimizes the necessity of leaving the field or changing the object of social comparison once it has stabilized. Thus, we are not likely to ask for a salary cut if we think we are overpaid, but we are more inclined to regard the work as more demanding.

The equity drive is so strong that people who are denied the opportunity to restore equity will derogate others. People choose an equity-restoration method that maximizes positive outcomes with the least expenditure of costs. If distortion must occur, people focus on the other person's inputs or outcomes before distorting their own, especially if such distortion threatens their self-esteem. Leaving the situation and changing the object of comparison involve the highest costs, because they disrupt the status quo and violate justice beliefs.

Retributive Justice: Don't Get Mad, Get Even

Groups develop norms, rules, and expectations concerning appropriate behavior and the distribution of rewards. However, rules and norms can be broken, the decisions of groups and organizations ignored, and negotiated settlements reneged (Tyler and Lind, 1992). The question of how to respond to rule breaking is central to the viability of organized groups and negotiated interactions (Tyler and Smith, 1995). Retributive justice concerns people's reactions to rule-breaking behavior and examines situations in which people feel that sanctioning is appropriate. Equity theory suggests that people feel the need to restore equity after they have been victimized. People often feel that the restoration of equity is inadequate as a response to rule breaking, however, and that violators should be punished in some way.

The enforcement of informal norms is achieved through social mechanisms such as ostracism or alienation, whereas enforcement of formal norms is undertaken by appointed authorities. Responses to rule violation are a function of the type of rule that has been broken. For example, violations that lead to material harms are evaluated less severely than violations that lead to psychological or social harms (Alicke, 1990; Rossi, Waite, Bose, and Berk, 1974).

The rules that regulate the activities of members of social groups may be classified into four categories (Tyler and Smith, 1995) relevant to negotiation:

- **Regulation of personal material resource transactions.** These rules refer to maintenance of equitable exchange, contracts, and norms of reciprocity in exchange. Restitution or compensation of those who have suffered some material or financial loss is often expected by the affected party and by observers. This is most clearly seen in the reciprocity effect in negotiation (Gouldner, 1960). The reciprocity effect is so powerful that, even in situations in which one person is at an advantage compared to another, both parties cooperate in the attainment of a system that rewards both equally. For example, in dilemma games in which one person has leverage and another has potential regret, the parties alternate: each person takes a turn being the "sucker" so that the other party can win (Murnighan, King, and Schoumaker, 1990).

- **Regulation of personal status resource transactions.** These rules support the social order by specifying how people of equal and unequal status should interact. Breaches of status rules involve social psychological resources that are difficult to specify or quantify. The goal of retributive justice in such instances is to restore the former status quo (Heider, 1958; Miller and Vidmar, 1981), with apologies demanded and expected. If apologies are not forthcoming, retaliation or vengeance is likely (Ohbuchi, Kameda, and Agarie, 1989) and conflict escalates (Hogan and Emler, 1981).

- **Regulation of the use of collective material resources.** These resources may include public funds, public property, and natural resources such as a safe environment, clean air, etc. Reactions to rule breaking are linked to the severity of the threat. For example, when people believe that crime is on the increase, they give more severe sentences to rule breakers (Heider, 1958).

- **Support of fundamental collective values.** These rules protect basic human rights. Violations of these types of norms or moral values may involve victims but also include victimless crimes. The goal of retributive justice in these instances is to restore the validity of the violated norms or values and to ensure that they are not violated further (Miller and Vidmar, 1981).

Relative Deprivation: One Step Forward and Two Steps Back

People evaluate their resources by comparing them to resources of other people and to what they have experienced in the past (Stouffer et al., 1949; Runciman, 1966). Relative deprivation is the experience that one's outcomes are less than what they have been in the past. Relative deprivation is linked to feelings of anger and resentment (Crosby, 1976, 1984; Runciman, 1966). As an emotional state, relative deprivation results from: (1) wanting a particular goal, (2) not having the goal, and (3) feeling entitled to the goal (Crosby, 1982, 1984; Olson, Roese, Meen, and Robertson, 1995).

Central to relative deprivation is the choice of a comparison referent. People with the same objective outcome can potentially feel very happy or angry depending upon their comparison choice. The choice of a comparison target is a sequence of steps (Berger, Fisek, Norman, and Wagner, 1983; Levine and Moreland, 1987; Walker and Pettigrew, 1984) whereby a person (1) chooses the dimension on which to compare; (2) chooses to compare oneself to others as opposed to oneself at other points in time; (3) if comparing to oneself, chooses the points in time with which to compare; (4) if comparing to others, chooses others; (5) chooses to compare oneself as an individual to other individuals or chooses to think of oneself as a group member and compare one's group to other groups; (6) chooses groups with which to identify; and (7) chooses a group with which to compare one's own group.

As an example, consider Bernard, a 28-year-old Hispanic male in a *Fortune* 500 company. In Bernard's company, people move ahead by winning the favor of key senior executive managers. For example, people who are asked to play golf with senior managers and are invited to informal parties are almost destined for success. Bernard is thinking about how he is treated on these dimensions relative to others. He compares himself to his two closest associates, Marc and Deborah. He also reflects on how he was treated during his first six months at the company. Bernard comes to the conclusion that relative to Marc and Deborah, he is not "in the loop." Furthermore, he feels less in the loop now than he did when he first joined the company. Bernard feels a mixture of anger, resentment, and anxiety.

Individual versus Group Relative Deprivation

An important distinction should be made between **egoistic deprivation,** which is produced by interpersonal comparisons, and **group-based fraternal deprivation,** which is produced by intergroup comparisons (Runciman, 1966). How do people determine whether they should evaluate their outcomes in individual or group terms? For example, does Bernard feel slighted as an individual or does he conclude that the firm discriminates against Hispanics? The most important distinction between group and individual relative deprivation is not the comparison target but whether people think of themselves as group members or as isolated individuals.

Two types of identity contribute to self-concept: **personal identity,** or the unique or idiosyncratic aspects of oneself, and **social identity,** or the membership groups and social categories with which individuals identify (Hogg and Abrams, 1988; Tajfel and Turner, 1986). If personal identity is salient, people are more likely to make interpersonal comparisons between themselves and others; if relevant social identity or group membership is salient, people are more likely to make intergroup comparisons between their membership group and out-groups.

Comparison with Self

We saw in chapter 10 that a person's satisfaction with a relationship is a function of her comparison of her real-life circumstances to what she expects she should have. People make comparisons of their own circumstances across time (Davis, 1959, 1962; Gurr, 1970; Taylor, 1982). There are three different patterns of relative deprivation, each of which focuses on discrepancies between a person's expectations and capabilities (Gurr, 1970):

- **Decremental deprivation:** Discrepancies that occur when expectations are constant but capabilities to meet them decrease. Consider Tyler, an employee at a small computer software firm. Tyler has been with the firm for five years. This year, it was announced that there would be no raises because of poor profits during the previous year. Tyler feels disappointed and resentful.

- **Aspirational deprivation:** Discrepancies that occur when people's capabilities remain constant but their expectations increase. Consider Joyce, a manager at an advertising company. Joyce has an MBA from a top university. Recently, Joyce asked for a promotion. When her supervisor asked why a promotion should be considered, Joyce replied that she "had been at the firm long enough to either move up or out."

- **Progressive deprivation:** Discrepancies that occur when both expectations and capabilities increase but expectations increase at a faster rate than capabilities. Ella, an associate professor at a large state university, received tenure four years ago. Her annual raises have been rather modest—about 3 percent to 4 percent. After some investigation at her public library, Ella learned that starting salaries for assistant professors increased an average of 6 percent a year. Ella told her department head she wanted to "catch up."

Social Comparison: Green with Envy

Social comparison concerns when and how people make comparisons with others. People have a basic drive to evaluate their opinions and abilities accurately (Festinger, 1954). In the absence of direct, objective, physical standards, people evaluate themselves by comparison with other people. Three general social comparison targets may be distinguished: upward comparison, downward comparison, and comparison with similar others.

- **Upward comparison** occurs when people compare themselves to someone who is better off, more accomplished, or higher in status. The young entrepreneur starting his own software company may compare himself to Bill Gates. Oftentimes, people compare themselves upward for inspiration and motivation.

- **Downward comparison** occurs when people compare themselves to someone who is less fortunate, able, accomplished, or lower in status. For example, when a young manager's marketing campaign proves to be a complete flop, he may compare himself to a colleague whose decisions led to the loss of hundreds of thousands of dollars. Downward comparison often makes people feel better about their own state.

- **Comparison with similar others** occurs when people choose someone of similar background, skill, and ability with whom to compare. For example, John compares himself with other first-year MBA students when he wants to assess his skills in finance. Comparison with similar others is useful when people desire to have accurate appraisals of their abilities.

People make comparative judgments not only about their ability and opinions but also about their emotions, personality, and outcomes in social events. A number of goals and motives may drive social comparison, including:

- **Accurate self-evaluation:** The desire for truthful knowledge about oneself (even if the outcome is not favorable).

- **Self-enhancement:** The desire to maintain or enhance a positive view of oneself. This leads people to bias information in self-serving ways. Rather than seek truth, people seek comparisons that show them in a favorable light. People make downward comparisons with others who are less fortunate, less successful, and so forth (Wills, 1981).

- **Self-improvement:** People compare themselves with others who can serve as models of success (Taylor and Lobel, 1989). For example, a beginning chess player may compare him- or herself with a grand master. Upward comparison provides inspiration, insight, and challenge, but it can also lead to feelings of discouragement and incompetence.

Self-evaluation Maintenance

Social comparison is an inevitable fact of life in organizations and relationships. Even if we do not desire to compare ourselves with others, we inevitably hear about someone's higher salary, larger office, special opportunities, and grander budget. Social situations are constant reminders of how others—strangers, acquaintances, and friends—compare with us in terms of fortune, fame, and happiness. How do we react to social comparisons? Are we happy for other people—do we bask in their glory when they achieve successes—or are we threatened and angry?

People behave in ways that maximize their self-evaluation and minimize their losses in self-evaluation (Tesser, 1988). That is, people "regulate" their behaviors and cognitions to maintain positive self-regard. When does performance of another individual enhance our personal self-evaluation and when does it threaten our self-worth?

Antecedent Conditions   When we compare ourselves to another, we consider the relevance of the comparison to our self-concept. In chapter 7, we introduced self-schemas and noted that people have beliefs and values which reflect their central dimensions of the self. Some dimensions are highly self-relevant; others are irrelevant. It all depends upon how a person defines him- or herself. For example, consider Tim, a new account manager in a large firm. Tim prides himself on being a financial wizard, able to work the numbers, play the market, and manage his money successfully. On the other hand, Tim is not an athlete; he does not care about sports nor play them.

Performance   A second critical ingredient in the self-evaluation maintenance model is the quality of our own and the other person's performance on a particular dimension. For example, Tim probably has some idea of how well he is doing financially as compared to other account managers by looking at stock reports or asset portfolios.

Closeness   The final critical piece of the puzzle is the relationship between ourself and the target person. The performance of other people can affect our self-evaluation, especially when we are psychologically close to them. We focus on situations in which people who are close to us perform better than we do. For example, Tim compares himself to Laura, who is an accounts manager for a sister product in the firm.

The Comparison Effect   When we observe someone who is close to us performing extremely well in an area that we highly identify with, our self-evaluation is threatened. Such "upward" comparisons can lead to envy, frustration, anger, and even sabotage. Upon hearing that a member of one's cohort made some extremely timely investments in companies that have paid off multifold and is now a millionaire three times over, people probably feel threatened if they pride themselves on their financial wizardry. The fact that our colleague excels in an area that we pride ourselves on rubs salt in the wounds of the psyche. For example, if Tim learns that Laura did well in her performance review this year, he is likely to feel threatened and envious.

The Reflection Effect   When another person outperforms us on a behavior that is irrelevant to our self-definition, the better their performance and the closer our relationship, the more we gain in self-evaluation. We take pride in their success. Imagine, for example, that

Tim heard that his best friend, Jean, won an international sailboat race. Because sports are irrelevant to Tim's self-definition, Tim is not threatened. Furthermore, because Tim feels a connection to Jean, Jean's success reflects positively on Tim's evaluation of himself.

Responses to Comparison Effects   Jan and Ida are top salespeople at a competitive advertising agency; each of them vie for the biggest account. This situation has the makings of an uncomfortable social comparison effect. What choices do Jan and Ida have to handle the inevitable feelings of threat, anger, and contempt? They may each reduce their degree of closeness to the other. For example, they may minimize their friendship and invest in others who are less threatening to their self-definition, or Jan may decide to leave the company to reduce the feelings of constant threat. Another alternative is to change one's self-definition. Ida may pursue another area of interest, a different hobby, or redirect her personal pursuits to change the direct comparison. Another alternative is to change performance by improving. In some cases, this may be easy to do: Ida may sign up for a special training course that gives her an advantage over Jan. In other cases, this may be less feasible, especially if people perceive themselves as having invested all they can in their chosen domain.

Procedural Justice: It's Not Whether You Win or Lose . . .

Whereas distributive justice concerns the allocation of outcomes, **procedural justice** focuses on the manner in which allocators implement justice and the mechanisms and practices by which allocation is enacted (Thibaut and Walker, 1975). People are concerned with the *way* outcomes are distributed in groups (Thibaut and Walker, 1975, 1978; Leventhal, 1976, 1980). In addition to evaluating the fairness of outcomes, people evaluate the fairness of the procedures by which those outcomes are determined. People's evaluations of the fairness of decision-making procedures influence their reactions to the outcomes of those procedures, which is distinct from their reactions to the outcomes themselves. People's evaluations of the fairness of procedures determine their satisfaction and willingness to comply with outcomes.

There are two ways of factoring procedural justice into social justice concerns (Lind and Tyler, 1988). One is the traditional model of informed self-interest (Thibaut and Walker, 1978; Leventhal, 1980). The other has to do with group identification processes.

Procedural Justice Based on Self-Interest

According to the self-interest perspective, people seek control over their decisions because they are fundamentally concerned with their own outcomes (Thibaut and Walker, 1978). The shift from concern with decision outcomes to processes of reaching decisions posits a recognition by people that they cannot always maintain complete control over their outcomes when interacting with others. People join and remain in groups because they believe they will gain in the long run. In this sense, people must balance two conflicting objectives: (1) short-term personal gain and (2) long-term relationship maintenance. Concerns about group harmony emphasize the importance of procedural justice.

Procedural Justice Based on Group Values

According to the group value model, procedures carry symbolic information about how members of a group are viewed by their organization (Lind and Tyler, 1988). People often focus on this symbolic information (rather than instrumental concerns) to evaluate the fairness of organizational procedures and policies, and seek identification with groups for reasons above and beyond pure self-interest. Why should people care about procedures? Procedural aspects of justice communicate two symbolic messages about group membership: (1) whether individuals are respected members of a group, and (2) whether they should feel pride in the group (Tyler, Degoey, and Smith, 1996). These messages are conveyed by three relational aspects of the actions of authorities: actions that indicate neutrality, trustworthiness, and status recognition.

Group procedures in accord with fundamental values of the group increase procedural justice. Evaluation of the group, commitment to the group, and loyalty increase to the extent that group members view the group processes as "fair."

If people were purely motivated by self-interest, they would positively evaluate outcomes that were good for themselves and negatively evaluate outcomes that were not so good. How such outcomes occurred would not be important to them. Consider Conlon's (1993) examination of the procedure for appealing parking violations on a university campus. Faculty and staff (who were found to have greater levels of commitment to the university than students) perceived greater procedural justice than students when their appeals were granted but less procedural justice when their appeals were denied—clearly suggesting that the outcome influences fairness perceptions. Granted appeals resulted in more favorable perceptions of procedural justice, distributive justice, and appeal board satisfaction, however, than did denied appeals, supporting the self-interest perspective.

Group Balance: Attraction and Respect

What does it take for a group to be successful? As we saw in chapter 9, it certainly helps for a group to be cohesive—that is, for the members to like one another. However, cohesion is not enough to ensure success. Groups also need to have the support and respect of relevant organizational authorities. So, groups need two things: attraction among members and respect from relevant outside authorities (Thompson, Kray, and Lind, 1994). A typology of decision-making groups may be derived from these two sources of support, as shown in Figure 11–1.

The "inner circle" is a group whose members are highly attracted to one another and whose decisions are respected by authorities. "Mutual admiration" groups are those with members who are highly attracted to one another but, as a group, receive little or no respect from

FIGURE 11–1. Group Balance Model of Decision Making

Respect from relevant authorities	Attraction among group members: Low	Attraction among group members: High
Low	"Tokens" • Low cooperation • High criticism	"Mutual admiration" • High cooperation • Low criticism
High	"Chosen" • Low cooperation • Low criticism	"Inner circle" • High cooperation • High criticism

outside authorities. "Chosen" groups are those with little attraction among members, but which are accorded high respect from organizational authorities. "Tokens" are groups composed of members who have little or no common bonds and whose decisions as a group are not valued.

Consider how well each of these groups would do facing two types of tasks: one calling for high cooperation and trust for success; the other calling for high criticism to avoid disastrous group think. (If groups are low on criticism, they make bad choices.)

Only the inner circle groups do well on tasks that call for cooperation and critical judgment (Thompson, Kray, and Lind, 1994). Mutual admiration groups cooperate but do not exercise critical judgment, presumably because they are reluctant to criticize others. The "chosen" fare poorly in both tasks; the "tokens" fail to cooperate.

Distributed versus Concentrated Unfairness

Within an organizational setting, many acts of unfair or unjust behavior may occur. For example, a person of color may be passed over for a promotion. A woman with managerial skills may be relegated to administrative and secretarial tasks. How do employees react to injustice in the organization? Consider two hypothetical companies: A and B. In each company, the overall incidence of unfair behavior is identical. In company A, the unfair incidences (i.e., percentage of total acts) are targeted toward a single individual—a black female; in company B, the unfair incidences are spread among three individuals—a black female, a Hispanic male, and an older, handicapped white male. The fact that the incidences are concentrated on a single individual or spread out over many organizational members should be irrelevant, if the overall incidence of unfairness in each organization is the same. In practice, however, this is not what happens.

In a simulated organization, each of three employees was victimized in one out of three interactions with a manager. In another company, one of the three employees was victimized in all three out of three interactions with a manager; the two other employees were treated fairly. Thus, in both companies, the incidence of unfairness was identical. However, groups' overall judgment of the unfairness of the manager was greater when the injustice was spread across members than when it was concentrated on one individual. Most disconcertingly, targets of discrimination were marginalized by other group members. Blaming-the-victim-effects may be more rampant when individuals are the sole targets of discrimination—ironically, when they need the most support (Lind, Kray, and Thompson, 1996).

SELF-INTEREST AND FAIRNESS IN NEGOTIATIONS

Imagine that you are being recruited for a position in firm A. Your colleague, Jay, of similar background and skill, is also being recruited by firm A. Firm A has made you and Jay the following salary offers:

Your salary:	$75,000
Jay's salary:	$95,000

Your other option is to take a position at firm B, which has made you an offer. Firm B has also made your colleague, Ines, an offer:

Your salary:	$72,000
Ines' salary:	$72,000

Which job offer do you take, firm A's or firm B's? If you follow the principles of rational judgment outlined in chapters 5 and 6, you take firm A's offer—it pays more money. However, if you are like most people, you prefer firm B's offer—you don't like feeling you're being treated unfairly (Bazerman, Loewenstein, and White, 1992).

Fairness and Social Utility

The example above illustrates that people do not always try to maximize their self-interest; they are concerned about the outcomes of others in their organizations or comparison groups. Concern for the outcomes of others exemplifies **social utility** (as opposed to individual utility).

Consider the following situation: You and a college friend have developed a potentially revolutionary (and profitable) idea for a new kind of water ski (see Loewenstein, Thompson, and Bazerman, 1989). You've spent about half a year in your dorm basement developing a prototype of the new invention. Your friend had the original idea; you developed the design and materials and assembled the prototype. The two of you talk to a patent lawyer about getting a patent, and the lawyer tells you that there is a pending patent on a similar product, but the company will offer you $3,000 for one of the innovative features of your design. You and your friend gladly accept. What division of the $3,000 between you and your friend would you find to be most satisfying?

People's preferences for several possible distributions of the money for themselves and the other person were assessed (Loewenstein, Thompson, and Bazerman, 1989). People's utility functions were social rather than individual, meaning that individual satisfaction was strongly influenced by the payoffs received by the other as well as the payoffs received by the self (see Figure 11–2). Social utility functions were tent-shaped. The most satisfying outcome was equal shares for the self and other ($1,500 apiece). Discrepancies between payoffs to the self versus the other led to lower satisfaction. However, social utility functions were lopsided in that advantageous inequity (self receives more than other) was preferable to disadvantageous inequity (other receives more than self). Further, the relationship people had with the other party mattered: In positive or neutral relationships, people preferred equality; in negative relationships, people preferred advantageous inequity.

People will pass up outcomes that entail one person receiving more than others and settle for a settlement of lower joint value but equal-appearing shares (McClelland and Rohrbaugh, 1978). This is especially true when resources are "lumpy" (i.e., hard to divide into pieces) such as an oriental rug (Messick, 1993). Concern for fair outcomes often thwarts the attainment of level 2 and 3 integrative agreements.

Fairness and Strikes

The likelihood and length of strikes may be directly predicted by the difference in perceived fair wages between management and union (Thompson and Loewenstein, 1992). That is, if management and union have widely differing perceptions of what constitutes a fair settlement, a strike is more likely. Even more disconcertingly, providing each party (management and labor) with additional unbiased information concerning the dispute has the effect of exaggerating each party's perceptions of fair settlement outcomes and excluding parties in their positions. This is a good example of how more information is not always better in negotiations.

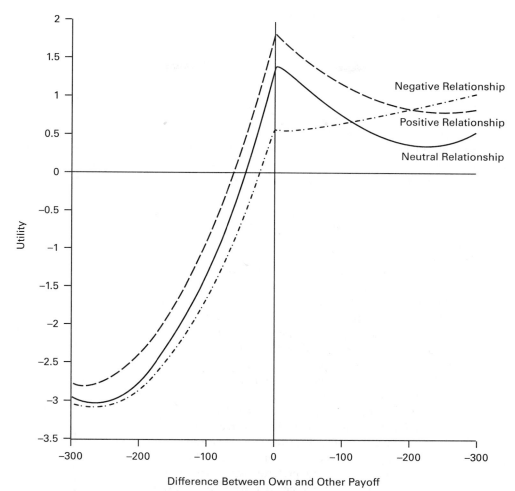

FIGURE 11–2. Social Utility as a Function of Discrepancy between Our Own and Others' Outcomes
Source: Loewenstein, G. F., L. Thompson, and M. H. Bazerman (1989). Social utility and decision making in interpersonal contexts. *Journal of Personality and Social Psychology* **57**(3): 426–441.

Ruthless Competitors, Saints, and Loyalists

Have you ever wondered whether most people are truly interested in other people or are only concerned about their own profit? To examine this question, MBA students were given several hypothetical scenarios, like the situation involving the ski invention, and asked what division of resources (and in some cases, costs) they preferred. Further, people made responses for different kinds of relationships: friendly ones, antagonistic ones, and neutral ones (Loewenstein, Thompson, and Bazerman, 1989). Three types of people were identified:

- **Loyalists** prefer to split resources equally, except in antagonistic relationships (27 percent).
- **Saints** prefer to split resources equally no matter whether relationships are positive, neutral, or negative (24 percent).

- **Ruthless competitors** prefer to have more resources than the other party, regardless of relationship (36 percent).

Competitors and Cooperators and Triangles

Michael thinks it's a dog-eat-dog world, so he behaves competitively. In contrast, Sheila thinks that the world is more complex. She thinks some people are competitive and others are cooperative. How do Michael and Sheila's views of the world affect their behavior? According to the **triangle hypothesis** (Kelly and Stahelski, 1970), people like Michael see the world to be more homogeneous than is really the case, and so they act competitively with everyone. In contrast, people like Sheila see the world as more complex, with two kinds of people: cooperators and competitors. Consequently, they adjust their behavior to respond to whom they are dealing with. What happens when a cooperator meets a competitor? The cooperator will begin by being cooperative, but then become competitive. This, of course, feeds into competitors' views that the world is full of competitive people.

The Problem of Fairness: What Goes Wrong?

If people care about fairness, why should there be conflict at all? Negotiated agreements are difficult to reach, despite people's apparently benevolent motivations. So what is wrong? Are people lying when they say that they care about fairness? Not necessarily. To address this enigma, we need to consider three things: (1) the relationship between fairness and satisfaction, (2) the relationship between satisfaction and choice, and (3) interpretations of fairness.

Fairness and Satisfaction

We might assume that fairness is highly related to satisfaction: Fair situations would seem to be regarded as more satisfying. But this is not necessarily so. The processes and factors that govern satisfaction are different from those that govern fairness (Messick and Sentis, 1983). Social and historical factors influence judgments of satisfaction. In contrast, the main determinant of fairness judgments is social comparison. People want or prefer more than what they regard as fair (the hedonic principle in equity theory). In short, our preferences are more primary, or immediate, than our social concerns. People are more in touch with their own preferences than with the concerns of others. We have immediate access to our preferences; fairness is a secondary judgment. For this reason, fairness judgments are likely to be tainted by preferences. Because preferences are primary and immediate, they often color a person's evaluation of fairness in a self-serving fashion. In a sense, our preferences act as a self-serving prime (chapter 7) on our judgments of fairness.

Satisfaction and Choice

Consider the following in terms of how satisfying you find these allocations of money: a $400 self/$400 other versus a $600 self/$800 other split. Most people evaluate the equal division of resources—the $400/$400 split—as preferable to the unequal allocation. When faced with an actual choice between the two options, however, most prefer the split that offers them the larger amount of resources: Most people choose the $600/$800 split over the $400/$400 split. People are concerned primarily with their own payoffs when choosing between options, but they focus on interpersonal comparisons when evaluating abstract situations (Bazerman, Loewenstein, and White, 1992).

Interpretations of Fairness

Fairness is not a normative or absolute construct; it is socially defined. What is fair to one person may not be fair in the eyes of another. There are multiple interpretations of fairness—all equally valid in different situations. As we saw in the coalition example in chapter 9, there is no single prescriptive method of fair allocation (Raiffa, 1982). For example, consider a group of three individuals who go out for dinner. One person orders a bottle of expensive red wine, an appetizer, and a pricey main course. Another abstains from drinking and orders two inexpensive side dishes. The third orders a moderately priced meal. Then the bill arrives. The wine drinker immediately suggests that the group split the bill into thirds, explaining that this is the simplest approach. The teetotaler winces and suggests that the group ask the waitress to bring three separate bills. The third group member argues that, because he is a graduate student, the two others should cover the bill, and he invites the two over to his house the next week for pizza. This example illustrates that in any situation, there are as many interpretations of fairness as there are parties involved. Two people may both truly want a fair settlement, but they may have very different and equally justifiable ideas about what is fair.

Egocentric Interpretations of Fairness   You have worked for seven hours and have been paid $25. Another person has worked for ten hours. It is piecemeal work. How much do you think the other person should get paid? If you're like most people, you believe the other person should get paid more for doing more work—about $30.29 on average. This is hardly a self-serving response. Now, let's turn this question on its head: The other person has worked for seven hours and been paid $25. You have worked for ten hours. What is a fair wage for you to be paid? The average response is $35.24 (Messick and Sentis, 1979). The difference between $35.24 and $30.29 is about $5, and illustrates the phenomenon of egocentric bias: People pay themselves substantially more than they are willing to pay others for doing the same task.

Allocating more money to ourselves is only one way that people show egocentric bias. Egocentric judgments of fairness also emerge in other ways. For example, people select fairness rules in a self-serving fashion: When people make minimal contributions, they often prefer equality rather than equity; however, when people's contributions are substantial, they opt for equity rather than equality (van Avermaet, 1974). Even if people agree to use the same fairness rule, they think it is fair for them to get more than others in a similar situation because they think they would have contributed more (Messick and Rutte, 1992).

Another way people can engage in egocentric evaluation is to selectively weight different aspects of the exchange situation in a way that favors themselves. Consider a situation in which participants are told how many hours they had worked on a task of assembling questionnaires as well as how many questionnaires they completed. The key dimensions are hours worked and productivity. Participants are then asked to indicate what they believe is fair payment for their work. Those who worked long hours but did not complete many questionnaires emphasize the importance of hours; in contrast, those who worked short hours but completed many questionnaires emphasize quantity completed. Thus, people emphasize the dimension that favors themselves (van Avermaet, 1974).

Appeals to equality can also be self-serving (Messick, 1993). At a superficial level, equality is trivially simple. Employing equality as a division rule in practice, however, is very complex because there are several dimensions on which equality may be established (see Harris and Joyce, 1980). Furthermore, equality is not consistently applied. For example, when the outcome is evenly divisible by the number in the group, people will use equality more than when even division is not possible (Allison and Messick, 1990).

Thus, appeals to equity and equality are often self-serving. Why is this? There are three reasons: disguised self-interest, cognitive factors, and motivated cognition.

Disguised self-interest.   The examples above suggest that people are fairly transparent; they immediately seize upon any opportunity to favor themselves. However, fairness is not always a thin subterfuge for real self-interest. In many situations, people would ultimately be better off by not having egocentric views. Consider arbitration situations: People's predictions of judges' behavior are biased in a manner that favors their own side. Efforts to de-bias litigants meet with virtually no success. Informing parties of the potential bias or providing them with information about the opponent's point of view do little to assuage biased perceptions of fairness, suggesting that egocentric biases are deeply ingrained (Babcock, Loewenstein, Issacharoff, and Camerer, 1995).

Cognitive factors.   A more benign cause of egocentric judgments holds that people really do care about fairness (social utility), but they do not realize that they are behaving in a self-interested fashion. Egocentric judgments of responsibility and fairness are attributable to ways in which people process information. There are several cognitive mechanisms by which egocentric judgments could develop:

- **Selective encoding and storage.** Our own thoughts attract attention away from thinking about the contributions of others. We rehearse our own actions and fit them into our own cognitive schemas, which facilitates retention and subsequent retrieval. If encoding mechanisms lead to self-serving judgments of fairness, then a person who learns of the facts before knowing which side of a dispute he or she is on should not be egocentric. However, the egocentric effect still emerges even when the direction of self-interest occurs subsequent to the processing of information, suggesting that encoding is not the sole mechanism producing egocentric judgment.

- **Differential retrieval.** When making judgments of responsibility, people ask themselves, "How much did I contribute?", and they attempt to retrieve specific instances (Ross and Sicoly, 1979). Because people's self-schemas are so well developed (chapter 7), it is cognitively easier to retrieve instances involving oneself. There is a positive correlation between recall and responsibility attributions, similar to the availability bias (Kahneman and Tversky, 1982).

- **Informational disparity.** People are often not privy to the contributions made by others. This suggests that information, not goals, mediates the self-serving effect. Even when information is constant but goals are manipulated, however, the self-serving effects emerge (see Thompson and Loewenstein, 1992), suggesting that information itself is not solely responsible for the egocentric effect (see Camerer and Loewenstein, 1993).

Motivated cognition.   Most situations are ambiguous enough that people can construe them in a fashion that favors their own interests. One unfortunate consequence is that people will develop different perceptions of fairness even when they are presented with the same evidence.

Consider a strike situation in which people are provided with background information on a hypothetical teachers' union and board of education. The background material is constructed so that some facts favor the teachers and other facts favor the board of education. On balance, the facts are equal. In one condition, both disputants are presented with extensive, identical background information concerning the dispute. In another condition, disputants are presented with abbreviated, much less extensive background information. Those who have extensive information are more likely to go on strikes which last longer and are more costly to both parties, compared to disputants who do not have extensive information, even though information is identical for both sides (Thompson and Loewenstein, 1992). Information, even when shared among parties, creates ambiguity and provides fertile ground for unchecked self-interest to operate.

Fairness as a Social Decision Heuristic

The distribution of resources is an unavoidable and inevitable aspect of negotiation. What qualities should we look for in a good social decision heuristic? Messick (1993) suggests the following: consistency, simplicity, effectiveness, and justifiability. Further, fairness heuristics should not violate the prescriptions of economic models, produce pareto-suboptimal agreements, nor be inconsistent (Bazerman, 1993). To this list of qualities we add consensus, generality, and satisfaction (Levine and Thompson, 1996).

Consistency

One of the hallmarks of a good social decision heuristic is consistency or invariance across settings, time, and with respect to the enforcer of the procedure. For example, most of us would be outraged if those managers up for performance review did better if the meeting was scheduled in the morning versus the afternoon. This is a clear bias of the interviewer. Fairness procedures are often inconsistent because of heuristic decision making. Heuristic judgment processes are necessary when normative decision procedures are absent or when their application would be inefficient. Unfortunately, people are typically unaware of the powerful contextual factors that affect their judgments of fairness.

Simplicity

Social justice procedures should be clearly understood by the individuals who employ them and those who are affected by them. Group members should be able to articulate easily the procedure used to allocate resources. This allows the procedure to be implemented with full understanding and the outcomes of the procedure to be evaluated against a clear criterion.

Effectiveness

Social justice procedures should produce a choice; the allocation procedure should yield a clear decision. If the procedure does not produce such a decision, then conflict may erupt among group members who try to identify and implement a decision post hoc.

Justifiability

Social justice procedures should be justifiable to other parties. A social justice procedure may be consistent, simple, and effective, but if it cannot be justified, it is not likely to be successful. For example, suppose that a manager of an airline company decides that raises will be based upon hair color: Blondes get big raises, brunettes don't. This policy is consistent, simple, and effective, but hardly justifiable.

Consensus

Group members should agree upon the method of allocation. Effective social justice procedures are often internalized by group members, and norms act as strong guidelines for behavior and decision making in groups. Because social justice procedures often outlive current group members, new members are frequently indoctrinated with procedures that the group has found useful in the past (Bettenhausen and Murnighan, 1985; Levine and Moreland, 1994).

Generalizability

The social justice procedure should be applicable to a wide variety of situations. Procedures and norms develop when intragroup conflict is expected, enduring, or recurrent, and effective policy therefore specifies outcome distribution across situations.

Satisfaction

The procedure should be satisfying to group members. This increases the likelihood they will use it in the future and contributes to the survival of the group.

CONCLUSION

We have examined the ways in which issues of social justice and fairness affect the processes and outcomes of negotiation. Fairness is not an objective construct; there is no rational method for fair allocation. There are as many different ways to implement fairness as there are people involved in conflict. Even if a method is agreed upon by interdependent parties, there is no guarantee that the method will produce an integrative agreement.

TAKE-AWAYS

- Be aware of which social justice principle (equity, equality, or need) operates in a particular situation.
- If conflict erupts, don't ask yourself or the other party *whether* you want to be fair. Rather, ask each other what *principle* of fairness you are employing.
- Look for egocentric bias in your own judgments of fairness.
- Remember: More information (even ambiguous information) can often fuel the fires of conflict.
- When designing and implementing a system for allocating scarce resources (like raises, promotions, awards, etc.), focus on consistency, simplicity, effectiveness, justifiability, consensus, generalizability, and satisfaction of the parties involved.

CHAPTER 12

Social Dilemmas and Other Noncooperative Games:
We're All in This Together

Several members of a well-respected, decentralized research and development department in an organization had a need for laboratory space. The department made a decision several years ago that each organizational member should develop and maintain his or her own laboratory space so as to allow for specialization and reduce bureaucratic control and overhead. The organization realized that such a system might lead to an eventual shortage of laboratory space, however, and it was agreed that, each year, members would make a laboratory facilities request that would be considered by a committee. The committee was charged with the task of allocating research space on a yearly basis. External funding was the primary criteria that determined allocations: The greater one's external funding, the more laboratory resources were granted.

The committee began to encounter a problem as the organization grew in personnel, but not in physical facilities. Every year, each member requested his or her previous allocation of laboratory facilities and augmented this with an additional request for more resources. Each year, the committee struggled to meet basic needs, and turned down all new requests. Precedent became the key factor in determining allocations.

As the organization aged, it acquired more and more organizational members, each with their own idiosyncratic laboratory needs. The physical facilities of the organization were at a maximum. This had several undesirable consequences: First, organizational members who did not require laboratory space continued to request it for fear of not having space in the future when and if they needed it.

Second, and most seriously, the space shortage drastically curtailed the selection of new organizational members. Whereas the department realized that attracting new members was ultimately necessary for the survival and development of the organization as a whole, old-timers were reluctant and often outright opposed to recruiting new members, especially those who had expansive laboratory needs.

When the department approached the larger organization about the dilemma, they were politely told to solve the problem internally, and recommended that members share space. The organizational members were strongly opposed to this suggestion. Morale and cooperation in the department declined steadily. After several lean hiring seasons, the organization's reputation and overall productivity suffered seriously. When asked to explain the ultimate demise of the R&D group, individual members pointed to the unbridled greed of others in the department.

It seems preposterous that intelligent and well-meaning people could engage in behaviors that seem so insensible. The R&D group is not unique. Similar examples of competitive behavior leading to huge financial losses occurred in the cola advertising wars and the airline wars of the 1980s, and the telephone long-distance rate wars of the 1990s. Other examples include population control, free trade, the budget deficit, cartels, and unionization.

So far, we have focused on cooperative bargaining situations, wherein people must be in mutual agreement for an outcome to be binding. In non-cooperative bargaining situations, parties are **interdependent** with respect to outcomes, but make **independent** decisions. Such bargaining situations are **noncooperative,** because parties do not need to cooperate for an outcome to be reached. For example, a cola company may decide to engage in a negative advertising campaign. The company's main competitor may then start to advertise negatively. As a result, both companies suffer.

Suppose that you are the head of a large airline company and it has been announced that a smaller airline is for sale. You would love to acquire the smaller airline. However, you know your competitors would also like to acquire the airline. Do you make an offer? Will you engage in a bidding war?

Noncooperative games focus on the distributive dimension of negotiation—that is, how much of the pie each party claims. Nevertheless, the integrative dimension is still present: Because most situations involve costs for delay, parties have an incentive to settle quickly; their outcomes deteriorate by prolonging settlement. However, this places negotiators in a weak position; if a negotiator has costs for time, and the other party knows this, he or she may be exploited. These situations—cola wars and bidding wars—are social dilemmas because the negotiator is unsure how to make choices. Some choices risk exploitation; other choices risk antagonizing others.

COMMON MYTHS ABOUT INTERDEPENDENT DECISION MAKING

In approaching dilemma-type situations, people are often guilty of mythological thinking. Next, we expose the three leading myths that impair decision making before presenting what we believe is an effective decision-making strategy.

Myth 1: "It's a Game of Wits: I Can Outsmart Them"

Many people believe that they can stay one move ahead of their competitor. However, effective decision making in noncooperative situations is not about outsmarting people. It is unrealistic to believe we can consistently outwit others—an egocentric illusion. A better and more realistic goal is to understand the incentive structure in the situation and take the perspective of the other party. For example, imagine that the person you are dealing with is your identical twin—it's pretty hard to outwit yourself!

Myth 2: "It's a Game of Strength: Show 'em You're Tough"

This negotiator goes into battle fighting fire with fire. The problem is that this behavior can unnecessarily escalate conflict situations, especially if people have a false sense of uniqueness (see chapter 8).

Myth 3: "It's a Game of Chance: Hope for the Best"

This negotiator believes that outcomes are not predictable and depend on ever-changing aspects of the situation: personality, mood, time of day, and so on. This person erroneously believes that it either takes a long time to figure out a good strategy or it's just downright impossible.

In this chapter, we suggest that dilemma-type situations are neither games of wits, strength, or chance, but decision opportunities. We'll use the principles of logic, game theory, and psychology to optimally deal with these situations.

DILEMMAS

In organizational and group life, our outcomes depend upon the actions of others. The situation that results when people engage in behaviors that seem perfectly rational on an individual basis but lead to collective disaster, such as a bidding war or what happened in the R&D department, is a social dilemma. Next, we discuss two kinds of social dilemmas: two-person dilemmas and multiperson dilemmas. The two-person dilemma is the **prisoner's dilemma;** the multiperson dilemma is a **social dilemma.** We'll discuss both dilemmas as problems for people and groups in conflict and how they may be effectively handled.

THE PRISONER'S DILEMMA

Thelma and Louise are common criminals who have just been arrested on suspicion of burglary. There is enough evidence to convict each suspect of a minor breaking-and-entering crime, but insufficient evidence to convict the suspects on a more serious felony charge of burglary and assault. The district attorney separates Thelma and Louise immediately after their arrest. Each suspect is approached separately and presented with two options: confess to the serious burglary charge or remain silent (not confess). The consequences of each course of action depend on what the other decides to do. The catch is that Thelma and Louise must make their choices independently. They cannot communicate in any way prior to making an independent, irrevocable decision. The decision situation that faces each suspect is illustrated in Figure 12–1.

Louise \ Thelma	Do not confess (remain silent)	Confess
Do not confess (remain silent)	A T = 1 yr L = 1 yr	B T = 0 yrs L = 15 yrs
Confess	C T = 15 yrs L = 0 yrs	D T = 10 yrs L = 10 yrs

FIGURE 12–1. Consequences of Thelma and Louise's Behaviors
Note: Entries represent prison term length. T = Thelma's term length; L = Louise's term length.

Inspection of Figure 12–1 indicates that Thelma and Louise will go to prison between 0 and 15 years, depending upon what the other partner chooses. Obviously, this is an important decision. Imagine that you are an advisor to Thelma. Your concern is not morality or ethics; you're simply trying to get her a shorter sentence. What do you advise her to do?

Ideally, it is desirable for both suspects to not confess, thereby minimizing the prison sentence to one year for each (cell A). This option is risky, however. If one confesses, then the suspect who does not confess goes to prison for the maximum sentence of 15 years—an extremely undesirable outcome (cell B or C). In fact, the most desirable situation from the standpoint of each suspect would be to confess and have the other person not confess. This would mean that the confessing suspect would be released and his or her partner would go to prison for the maximum sentence of 15 years. Given these contingencies, what should Thelma do? Before reading further, stop and think about what you think her best course of action is.

THE DILEMMA AND THE PARADOX

The answer is not easy, which is why the situation is a dilemma. It will soon be demonstrated that when each person pursues the course of action that is most rational from her point of view, the result is mutual disaster. That is, both Thelma and Louise go to prison for 10 years (cell D). The paradox of the prisoner's dilemma is that the pursuit of individual self-interest leads to collective disaster. There is a conflict between individual and collective well-being that derives from rational analysis. It is easy for Thelma and Louise (as well as for the R&D department members) to *see* that each could do better by cooperating, but it is not easy to know *how* to implement this behavior. The players can get there only with coordinated effort.

Cooperation and Defection as Unilateral Choices

We will use the prisoner's dilemma situation depicted in Figure 12–1 to analyze players' decision making. We will refer to the choices that players make in this game as **cooperation** and **defection,** depending upon whether they remain silent or confess. The language of cooperation and defection allows the prisoner's dilemma game structure to be meaningfully extended to other situations that do not involve criminals, but nevertheless have the same underlying structure, such as whether an airline company should bid for a smaller company, whether a cola company should engage in negative advertising, or whether a department member should demand lab space.

Rational Analysis

We will use the logic of game theory to provide a rational analysis of this situation. In our analysis, we will consider three different cases: (1) one-shot, nonrepeated play situations (as in the case of Thelma and Louise); (2) the case in which the decision is repeated for a finite number of terms (such as might occur in a yearly election for a position on a five-year task force); and (3) the case in which the decision is repeated for a potentially infinite number of trials or the end is unknown (such as might occur in industries like phone companies, airlines, and cola manufacturers).

Case 1: One-shot Decision

As we noted in chapter 4, game theoretic analysis relies on the principle of dominance detection. That is, the easiest and first principle we should try to invoke is to detect whether one strategy, confession or remaining silent, is dominant. We want to search for a strategy that will result in a better outcome no matter what the other decides to do.

Suppose that you are Thelma and your partner in crime is Louise. First, consider what happens if Louise remains silent (does not confess). Thus, we are focusing on the first row in Figure 12–1. If you remain silent, this puts you in cell A: You both get one year. This outcome is not too bad, but maybe you could do better. Suppose that you decide to confess. This puts you in cell B: You get 0 years and Louise gets 15 years. If Louise remains silent, what do you want to do? Certainly no prison sentence is much better than a one-year sentence, so confession seems like the optimal choice for you to make, given that Louise does not confess.

Now, what happens if Louise confesses? In this situation, we are focusing on row 2. If you remain silent, this puts you in cell C: You get 15 years and Louise gets 0 years. This is not very good for you. Now, suppose that you confess; this puts you in cell D: You both get 10 years. Neither outcome is splendid, but 10 years is certainly better than 15 years. Given that Louise confesses, what do you want to do? The choice amounts to whether you want to go to prison for 15 years or 10 years. Again, confession is the optimal choice for you.

We have just illustrated the principle of dominance detection: No matter what Louise does (remains silent or confesses), it is better for Thelma to confess. Confession is a dominant strategy; under all possible states of the world, players in this game should choose to confess. We know that Louise is smart and has looked at the situation and its contingencies in the same way as Thelma and has reached the same conclusion. In this sense, mutual defection is an **equilibrium outcome.** No player can unilaterally (single-handedly) improve her outcome by making a different choice.

Thus, both Thelma and Louise are led through rational analysis to confess and they collectively end up in cell D, where they both go to prison for a long period of time. This seems both unfortunate and avoidable. Certainly, both suspects would prefer to be in cell A than in cell D. Is there some way to escape the tragic outcomes produced by the prisoner's dilemma? Are we doomed to collective disaster in such situations?

It would seem that players might extricate themselves from the dilemma if they could communicate, but we have already noted that communication is outside of the bounds of the noncooperative game. Further, because the game structure is noncooperative, any deals that players might make with one another are nonbinding. For example, antitrust legislation prohibits companies from price fixing, which means that any communication that occurs between companies regarding price fixing is unenforceable, not to mention punishable by law.

What other mechanism might allow parties in such situations to avoid the disastrous outcome produced by mutual defection? One possibility is to have both parties make those decisions over **multiple trials.** That is, suppose that the parties did not make a single choice but instead made a choice, received feedback about the other player's choice, experienced the consequences, and then made another choice. Perhaps repeated interaction with the other person would provide a mechanism for parties to coordinate their actions. If the game is to be played more than once, players might reason that by cooperating on the first round, cooperation may be elicited in subsequent periods. We consider that situation next.

Case 2: Repeated Interaction over a Fixed Number of Trials

Instead of making a single choice and living with the consequence, suppose that Thelma and Louise were to play the game in Figure 12–1 a total of ten times. It might seem strange to think about criminals doing this, so it may be useful to think about two political candidates deciding whether or not to engage in negative campaigning (hereafter referred to as campaigning). There are term limits in their state—they can run and hold office for a maximum of five years. There is an election every year. During each election period, each candidate makes an independent choice (to campaign or not), then learns of the other's choice (to campaign or not) and experiences the resultant outcome. After the election, the candidates consider the same alternatives once again and make an independent choice; this continues for five separate elections.

How does game theory allow us to analyze this situation? We will use the concept of dominance as applied above, but we need another tool that tells us how to analyze the repeated nature of the game. Fortunately, game theory provides such a mechanism. **Backward induction** is the mechanism by which a person decides what to do in a repeated game situation, by looking backward from the last stage of the game.

We begin by examining what players should do in election 5 (the last election). If the candidates are making their choices in the last election, the game is identical to that analyzed in the one-shot case above. Thus, the logic of dominant strategies applies, and we are left with the conclusion that each candidate will choose to campaign. Now, given that we know that each candidate will campaign in the last election, what will they do in the fourth election?

From a candidate's standpoint, the only reason to cooperate (or to not campaign) is to influence the behavior of the other party in the subsequent election. That is, a player might signal a willingness to cooperate by making a cooperative choice in the period before. We have already determined that it is a foregone conclusion that both candidates will defect (choose to campaign) in the last election, so it is futile to choose the cooperative (no campaigning) strategy in the fourth election. So, what about the third election? Given that candidates will not cooperate in the last election, nor in the second-to-last election, there is little point to cooperating in the third-to-last election for the same reason that cooperation was deemed to be ineffective in the second-to-last election. As it turns out, this logic can be applied to every election in such a backward fashion. Moreover, this is true in any situation with a finite number of elections. This leaves us with the conclusion that defection remains the dominant strategy even in the repeated trial case. Formally, if the prisoner's dilemma is repeated finitely, all Nash equilibria of the resulting sequential games have the property that the noncooperative outcome, which is pareto-inferior, occurs in each period, no matter how large the number of periods.

This is surely disappointing news. It suggests that cooperation is not possible even in long-term relationships. This runs counter to intuition, observation, and logic, however. We must consider another case, arguably more realistic of the situations we want to study in most circumstances, in which repeated interaction continues for an infinite or indefinite amount of time.

Case 3: Repeated Interaction for an Infinite or Indefinite Amount of Time

In the case in which parties interact with one another for an infinite or indefinite period of time, the logic of backward induction breaks down. There is no identifiable end point from which to reason backward. We are left with forward-thinking logic.

If we anticipate playing a prisoner's dilemma game with another person for an infinitely long or uncertain length of time, we reason that we might influence their behavior with our own behavior. That is, we may signal a desire to cooperate on a mutual basis by making a cooperative choice in an early trial. Similarly, we can reward and punish their behavior through our actions.

Under such conditions, the game theoretic analysis indicates that cooperation in the first period is the optimal choice (Kreps, Milgrom, Roberts, and Wilson, 1982). Should our strategy be to cooperate no matter what? No! If a person adopted cooperation as a general strategy, this would surely lead to exploitation. So, what strategy would be optimal to adopt? Before reading further, stop and indicate what is a good strategy.

The Tournament of Champions

In 1981, Robert Axelrod, a leading game theorist, posed this very question to readers in an article in *Science* magazine. Axelrod spelled out the contingencies of the prisoner's dilemma game and invited members of the scientific community to submit a strategy to play in a prisoner's dilemma tournament. To play in the tournament, a person had to submit a strategy (a plan that would tell a decision maker what to do in every trial under all possible conditions) in the form of a computer program. Axelrod explained that each strategy would play all other strategies across 200 trials of a prisoner's dilemma game. He further explained that the strategies would be evaluated in terms of the maximization of gains across all opponents they faced. Hundreds of strategies were submitted by eminent scholars from around the world.

The Winner Is a Loser

The winner of the tournament was the simplest strategy that was submitted. The FORTRAN code was only four lines long. The strategy was called **tit-for-tat** and was submitted by Anatol Rapoport. Tit-for-tat accumulated the greatest number of points across all trials with all of its opponents. The basic principle for tit-for-tat is simple. Tit-for-tat always cooperates on the first trial, and on subsequent trials, it does whatever its opponent did on the previous trial. For example, suppose that tit-for-tat played against someone who cooperated on the first trial, defected on the second trial, and then cooperated on the third trial. Tit-for-tat would cooperate on the first trial and the second trial, defect on the third trial, and cooperate on the fourth trial.

Tit-for-tat never beat any of the strategies it played against. Because it cooperates on the first trial, it can never do better than its opponent. The most tit-for-tat can do is earn as much as its opponent. If it never wins (i.e., beats its opponent), how can tit-for-tat be so successful in maximizing its overall gains? The answer is that it induces cooperation from its opponents. How does it do this? Several characteristics make tit-for-tat an especially effective strategy for inducing cooperation.

Psychological Analysis of Why Tit-for-Tat Is Effective

Not Envious

One reason why tit-for-tat is effective is that it is not an envious strategy. That is, it does not care that it can never beat the opponent. Tit-for-tat can never earn more than any strategy it plays against. Rather, the tit-for-tat strategy is designed to maximize its own gain in the long run.

Nice

Tit-for-tat always begins the interaction by cooperating. Furthermore, it is never the first to defect. Thus tit-for-tat is a nice strategy. This is an important feature because it is difficult for people to recover from initial defections. Competitive, aggressive behavior often sours a relationship. Moreover, aggression often begets aggression. The tit-for-tat strategy neatly avoids the costly mutual escalation trap that can lead to the demise of both parties.

Tough

Although tit-for-tat is a nice strategy, it is not a pushover. A strategy of solid cooperation would be easily exploitable by an opponent. Tit-for-tat can be provoked—it will defect if the opponent invites competition. Tit-for-tat reciprocates defection. This is an important feature of its strategy. By reciprocating defection, tit-for-tat conveys the message that it cannot be taken advantage of.

Forgiving

We have noted that tit-for-tat is tough in that it reciprocates defection. It is also a forgiving strategy in the sense that it reciprocates cooperation. This is another important feature of the tit-for-tat strategy. It is often difficult for people in conflict to recover from defection and end an escalating spiral of aggression. Tit-for-tat's eye-for-an-eye strategy ensures that its responses to aggression from the other side will never be more than it receives.

Not Clever

Ironically, one reason why tit-for-tat is so effective is that it is not very clever. It is an extremely simple strategy, and other people can quickly figure out what to expect from a player who follows it. This predictability has important psychological properties. When people are uncertain or unclear about what to expect, they are more likely to engage in defensive behavior. When uncertainty is high, people often assume the worst about another person. Predictability increases interpersonal attraction.

Not Egotistical

Another feature that makes tit-for-tat an effective strategy is that it is not egotistical in the sense of believing it may gain an advantage over the other. Tit-for-tat realizes it cannot outsmart its opponent. Tit-for-tat is successful because it induces the opponent to cooperate to maximize individual gain. The norm of reciprocity is an extremely powerful form of social influence and behavior.

In summary, tit-for-tat is an extremely stable strategy. Players who follow it often induce their opponents to adopt the tit-for-tat strategy. But tit-for-tat is not uniquely stable; there are other strategies that are stable as well. For example, solid defection is a stable strategy. Two players who defect on every trial have little reason to do anything else. The message is that once someone has defected, it is very difficult to recover from breaches of trust.

How to Build Cooperation

We have worked through the logic of the rational analysis of the prisoner's dilemma game, and we have examined the characteristics of the tit-for-tat strategy as a general principle, but what about behavior in real situations? What do people do when faced with dilemmas like these?

Many individual characteristics of people have been studied, such as men versus women, different races, machiavellianism, status, age, and so on (for a review, see Rubin and Brown, 1975). There are few, if any, reliable individual differences that predict behavior in a prisoner's dilemma game. People cooperate more than rational analysis would predict. Many investigations use a single trial or fixed number of trials in which the rational strategy is solid defection. When the game is infinite or the number of trials is indefinite, however, people cooperate less than they should. What steps can the manager take to build greater cooperation and trust among organization members?

Social Contracts: A Foot in the Door Is a Bird in the Hand

People are more likely to cooperate when they promise to cooperate. Although any such promises are nonbinding and are therefore "cheap talk," people nevertheless act as if they are binding. Why is this? According to the **norm of commitment,** people feel psychologically committed to follow through with their word (Cialdini, 1993).

The norm of commitment is so powerful that people often do things that are completely at odds with their preferences or that are highly inconvenient. For example, once people agree to let a salesperson demonstrate a product in their home, they are more likely to buy it. Homeowners are more likely to consent to have a large (over 10 feet), obtrusive sign in their front yard that says "Drive Carefully" when they agree to a small request made the week before (Freedman and Fraser, 1966). Why is this? In the foot-in-the-door technique, people are asked to agree to a small request, and then they are confronted with a large, more costly request. They often agree. Why? After complying with the smaller request, they view themselves as the kind of person who helps out on important community issues. Once this self-image is in place, people are more likely to agree to subsequent (often outlandish) requests (Cialdini, 1993).

Metamagical Thinking and Superrationality

In the prisoner's dilemma game, people make choices simultaneously and therefore one's choice cannot influence the choice that the other person makes on a given trial—only in subsequent trials. That is, when Thelma makes her decision to confess or not, this does not influence Louise, unless she is telepathic. However, people *act as if* their behavior influences the behavior of others, even though it logically cannot.

In an intriguing analysis of this perception, Hofstadter wrote a letter, published in *Scientific American,* to 20 friends (see Box 12–1 on page 222).

BOX 12–1

Letter from Douglas Hofstadter to 20 friends in Scientific American

Dear _____:

I am sending this letter by special delivery to 20 of you (namely, various friends of mine around the country). I am proposing to all of you a one-round Prisoner's Dilemma game, the payoffs to be monetary (provided by *Scientific American*). It is very simple. Here is how it goes.

Each of you is to give me a single letter: *C* or *D*, standing for "cooperate" or "defect." This will be used as your move in a Prisoner's Dilemma with *each* of the 19 other players.

Thus, if everyone sends in *C*, everyone will get $57, whereas if everyone sends in *D*, everyone will get $19. You can't lose! And, of course, anyone who sends in *D* will get at least as much as everyone else. If, for example, 11 people send in *C* and nine send in *D*, then the 11 *C*-ers will get $3 apiece from each of the other *C*-ers (making $30) and will get nothing from the *D*-ers. Therefore, *C*-ers will get $30 each. The *D*-ers, in contrast, will pick up $5 apiece from each of the *C*-ers (making $55) and will get $1 from each of the other *D*-ers (making $8), for a grand total of $63. No matter what the distribution is, *D*-ers always do better than *C*-ers. Of course, the more *C*-ers there are, the better *everyone* will do!

By the way, I should make it clear that in making your choice you should not aim to be the *winner* but simply to get as much *money* for yourself as possible. Thus, you should be happier to get $30 (say, as a result of saying *C* along with 10 others, even though the nine *D*-sayers get more than you) than to get $19 (by saying *D* along with everyone else, so that nobody "beat" you). Furthermore, you are not supposed to think that at some later time you will meet with and be able to share the goods with your co-participants. You are not aiming at maximizing the total number of dollars *Scientific American* shells out, only at maximizing the number of dollars that come to *you*!

Of course, your hope is to be the *unique* defector, thereby really cleaning up: with 19 *C*-ers, you will get $95 and they will each get 18 times $3, namely $54. But why am I doing the multiplication or any of this figuring for you? You are very bright. So are the others. All about equally bright, I would say. Therefore, all you need to do is tell me your choice. I want all answers by telephone (call collect, please) *the day you receive this letter.*

It is to be understood (it *almost* goes without saying, but not quite) that you are not to try to consult with others who you guess have been asked to participate. In fact, please consult with no one at all. The purpose is to see what people will do on their own, in isolation. Finally, I would appreciate a short statement to go along with your choice, telling me *why* you made this particular one.

Yours,

Doug H.

Source: Hofstadter, D. (1983). Metamagical thinking. *Scientific American* 248: 14–28.

Hofstadter raised the question of whether one person's action in this situation can be taken as an indication of what all people will do. He concluded that if players are indeed rational, they will either all choose to defect or all choose to cooperate. Given that all players are going to submit the same answer, which choice would be more logical? It would seem that cooperation is best (each player gets $57 when all cooperate and only $19 when they all defect). At this point, the logic seems like magical thinking: A person's choice at a given time influences the behavior of others at the same time. Another example: People explain that they've decided to vote in an election so that others will, too. Of course, it is impossible that one person's voting behavior could affect others in a *given* election, but people act as if it does. Hofstadter argues that decision makers wrestling with such choices must give others credit for seeing the logic that oneself has seen. Thus, we need to believe that others are rational (like ourselves) and that they believe that everyone is rational. Hofstadter calls this rationality **superrationality.** For this reason, choosing to defect undermines the very reasons for choosing it. In Hofstadter's game, 14 people defected and 6 cooperated. The defectors received $43; the cooperaters received $15. Robert Axelrod was one of the participants who defected, remarking that in a one-shot game, there was no reason to cooperate.

Imagine that you are playing a prisoner's dilemma game like that described in the Thelma and Louise case. You are told about the contingencies and payoffs in the game and then asked to make a choice. The twist in the situation is that you are either told that your opponent: (1) has already made his choice earlier that day, (2) will make his choice later that day, or (3) will make his choice at the same time as you. In all cases, you will *not* know the other person's choice before making your own. When faced with this situation, people are more likely to cooperate when their opponent's decision is temporally contiguous with their own decision—that is, when the opponent will make his decision at the same time (Morris, Sim, and Girrotto, 1995). Temporal contiguity fosters a causal illusion: the idea that our behavior at a given time can influence the behavior of others. This logical impossibility is not permissible in the time-delayed decisions.

Do the Right Thing: It's the Name of the Game

According to rational analysis, only the payoffs of the game should influence one's strategy. However, our behavior in social dilemmas is influenced by our perceptions about what kinds of behavior are appropriate and expected in a given context. In an intriguing examination of this idea, people engaged in a prisoner's dilemma task. The game was not described to participants as a "prisoner's dilemma," though. In one condition, the game was called the "Wall Street game," and in another condition, the game was called the "community game" (Ross and Samuels, 1993). Otherwise, the game, the payoffs, and the choices were identical. Whereas rational analysis predicts that defection is the optimal strategy no matter what the name, in fact, the incidence of cooperation was three times as high in the community game than in the Wall Street game, indicating that people are sensitive to situational cues as trivial as the name of the game.

Impression Management

Still another reason why people cooperate is that they want to believe that they are nice people. For example, one person attributed his decision to make a cooperative choice in the 20-person prisoner's dilemma game to the fact that he did not want the readers of *Scientific American* to think that he was a defector (Hofstadter, 1983). This is a type of impression management (Goffman, 1959).

Impression management raises the question of whether people's behavior is different when it is anonymous than when it is public. The answer appears to be yes. However, it is not always the case that public behavior is more cooperative than private behavior. For example, negotiators who are accountable to a constituency often bargain harder and are more competitive than when they are accountable for their behavior (see Carnevale, Pruitt, and Seilheimmer, 1981).

Signaling and Publicizing Commitment

In November of 1995, USAir announced that it was putting its company up for sale (for a full treatment, see Diekmann, Tenbrunsel, and Bazerman, 1998). Financial analysts speculated that the sale of USAir would lead to a bidding war between the major airlines, because whichever airline acquired USAir would have a market advantage. None of the airlines wanted to be in the position of not acquiring USAir and seeing another airline buy the company.

Following the announcement of the sale of USAir, a strange series of events followed that was not forecast by financial analysts: No one bid for USAir. Analysts did not realize that the major airlines had learned an important principle through their experience in the 1980s with the frequent flyer and triple mile programs. The frequent flyer and triple mile programs were designed to be competitive strategies to capture market share. However, the approach backfired in the airline industry when all of the major airlines developed frequent flyer programs and a price war began, which resulted in the loss of millions of dollars among airlines.

Robert Crandall, the chairman of American Airlines, was effective in averting a costly escalation war for USAir. How did he do this? Before reading further, stop and indicate how you would attempt to nip a bidding war in the bud.

Robert Crandall wrote and published an open letter to the employees of American Airlines that appeared in the *Chicago Tribune* (see Box 12–2). The letter clearly indicated that American Airlines was interested in avoiding a costly bidding war with United Airlines for USAir. The letter clearly stated the *intentions* of American not to make an opening bid for USAir. The letter further indicated that American would bid competitively if United initiated bidding for USAir.

The letter effectively **signaled** the intentions of American Airlines in a way that made bidding behavior seem too costly. Although the letter was addressed to the employees of American Airlines, it is obvious that the real targets of this message were the other airlines.

BOX 12–2

Letter to the Employees of American Airlines from Robert Crandall, Chairman

We continue to believe, as we always have, that the best way for American to increase its size and reach is by internal growth—not by consolidation. So we will not be the first to make a bid for USAir. On the other hand, if United seeks to acquire USAir, we will be prepared to respond with a bid, or by other means as necessary, to protect American's competitive position.

Source: S. Ziemba, *Chicago Tribune*, November 10, 1995.

Align Incentives

To the extent possible, managers interested in building cooperation should align the incentives of organizational actors to make defection less attractive. For example, by putting in "high vehicle occupancy" lanes on major highways, single drivers are more motivated to carpool.

Personalize Others

People often behave as if they were interacting with an entity or organization rather than a person. For example, an embittered customer claims that the airline refused her a refund when in fact it was a representative of the airline who did not issue a refund. To the extent that others can be personalized, people are more motivated to cooperate than if they believe they are dealing with a dehumanized bureaucracy.

Recovering from Breaches of Trust

Suppose that you're the manager of a large HMO. The managed health care industry is highly competitive, with different companies vying to capture market share by touting low deductibles and so on. You've analyzed the situation with your competitors to be a noncooperative game. You've thought about how your competitor must view the situation, and you've decided to take a cooperative approach and *not* engage in negative advertising. Later that week, you learn that your opponent has taken out a full-page ad in *The Wall Street Journal* that denigrates your HMO, by publicizing questionable statistics about your mortality rates, quotes from angry patients, and charges about physicians. You counter with some negative TV spots. You are spending a lot of money and are angry. Can you recover from an initial breach of trust? Probably so, if you consider the following three strategies.

Make Situational Attributions

We often blame the incidence of escalating, mutually destructive conflict on others' ill will and evil intentions. We fail to realize that we might have done the same thing as our competitor had we been in his or her shoes. Why? We punctuate events differently than do our opponents. We see our behavior as a defensive *response* to the other. In contrast, we view the other as engaging in unprovoked acts of aggression. The solution is to see the other side's behavior as a response to our own actions. In the situation above, your competitor's negative ad campaign may be a payback for your campaign a year ago.

Tiny Steps

Trust is not rebuilt in a day. We rebuild trust incrementally by taking tiny steps. For example, the **GRIT (graduated reduction in tension relations)** strategy calls for conflicting parties to offer small concessions. This reduces the risk for the party making the concession.

Getting Even and Catching Up

As we saw in chapter 11, people are hyperconcerned with fairness. The perception of inequity is a major threat to the continuance of relationships. One way of rebuilding trust is to let the other party "get even" and catch up. The resurrection of a damaged relationship may depend on repentance on the part of the injurer and forgiveness on the part of the injured (Bottom, Gibson, Daniels, and Murnighan, 1996). Even more surprising is that, it's the thought that counts: Small amends are as effective as large amends in generating future cooperation.

Not the Only Game in Town

The prisoner's dilemma is not the only noncooperative game of interest for the organizational actor. Other games that characterize organization life include: chicken, spite, battle of the sexes, and the volunteer dilemma (Murnighan, 1992). The **volunteer dilemma** is a situation in which at least one person in a group must sacrifice his or her own interests to better the group. An example is a group of friends who want to go out for an evening of drinking and celebration. The problem is that all cannot drink if one person must safely drive everyone home. A "designated" driver is a volunteer for the group. Most organized entities would not function if no one volunteered. The act of volunteering strengthens group ties.

SOCIAL DILEMMAS

Since the 1970s, there has been a trend toward "comparative advertising" in which companies compare their product with competitors' products and point out the advantages of their own product and the disadvantages of the competitors' products. Hardly any industry has managed to avoid comparative advertising. Advertisers have battled over milk quality, fish oil, beer taste, electric shavers, cola, coffee, magazines, cars, telephone service, banking, credit cards, and peanut butter. The ads attack the products and services of other companies. What is the effect of the attack ad? For the consumer, attack ads keep prices down and quality high. However, it can also lead to consumer resentment toward the industry. The effect is much more serious for the advertisers, who can effectively run each other out of business.

The Tragedy of the Commons

Imagine that you are a farmer. You own several cows and share a grazing pasture known as a "commons" with other farmers. There are 100 farmers who share the pasture. Each farmer is allowed to have one cow graze. Because the commons is not policed, it is tempting for you to add one more cow without fear of detection. By adding another cow, a herdsman can double his or her utility and no one will really suffer. If everyone does this, however, the commons will be overrun and the grazing area depleted. The cumulative result will be disastrous. What should you do in this situation if you want to keep your family alive?

The analysis of the "tragedy of the commons" (from Hardin, 1968) may be applied to many real world problems, such as pollution, use of natural resources, and overpopulation. In these situations, people are tempted to maximize their own gain, reasoning that their pollution, failure to vote, and Styrofoam cups in the landfill won't have a measurable impact on others. However, if everyone engages in this behavior, the collective outcome is disastrous: Air will be unbreathable, there will not be enough votes in an election, and landfills will be overrun. Thus, in the social dilemma, the rational pursuit of self-interest produces collective disaster.

In the social dilemma situation, each person makes behavioral choices similar to those in the prisoner's dilemma: to benefit oneself or the group. As in the prisoner's dilemma, the choices are referred to as cooperation and defection. The defecting choice always results in better personal outcomes, at least in the immediate future, but universal defection results in poorer outcomes for everyone than does universal cooperation.

A hallmark characteristic of social dilemmas is that the rational pursuit of self-interest is detrimental to collective welfare. This has very serious and potentially disastrous implications. In this sense, social dilemmas contradict the principle of hedonism and laissez-faire economics. That is, unless some limits are placed on the pursuit of personal goals, the entire society may suffer.

Types of Social Dilemmas

There are two major forms of the social dilemma: **resource conservation dilemmas** (also known as **collective traps**) and **public goods dilemmas** (also known as **collective fences;** see Messick and Brewer, 1983). In the resource conservation dilemma, individuals take or harvest resources from a common pool (like the herdsmen in the commons). Examples of the detrimental effects of individual interest include pollution, burning of fossil fuels, and water shortage. The defecting choice occurs when people consume too much. The result of over-consumption is collective disaster. For groups to sustain themselves, the rate of consumption cannot exceed the rate of replenishment of resources.

In public goods dilemmas, individuals contribute or give resources to a common pool or community. Examples include donations for public radio and television, payment of taxes, and voting. The defecting choice is to not contribute. Those who fail to contribute are known as defectors or free riders. Those who pay while others free ride are affectionately known as suckers.

Determinants of Cooperation in Social Dilemmas

Most social groups could be characterized as social dilemma situations. Some people view groups within organizations as social dilemmas (Kramer, 1991; Mannix, 1993). Members are left to their own devices to decide how much to take or contribute for common benefit. Consider an organization in which members are allowed to monitor their use of supplies and equipment, such as computer manuals, Xerox paper, stamps, and envelopes. Each member may be tempted to overuse or hoard resources, thereby contributing to a rapid depletion of supply.

What determines whether and how much people will cooperate in social dilemma situations? The key determinant of cooperation is **communication** (Messick and Brewer, 1983; Liebrand, Messick, and Wilke, 1992; Komorita and Parks, 1994; Sally, in press). If people are allowed to communicate with the members of the group prior to making their choices, the incidence and level of cooperation increases dramatically (Sally, in press). Why is this?

The Power of Commitment

Communication is thought to be important for increasing cooperation for two reasons. First, communication provides a mechanism by which members of groups may make commitments to one another. Although the social dilemma, like its cousin the prisoner's dilemma, is a noncooperative game, such that players may not make binding agreements, players in social dilemmas nevertheless treat verbal commitments as if they were binding.

When people communicate with one another in social dilemma situations, they elicit commitments of cooperation from one another. Verbal commitments in such situations do two important things. First, they indicate the willingness of others to cooperate. In this sense, they reduce the uncertainty that people have about others in such situations and provide a measure of reassurance to decision makers. Second, commitments shape subsequent behavior. People are extremely reluctant not to follow through with their word, even when their words are nonbinding. If people are prevented from making verbal commitments, they will attempt to make nonverbal ones. For example, some students who engaged in a prisoner's dilemma situation rubbed their tattoos prior to making an independent decision as a sign of commitment!

Social Identity

The other reason why communication is effective in engendering cooperation is that it allows group members to develop a social or group identity: Communication allows people to get to know one another and feel more attracted to their group. People derive a sense of identity from their relationships to social groups (Tajfel, 1979). When our identity is traced to the relationships we have with others in groups, we seek to further the interests of these groups. This leads to more cooperative, or group-welfare, choices in social dilemmas.

How might social identity develop among members in groups? Social identity often arises from the mere categorization of people into groups. Sometimes these categories are meaningful, such as different organizational and industrial affiliations; sometimes they are trivial, such as different sides of a room or type of dress.

Imagine that you are sitting in a group of 20 people. A box with two kinds of letters, alphas and betas, is passed around. People randomly draw a letter out, and two groups are formed: alphas and betas. People are told of their group affiliation and then asked to rate their group and the other group on things like intelligence, competence, personal warmth, and sincerity. What do you think happens? Although the members of each group are complete strangers, people show an in-group bias: They rate their own group as superior to the out-group (Tajfel, 1968). Furthermore, when asked to allocate rewards to members of in-groups and out-groups, people give more to their own group than to the out-group, even when this has no implications for their own financial outcomes (Doise, 1978).

The Ties That Bind

As a consequence of population growth, the politics of water distribution, and five years of drought, California had widespread shortages of water in 1991. Residents of many areas were encouraged to voluntarily conserve water and were subjected to regulations imposed by the Public Utilities Commission. A telephone survey of hundreds of residents of the San Francisco area revealed that people were more willing to support authorities when they had strong relational bonds to the authorities (Tyler and Degoey, 1995). The effectiveness of authorities in eliciting cooperation in water-shortage dilemmas is linked to the social bonds that they share with community members.

Structural Factors

Communication is not the only means by which cooperation may be induced in social dilemmas. Structural factors may increase incidence of cooperation (Messick and Brewer, 1983). Structural characteristics are aspects of the situation or environment (as opposed to internal factors, such as cognition and motivation) that affect behavior. For example, monetary incentives for cooperation, privatization of resources, reduction in group size, election of a leader, and a monitoring system all increase the incidence of cooperation. Structural factors are powerful, but they are not easily modified or enacted by group members.

PRISONER'S DILEMMA VERSUS SOCIAL DILEMMA

What's the difference to the manager who finds himself in a prisoner's or social dilemma? The prisoner's dilemma differs from the social dilemma in terms of the number of players. The prisoner's dilemma involves two parties; the social dilemma involves several parties. The size difference is important. First, in the prisoner's dilemma, the costs of choosing the dominating or defecting strategy is borne by one other player; in the social dilemma, the costs are spread out across several or many others. Second, the defecting choice in the two-person dilemma guarantees a certain minimal payoff to the party, but this is not true in the social dilemma, which is risky for the cooperating member. The defecting choice in the social dilemma does not guarantee a certain minimal payoff. Third, when someone defects in the two-person group, the other person knows who did it. Anonymity is impossible. This is not the case in larger groups. Fourth, each person in a two-person group has **fate control**—i.e., can affect the outcome of the other (Kelley and Thibaut, 1978). By choosing defection, one person may punish the other; by choosing cooperation, one can reward the other. A direct linkage of behavior between each person's outcomes does not characterize collective dilemmas.

We have discussed the prisoner's dilemma and social dilemmas as situations in which the pursuit of individually rational behavior leads to collective disaster. We now turn our attention to two other noncooperative games that negotiators often face: ultimatums and double-auctions.

ULTIMATUMS

In an ultimatum bargaining situation, one person makes a final offer—an ultimatum—to another person. If the other person accepts the offer, then the first player receives the demand that he or she made, and the other player agrees to accept what was offered to him or her. If the offer is refused, then no settlement is reached—an impasse occurs—and negotiators receive their respective reservation points.

How should we negotiate in ultimatum situations? What kind of a final offer should we make to another person? When the tables are turned, on what basis should we accept or refuse a final offer someone makes to us?

Suppose someone with a $100 bill in hand comes up to you and the person sitting on the bus beside you. This person explains that the $100 is yours to share with the other person if you can propose a split that the other person will agree to. The only hitch is that the division you propose is a once-and-for-all-decision: You can't discuss it with the other person, and you have to propose a take-it-or-leave-it split. If the other person accepts your proposal, the $100 will be allocated accordingly. If the other person rejects your proposal, no one gets any money and you do not have the opportunity to propose another offer. Faced with this situation, what should you do? (Before reading further, indicate what you would do and why.)

It is useful for us to solve this problem using the principles of decision theory and then see if the solution squares with our intuition. Once again, we use the concept of backward induction, working backward from the last period of the game. The last decision in this game is an ultimatum. In this game, player 2 (the person beside you on the bus) must decide whether to accept the proposal offered by you or reject the offer and receive nothing. From a rational standpoint, player 2 should accept any positive offer you make to him or her because, after all, something (even 1 cent) is better than nothing.

Now we can examine the next-to-last decision in the game and ask what proposal player 1 (you) should make. Because you know that player 2 should accept any positive offer greater than $0, the game theoretic solution is for you to offer $.01 to player 2 and demand $99.99 for yourself. This is a **subgame perfect equilibrium** (Selten, 1975) because it is rational within each period of the game. Said in a different way, even if the game had additional periods to be played in the future, your offer of $99 (to you) and $.01 to the other person would still be rational at this point.

Contrary to game theoretic predictions, most people don't do this. That is, most player 1s propose amounts substantially greater than $.01 for player 2, often around the midpoint, or $50. Further, player 2s often reject offers that are not 50–50 splits. Thus, some player 2s choose to have $0 rather than $1, or $2—or even $49. Player 1s act nonrationally and so do player 2s. This seems completely counter to one's interests, but, as we saw in the chapter on fairness, people are often more concerned with how their outcomes compare to others than with the absolute value of their outcomes (see Loewenstein, Thompson, and Bazerman, 1989; Messick and Sentis, 1979).

Chickens and Eggs

If you are playing an ultimatum game and the other person offers you a 50–50 split, should you assume that they like you or that they don't want their offer to be rejected? That is, are they a *saint* or are they *strategic*? Are people really concerned with others' outcomes (social utility), or do they rationally try to maximize their outcome, knowing that they are dealing with a person who rejects positive offers that are less than an equal split? (Before reading further, speculate about how you could determine the answer to this question.)

One way of addressing this question is to study behavior in **dictator games,** which are like ultimatum games, except that player 2 does not have the option to reject. That is, player 1 proposes a split, and the other party just lives with it. Presumably, behavior in dictator games is a pure expression of preference because player 2 has no say in the matter; he or she can't reject the proposal player 1 makes. In the dictator game, the modal offer is $0 to player 2 (36 percent) (Forsythe, Horowitz, Savin, and Sefton, 1994). Certainly, this suggests that people are not saintly.

However, we also observe a concentration of equal division proposals in the dictator game. Clearly, this cannot reflect self-interest. In conclusion, some people may be primarily motivated by considerations of fairness, but the high concentration of equal division offers in the ultimatum game cannot be attributed to simple desire for fairness. Therefore, there is a "chicken and egg" problem: The strategic environment may be influenced by ideas about fairness, and ideas of fairness are influenced by the strategic environment. That is, although people may have clear ideas about what is fair in a variety of circumstances, they may adapt their ideas about what is fair in response to their experience, in ways that may be heavily influenced by strategic considerations.

How can normative analysis explain why people reject positive offers? Why on earth would someone turn down $49 and get nothing? The simple answer is: Spite. A player's preference for more money is counterbalanced by a preference for disagreement over amounts he perceives as very small relative to his playing partner's share. This sounds like sour grapes. Is it rational? This is a rational model because it assumes that player 1 proposes fair division because he or she is concerned that player 2 will punish player 1 by rejecting the offer. Only by rejecting offers can player 2s be perceived as credible.

DOUBLE AUCTIONS

Another type of noncooperative game that has a similar underlying structure to the ultimatum game is the **double auction.** The double auction is the situation in which one player owns a good and the other player is a potential buyer.

The double auction game involves a buyer and a seller. Consider, for example, a car buyer talking to a car seller. The seller owns a car that is worth some amount to him or her; the buyer values the car to be worth some amount. In this sense, both seller and buyer have reservation prices. The object of the game is for the buyer to buy the good at a price less than his or her valuation of the good and, simultaneously, for the seller to sell the good for more than he or she values it. The buyer's value and the seller's cost for the good are private information.

In the game, the buyer and seller simultaneously submit an offer and a demand, respectively. If the buyer's offer exceeds the seller's demand, then a trade occurs at a price halfway between the two; otherwise, no trade occurs. In our situation, you will write down a price for the car, as will the seller. For example, if you think the car is worth $9,000, you might offer $8,300. If the seller thinks the car is worth $7,500, he might demand $8,000. If so, the sale would take place at $8,150.

Given this set of constraints, what price should the buyer offer and what price should the seller demand? Obviously, each party wants to name a price that ensures that trade will occur if there is a positive bargaining zone, but each party also wants to name a price that affords him or her a large share of the bargaining zone. In this sense, the dilemma that negotiators face is identical to the situation we discussed in chapter 2 on distributive negotiation: How do negotiators maximize surplus?

This situation is a noncooperative game, whereas the situation faced by negotiators in the bargaining problem is a cooperative game. Recall that the difference is that in noncooperative games, players make independent moves and their communication is not binding. In short, each player makes a choice, and they live with the consequences. In the cooperative context, outcomes are not binding until parties mutually consent to the terms of the agreement.

In the double auction with private information, parties have only one chance to name a price that will determine their outcomes. What should each do?

Strategy

Fortunately, game theory provides a mechanism for analyzing the optimal strategy for players to adopt in this double auction game. Ironically, there is no strategy that the players would be willing to play that would guarantee an efficient outcome (Myerson and Satterthwaite, 1989). Said differently, there is no feasible solution that ensures that players will reach agreement if the bargaining zone is positive. This means that players will sometimes fail to reach a level 1 integrative agreement. This seems unfortunate. Is there any way around this? It seems tragically absurd that if you think Gino's car is worth $2,400 at the very least, and Gino is willing to part with it for $2,200, that you would fail to trade.

One suggestion is that each party could name his or her reservation price. This would ensure that an agreement would be reached if there was positive overlap, and that the midpoint would nicely split the bargaining surplus between the two parties. This is not a feasible strategy, however, because players cannot verify that the other party is naming his or her valuation. Each is tempted to maximize his or her share of the surplus by shading his or her bid—buyers would offer less than the good is actually worth to them and sellers would demand more. This means that when the bargaining zone is small, but positive, players would fail to reach agreement.

Communication

It seems unfortunate that players are unable to reach mutually beneficial outcomes. Perhaps if players communicated with one another prior to making their irrevocable bids, they could discern whether trade was possible and perhaps coordinate their bidding.

This possibility was examined in a repeated-trial, double auction game (Valley, Thompson, Gibbons, and Bazerman, 1997). In the game, each player played the double auction a total of six times. In a third of the cases, players just played the auction and were not allowed to communicate with the opponent. In another third of the cases, players were allowed to write messages to their opponent for a total of 12 minutes before making their final bids. In the final third of the cases, players communicated face to face in an unrestricted fashion for six minutes before making their final bids.

Communication, whether written or face to face, dramatically improved the incidence of level 1 integrative agreements (trades) when the bargaining zone is positive. A total of 92 percent of negotiators who communicated face-to-face or in writing achieved trades when bargaining zones were positive, compared to only 60 percent of those who did not communicate. The beneficial effects of communication were even more dramatic when the bargaining zone was especially narrow (but still positive): 80 percent of those who communicated achieved trade compared with only 33 percent of those who did not communicate.

Coordination and Revelation

How did negotiators who communicated beat the predictions of game theory? They achieved trades via one of two mechanisms: (1) coordinating on a single price, or (2) mutually bidding their valuations. Of the two mechanisms, coordination was more common, occurring in 50 percent of the dyads where there was a positive bargaining zone, as opposed to 20 percent for the mutual bidding of valuations. A substantial number of negotiators in the communication conditions revealed their valuation to the other party (58 percent in the positive bargaining zone case). Value revelation was often mutual (26 percent).

CONCLUSION

In this chapter, we have analyzed noncooperative bargaining games. We have examined the game theoretic analysis of these games, which often leads to less than desirable outcomes. We have explored the various conditions that may allow negotiators to reach more optimal outcomes in these situations. Game theory does not account for the mechanisms that induce cooperation in dilemmas; social psychology provides insights as to when and why people cooperate. The analysis of noncooperative games is important and intriguing because of the many parallels it shares with situations in which people make unilateral decisions that have far-reaching implications for their own and others' welfare.

TAKE-AWAYS

- Noncooperative situations are characterized by the absence of enforcement mechanisms.
- The best way to build in enforcements is to (1) change the perceived time horizon of the situation, (2) obtain verbal commitments, and (3) build social identity with one's opponent.
- A good strategy is one in which you (1) use backward induction and (2) think about what the other players will do given the contingencies.
- You can maximize your bargaining effectiveness by focusing on *your* outcomes in the *long-run*; short-run gains and comparisons to others can lead to inefficient and potentially disastrous outcomes.

CHAPTER 13

Experience, Expertise, and Learning: *Best Practices for Peak Performance*

Jim bit his lip for the third time in his conversation with the Mullers. After showing the young couple more than 175 houses over a four-month period, he had thought that they were finally ready to make an offer on a property in the northwest of town. The Mullers had called Jim in the morning to explain that they wanted to make an offer on the property that day. Stunned and relieved, Jim spent the morning hours assembling the paperwork, calling the attorney and the bank, and canceling a lunch so that he could meet with the Mullers.

As Jim stood with the papers in his hand ready for final signature, the Mullers explained that they would also like to make an offer on a property they saw last week in the northeast end of town. Jim stopped short. In his 17 years of experience, he had never heard of a buyer making two offers at the same time. This ran counter to every principle of moving property Jim had been trained in. With great restraint, Jim said, "I would not advise that." But the Mullers were insistent, "There's no law that says we can't, is there?" "Well, no, but it is not normally done. It sends the wrong message to the seller," Jim explained. "But, that is exactly the point," offered Mr. Muller. "Yes," said Mrs. Muller, chiming in, "by making two offers, we increase our BATNA." "Your what?" asked Jim, nearly at the end of his rope.

Through their months of working together, the Mullers had told Jim the story of their first house purchase, which they regarded as a negotiation failure. They had made the mistake of falling in love with a house and made too generous an offer; they had paid about 99 percent of the asking price. "We learned a lot from experience," explained Mr. Muller.

W hat did the Mullers learn from their first house-buying experience that led them to behave differently in the purchase of their next home? Will their behavior be more effective in the purchase of their second home? Most of our negotiation experiences are those that we engage in several times. Even the "big three" negotiations—car, house, and job—are rapidly becoming repeated experiences for people who go through several jobs, cars, and houses during their lives. This stands in sharp contrast to the era in which people stayed in one job and one house, and drove one car for most of their lives. Now, people frequently trade up.

A cornerstone of psychological theory is that people learn from experience. Whereas considerable debate exists about the most effective methods of learning, it seems obvious that people learn from and improve with experience. Do people learn from their negotiation experiences? In this chapter, we examine *what* people learn from experience and *how* they learn.

NAÏVES, NOVICES, AND EXPERTS

To understand principles of learning, it is important to distinguish between naïves, novices, and experts. Below are some definitions that provide sharper distinctions to the discussion that follows:

- **Naïve person:** A person who has not received formal training in an area or domain. The student who has not taken a course in negotiation is naïve when he or she negotiates his or her first job offer.
- **Novice:** A person who is currently receiving training or has received training and is becoming an expert.
- **Experienced person:** A person who has undergone several trials of natural experience but no formal training.
- **Expert:** A person who has years of experience in a domain. Typically, experts have 10 or more years of experience (Ericsson and Smith, 1991). For example, no one—not even Mozart—composes outstanding music without first having ten years of intensive musical preparation (Hays, 1981).
- **Learning:** The act of acquiring new skills.
- **Creativity:** The ability to form new concepts using existing knowledge (Guilford, 1959, 1967), as well as the ability to form new relations *between* existing concepts (for a review, see Sternberg, 1988). The genius finds connections where other people do not (Koestler, 1964).

LEARNING

The goal of experience is to learn. What do negotiators learn through experience? Ideally, negotiators need a **strategic conceptualization** of negotiation to reach integrative solutions (Northcraft and Neale, 1991). A strategic conceptualization is a cognitive framework that allows an individual to understand and apply integrative strategies to different negotiation situations. There are several different types of learning, as depicted in Figure 13–1.

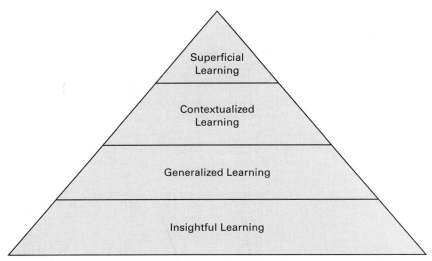

FIGURE 13–1. A Pyramid Model of Stages of Learning

Think of the diagram in Figure 13–1 as an iceberg. Typically, about one-ninth of the total volume of an iceberg is visible on the surface; eight-ninths is submerged. The tip of the iceberg represents **superficial learning,** or the ability to parrot back an idea or behavior that a person has observed or enacted. For example, a person might observe a negotiation in which one party asks for a 15 percent increase in salary over her current level. She may then ask for a 15 percent increase in all subsequent salary negotiations. This may result in desired outcomes for the negotiator; however, she may sometimes walk away from potentially profitable opportunities and occasionally fall prey to lose–lose outcomes.

Contextualized learning is a deeper thought process, in which a person generalizes an idea to another problem in the same context. For example, in talking with her employer, Janice realizes that a mutually beneficial tradeoff can be made between flexible time and salary. Janice would be willing to take a 10 percent salary cut in exchange for working 3.5 days per week. To the extent she identifies similar tradeoffs in her subsequent employment negotiations, she exhibits contextualized learning.

Generalized learning is the ability to generalize an idea or behavior to a different context. Janice extends the principle of mutually beneficial tradeoffs (logrolling) to a completely different context—this time with her neighbor concerning the construction of a fence and landscaping.

Insightful learning is the ability to develop a new insight based upon existing concepts. This is the creative aspect of learning. For example, Janice has an insight during a negotiation in which she and a supplier have different projections about future sales. Janice suggests they bet on their different expectations. If sales are higher than X, then Janice gets a discount from the supplier; if sales are less than X, Janice pays a surcharge to the supplier. By developing a contingency contract, Janice adds more value to the deal and avoids a nasty dispute about the future, which is uncertain.

As we have seen, people often fail to resolve conflicts in an integrative fashion, and negotiated outcomes frequently fall far short of the pareto-efficient frontier. For a variety of reasons, people's behavior does not follow principles of normative decision making. This is due to cognitive, emotional, motivational, and social reasons.

When their shortcomings are pointed out to them, most people are upset and wish that they could have done better. The standards of performance derived from normative models that we have described have intuitive appeal. It would be very difficult to attempt to change behavior if people did not have an appreciation of normative principles.

THE LEARNING CURVE

What is the typical learning curve for negotiation? Initially, negotiators fail to discover and capitalize on integrative potential in bargaining situations; they usually attain level 1 outcomes. With repeated experience, they quickly get better at learning skills, like logrolling, but their performance usually levels off before they attain level 3 outcomes. A typical learning curve is presented in Figure 13–2.

The classic learning curve is known as the **power law of practice** (Newell and Rosenbloom, 1981). The power law of practice states that the benefits of practice are most dramatic early on; the benefit of further practice rapidly diminishes. Yet, no matter how much practice we have had, additional practice helps. There are three basic ideas in the power law of practice (Newell, 1990):

- People **chunk** (i.e., group together) information at a constant rate. Every time we get more experience, we build additional chunks. For example, when a beginner chess player first plays, the "chunks" might be the individual pieces and particular moves. As the chess player becomes more experienced, chunks represent larger sequences of moves. The expert chess player chunks at the level of games.

- Performance of a task is faster the more chunks we have built that are relevant to the task.

- The structure of the environment implies that higher-level chunks recur more rarely. For example, if one chunk is a negotiation that involves a potential strike and another chunk is a negotiation that involves coalition potential, a negotiator should see each of these situations more frequently than a negotiation that involves both a strike and coalition potential.

FIGURE 13–2. Learning Curve in Negotiation

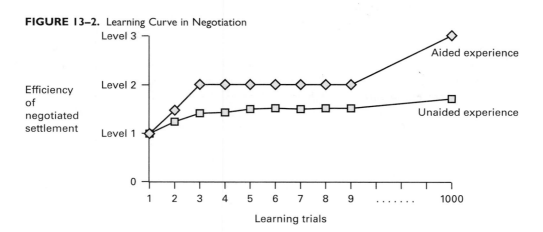

HOW DO WE LEARN FROM EXPERIENCE?

What is it about experience that allows people to learn? What is the best way to develop insightful learning?

The Economic Argument: The Self-correcting Market

According to rational expectations theory, the market is a self-correcting mechanism. The argument goes something like this: If people behaved in a suboptimal fashion, their outcomes would suffer, and they would quickly adapt by altering their behavior. If people failed to adapt, they would be selected out of the marketplace. For example, consider Willy, a salesman, who is not very successful. He knows nothing about the key social influence principles, like reciprocity and scarcity, that we presented in chapter 3. If Willy does not make a certain volume of sales, he does not make any commission. If he doesn't make a commission, he cannot pay his rent. If Willy improves his sales performance, he stays in the sales business. If he doesn't, he is fired or quits and goes into another line of work. The point is: Willy cannot survive as a salesman if he is inept. The market shapes his behavior. The notion of the self-correcting market is based upon the **equilibrium principle:** People choose the behavior that maximizes their interest; behavior is stable in the sense that they will not want to move away from a course of action because it will reduce their utility.

Deeper reflection reveals that this argument is tautological in nature. The market sets its own standards, and whatever behavior is observed in the market is regarded to be optimal. However, we might well imagine that some markets are inefficient and people survive because their outcomes are good enough, although far from optimal. The economic argument of why experience should improve performance is reminiscent of the corrigible rationalist perspective spelled out in chapter 8.

Learning by Analogy

Consider the following breakthrough discoveries:

- Friedrich August von Kekulé discovered the ring structure of benzene after visualizing a snake biting his own tail.
- Rutherford formed a new model of the atom by likening it to the solar system, wherein the planets revolve around the sun.
- Johannes Kepler developed a causal theory of planetary motion by likening gravity to light.

In each of these examples, a breakthrough discovery was made through the process of analogical reasoning. The people who had the spark of insight were ordinary individuals who saw a connection between their problem and a remote analogy. This is creative genius in action.

As these examples illustrate, one of the most effective means by which people solve problems is through analogical reasoning (Gick and Holyoak, 1983; Hesse, 1966; Gentner and Gentner, 1983; Sternberg, 1977). Analogy is the process by which a problem solver maps the solution for one problem into a solution for another problem. Sometimes the analogy process can be straightforward. At other times the transformations can be more complex, as when Rutherford used the solar system as a model for the structure of the atom in which electrons revolve around the atom like planets revolve around the sun (Koestler, 1964; Gentner and Gentner, 1983).

Analogical reasoning involves noticing that a solution to a problem from the past is relevant, and then mapping the elements from that solution to produce an operator for the current problem. In any act of analogy it is necessary to map the elements from the source to the target. For example, consider a simple analogy, like red is to stop as green is to go, or red:stop::green:go or A:B::C:D. (Mayer, 1983). There are five key cognitive processes in the solving of such a problem: encoding, inference, mapping, application, and preparation–response (Sternberg, 1977).

- **Encoding:** Each of the four stimulus items is translated into an internal representation (see chapter 7 for a discussion of mental representations).
- **Inference:** A rule is found that relates the A term of the analogy (red) to the B term (stop). For example, a red traffic light is a signal to stop.
- **Mapping:** A higher-order rule is found that relates the A term with the C term (green). For example, red and green are colors of traffic signals.
- **Application:** A rule is applied to C in order to generate a final term, D (go). For example, green is the signal for go. If this answer matches the answer given for the D term, the answer regarding the analogy is yes; otherwise, the answer is no.
- **Preparation–response:** This includes all the remaining time that is used in preparing to solve the analogy and carrying out the response.

An example of the power of analogy in problem solving is provided in the following example (based on Gick and Holyoak, 1980). People are presented with the problem in Box 13–1 (adapted from Duncker, 1945). The problem is how to cure an inoperable tumor when enough radiation to kill the tumor would also kill the surrounding flesh.

Before reading any further, stop and try to solve the problem. This is a very difficult problem, and few people are able to immediately solve it. The solution is to attack the tumor from several different directions at once so that the healthy tissue is exposed to only a fraction of the ray but the target site (or tumor) receives the full amount of rays.

The solution to converge on the tumor with several weak beams of radiation is normally discovered by only 10 percent of people who try to solve the problem. However, if

---

BOX 13–1

Analogical Reasoning Problem

Suppose you are a doctor faced with a patient who has a malignant tumor in his stomach. It is impossible to operate on the patient, but unless the tumor is destroyed, the patient will die. There is a kind of ray that can be used to destroy the tumor. If the rays reach the tumor all at once at a sufficiently high intensity, the tumor will be destroyed. Unfortunately, at this intensity, the healthy tissue that the rays pass through on the way to the tumor will also be destroyed. At lower intensities, the rays are harmless to the healthy tissue, but they will not affect the tumor either. What type of procedure might be used to destroy the tumor with the rays and at the same time avoid destroying the healthy tissue?

Source: Duncker, K. (1945). On problem solving. *Psychological Monographs* **58**: 270; Gick, M. L. and K. J. Holyoak (1983). Schema induction and analogical transfer. *Cognitive Psychology* **15**: 1–38.

participants are given a prior analogous story in which soldiers converged on a fort from several different directions at once, three times as many produce the correct answer. This indicates that spontaneous analogical transfer can occur.

Many problems may be solved through the application of appropriate analogies, but often a single analogy is insufficient to instigate the crucial mapping that precedes analogical reasoning (Gick and Holyoak, 1983). When two analogies are given, problem solvers often derive a problem schema as an incidental product describing the similarities of the analogy. Analogical reasoning is most effective when the problem solver abstracts key elements, and abstraction is facilitated when problem solvers are exposed to two analogies. In learning negotiation skills, like logrolling, presenting negotiators with a single analogy is not sufficient to obtain transfer (Fulton, Thompson, and Gonzalez, 1997).

Learning by Feedback

Sometimes people learn through their own behavior (Einhorn and Hogarth, 1978). Consider the feedback model in Figure 13–3. Outcomes follow from people's initial judgments and predictions, which are then used to determine their actions and choices. This occurs within a particular **environment,** which includes factors that may influence the outcome, including structural characteristics of the task, such as the amount of random variation. The combina-

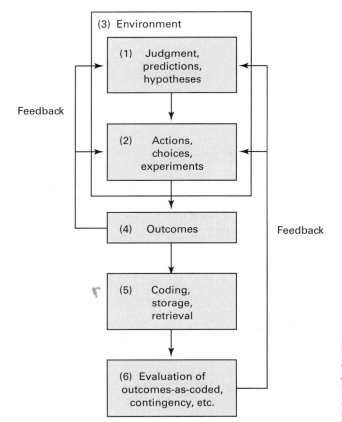

FIGURE 13–3. Feedback Model
Source: Hogarth, R. M. (1987). *Judgment and Choice.* New York: Wiley. Copyright © John Wiley & Sons Limited. Reproduced with permission.

tion of judgments, actions, and the environment produces outcomes. Outcomes produce two feedback mechanisms: a **direct effect** on subsequent judgments and actions and an **indirect effect** based upon a person's interpretation or evaluation of the outcomes.

Not All Feedback Is Created Equal

There are two types of feedback: outcome feedback and process feedback (Balzer, Doherty, and O'Connor, 1989). **Outcome feedback** is simply the knowledge of the results of a decision. **Process feedback** refers to information about relations in the environment rather than outcomes. Outcome feedback is knowledge of the outcome of a judgment, whereas process feedback provides information concerning the relations between the cues in the environment and the criterion—the thing that is the subject of one's judgment.

Consider a hiring situation in which we recruited and hired a brand manager. Outcome feedback is simply knowing whether the person we hired is working out or not. Process feedback concerns our knowledge of the relationship between various cues (the employee's work history, experience, and technical expertise) and success on the job. For example, process feedback would let us know that all of the people hired into the organization with less than three years of work experience are less productive than those with three or more years of experience. In general, outcome feedback is not as effective in improving accuracy and performance as is process feedback (Balzer et al., 1989). Process feedback is an important corrective mechanism for judgment (Balzer et al., 1989; Hammond et al., 1975; Hammond, Summers, and Deane, 1973).

An Eyeglass Prescription for Looking at the World

In many judgment situations, we are faced with making a prediction or a judgment about someone or something in the face of uncertainty. For example, imagine that you are hiring someone for your company and you want to know if that person will be successful. Obviously, it will be some time after the person is hired before it can be determined whether the hire is successful.

One way of trying to answer this question is based upon a lens model (Brunswik, 1952). The lens model maps the interrelation between two systems. One system is the actual relationships that characterize the real world; the other is the relationships that an individual perceives to be true. Thus, the lens model employs a principle of **parallel concepts.**

For example, imagine that you are trying to predict whether a particular job candidate is a good investment for your company. The key thing to remember is that you are trying to figure something out that you cannot observe directly. Rather, you look at cues to make a guess. The accuracy of your judgment in this situation hinges upon the operation of two systems. System 1 is the economic environment that includes the real relationships between qualities of the job candidate (experience, board scores, etc.) and her real value. This system is the "truth" that we cannot know or directly observe. System 2 represents your mind and includes the relations you perceive or imagine between qualities of the job candidate and your prediction of her value. The accuracy of your prediction, therefore, depends on the extent to which your system matches that of the environment system (e.g., in terms of which qualities to assess, relations between various qualities and between qualities and job success), as well as the relative importance of the qualities.

Consider the lens model analysis in Figure 13–4. As we can see, the success of this job candidate is most determined by her previous work experience. Her board scores have little predictive validity in determining success on the job, but technical and group skills are im-

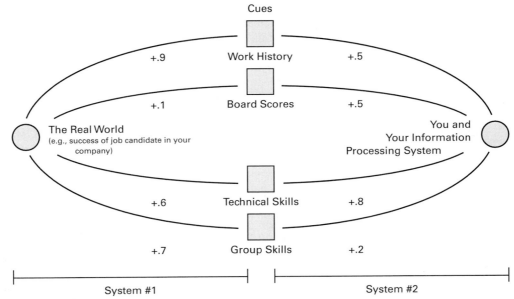

FIGURE 13–4. Lens Model

Source: Hammond, K. R., J. Rohrbaugh, J. Mumpower, and L. Adelman (1977). Social judgment theory: Applications in policy formation. In *Human Judgment and Decision Processes in Applied Settings*, M. F. Kaplan and S. Schwartz (eds.), New York: Academic Press.

portant. (*Note*: these relationships are totally hypothetical.) Now imagine that as the employer, you think that technical skills are essential, board scores and work history may be important, and group skills are less important. Clearly, your model (depicted by system #2) of what qualities are important for successful performance in your company differ from that of the real world. Presumably, if you watch closely what happens to each candidate you hire, you can revise your model to be more accurate. However, this is hard to do because (1) people are egocentric—they think they are accurate; and (2) feedback about the real world is often delayed or ambiguous (i.e., it might take years to determine whether a particular candidate is successful on the job).

Now, imagine that you make all of your firm's hiring decisions with your partner, Roy, who has a different view of what it takes to be successful. Unlike you, Roy likes to give each potential recruit a psychological test and subject them to a stress interview. We're now dealing with three systems: (1) the world, (2) you, and (3) Roy. You and Roy may be in conflict on what qualities are important; neither or both of you could be accurate. The more complex the problem (i.e., many, varied relationships between cues and criterion), the greater the obscurity of the judgment process, and the more difficult it will be for you to resolve disagreement. This means that people are less able to discover the true source of their disagreement but will attribute their disagreement to ill will, hidden agendas, and extremism (all erroneous causes). Specifically, interpersonal conflict may erupt and be augmented by several factors, including: different cues, differential weighting of cues, different functional relations between cues and judgment, different ways of organizing information into a judgment, and cognitive control.

Different cues: People base their judgments on cues or indicators. For example, our judgment about the qualifications of a job candidate may be based on the following cues: (1) previous employment history, (2) letters of reference, and (3) aptitude scores. Obviously, conflict can erupt when people rely on different cues to assess the value or make a prediction about a candidate (e.g., you look at job history; Roy focuses on projective tests).

Differential weighting of cues: Even if two people agree on which cues to use, they may differ on how *important* they think each is. For example, some managers may consider only aptitude scores; others only value letters of reference. The weight an individual places on a cue may not match the real relationship between the cue and the criterion (**ecological validity**) and may clash with another person's views.

Different functional relations between cue and judgment: Even if people agree on which cues should be used and agree on how important they think they are, they may still disagree about whether it's better to be low, high, or in the middle on each. Any of four functional forms characterize the relationship between a cue and judgment: positive, negative, curvilinear, and no relationship (see Figure 13–5). For example, two managers may have different function forms related to the previous work experience of a job candidate. One may believe that "more is better," that is, apply a linear function form to experience and job success. The other may have a curvilinear relationship and believe that no experience is bad and some experience is good, but that after too much experience, people become jaded and set in their ways.

Organizing information: The information from all of the cues must somehow be combined into an overall judgment; for example, suppose that we learn that Ingrid has a lot of technical training, moderate team experience, and high board scores. What do we think of her overall? Do we want to hire her? The manner in which we combine these qualities, or cues, to reach an overall judgment is our organizing principle. People may reach an overall judgment by simply adding up everything they know about a person. This is known as an additive model and follows the MAUT principle we discussed in chapter 6. However, people may organize information in other ways that involve multiplicative or interactive principles (e.g., experience combined with high board scores is good, but high scores in the absence of experience is bad).

Cognitive control: Imagine that you are a manager who makes several hundred hiring decisions each year. If someone were to observe how you make your judgments, that person could reliably model your **judgment policy. Cognitive control** is how *consistent* you are in employing your own judgment policy, regardless of the question of how accurate your policy is.

Unfortunately, most people are not as "in control" as they would like to be when it comes to making decisions. One shocking implication is that a model of a person's judgment policy will lead to wiser decisions than allowing that same person to actually make judgments. Consider a senior human resource manager who hires middle-level managers in a large, decentralized organization. The senior manager considers several pieces of information—experience, letters of reference, job history, academic training, and ability to work

FIGURE 13–5. Functional Forms Depicting Hypothetical Relationships between Work Experience and Performance

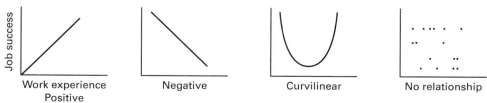

with others. A model of the senior manager's judgment policy could be obtained by watching who she hires and does not hire over a period of time. This would allow us to determine (1) which cues she is actually using and (2) how she is factoring them into her hiring decisions. Using a regression equation, we could then model her judgment policy. An example might be the following:

$$\text{Hire decision} = .9E + .6A - .5G + .09L$$

$$\text{where} \quad E = \text{previous experience}$$
$$A = \text{academic training}$$
$$G = \text{ability to work with others}$$
$$L = \text{letters of reference}$$

This regression equation says the following:

- The employer primarily uses previous experience as the key determinant of her hiring decisions.
- Academic training is positively related to hiring decisions but doesn't guarantee someone a job in the company.
- The ability to work with others is negatively related to her hiring decisions.
- Letters of reference are virtually inconsequential in hiring decisions.

It should be noted that this hiring policy is in no way accurate or appropriate in a normative sense—it is simply a hypothetical empirical model of how this person makes decisions. It is a mathematical representation of a hiring policy. The important point is that *everyone* has a hiring policy. The disturbing fact is that people (1) don't know what cues they use to make decisions and (2) are inconsistent in their judgments. Decision makers are rarely, if ever, aware of their own decision-making models. In general, people believe that they use more information than they really do.

Would it be better to use the personnel officer's model to make hiring decisions or to let the officer make decisions as she always has—through face-to-face interviews? Most people would prefer the latter. Here, we make an argument for the former.

The University of Oregon's graduate psychology program developed a model for admitting students that assigned each applicant a score based upon factors proved to be important for graduate study success (e.g., board scores, grade point average, letters of reference, and so on) (Dawes, 1980). A computer program generated an overall score for each applicant and those who had scores above a certain threshold were admitted; those falling below were not.

To some, this process seemed cold and calculated and lacked the human element that comes from impressions based on face-to-face interaction. However, if we consider the fact that humans are fallible decision makers, whose otherwise accurate judgments are affected by random noise, it would seem more human to make decisions systematically, without the bias that often occurs in face-to-face situations.

Assessing the Quality of Policies

How can the quality of a decision policy be assessed? In short, how do we know if our hiring policy is a good one? An obvious answer is to measure the success of our decisions by seeing which candidates succeed in our company (i.e., if the managers we hire using our policy are successful, then our model would seem to be a good one). However, assessing the suc-

FIGURE 13–6. Four Pieces of Information about Training and Performance Relationship
Source: Adapted from Einhorn, H. and R. Hogarth (1978). Confidence in judgment: Persistence in the illusion of validity. *Psychological Review* **85**: 395–416.

cess of the people we hire is only half of the picture. To assess the accuracy of our hiring policy, we also need to assess the performance of those whom we do not hire.

To see how this may be done, engage in the following exercise: Your task is to test the claim that students who receive their MBAs from Temworkzfun University make excellent managers of work groups. Imagine that you have access to the four pieces of information in Figure 13–6 (based on Einhorn and Hogarth, 1978).

Imagine that A, B, C, and D are cards. One side of each card indicates where the student was trained (either at Temworkzfun or Idoitalone University), and the other side indicates their performance during the first year on the job. By turning over cards A and B, we learn about these students' performance on the job, and by turning over cards C and D, we learn where these students were trained.

You want to check the validity of the claim that students trained at Temworkzfun University are excellent at managing groups. Which cards would you turn over to check your hypothesis?

Most people choose to turn over card A. If the other side of the card reveals that the student is a successful manager, then this lends direct support to the hypothesis. Some people also turn over card C, in which they expect to see that the successful manager was trained at Temworkzfun University. Whereas card C can add *confirming* evidence to card A, it does not provide *unique* information.

So far, so good. However, the manager who stops at this point is in danger of committing a **confirmation error.** That is, this manager has not tried to falsify his claim. Only by attempting to refute one's beliefs can we gain support for them if they survive our attempts at disconfirmation.

Consider card B. What will this card reveal? Nothing—because we do not have any particular hypotheses concerning Idoitalone University.

Now, consider card D. This is the important one to test. If our hypothesis is right, then we should expect the student to have been trained elsewhere, but not at Temworkzfun University. However, if the student was trained at Temworkzfun University, this *disconfirms* our beliefs. Thus, cards A and D are the crucial ones to turn over to adequately test our hypothesis.

This logic is easy to see in retrospect, but very hard to see prior to solving the problem. For example, in a group of 23 statisticians, only five correctly chose cards A and D. Thus, even experts fall prey to the confirmation bias (Einhorn and Hogarth, 1978).

Why Is It Hard to Learn from Experience?

Considering that most of us negotiate and make decisions every day of our lives, then by some definition, we should all be experts at negotiation. However, the disconcerting truth is that most of us consistently fall short of ideal performance at the negotiation table and squander valuable resources. The consequences of inefficiency are serious and dramatic. Hundreds of thousands of dollars go wasted, interpersonal relations are strained, and much valuable time is ill spent (Thompson and Hrebec, 1996).

Obviously, mere experience does not guarantee the development of effective negotiation skills. Why? Four factors hinder our ability to learn optimally from experience: delayed outcomes, variability in the environment, counterfactual thinking, and unique decisions.

Delayed Outcomes: I Wish I'd Known Then What I Know Now

Often, the results of the choices that we make in life are delayed. We make a decision and only later experience the consequences of our choice. Consider a student faced with the decision of which graduate school to attend. Out of five possibilities, the student may select only one. After choosing to go to a Midwestern university, the student may wonder whether she made the right decision. It may take her several years to realize the outcome of her education on her professional life. Furthermore, the choice she makes is confounded by many other circumstances. At the time the student attends graduate school, she meets her future husband and has a baby. So, it becomes very difficult to unambiguously connect a given effect—in this case, the student's success on the job market—with a particular cause—her choice of graduate school.

Variation

Two people were embroiled in a bitter conflict situation. One of the parties attempted to bridge their differences by suggesting that both make a concession. He left a message on an answering machine for the other party. His suggestion for a "bilateral" concession was misinterpreted by a receptionist at the other end who wrote "unilateral" concession on a memo. The conflict worsened. This is a tragicomic case of how perturbations in the environment can obscure us from perceiving the truth.

Consider the causes of a labor strike at Dow Chemical Company (Hammond et al., 1975). Both management and union representatives were interviewed about the issues in the conflict, their preferences concerning the issues, and their perceptions of the other party's preferences. Each side did not have an accurate view of the interests of the other party nor those of their own side. In fact, both union and management preferred the same wage settlement but failed to realize this at the time of the strike.

The Road Less Traveled

In a famous poem, Robert Frost writes about the road less traveled—what life would be like had the narrator taken some other path. Unfortunately, life does not offer us the opportunity to experiment with different courses of action; we can't do two different things and pick the one with the best results. We accept jobs, buy houses, sell cars, embark on research projects, and never get a chance to know what would have happened if we had made a different decision.

Nevertheless, we think about the roads not traveled. The act of thinking about how things might have turned out differently is counterfactual thinking (Kahneman and Miller, 1986). Sometimes this can lead to feelings of regret. The inability to see the outcomes of different choices we make severely handicaps our ability to learn from experience. That is, we may not realize that by having taken a different course of action, we actually would have been better off.

Uniqueness

Many important decisions are unique. For example, choosing a spouse, a job, or a particular joint venture are decisions that only come around once in a while. Consequently, there is little opportunity for learning. If people don't have an opportunity to learn, they fall back on surface features; that is, they make decisions and judgments using superficial, meaningless cues rather than diagnostic information. For example, when people are presented with sayings or morals such as "all that glitters is not gold," "every cloud has a silver lining," and "don't judge a book by its cover," judgments of the similarity of the sayings are based upon surface similarity, such as the presence of similar words (e.g., "all that glitters . . ." is seen as similar to ". . . silver lining"), rather than on deeper meaning (e.g., "all that glitters . . ." and "don't judge a book . . .") (Gentner and Gentner, 1983).

IMPROVING NEGOTIATION PERFORMANCE: BEST PRACTICES

What do empirical data reveal about the best method for learning in negotiation tasks? We consider the three most common learning situations: (1) bargaining markets, (2) repeated dyadic interactions, and (3) structured training programs.

Bargaining Markets

We discuss two types of markets. One we'll call the **transaction market,** where the objective is to complete as many profitable transactions as possible. The other we'll call the **relationship market,** where the objective is to find the best match in a market.

Transaction Markets

Consider a typical transaction market: a local arts and crafts festival. Merchants and vendors spend summer and fall traveling around the country to sell their crafts and artwork in streets, convention halls, gymnasiums, and parking lots. Their goal is to complete as many profitable transactions as possible in a typical weekend craft show. Another transaction market is the stock market.

In transaction markets, there are two types of people: buyers and sellers. In a typical market simulation, buyers and sellers are instructed to complete as many profitable transactions with members of the other type as possible within a given amount of time (i.e., before the close of the business day). In simulations of transaction markets, the only restriction is that parties may not negotiate a deal with the same person more than once. In the typical simulation, buyers and sellers are clones; that is, all buyers are identical in terms of their preferences, as are sellers.

The quality of negotiated outcomes in bargaining markets may be examined in terms of the extent to which negotiators reach level 3 integrative agreements and the number of successful transactions that they complete. In this sense, there is a quality and quantity aspect to performance. The vendor at the craft show wants to sell as many lava lamps as possible at a good price.

The average value of negotiated transactions is more profitable over time, approaching the pareto-optimal frontier (Bazerman, Magliozzi, and Neale, 1985). However, it is unclear whether negotiators are learning skills that generalize across different negotiation situations or whether performance is task specific and represents just the tip of the learning iceberg.

Relationship Markets: Finding a Good Match

Consider a relationship market: Sandy is a second-year MBA student at a leading university; she seeks a position at a consulting firm. Sandy is on the job market along with many of her colleagues. She is attempting to distinguish herself from the other applicants. On the other side of the market, a similar process is occurring. Consulting firms in Chicago, San Francisco, New York, and Boston are competing for the "best" students on the market to fill what they see as too many positions in a lean market.

In relationship markets, the objective is not to complete as many profitable transactions as possible but rather to make the best single match from among many possible alternative matches. Imagine that you are presented with a series of houses to look at, all listed at the same price. There are 100 houses that are ranked from 1 to 100 in terms of quality. You may look at each one and then make a decision whether or not to buy it. If you decide to buy it, the search stops and you don't see any more houses. However, if you decide to pass it over, you cannot go back to it at a later time when it is off the market. You know in advance that you will see 100 houses of different quality and that they will be presented in a random order in terms of quality. What do you do? How do you know when to stop looking? There are two tragedies that could result: (a) you could pass over a great house and have to settle for a less great house, or (b) you could too quickly choose an average house when a great house could have been had by waiting.

Imagine a similar situation in which you are interviewing for jobs with several different employers. You have a series of interviews lined up for spring term. The first company you interview with makes you an "exploding" offer that will quickly expire. Should you take it? You still have four interviews scheduled. You believe that you have a "best match" out there, but the question is: How do you know it when you see it?

Sondak and Bazerman (1989) studied a version of this problem by creating a simulation involving a large group of job candidates and employers. In reality, there did exist a "best match" between pairs of candidates and employers, but there was also time pressure among candidates to land a job and among firms to sign candidates. Members of the market often failed to meet their match. In fact, markets fell far short of a rational set of solutions.

One solution for such situations is to use an algorithm that matches candidates with firms, such as is done in medical internship placements. People are often reluctant to rely on such mechanisms, however, fearing that the loss of control will result in worse outcomes. In actuality, outcomes are usually better from the perspective of parties on both sides of the market, although it is true that a matching algorithm must be biased toward one side of the market, either the employer's or the candidate's. In the case of medical students and teaching hospitals, the market is biased for the hospital; that is, the hospital is more likely to get its top candidate than is the top student.

Can Experience Be Detrimental to Learning?

Most of the time we think of experience as having beneficial effects on performance. There may be situations in which experience can backfire, however. Probably the most dramatic illustration of this is the functional fixedness effect (Maier, 1931). As an illustration, consider the diagram in Figure 13–7. The goal is to try to attach the candle to the wall (using only the materials provided) so that it burns properly in an upright position.

Most people who attempt to solve this problem have a difficult time because they are used to thinking about the objects as they normally use them. The solution to the problem re-

FIGURE 13–7. The Candle Problem

Source: Adapted from Anderson, J. R. (1995). *Cognitive psychology and its implications*, 4th ed. New York: W. H. Freeman. 265. Copyright © 1995 by W. H. Freeman. Used with permission.

quires thinking about the objects in a completely different way from their common usage. (The solution to this situation, incidentally, is to create a sturdy platform for the candle by using the box of tacks as a candle holder and attaching the box to the wall with the tacks.)

Can experience hinder negotiators' ability to reach integrative agreements? To examine this, Thompson (1990b) had negotiators engage in two bargaining tasks. One group of people engaged in a task that had integrative potential (e.g., contained issues that could be logrolled and were compatible). Another group engaged in a similar task, but this task did not have integrative potential. It was a purely fixed-sum task. It was predicted that negotiators who engaged in a purely fixed-sum negotiation would develop fixed-pie perceptions about negotiation that would hinder their ability to reach integrative agreements in a subsequent task that contained integrative potential. Negotiators who had experience in tasks with logrolling potential performed better in subsequent integrative tasks than did those whose experience was in a purely fixed-sum task. Those who engaged in the fixed-sum task during the first period were not worse off than those who did not have any experience. Thus, experience in negotiation doesn't hurt subsequent performance, but it doesn't always help.

Can Experience Buy a Relative Advantage?

Is a negotiator who has more or less experience than his or her opponent at an advantage at the bargaining table? Is he or she able to claim a larger share of resources?

To examine this question, Thompson (1990a) had 20 negotiators engage in a total of seven bargaining tasks. Each of the tasks was unique, but all contained the potential for integrative agreement, so a common index of performance was used to measure outcomes across all of the tasks. Specifically, each task contained a pair of issues which could be logrolled to maximize joint gain and a compatible issue for which negotiators had identical preferences. The 20 negotiators in the "high experience" group negotiated on each task with "naïves," people who had either one previous negotiating experience or none at all.

Performance results were plotted over time as the "high experience" group gained experience (see Figure 13–8). Some interesting patterns emerged: (1) In general, negotiators' ability to logroll, or make mutually beneficial tradeoffs, improved as they gained experience; (2) negotiators were more successful in logrolling when the naïve member of the bargaining pair had just a single previous bargaining experience as opposed to no previous experience; (3) highly experienced negotiators claimed a larger share of the pie of resources at the expense of naïve counterparts; and (4) the advantage of experienced negotiators increased over time (i.e., as they gained more experience).

The beneficial results for experience were qualified by an important caveat: Experience did not improve negotiators' ability to recognize compatible issues. At least one negotiator in 71 percent of all pairs failed to realize that they had some interests that were perfectly compatible with those of the other party; 20 percent reached lose–lose agreements.

Process and Outcome Feedback

In all of the examinations of experience we have discussed thus far, negotiators engage in a task and then move on to another task without ever knowing how well they did in the previous task. However, as we saw in chapter 11, people often seek social comparison information as a way of assessing their own performance. Such information may serve a potentially use-

FIGURE 13–8. Logrolling Performance

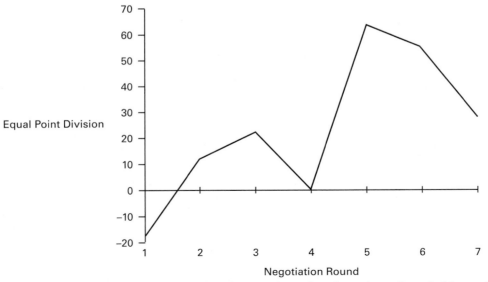

Source: Thompson, L. (1990a). An examination of naïve and experienced negotiators. *Journal of Personality and Social Psychology* **59**: 86. Copyright © 1990 by the American Psychological Association. Reprinted with permission.

ful purpose, by providing feedback to negotiators about the relationship between their own and the other party's interests.

As a way of examining this idea, Thompson and DeHarpport (1994) had negotiators engage in a series of four negotiations. Each task was unique and therefore required a different agreement to reach an integrative outcome. All tasks contained integrative potential, however, and so comparisons of performance across tasks were possible.

Negotiators received one of three different types of feedback between each task. Those in the "no feedback" condition did not receive any information about either the other party or the underlying structure of the task. They were given a blank sheet of paper and asked to write some comments about the nature of their experience on the previous task. Those in the "outcome" feedback condition were told how much the other party received in the previous negotiation. This feedback provided important information for negotiators in terms of clues about the underlying structure of the task. Finally, those in the "process" feedback condition were given complete information about the preferences of their opponent for each of the issues in the previous task. To ensure that negotiators considered the information carefully, they were asked to study the information and write down their observations and thoughts.

Negotiators who received process feedback were the most likely to recognize the integrative potential of subsequent negotiation tasks and abandon the pervasive fixed-pie assumption. They were also more likely to effectively logroll their interests to increase joint gain and to abandon the fixed-pie perception, compared to those who did not receive feedback. Negotiators who received only outcome feedback were midway between the no-feedback and process feedback groups.

Even among negotiators who received process feedback in which the learning conditions were nearly ideal, a significant number (14 percent) still failed to reach integrative agreements. Furthermore, a significant number (36 percent) failed to develop an accurate perception of the integrative structure of the task, despite the perfect feedback. These results attest to the robust nature of the fixed-pie perception.

The Power of Information

One of the key mechanisms that improves performance in negotiation is information seeking. As we saw in chapter 4, negotiators usually lack the information necessary to determine what an optimal agreement would be and, more to the point, to know the most they could possibly claim in the negotiation while ensuring that an agreement is reached.

Thompson (1991) set up a situation in which negotiators either provided, sought, or were alerted about other parties' interests. All of these groups were compared to a group of naïve negotiators. Negotiators bargained over the course of three different trials, each requiring different tradeoffs to reach integrative agreement. There were three notable effects: (1) Negotiators who provided or sought information were more likely to reach integrative agreements compared to naïve negotiators; (2) these groups improved at a faster rate or had a steeper learning curve than the naïve negotiators; and (3) negotiators in the alerted and naïve groups did not spontaneously exchange much information (20 percent sought information and 7 percent provided information).

The Information Advantage

It is not too surprising that when both people in a negotiation provide information to one another, joint outcomes increase; however, we can't always count on the other person to give us information. What are the implications when information is asymmetric?

Imagine a negotiation in which only one person in each dyad provides or seeks information to or from the other. Is it sufficient for only one "enlightened" party to reach integrative agreement? Would the asymmetric information lead to a distributive advantage for the "disclosing" negotiator?

Negotiators who provide or seek information are successful in maximizing joint outcomes in a single-handed fashion (Thompson, 1991, Experiment 2). Surprisingly, there is no evidence of a distributive advantage for the party who had information about the opponent, suggesting that providing opponents with information about our priorities does not place the negotiator at a competitive disadvantage.

Training Programs

Every year, thousands of managers and managers-to-be engage in negotiations training programs. How effective are these training programs?[1] In a typical training program, managers are introduced to the topic of negotiation and then provided with a set of skills and techniques for reaching integrative agreement. This may be done in a purely didactic method or supplemented with simulations and role play.

In one examination, Neale, Northcraft, and Early (1990) had participants engage in a bargaining market exercise. The next day, participants attended a seminar on the basic principles of negotiation, wherein negotiation was defined and described, distributive versus integrative negotiation concepts were introduced, and strategies for moving from distributive to integrative agreements were included. On the final day, the participants again engaged in a bargaining market exercise. Those who had received training were more likely to reach integrative agreements in the second market exercise if they had also set specific goals compared to those who merely tried to "do their best." Apparently, training programs like this can improve negotiation performance—provided that negotiators set goals.

Evaluating Program Effectiveness

How can we evaluate the success of negotiation training programs? Two groups of people, identical in most respects, must be randomly assigned to a training group or to a control group, and the performance of each group must be measured on criteria of interest. This last point is important. Imagine a situation in which negotiators engaged in a task and their performance was then measured on the same task. This would be like assessing the effectiveness of a GMAT preparation course by using the actual test items that students would ultimately be tested on! This would result in very high scores, but we would not know whether the students were really smart. Ideally, we want our criterion measure of performance to be different enough from the training program so as to assess the ability of negotiators to apply concepts to novel tasks in creative ways—that is, to get to the core of the learning iceberg. This is the essence of real learning. If we just measured the success of each group on the training task, this wouldn't tell us whether the learning could be extended to meaningful applications.

How can we assess long-term change? Consider a manager who attends a course on negotiating skills. How can the effectiveness of the training program be measured? Should we look at his or her sales pre- and post-training? Self-reports? Company profit? This is a very difficult question to assess. The challenge is to use a measure of performance that is important enough to care about, but that can be objectively assessed and not influenced by extraneous factors.

---

[1] In this chapter, we do not address the vast differences in the *content* of training programs.

Experience in Competitive Judgment Tasks

In some cases, negotiators are faced with a competitive situation in which they must make a decision. How well do negotiators think about such problems? Bazerman and Carroll (1987) presented individuals with the problem in Box 13–2.

BOX 13–2

Acquiring a Company

INSTRUCTIONS

You represent company A (the acquirer), which is considering acquiring company T (the target) by means of a tender offer. You plan to tender in cash for 100 percent of company T's share but are unsure how high a price to offer.

The main complication is this: The value of company T depends directly on the outcome of a major oil exploration project it is currently undertaking. Indeed, company T's very viability depends on that outcome. If the project fails, the company under current management will be worth nothing. But if the company succeeds, the value of the company under current management could be as high as $100/share. All share values between $0 and $100 are considered equally likely.

By all estimates, the company will be worth considerably more in the hands of company A than under current management. In fact, whatever the ultimate value under current management, *company T will be worth 50 percent more under the management of A*. If the project fails, the company is worth $0/share under either management. If the exploration project generates a $50/share value under current management, the value under company A is $75/share. Similarly, a $100/share value under company T implies a $150/share value under company A, and so on.

Company A's board of directors has asked you to determine the price they should offer for company T's shares. This offer must be made now, *before* the exploration outcome is known. From all indicators, company T would be happy to be acquired by company A, *provided it is at a profitable price*. Moreover, company T wishes to avoid, at all cost, the potential takeover bid by any other firm. You expect company T to delay a decision on your bid until the results of the project are in and then accept or reject your offer before the news of the results reaches the press.

Thus, you (company A) will not know the result of the exploration project when submitting your price offer, but company T will know the results when deciding whether or not to accept your offer. In addition, company T is expected to accept any offer by company A that is greater than the (per share) value of the company under current management.

As the representative of company A, you are deliberating over offers in the range of $0/share (this is tantamount of making no offer at all) to $150/share. What price per share would you tend for company T's stock?

$_____/share

Source: Samuelson, W. F. and M. H. Bazerman (1985). Negotiating under the winner's curse. In *Research in Experimental Economics*. V. Smith, ed. New York: JAI Press: 3. Reprinted by permission of JAI Press, Inc.

Most people faced with this situation bid somewhere between $50 to $75 for the shares of the company. Their logic goes something like this: "On average, the firm is worth $50 to target and $75 to acquirer. Consequently, a transaction in this range will, on average, be profitable to both parties."

Deeper reflection reveals a problem with this logic. Suppose that a person offers $60/share to acquire the firm. This means that the offer will be accepted, on average, 60 percent of the time, or whenever the firm is worth between $0 and $60 to the target. Because all values are equally likely between $0 and $60, the firm will, on average, be worth $30/share to the target when the target accepts a $60/share offer and will be worth $45/share to the acquirer. This, of course, results in a loss of $15/share. Consequently, an offer of $60/share is unwise because it results, on average, in a loss. As it turns out, this same reasoning extends to any positive offer an acquirer could make. On average, the acquirer obtains a company worth 25 percent less than the price offered when its offer is accepted.

The paradox of the situation is that, even though in all circumstances the firm is worth more to the acquirer than to the target, any offer above $0 leads to a negative expected return to the acquirer. The source of the paradox lies in the high likelihood that the target will accept the acquirer's offer when the firm is least valuable to the acquirer—in other words, when it is a "lemon" (Akerlof, 1970).

At this point, we might employ rational expectations theory and argue that, whereas decision making may be suboptimal in a one-shot situation, if people had repeated experience, their behavior would quickly adapt. To investigate this, Ball, Bazerman, and Carroll (1991) had students trained in game theory engage in 20 trials of the "acquiring a company" problem. After each trial, they received feedback about the value of the firm to them. The startling finding was that there was no obvious learning trend. That is, even on the last trial, the average offer for the firm was $50 to $75/share!

Mental Models

Consider the brain teaser in Box 13–3.

What is going on in this situation? The events don't seem to make much sense until we learn that the man who walked into the bar had a case of the hiccups. The bartender apparently realized this and attempted to scare the daylights out of the man. Some people are able to solve this problem immediately; others are not.

Mental models are the ways in which people think about solving problems (Johnson-Laird, 1983; Rouse and Morris, 1986). Consider a person's mental model of how the thermostat operates to control the temperature in his house (Gentner and Gentner, 1983). One person may use a mental model of his car to understand the process of the thermostatic

---

BOX 13–3

Brainteaser

A man walks into a bar and asks for a glass of water. The bartender points a shotgun at the man. The man says "Thank you," and walks out.

Source: Dayton, T., F. T. Durso, and J. D. Shepard (1990). A measure of the knowledge reorganization underlying insight. In *Pathfinder associative networks: Studies in knowledge organization*. R. W. Schraneveldt, ed. Norwood, NJ: Ablex.

temperature control. He may assume that the dial on the thermostat is like the gas pedal in his car. By turning up the heat (pressing on the pedal), the house gets warmer faster (the car goes faster). Another person may have a quite different mental model of how the thermostat operates. She reasons that the dial on the thermostat is like the dial on her oven. By turning up the heat on the thermostat (turning the oven on 400 degrees), the house reaches that temperature (the oven is preheated to the specified temperature). She correctly realizes that the house (and her oven) will reach the desired temperature (400 degrees) equally fast no matter whether the oven is turned to 500 or 400 degrees initially. However, if an oven is turned up to 500 degrees, it will get too hot. People often misapply mental models, such as the person who operates his home thermostat like his gas pedal. The result is higher utility bills and an uncomfortable house. If faulty mental models are applied to negotiation situations, the outcomes will be less efficient.

Negotiators have different kinds of mental models that they apply to negotiation situations. People who effectively resolve negotiation situations construct mental models that make the discovery and implementation of integrative agreements more likely. There are two primary ways of thinking about negotiation: the "fixed-pie" model and the "creative problem-solving" model (Van Boven and Thompson, 1996).

Fixed-pie Model

The fixed-pie model assumes that each negotiator wants to claim as much of a fixed pie of resources as he or she can for him- or herself. Outcomes are determined by a contest of wills (i.e., who can hold out the longest or bully the other) or through compromise (wherein both parties make concessions from their target points). Consider, for example, a negotiation between a potential car buyer and car salesperson. The buyer warily approaches the salesperson and makes the lowest bid he or she can without risking being laughed at. The car dealer disappears and returns with a counteroffer. The buyer makes another concession. The car dealer then makes a concession, and this process of offer–counteroffer–concession continues until one party suggests splitting the difference.

Creative Problem-solving Model

A quite different mental model views negotiation as requiring creative problem solving (Pruitt and Carnevale, 1993). Creative problem-solving models do not assume that parties' interests are completely opposed but rather that negotiators must exchange information to discover the other person's interests. Once the other party's interests are known vis-à-vis one's own interests, then resolutions may be proposed so as to capitalize on divergence of interests. Consider, for example, a negotiation between an employee and an employer concerning salary, benefits, and support staff. The employer may be concerned with keeping medical coverage down; whereas the employee is more concerned with support staff. An integrative solution to this situation involves a tradeoff between benefits and support staff: The employee is hired with few medical benefits but with a lavish support staff. The key to discovering integrative solutions is for parties to realize that they have different preferences for the issues to be negotiated. In other situations, integrative agreement may be reached by identifying interests that the parties share (Thompson and Hrebec, 1996).

Do the mental models of negotiators who effectively resolve their conflicts differ in fundamental ways from those who fail to resolve conflicts or reach inefficient outcomes? A major difference between the fixed-pie mental model and the creative problem-solving mental model is the incidence of information exchange. Further, because negotiation is a collaborative activity, negotiators who have mental models more similar to those of their opponent should be more likely to resolve the conflict in a mutually beneficial or integrative fashion. This is the contagion idea that we talked about in chapter 10.

In a recent study, pairs of people were instructed to negotiate against one another on a negotiation task which contained potential for integrative agreement via tradeoffs and compatible issues. We identified those who reached level 3 integrative agreements (solvers) and those who failed to reach level 3 integrative agreements (nonsolvers). We then measured negotiators' mental models using a technique known as similarity-judgment ratings (Van Boven and Thompson, 1996).

The solvers had a different mental picture of the negotiation compared to nonsolvers. There were four key differences between solvers and nonsolvers:

- The mental models of solvers (negotiators who reached level 3 integrative agreements in negotiation) were structurally different from those of nonsolvers (those who failed to reach pareto-optimal agreements. The key structural difference was the centrality of "exchange information."

- Another major structural difference between solvers' and nonsolvers' mental models was the prominence of each party's most important issue; the priority of issues to negotiators is key in the development of integrative tradeoffs between differentially valued issues.

- Negotiators with problem-solving models made more accurate judgments about their opponents' interests.

- The mental models of solvers were more similar to those of their opponents than were the mental models of nonsolvers, suggesting that convergence of mental models—contagion—is key for negotiation success.

Trained versus Naïve Negotiators

In a follow-up investigation, we compared "trained" versus "nontrained" negotiators. Arguably, trained negotiators have a much larger repertoire of skills than do nontrained negotiators. Accordingly, we designed training conditions for creating expertise in one group of participants but not in others. We offered a negotiation skills course to a group of students for a period of 10 weeks.

What differences were there between the trained group and the naïve group?

1. Trained negotiators efficiently resolved the negotiation; most reached level 3 outcomes. The trained negotiators reached outcomes that were clearly superior to nonsolvers.

2. The mental models of trained negotiators were structurally more similar to solvers than nonsolvers. Specifically, trained negotiators were more likely to have "exchange information" as a central node and they were more likely to link each negotiator to his or her most important issue. These two structural features were the main ways that solvers' mental models differed from nonsolvers'.

3. Trained negotiators had fewer links in their mental models than both solvers and nonsolvers. The creative problem-solving model is more refined and parsimonious than the fixed-pie model.

4. Analyses of the mental models of each trained participant corroborate the aggregate mental model; that is, the models of trained negotiators were more similar to the solvers than to the nonsolvers. Trained negotiators each had a greater number of links to exchange information.

5. Trained negotiators showed greater insight into their opponents' interests than did nonsolvers, but had less insight than solvers.

6. Finally, the mental models of trained negotiators showed remarkable convergence: The mental models of opponents were highly similar, suggesting that trained negotiators developed shared representations of the task system (Klimoski and Mohammed, 1994).

In sum, creative problem-solving mental models of negotiation may be reliably created through experience. The implication for negotiation training is clear: The negotiators in study 2 were challenged with a novel negotiation task that they had not seen during their 10-week training period. Yet, they were able to apply effective negotiation strategies to resolve the situation.

SPECIAL FOCUS: EXPERTS

So far, we have limited our focus to examinations of naïve and novice negotiators. Might we learn something more about negotiation by studying experts—people who negotiate for a living and who are successful at what they do? What do studies of real experts reveal about negotiation? The findings are surprising.

Greater Confidence, Less Accuracy

Experts are more *confident* about their judgments, but not more *accurate* than naïve decision makers. For example, experts' ability to make accurate diagnoses of patients' mental illnesses was compared to diagnoses made by secretaries (Chapman and Chapman, 1967). Real doctors and their secretaries were given the results of a "draw-a-person" test (a common projective test used in clinical assessment). Psychiatrists made diagnoses of patients; secretaries (with no clinical expertise) also made diagnoses. Shockingly, there was no difference in the accuracy of diagnosis between the two groups.

Similar findings apply to experts in other domains, such as financial analysis. One exception to this general rule is weather forecasters, who are more accurate and calibrated than other experts. The reason for this is the availability of immediate feedback. Weather forecasters know immediately whether their prediction was correct or not and can quickly update their mental models for predicting weather.

Although evidence for unrealistic optimism is considerable, people abandon their optimism and even become pessimistic in anticipation of self-relevant feedback. For example, when college sophomores, juniors, and seniors estimate their likely salary at their first full-time job after graduation, only seniors grow less optimistic as graduation approaches (Sheppard, Ouellette, and Fernandez, 1996). The same pattern happens when students predict their exam scores: Unrealistic optimism gives way to pessimistic forecasts as exam time approaches.

Complex Thoughts or Simple Minds?

It would seem that experts would have greater insight into how they make judgments than would naïve persons. An intriguing study by Northcraft and Neale (1987) suggests that this is not the case. Northcraft and Neale presented a group of experts (real estate appraisers) and a group of nonexperts with a task that involved assessing the value of a piece of real estate. Each participant was presented with a large packet of information on which to base his or her decision, among which included the list price of the property. After making their judgments about the value of the property, experts and naïves were asked to what extent the list price figured prominently in their appraisal. The experts uniformly denied that they used list price and instead described a complex formula involving a number of variables to arrive at an overall evaluation of the property.

Despite their claims, analysis showed that experts relied almost exclusively on the property's list price to determine their appraisals. Experts showed a profound lack of insight into their own judgment policies and, in general, believed that they were more complex than they really were. For most judgments, ranging from the selection of graduate students to the diagnosis of diseases, people tend to rely on one or two prominent cues to make their decisions, but believe that they consider several.

Expertise and Integrative Bargaining

It would seem that experts in negotiation should do better at the bargaining table than naïves. Consider experts' versus amateurs' performance on an integrative bargaining task (Neale and Northcraft, 1986). The experts were corporate real-estate executives with an average of 10 years' experience. The amateurs were students at a state university. The experts were more successful in reaching integrative agreements in novel bargaining tasks than were the amateurs, but the rate of learning was higher for naïves than for experts. A likely explanation is the presence of a **ceiling effect:** Experts had less room to show dramatic improvement compared to naïves.

However, experts do not consistently outperform naïves in novel tasks. For example, professionals (head buyers for West German department stores) and nonprofessionals (vocational retraining students) engaged in an integrative bargaining task did not differ (Sholtz, Fleisher, and Bentpup, 1982). The professionals resolved conflicts more quickly than did nonprofessionals, but they did not differ in terms of joint outcomes (pareto-efficiency).

In Search of Expertise?

What is the best way to study experts? One suggestion is to identify a sample of experts (e.g., senior executive managers) and study their behavior. However, this methodology raises several thorny issues.

Baseline for comparison. If we find that experts engage in a particular behavior, the question remains as to whether we are learning something unique about experts or about human behavior in general. This question can be answered only if we identify a **control group** of experts that serves as a basis for comparison. However, the presence of a control group does not completely solve the problem. There are many ways that experts differ from others, which means that any number of things could be the cause for seeing a difference.

Self-report. A common way to study experts is to conduct an interview and question experts about their behavior and thoughts. However, there are several serious problems with using self-report data (Ericcson and Simon, 1980). Self-reports are plagued with inaccuracy. People remember events in self-serving ways. They also tend to use stereotypical sequences to fill in missing pieces of information. Further, the mere recollection of events tends to alter our evaluation of them (Millar and Tesser, 1986). Egocentric biases and schematic information processing encroach on our memory.

Information and ignorance. To get a complete picture of a negotiation, we need to have an analysis of both parties (i.e., the seller and the buyer) to accurately determine the pareto frontier. For example, Balke, Hammond, and Meyer (1973) performed a post hoc investigation of the labor strike at Dow Chemical Company. Interviewing either labor or management alone would have provided an incomplete picture of the negotiation. Only by conducting interviews with both management and union representatives were Hammond and his colleagues able to determine the issues in conflict and the pareto frontier of possible solutions.

What do we want experts to tell us? As we have seen, game theory provides a compelling analysis of the tensions, goals, and most desirable outcomes in negotiation situations. Furthermore, behavioral negotiation theory provides a compelling analysis of the strategies that negotiators may employ to reach integrative agreements and maximize their share of bargaining surplus. This raises the question of what exactly it is that we want experts to tell us. Do we want to examine whether they think in a game theoretic fashion? Do we want to see how they implemented strategies? Starkly stated, we have a well-developed normative theory of behavior. What more do we want to know? What is it that we expect experts to do?

Distribution, not creation. One hazard in the study of experts in negotiation is the temptation to focus on the distributive, rather than the integrative, aspect of negotiation. This is a mistake, because the distributive and integrative aspects of negotiation are intertwined; we cannot understand distribution without an appreciation of integration and vice versa. Most negotiators don't need help with the distributive aspect of negotiation; the integrative aspect is the most challenging.

DEVELOPING THE CREATIVE MIND

Creativity is one of the most important negotiation skills. Many managers of organizations would like to unleash their creative thought processes and those of their work groups. The typical approach is to focus on the individual. However, organizational creativity and innovation are never solely the result of individual action; they are the product of three main shaping forces (Csikszentmihalyi, 1988) (see Figure 13–9).

- The **field:** A set of social institutions that selects from the variations produced by individuals those that are worth preserving.
- The domain: A stable culture that will preserve and transmit the selected new ideas to the following generations.
- The person: The person who brings about some change in the domain that the field considers to be creative.

In an examination of creativity in microbiology labs, the labs that were the most creative did three things (Dunbar, 1995):

- used analogies freely
- paid attention to inconsistencies
- had heterogeneous teams

What individual attributes does it take to be creative? Persistence, commitment, and determination. Creative scientists typically work 70 to 80 hours a week. In addition, there is an extended period of preparation. It typically takes people at least 10 years to learn their domain.

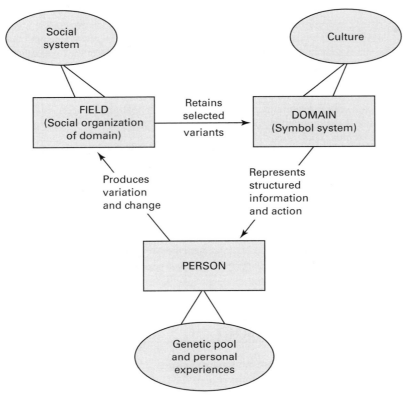

FIGURE 13-9. The Locus of Creativity

Source: Csikszentmihalyi, M. (1988). In *The nature of creativity: Contemporary psychological perspectives*. R. Sternberg (ed.). New York: Cambridge University Press. Reprinted with permission of Cambridge University Press.

In most ways, experts are ordinary people. What makes them unique is that they see or structure problems differently than average people. For example, master chess players do not use special tricks; their strategies are not exceptional, but their **representation** of the problem is (DeGroot, 1965). The key to solving a problem lies in the way that it is represented.

CONCLUSION

In this chapter, we have wrestled with some of the most challenging issues that face negotiators who want to improve their performance. All of us engage in negotiations that call upon our previous experiences. Ideally, we would like to become experts. Understanding how to unlock integrative potential and best serve our interests is a fundamental goal for the negotiator. We have pointed to some of the stumbling blocks on the road to expertise.

TAKE-AWAYS

- An expert negotiator is able to see parallels across many different kinds of negotiation tasks and unlock the hidden integrative potential in almost any bargaining situation.

- There are many different ways to learn, but reasoning by analogy and using feedback are two of the most common and successful approaches.

- It is hard for us to capitalize from unaided experience because feedback is often delayed, faulty, or ambiguous.

- The most effective negotiators use principles of disconfirmation to test their hypotheses.

- To assess the effectiveness of a training program, it is necessary to identify a clear measure of what constitutes "success" in the workplace.

CHAPTER 14

Environmental, Technological, and Cultural Clashes:
When the Going Gets Tough

The Arctic National Wildlife Refuge is a 19 million acre area in the northwest corner of Alaska, created by President Jimmy Carter in 1980. Environmentalists call it the last intact and protected Arctic ecosystem. The refuge, the chief calving ground for the porcupine caribou herd, 150,000 of which migrate the shores of the Arctic Ocean during the summer, is also believed to be the last chance for a major oil strike in the United States, according to Alaskan leaders and oil-industry officials. The dispute over oil drilling in the refuge focuses on the potential effects of development on the caribou and the impoverished Gwich'in Indians, who depend on the herd for food.

The dispute is a complex tangle of issues, parties, values, beliefs, information, and ideology. Bob Childers, an advocate for Alaska's Gwich'in Indians, opposes the drilling. The state of Alaska has struggled for more than two decades to open the refuge to oil and gas exploration, which improves the lives of Alaskans. Polls indicate, however, that a majority of Americans oppose developing a remote refuge that few will ever see. The Republican-controlled Congress approved oil drilling in the preserve in a measure intended to raise $1.3 billion to reduce the deficit, but a dispute developed within the Republican ranks. Moderate Republicans showed weak support for the drilling, and a disagreement over how to split the drilling revenues erupted. The economic arguments against drilling were bolstered when the U.S. Geological Survey halved its initial estimate of how much oil lies beneath the land.

There are many benefits to oil drilling. Neighbors of the Gwich'in, the Ipupiat people, who initially feared environmental damage from drilling, now fear that they will lose the benefits flowing in from the $120 million in current oil-related revenues each year from the Alaskan pipeline. As Isaa Akootchook, a village leader for the Inupiat, said as he watched Monday night football on his TV, "We used to be against [oil development] because we didn't know about these things. This [drilling] will be good for the Inupiat people"
(Chicago Tribune, November 14, 1995).

The Alaskan refuge battle, carried out with extensive direct-mail campaigns and full-page ads in far-off newspapers, is an example of how the environment is a symbol for our self- and world-views as well as a resource to be allocated. Our position on environmental issues provides a medium for the expression of fundamental values, beliefs, and ethics concerning the world. In this chapter, we deal with very difficult conflict situations involving clashes of value, as in the Alaskan situation, clashes of technology, and clashes of cultures. In the sections that follow, we (1) analyze environmental disputes, negotiations conducted via technology, and clashes of culture; (2) identify the key obstacles to effective dispute resolution; and (3) show how to create movement in these seemingly intractable disputes.

CONSENSUS CONFLICT VS. SCARCE RESOURCE COMPETITION

In chapter 1, we distinguished consensus conflict from scarce resource competition in our conflict tree model. Virtually all of the conflicts we have addressed thus far have been ones where scarce resources are at stake. However, many conflicts arise not because of competing interests, but because parties do not share the same conceptualization of the situation, such as when people have divergent ideologies and values. The mode of resolution for such conflicts is not compromise, concessions, or the integrative bargaining model. Resolution requires an altered understanding of the situation by one or both people.

Consider the framework in Table 14–1, which presents a four-cell table for analyzing the nature of conflict.

For any given conflict, people's interests concerning scarce resources may be at stake and/or their beliefs about the nature of the world may be in conflict. Below, we consider four different conflict scenarios:

- **No conflict.** Parties are in agreement both in terms of their ideologies and the distribution of resources.
- **Scarce resource conflict.** People share a similar understanding of the situation, but are in disagreement concerning the allocation of resources. For example, an employee wants a higher wage than his employer is willing to give; Stan wants to put an addition on the house but his spouse doesn't want to spend the money; Georgia wants to outsource more product components, but her supervisor doesn't.
- **Ideological conflict.** People are in disagreement concerning their ideologies or the facts of a situation but do not have to apportion scarce resources (also see Keeney, 1992). For example,

TABLE 14–1. Typologies of Conflict

Conflict of Values (Ideology)	*Conflict of Interest (Scarce Resources)*	
	No	*Yes*
No	**No Conflict** Parties in agreement on issues and ideology	**Scarce Resource Conflict** Parties in disagreement about apportionment of resources but agree ideologically about the nature of the dispute
Yes	**Ideological Conflict** Parties in disagreement about nature of world, correct view, what should or ought to be; no disagreement concerning apportionment of resources	**Complex Conflict** Parties in disagreement about resources and about ideology

Source: Thompson, L. and R. Gonzalez (1997). Environmental disputes: Competition for scarce resources and clashing of values. In *Environment, ethics, and behavior.* M. Bazerman, D. Messick, A. Tenbrunsel, and K. Wade-Benzoni, eds. San Francisco: New Lexington Press: 84. Copyright © 1997 The New Lexington Press. Reprinted with permission. All rights reserved.

Gerry and Rita disagree about the mission of their product development team; Ann thinks John should be promoted but Harriet does not; Cara solves problems with rationality, while John relies on intuition and emotion.

- **Complex conflict.** People are in disagreement concerning their ideologies, and scarce resources are at stake. For example, Carla and Jose are in disagreement over who to hire for a junior management position; the conflict centers on racial and gender diversity as well as resources. We suspect that most conflicts concerning environmental issues are of this complex type.

Principles of rationality and integrative bargaining can only take us so far in understanding how these complex conflicts may be effectively resolved. In this chapter, we identify social psychological processes that prevent efficient dispute resolution, and suggest ways to resolve disputes that include conflict over fundamental beliefs and values.

Obstacles in the Effective Resolution of Conflict

Environmental conflicts involve competition for scarce resources and clashes of ideology. What problems might negotiators or third parties encounter as they attempt to fashion tradeoffs among issues in environmental disputes? Next, we highlight some of the key social psychological obstacles to the development of mutually beneficial, integrative agreements in environmental disputes.

Sacred Values and Taboo Tradeoffs: What Kind of Person Do You Think I Am?

Howard is involved in a negotiation with Rick concerning the sale of a piece of expensive property. Howard is selling the property in part because his wife is terribly ill with a rare lung disease and desperately needs a new lung. Hoping to liquidate most of his assets to help pay for medical bills, Howard is disappointed to learn that Rick does not have enough money to buy the property. Rick suggests that he give one of his lungs to Howard's wife in exchange for the property. Howard is shocked and horrified. Most people who hear about Rick's proposal are also horrified. Why? Rick has made a **taboo tradeoff** (Tetlock, Peterson, and Lerner, 1996).

Most people are equally horrified and shocked when parents offer to sell their children, citizens sell their right to a jury trial, and immigrants buy voting privileges. However, consider O. Henry's famous story "The Gift of the Magi," in which a woman sells her hair to buy her husband a watch fob for Christmas. This is a tender and acceptable tradeoff. Consider the "oldest profession," in which people buy and sell sexual pleasure. Clearly, there is a very thin line between acceptable and taboo tradeoffs. What if Rick were to offer free physical therapy or home care in exchange for the property? On a purely theoretical level, Rick is simply employing the powerful **tradeoff** principle we discussed in chapter 4 on integrative bargaining.

The tradeoff principle is ideal for handling scarce resource conflicts that contain issues that are fungible. The behavioral negotiation framework assumes that people are able to compare resources and make apple and orange comparisons among resources and trade them in a way that maximizes their outcomes. Remember in chapter 5 when we compared a dime, a nickel, and being shot at dawn. Normative bargaining theory assumes that everything is comparable and has a price. However, the notion of trading becomes unconscionable in some conflict situations (Tetlock, Peterson, and Lerner, 1996). People sometimes refuse to place a monetary value on a good or even think of trading it. To even suggest a trade is cause for moral outrage and soured negotiations. **Sacred issues** are deemed by the decision maker as those that cannot be compromised, traded, or even questioned[1] (Tetlock, Peterson, and Lerner, 1996); sacred issues are distinguished from their fungible cousin so common in the negotiation paradigm—**secular issues.** Attaching a monetary value to a bottle of wine, a house, or the services of a gardener can be a cognitively demanding task but raises no questions about the morality of the individual who proposes the sale or trade. In contrast, attaching monetary value to human life, familial obligations, national honor, and the ecosystem seriously undermines one's social identity or standing in the eyes of others (Schlenker, 1980). In a dispute concerning the construction of a dam that would remove native Indians from their ancestral land, a Yavapia teenager said, "The land is our mother. You don't sell your mother" (from Espeland, 1994).

Proposals to exchange sacred values (e.g., environmental resources) for secular ones (for example, money, time, or convenience) constitute taboo tradeoffs. Given the inherently sacred values that operate in environmental disputes, the familiar notions of trading and logrolling, so important to the theory of behavioral negotiation, are likely to be considered unacceptable and reprehensible to the environmentalist.

Yet, sacred and secular issues are contextually defined (Tetlock et al., 1996); there are no absolutes. Sociocultural norms affect the sacredness of certain positions, such as smoking, which is now generally considered baneful but in the recent past was completely acceptable. The sanctity of issues is also influenced by the labels and names used to define conflicts. For example, in 1994, all three members of Alaska's congressional delegation began referring to the part of the Arctic National Wildlife Refuge that would be subject to oil exploration as the "Arctic Oil Reserve." The group believed that this term was more accurate because that part of the refuge was not officially classified as either wilderness or refuge. Environmentalists, on the other hand, objected to this term and did not even like the use of the acronym ANWAR (Arctic Natural Wildlife Refuge), because they worried that unless the words "wildlife refuge" were clearly stated, the public wouldn't understand the value of the land.

---

[1] Whereas it might seem that a behavioral decision theorist may account for sacred values by attaching a very high monetary value, this is conceptually dissatisfying and doesn't address psychological aversion to trade.

Truly sacred values cannot exist because, by definition of the utility function (chapter 5), everyone "has their price." With sufficient compensation, people are willing to trade off a "sacred" value. The critical issue is not how much it takes to compensate someone for a sacred issue but, instead, what factors allow tradeoffs to occur on sacred issues.

The term "sacred" describes people's preferences on issues on which they view themselves as uncompromising. It immediately becomes obvious, however, that labeling an issue as sacred may be a negotiation ploy, rather than a reflection of heartfelt value. By anointing certain issues as sacred, and removing them from bargaining consideration, a negotiator increases the likelihood of a favorable settlement. The strategy is similar to the irrevocable commitment strategy (Schelling, 1960). We refer to issues that are not really sacred, but positioned as such, as **pseudosacred.**[2] Thus, for example, if the Yavapia Indians would trade one acre of land for a hospital, new school, or money, then the land is not truly sacred but pseudosacred.

Affiliation Bias: It's OK When I Do It, But Not When You Do It

A chemical company and an environmental advocacy group each leave a park picnic area without disposing of their waste products. Which group is judged most harshly? According to the affiliation bias, the chemical company group is judged more harshly than the environmental group, even when their actions are identical. The **affiliation bias** occurs when people evaluate a person's actions on the basis of their affiliations rather than on the merits of the behavior itself. For example, when football fans watch a game, they believe the other side commits more infractions than does their own team (Hastorf and Cantril, 1954).

Consider the following actions that a country could take: establishing a rocket base close to the borders of a country with whom it has strained relations; testing a new assault weapon; and establishing trade relations with a powerful country. People's perceptions of the acceptability of these actions differ dramatically as a function of the perceived agent. For example, during the time of the Cold War, U.S. citizens regarded the above actions to be much more beneficial when the U.S. was the one responsible than when the then U.S.S.R. had engaged in the same actions (Oskamp, 1965). People perceive the same objective behavior as either sinister or benign, merely as a consequence of the agent's affiliation.

Punctuation and Causal Chunking: You Leave Me No Choice

At noon, you have lunch with your friend, Melanie, who tells you that her colleague, Peter, tried to steal the database that had taken her months to compile. Melanie explains that she noticed that Peter had included her data in a proposal for a client. Melanie flew into a rage and called the client and effectively killed the deal. That evening Peter calls you and explains his version of the story: He had a great idea for a database for a project; he shared the idea with Melanie, who did most of the legwork in getting it compiled. She talked about charging clients to use it, so Peter included it in a proposal. Each person recounted the same event, but told a completely different story. Melanie views her own behavior as a reasonable response to Peter's malicious ploy to steal her database; Peter views his own behavior as his only response to Melanie's unprovoked accusation. In short, each person views him- or herself as responding to the other party's unprovoked actions.

Melanie's and Peter's behaviors are a continuous stream of cause-and-effect relationships; each person's actions influence the actions of others (Jones and Gerard, 1967). To an

---

[2] We are indebted to Max Bazerman for this term.

outside observer, their interaction is an uninterrupted sequence of interchanges. However, people who are actively engaged in conflict do not always see things this way. Instead, they organize their interactions into a series of discrete causal chunks (Swann, Pelham, and Roberts, 1987), a process known as causal chunking or punctuation (Whorf, 1956).

Causal chunks influence the extent to which people are aware of their influence on others, as well as their impressions of others. There are two kinds of chunking patterns: self-causal and other-causal. People form self-causal chunks (for example, my action causes my partner's action) when they possess an offensive set and other-causal chunks when they possess a defensive set.

The **biased punctuation of conflict** occurs when people interpret interactions with their adversaries in self-serving and other-derogating terms (Kahn and Kramer, 1990). An actor, A, perceives the history of conflict with another actor, B, as a sequence of B-A, B-A, B-A, in which the initial hostile or aggressive move was made by B, causing A to engage in defensive and legitimate retaliatory actions. Actor B punctuates the same history of interaction as A-B, A-B, A-B, however, reversing the roles of aggressor and defender.

Disagreement about how to punctuate a sequence of events and a conflict relationship is at the root of many environmental disputes. When each side to the dispute is queried, they explain their frustrations and actions as defenses against the acts of the other party. As a result, conflict escalates unnecessarily.

Perceived Efficacy of Coercion and Conciliation in Conflicts: I'd Rather Fight Than Switch

During World War II, the American journalist Edward R. Murrow made a nightly broadcast from London, reporting on the psychological and physical consequences of the Nazi bombing of British cities (Rothbart and Hallmark, 1988). Contrary to Nazi intent, the bombing did not move the British toward surrender. It had quite the opposite effect, strengthening rather than diminishing British resolve to resist German domination. Shortly after the United States entered World War II, the Americans joined the British in launching costly bombing raids over Germany. In part, the intent was to decrease the German people's will to resist. Later research reported by the Office of Strategic Services that compared lightly and heavily bombed areas found only minimal differences in civilians' will to resist.

Several other conflicts follow the same psychological pattern, such as Pearl Harbor, South Africa, and North Vietnam. Each of these instances point to important differences in countries' perceptions of what will be effective in motivating an enemy and what will be effective in motivating themselves or their allies. Coercion is viewed as more effective with our enemies than with ourselves, whereas conciliation is viewed as more effective with ourselves than with our enemies. The unfortunate consequence, of course, is that this perception encourages aggressive rather than constructive action.

There are three key reasons why this occurs (Rothbart and Hallmark, 1988). A preference for punitive strategies with one's enemies may reflect a desire to inflict injury or pain, as well as a desire to influence behavior in a desired direction. The relative preference for punishment is based on an incompatible desire to both injure and modify the behavior of the enemy. Alternatively, people may be inclined to use more coercive strategies with an opponent because the appearance of toughness conveys information about their motives and intentions, which, in the long run, may bring about the desired result (remember the Gulf War example in chapter 10). Finally, the mere creation of mutually exclusive, exhaustive social categories (e.g., "them" and "us") leads to different assumptions about members of such groups: more favorable attributes are assigned to in-group than to out-group members (Brewer, 1979; Tajfel, 1970). Social categorization processes may be particularly powerful in environmental disputes because of the well-defined camps. Some of the tactics used in environmental disputes may raise the hurdle that needs to be overcome for a successful renegotiation. Tactics such as chaining oneself to a fishing boat or placing metal spikes in trees to damage logging equipment might strengthen the resolve of the other side.

Exaggeration and Polarization of Others' Views: They're All Alike

There is a heated debate among English teachers concerning which books should be on the required reading list for American high school students. The Western Cannon Debate features traditionalists, who prefer to have classics on the reading list, and revisionists, who believe that the reading list should be more racially, ethnically, and sexually diversified. In a recent analysis, traditionalists and revisionists were interviewed about their own and the other party's preferred books (Robinson and Keltner, 1996). Most strikingly, each party exaggerated the views of the other side in a way that made their differences bigger rather than smaller. Traditionalists viewed revisionists to be much more extreme than they really were; revisionists viewed traditionalists to be much more conservative. In fact, the groups agreed on 7 out of the 15 books on the reading list! Nevertheless, each group greatly exaggerated the difference between their own and the other's belief systems in a way that exacerbated the conflict. Further, people perceived the other side to be more uniform in their views, whereas they perceived their own views to be more varied and heterogeneous (Linville, Fischer, and Salovey, 1989). This faulty perception, of course, leads to beliefs such as "They're all alike." Ideological conflict is often exacerbated unnecessarily as partisans construe the other person's values to be more extremist and unbending than they really are.

Sinister and Fanatical Attribution Errors

In 1995, Republican Congressman George Gekas of Pennsylvania was accused by the opposing partisan party of espousing antienvironmental attitudes. The angered Gekas mocked the accusation: "Mr. Speaker and members of the House, I hate clean air. I don't want to breathe clean air. I want the dirtiest air possible for me and my household and my constituents. That's what the supporters of this motion want people to believe about our position on these riders. Now, you know that's absolutely untenable" (National Public Radio, November 3, 1995).

The **fundamental attribution error** occurs when people explain the causes of the behavior of others in terms of their underlying dispositions and discount the role of situational factors (Ross, 1977). Many environmental disputes involve a group that is believed to be interested in the economic development of the environment and an opposing group which represents the interests of the ecosystem. According to the fundamental attribution error, when each group is asked to name the cause of the dispute, each will attribute the negative aspects of conflict to the dispositions of the other party. Specifically, developers regard environmentalists to be fanatic lunatics; environmentalists regard developers to be sinister and greedy.

Heartfelt versus Calculated Interests

The Blue Moon was a bar in a university district that was somewhat run down and often attracted a rough crowd. Many considered it to be a seedy eyesore. The city legislature drew up a plan to tear down the Blue Moon and replace it with commercial building space. A group of citizens opposed the new project on the grounds that the Blue Moon was a "historical landmark." (Historical landmarks are structures which have to meet specific criteria and are preserved by the city or state.) A debate ensued about whether the Blue Moon was really an architectural gem or just a run-down bar that some people wanted to keep open for their own interests.

The debate over the Blue Moon raises the dilemma of whether interests are heartfelt or calculated. Was the building truly a historical landmark, or was this a ploy to protect partisan interests? In short, how can we tell whether someone's interests are sincere or calculated?

Consider two models for understanding the interplay between heartfelt values and economic interests: value-driven interests and interest-driven values. In the **value-driven interests** model, a person's interests reflect his or her underlying values. In the **interest-driven values** framework, a person's interests drive or dictate their values. The difference between these two models is based, in short, on whether one's values are **heartfelt** or calculated. The distinction rests on whether one's interests are driven by social and moral values that are independent of self-interest, or whether self-interest shapes one's values. Either can hinder the effective resolution of conflict.

Most people view their values as dictating and shaping their interests but view others as expressing values that serve their self-interest. Thus, we view the values held by our opponents as arising from unbridled greed and self-interest. In contrast, we regard our own interests to be an expression of our underlying values. Consequently, we believe that others' values are more capricious than our own. We believe that, at the right price, others can be bought or persuaded, whereas we cannot.

Environmentalists' and developers' views of one another are often not symmetric. Environmentalists may accuse developers of harboring evil, calculated interests; whereas developers often view environmentalists to be naïve and idealistic. Why do we see our own interests as heartfelt and others' as calculated? It is difficult for people to grant that there may, in fact, be more than one valid view of the world (Ross and Ward, 1994). The presence of more than one value system is psychologically disturbing for the person who wants to believe that there is a single, objective truth.

Outsmarting Versus Convincing

Charlie negotiated with his supervisor for a raise by pointing to an ambiguous legal clause in his contract that could be loosely interpreted as entitling him to a raise. Susan also negotiated with her supervisor for a raise; she listed a number of her accomplishments in the past year which had not been obvious to her supervisor. Both Charlie and Susan were given raises. Charlie outsmarted his supervisor; Susan convinced her supervisor. Who feels more satisfied? The most satisfaction comes from rational, persuasive argument, rather than clever tricks; Susan should feel more satisfied (by convincing her supervisor) than should Charlie (who outsmarted his supervisor) (Rapoport, 1960). Convincing someone about the correctness of our own views validates our views and has a more lasting impact than outsmarting someone. In environmental disputes, which often involve sacred values, people desire to convince, rather than outsmart, others.

Argument, or convincing others, serves at least five useful purposes that all serve to maximize self-interest (Elster, 1995).

- If others believe that a person is truly arguing from principle, they may be more willing to back down because they might regard the other as willing to suffer a loss rather than accept a compromise (Frank, 1988).

- The use of ideology and principle is often a subterfuge used for political purpose to hide what is, in reality, a deal among special interests.

- Arguments are effective persuasion and informational influence tools (Deutsch and Gerrard, 1955).

- Social norms often prescribe that people should take positions that are beneficial to the collective. Discussions of values and principles provide an acceptable means of dialogue when the social context does not tolerate the discussion of interests.

- Parties to a dispute might use arguments to avoid humiliating an opponent: If the stronger party articulates an impartial reason that allows the weaker party to save face, both gain.

The problem is that most people are not very persuasive spokespersons for their own ideology. This is because we associate with people who share our views (biased selection), so we have little opportunity to focus on the other side. Second, we frequently confuse rational argument with ideology. For example, when people are pressed to justify their political preferences, all inquiry ultimately terminates in the expression of values that people find ridiculous to justify any further (Tetlock, Peterson, and Lerner, 1996). For example, environmentalists consider "protection of the environment" as self-evident for their position just as pro-drilling Republicans consider "economic development" a self-justifying explanation for their position to drill for oil in the refuge. When people are questioned about why they hold a given view, they often restate their views rather than provide reasons for holding the view. Our own ideology is persuasive to us but not to others.

Prescriptive Implications

Having focused on the factors that make environmental disputes less amenable to successful application of negotiation principles, what prescriptive steps may be taken to facilitate integrative outcomes in environmental disputes?

Using Resources to Change Values

One way of solving conflicts is to use the endowment effect (discussed in chapter 6). We might very well imagine that the Alaskan Indian enjoying Monday night football was initially opposed to development of the wildlife refuge. However, once people have experienced something pleasurable, they are reluctant to give it up (due to loss aversion and relative deprivation). The Inupiat Indians in Alaska were initially opposed to the drilling but have come to enjoy the amenities of modern life, such as television, made possible by oil exploration in their community. The key obstacles to overcome when implementing this strategy are issues of face saving (Brown, 1968) and maintaining self-identity. People don't want to look like they can be bought or have sold out.

The Necessity of Tradeoffs

No one can live without making choices among sacred issues. For everything that we choose, something is not chosen. Even Gwich'in Indians who value hunting caribou in the pristine wilderness trade off the longevity of their tribe and children (forgoing benefits of formalized medicine and education). Tradeoffs are inevitable; people constantly make decisions that affect their own and others' welfare. When people buy cloth diapers, they affect the water supply; when they use plastic diapers, they add to landfills. It is impossible not to affect the welfare of others. Yet, when such tradeoffs are pointed out, people deny them. Why is it so hard for people to realize the tradeoffs that they make? People don't like to make sacrifices.

The Sticky Slope

Movement is blocked in many conflicts because people fear a slippery slope—if they give in on one issue, they will eventually lose all ground. If they could receive assurance that a concession in one area would not start an avalanche of capitulation, they might develop more creative and mutually beneficial negotiated agreements. A **sticky slope** is the opposite of a slippery slope. A sticky slope is created when the party who makes a concession is assured that further ground is not also imperiled. The trick, of course, is creating meaningful sticking points. When parties have different perceptions about the state of the world, instead of arguing about what is or will likely be, they can bet upon their differences. For example, consider the conflict of building a bridge in a wetlands area: Developers like the idea; environmentalists are concerned about wildlife. The developers do not believe that the construction will have adverse effects. Parties to the dispute may fashion a bet such that the animal population will be monitored following construction; if a critical number of animals suffer adverse effects, then the developers will remove the bridge and, furthermore, donate moneys to special habitat preserves. If the animal population is not harmed, however, additional development exploration will be allowed. The essential feature of such a bet is that uncertainty about future conditions is used to leverage agreement. Both sides to the dispute are provided with an insurance policy that protects them from losing ground should things go awry.

Changing the Sociopolitical Context

The social context of a negotiation often determines whether tradeoffs are taboo or not. When people anticipate that their decisions and actions will be scrutinized by others, they often make worse decisions (Heath, 1996). One way to facilitate negotiation is to remove accountability pressures. It may be possible to create teams of decision makers to diffuse responsibility (Gruenfeld et al., 1996). Another way of altering the sociopolitical context is to create scapegoats and mutual enemies.

Introduce a Common Goal

The "rattlers" and the "eagles" were two rival groups at Robber's Cave, a boy's summer camp. The boys were separated into two groups before spending several days hiking, swimming, and playing sports. During that time, friendship bonds, norms, and rituals developed within each group, along with animosity toward the other group. When the two groups met in a series of competitive games, tempers flared and hostility raged. Unbeknownst to the boys, the camp was part of a field study of social behavior (Sherif, et al., 1961). When hostilities reached a physical level, observers interviewed and separated the two groups. They then staged a series of situations that could be solved only if the groups cooperated with each other. One problem required locating a leak in the camp's water supply. Another necessitated moving a broken-down truck. During the pursuit of these goals, animosity between the two groups diminished.

The conflict at the summer camp illustrates the power of a common goal. A common goal, like a common enemy, removes the perception that the parties' interests can be completely opposed, and builds a new value that represents a higher-order principle that both parties find acceptable, and perhaps superior to their previously espoused values.

In environmental disputes, the common goal may take the form of a new paradigm or ideology that encompasses developers' interests and environmentalists' goals: sustainable development. Hoffman and Ehrenfeld (1995) outline the components for the creation of a paradigm shift that encompasses two opposing value systems. In particular, they argue that ecodevelopment, "sustaincentrism," or, more commonly, sustainable development as an ideology, is compatible with both frontier economics and deep ecology, two currently opposing ideologies.

Precedented Agreement

An interesting phenomenon occurs when people are asked to solve brain teasers or puzzlers: Their effort and persistence are much greater when they believe a solution exists than when they doubt its solubility. In the same way, a precedent of agreement in a dispute context creates the very mechanisms necessary for agreement: persistence and creativity. If disputants believe that a solution is possible, they are more likely to reach agreement (Ross and Ward, 1994). For example, a history of no strikes at a company or unanimous voting in an organization can act as a powerful norm for reaching settlement. No one wants to break tradition.

Creating Ideological Illusions

In the 1992 presidential election debates, supporters of each of the three presidential candidates—George Bush, Bill Clinton, and Ross Perot—all claimed victory. Of course, it is a logical impossibility that all parties could win the debates. Nevertheless, through enough rhetoric, bolstering, and judicious selectivity of perception, constituents may be confident and multiple illusions can be maintained. In a similar fashion, mediators may facilitate tradeoffs that maintain the illusion that parties' core values have been preserved. The key is to reframe values in terms of general principles, not as specific positions. This provides sufficient ambiguity so that parties will be flexible about the means of achieving their values.

Postscript on Environmental Dispute Resolution

We have suggested some of the complexities that arise in complex conflicts and how the behavioral negotiation model cannot address these problems. We have also suggested some ways of overcoming these problems and facilitating integrative agreements in environmental conflicts.

Some may accuse us of arguing that people should be willing to negotiate anything and place a price on core values. Certainly, it would seem that some things in life do not have a price (e.g., health, children, and marriage). The refusal to consider trading certain things is part of a deeply rooted value system. Whether people are aware of it or not, they do make choices that involve tradeoffs. The problem is that people do not realize when they make tradeoffs. Instead, when values are involved, people fall into a **lexicographic decision mode,** in which their values drive the choice in a manner that does not make tradeoff seem relevant—they pick the option that appears best on the important value without regard to other values and their tradeoffs.

People's interests are influenced by their beliefs and values. Values often serve as self-justifying systems for the pursuit of interests. By pulling down the value smoke screens that hide the choices and tradeoffs that we make, we may pave the way toward more effective conflict resolution, even in the most complex and heated debates, such as those involving environmental issues.

NEGOTIATION VIA TECHNOLOGY

Something interesting is happening in Leona's job. After years of meeting with key clients in hotel lobbies and business suites, she now communicates with clients via telephone, fax, tele-conference, videoconference, and electronic mail. In years past, Leona took her large brief-case on the airplane and sipped coffee while she pored over reports and papers. She would rest in the evening and then have meetings all morning. Now, her clients call her and in sec-onds, three or four other people are on the line, ready to talk and work out the details. Leona's scenario is commonplace in organizations, illustrating three facts of organizational life:

- People are busy.
- People are in different places.
- Information is not always where it is needed.

Whereas the most common form of negotiation is unrestricted, face-to-face interaction, other forms of communication are increasingly common. More and more, people are using technology to overcome time and space constraints, improve their performance, and increase the range and speed of access to information (McGrath and Hollingshead, 1994). The issue for Leona is not technical—she can easily figure out how to use the technology—rather, the issue is strategic. She wonders whether the modes of communication she uses affect her ne-gotiation. As it turns out, her intuition is right: Mode of communication does affect the qual-ity of interaction. In this section, we examine how.

You Can't Fight Progress

Leona, like many managers, knows that she can't fight progress. The information age is here (Tapscott, 1996). To be successful, negotiators must not only know how to negotiate via technology but also understand the social dynamics that it produces.

With the development of any technology, there are first- and second-level effects (Sproull and Keisler, 1991). First-level effects are those associated with efficiency. They are the direct, intended effects. Second-level effects are those that are not intended, predicted, or anticipated. They have to do with how the social system is affected by technology. Indirect effects are caused by behavior that technology makes feasible and how people use options. Indirect effects lead to the development of new social roles. For example, the development of the computer led to the development of the hacker, user consultant, and management of in-formation specialist (MIS) (Sproull and Keisler, 1991).

A good example is the telephone (from Sproull and Keisler, 1991). The first-level effect of the telephone was that of an efficient replacement for the telegraph. It was originally sold as a tool for business. In 1878, the Pittsburgh telephone directory had 12 pages of entries, which were all for businesses and businessmen. Telegraph companies offering telephones for lease at $50/year advertised: "The telephone has ceased to be a novelty and has become a rec-ognized instrument for business purposes." A selling point for the business manager was that "no skill whatsoever" was required in the use of the instrument. The Bell Telephone Company partners decided to prepare for the distant possibility that people would use the telephone for social purposes as well. By the 1920s, Bell System was emphasizing the social character of the telephone with claims such as "Friends who are linked by telephone have good times," and "Friendship's path often follows the trail of the telephone wire." Today, the telephone is the backbone of virtually all social and organizational life. People once wondered if the telephone would increase the authority of the boss inside the firm by allowing him or her to call subordinates at any hour of the day. Instead, the telephone gave employees a chance to call their supervisors and each other. The telephone democratized more workplaces than it bureaucratized and networked more organizations than it created fiefdoms.

The full possibilities of new technologies are hard to foresee. The inventors and early adopters emphasize the planned uses and underestimate the second-level effects. For example, the first Internet, known as ARPANET, was developed in the 1960s so that academicians could communicate their research ideas and data (usually large reports). It was only after the Gulf War and the 1992 presidential election that the "information superhighway," the World Wide Web, and the Internet became common forms of communication for the lay person.

The unanticipated consequences of technology often have less to do with efficiency effects and more to do with changing social arrangements of interpersonal interactions, such as ideas about what is important and procedures/norms guiding behavior. Second-level effects often emerge somewhat slowly as people renegotiate changed patterns of behavior and thinking. Second-level effects are not caused by technology operating autonomously on a passive organization or a society. Instead, they are constructed by people as their design and use of technology interacts with, shapes, and is shaped by the technological, social, and policy environment. Second-level and unanticipated effects are not always positive and innovative. Place dependence can develop, wherein a group becomes dependent on technology to function, but they don't realize it. If the system is changed or altered, group productivity declines.

Negotiation in the Technological Age

For any negotiation or group task there are, broadly speaking, four possibilities, depicted in the place–time model in Table 14–2 (see also Johansen, 1988; Englebart, 1989).[3] In the traditional mode, people meet face-to-face at the same time and same place. Communication is unrestricted. Negotiators are more cooperative when interacting face to face rather than over the telephone (Drolet and Morris, 1995). Face-to-face communication (as opposed to telephone or more restricting forms) fosters the development of interpersonal synchrony and rapport, and thus leads to more trusting, cooperative behavior (Drolet and Morris, 1995). In the same-time, different-place mode, people communicate at the same time, but they are not physically present. The most common mode is the telephone; videoconferencing is another

Table 14–2. Place–time Model of Interaction

	Same Place	*Different Place*
Same Time	Face to face	Telephone Videoconference
Different Time	Single text editing Shift work	E-mail Voice mail

---

[3] A more sophisticated model of groups interacting with technology is the group communication support system model, developed by McGrath and Hollingshead (1994), which distinguishes contiguous versus distal modalities, synchronous versus asynchronous communication, and video/audio, audio, and text/graphics modes.

example. In the different-time, same-place mode, groups interact asynchronously, but have access to the same physical work space. An example might be shift workers who pick up the task left for them by the previous shift; another example would be two collaborators working on the same electronic document. After one colleague finishes, she gives the text to her partner, who further edits and develops it. Finally, in the different-place, different-time model, interactants communicate asynchronously in different places. The most common example is electronic mail: Jerry, who is in Seattle, sends a message to Sally, who is in Japan.

Face-to-face meetings are often ideal, especially for wrestling with complex problems. One exception might be when the topic is uncomfortable and we are interested in accuracy. People underreport socially undesirable behaviors more in personal interviews than in questionnaires. However, we don't always have the luxury of meeting face to face. People often turn to the telephone, but even then, people do not always reach their party. Some estimates suggest that up to 70 percent of initial telephone attempts fail to reach the intended party (Philip and Young, 1987). With electronic mail, both parties to a communication do not have to be available simultaneously for it to occur. However, electronic communication is no panacea. Because it is easy to send a message, people often write before they think. Further, greater information is not always better—some people receive several hundred electronic messages each day.

Technology and Interpersonal Relationships

Leona wants to know how technology affects her relationships, negotiation strategy, and development of rapport with her clients. As we saw in chapter 10, building rapport is critical for negotiation success. Rapport would seem more difficult to establish with impoverished mediums of communication.

The Great Equalizer

In virtually any group, people's contributions are not equal. Walk into any classroom, lunch discussion, or business meeting, and it will be immediately obvious that a handful of people do more than 75 percent of the talking. One person or one clique usually dominates the discussion. In face-to-face interactions, participation is not equal, even when performance depends on contributions. Most social interaction follows the form of that depicted in Figure 14–1.

Who dominates the discussion? Almost without exception, member status predicts domination. If there is no inherent organizational status system, groups rely on traditional symbols of status, such as gender, age, and race. Status cues can be amazingly superficial. The person who sits at the head of the table talks more than those on the sides, even if seating arrangement is arbitrary. Appearance can affect status: Those in business suits talk more than others. Dynamic cues can define status, such as nodding in approval, touching (high-status people touch those of lower status but not vice versa), hesitating, and frowning. Not surprisingly, managers speak more than subordinates, and men speak more than women. In mixed-status groups, higher-status people talk more than lower-status people. Further, these behaviors hold even when higher-status people are not more expert on a topic.

What happens when groups interact via technology, such as electronic mail? Because it is harder to discern status cues in electronic messages, high-status people do not dominate discussions. When social status cues are missing or weak, people feel distant from others and somewhat anonymous. People are less concerned about making a good appearance.

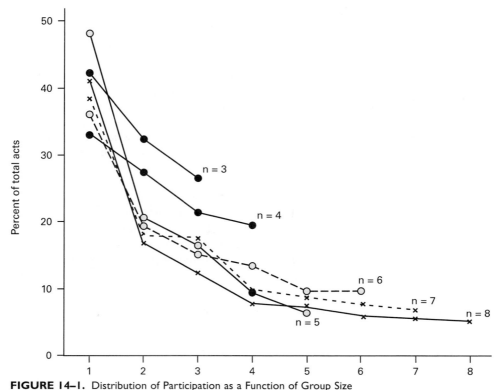

FIGURE 14–1. Distribution of Participation as a Function of Group Size

Source: Shaw, M. E. (1981). *Group dynamics: The psychology of small group behavior*, 3rd ed. New York: McGraw-Hill. 170. Reprinted with permission.

In electronic communication, static and dynamic cues about status and normative behavior are unavailable. For example, in most electronic networks, when people send e-mail, the only signs of position and personal attributes are names and addresses. The message address identifies the organization, but not subunits, job title, social importance, or level in the organization. The absence of these cues leads people to respond more openly and less hesitatingly than in face-to-face interaction. People are less likely to conform to social norms and other people when interacting via electronic communication. Overall, the amount of participation will be less in electronic versus face-to-face communication, but the contributions of members will be more equal (for a review, see McGrath and Hollingshead, 1994). For example, when groups of executives meet face to face, men are five times more likely than women to make the first decision proposal. When those same groups meet via computer, women make the first proposal as often as men do (McGuire, Keisler, and Siegel, 1987). Further, the time to complete a task is longer on e-mail than in face-to-face interaction, probably because people talk much faster than they write.

Networks and Resources

In traditional organizations, networks are determined by who talks to whom; in the new organization, networks are determined by who communicates with whom via technology. Peripheral people who communicate electronically become better integrated into their organization (Eveland and Bikson, 1988). Computerized interaction increases the resources of low-network people.

Is it sending or receiving messages that expands one's network and ultimate organizational commitment? The amount of e-mail a person sends (but not receives) predicts commitment (Sproull and Keisler, 1991). Thus, e-mail can provide an alternate route to letting people have a voice if they are low contributors in face-to-face meetings.

How do low-network people increase their resources? People use **weak ties** (i.e., relationships with acquaintances or strangers) to seek help that is unavailable from friends or colleagues (Granovetter, 1973). However, in the absence of personal relationships or the expectation of direct reciprocity, help from weak ties might not be forthcoming or could be of low quality. For example, consider employees of a global computer manufacturer in a geographically dispersed organization. Employees cannot always get useful advice from their local colleagues. People in organizations usually prefer to exchange help through strong collegial ties, which develop through physical proximity, similarity, and so forth. To solve problems, people must exchange technical advice. In one study, information providers gave useful advice and solved the problems of information seekers, despite their lack of personal connection with the seekers. On average, information seekers received 7.8 replies per question. Further, providers spent nine minutes per reply. Most notably, 50 percent of respondents said the reply solved their problem (Sproull and Keisler, 1991).

Quality of Group Decisions: The Risky Manager

In a study of risk taking, corporate managers (McGuire, Keisler, and Siegel, 1987) were presented with the following choices:

Option A: $20,000 return over two years

Option B: 50 percent chance of $40,000 return; 50 percent chance of nothing

Obviously, A is the "safe" (riskless) choice; B is the risky choice. Mathematically, options A and B are identical by virtue of the expected utility principle discussed in chapter 6. Further, recall that most people are risk averse for gains, but risk seeking when it comes to loss. Thus, we would expect people to choose A. Groups that meet face to face were risk averse for gain choices and risk seeking for loss. However, when the groups met electronically, they were risk seeking in all circumstances. Further, executives were just as confident of decisions, whether made through electronic communication or face to face.

Heightened Uncertainty: Who Am I Talking To?

In the TV show *Saturday Night Live*, Pat is a character whose sex is unknown. Pat has an androgynous name, wears baggy clothes, and does not display any stereotypical male or female characteristics or preferences. Most people find it maddening to interact with Pat without knowing his or her gender. Gender ambiguity also happens when interacting via technology. It is generally impolite to ask someone whether they are a man or woman. Therefore, we are left feeling uncertain. Uncertainty, consequently, increases paranoia. Paranoid people are more likely to assume the worst about another person or situation (Kramer, 1995).

When technological change creates new social situations, traditional expectations and norms lose their power. People invent new ways of behaving. Today's electronic technology is impoverished in social cues and shared experience. People "talk" to other people, but they do so alone (Sproull and Keisler, 1991). As a result, their messages are likely to display less social awareness. The advantage is that social posturing and sycophancy decline.

The disadvantage is that politeness and concern for others declines. Two characteristics of computer-based communication, the plain text and perceived ephemerality of messages, make it relatively easy for a person to forget or ignore his or her audience and consequently send messages that ignore social boundaries, disclose the self, and are too blunt (Sproull and Keisler, 1991).

Sparks and Flames

Consider the following exchange:

NEGOTIATOR A: "If I don't get your answer by tomorrow, then I assume that you agree with my proposal."

NEGOTIATOR B: "From my perspective, I don't see any rationale, or any incentive to transfer this revolutionary technology to your division."

NEGOTIATOR A: "I don't have to remind you how pushing the issue up the corporate ladder can prejudice both our careers."

NEGOTIATOR B: "Your offer is ridiculous."

NEGOTIATOR A: "It's my final offer."

Did this exchange occur in a meeting room or via the Internet? Most people correctly note that this exchange occurred on the Internet. This exchange is an example of "flaming," wherein interactants attempt to denigrate others' character, intelligence, and grammar. To flame is "to speak incessantly and/or rabidly on some relatively uninteresting subject or with a patently ridiculous attitude" (Steele, 1983, p. 65). The phenomenon of flaming suggests that through electronic mail, actions and decisions, not just messages, might become more extreme and impulsive (Sproull and Keisler, 1991). In fact, people are eight times more likely to flame in electronic discussions than face to face (Sproull and Keisler, 1991). Why? The absence of social context creates a feeling of anonymity. Conventional behavior, such as politeness rituals and acknowledgment of others' views decrease; rude, impulsive behavior such as flaming increases.

Control/Threat Opportunities

Electronic communication may be a great equalizer, but it can also be a powerful form of social control, both at an organizational and individual level. Virtually no one would disagree that computers keep a perfect record of communications: Even though messages that are composed and sent disappear from the screen, they are stored intact in several computer systems, accessible to virtually anyone intent on finding the information, even after they have been deleted. Yet, people act as if messages are ephemeral (Sproull and Keisler, 1991). For example, in his congressional hearing, Oliver North was extremely careful in his spoken interviews (presumably aware that the camera was on him indelibly recording every utterance); however, he was obviously much more lax in his computer mail (Sproull and Keisler, 1991).

Electronic Negotiations: What Every Manager Needs to Know

Christy is a consultant who received an electronic mail message from a manager of a Japanese firm. Christy had advertised a computer software program in a third-party resource publication. Over the course of a week, an electronic negotiation ensued wherein Christy and the Japanese manager negotiated the price of a software program, a warranty package, technical support, and the form of sale (e.g., purchase order in yen). The two never spoke.

Christy would find a message waiting for her on her computer at 8 A.M.; she would reply immediately, knowing that the Japanese manager might receive her message by the time he left work in the evening in Japan, depending upon the load on the system. What were the dynamics that operated?

Status Markers and Identity

When Christy first received the e-mail from the Japanese manager, she did not know the sender's status or, for that matter, whether the inquiry about her software was from a company, university, or independent user. As we have noted, electronic communication lacks many of the status markers common in face-to-face interaction. People who would normally not approach others in person are much more likely to initiate e-mail exchange.

Making Sense out of E-mail

We have made the point that electronic communication differs in fundamental ways from face-to-face communication in that it lacks much of the social context cues contained in face-to-face interaction. Whereas people think in terms of substance, they act and react on the basis of intention and intonation. Ninety-three percent of the meaning of a message is contained in facial and vocal cues, rather than text (Mehrabian, 1971). Facial and vocal cues are not present in electronic exchanges. So how do we make sense of electronic exchange?

Four types of information are important in e-mail:

- substance
- affect
- procedure
- relations

The substantive component is the content of the message. However, content by itself can be ambiguous and misinterpreted unless there is some other clue in the message about how to interpret the content. Consider, for example, the following statement in an e-mail message, "You are so right all the time." We don't know whether this person is displaying extreme deference, sarcasm, or apprehension.

The affective aspect of an e-mail message allows us to interpret the content. People communicate affect in words (e.g., "I am so angry"), but also in symbols or emoticons. Table 14–3 illustrates the most common emotional expressions in e-mail exchange.

It takes some time to become interpersonally skilled on e-mail. Many a novice has made an unwitting mistake only to be rebuffed and flamed. For example, one colleague we know is not a touch typist; he looks at the keyboard rather than the screen when typing. Unbeknownst to him at the time, the "caps lock" key was depressed during a long message. Not wanting to retype the message, he sent it in upper case. His recipient responded, "Why are you shouting at me—don't you know that is impolite?"

The substantive and affective aspects of an e-mail message are not sufficient to guarantee a productive and accurate exchange between people, however. Two other features are important: procedures and relations.

The procedural aspect of an e-mail message is the way in which communicators deal with and overcome the place/time constraints. The procedural aspect focuses on how people communicate about how they communicate (e.g., "I only read e-mail once every three days, so don't expect a quick reply"; "I would like to forward this to my committee, if you don't

TABLE 14–3. Emoticons in E-mail Communication Used to Express Emotion

Emoticon	Definition
:-)	The basic smiley. This smiley is used to inflect a sarcastic joking statement since we can't hear voice inflection over e-mail.
;-)	Winky smiley. User just made a flirtatious and/or sarcastic remark. More of a "don't hit me for what I just said" smiley.
:-(	Frowning smiley. User did not like the last statement or is upset or depressed about something.
:-T	Indifferent smiley. Better than a :-(but not quite as good as a :-).
:->	User just made a really biting sarcastic remark. Worse than a ;-).
>:->	User just made a really devilish remark.
>;->	Winky and devil combined. A very lewd remark was just made.
|-)	hee hee
|-D	ho ho
:-o	oops
:-P	nyahhh!

mind"). We know of a manager who became irate when she did not get a response for a week after sending an e-mail message to a government agency; only later did she realize that the recipient's gateway was blocked for security reasons during the Gulf War. In a different instance, a colleague was horrified to find that his e-mail message to a friend had been forwarded to 300 people. In yet another instance, a manager was shocked to learn on a site visit with her distant collaborator that the collaborator had not erased all of the messages that he had received from her in the past three years. The manager insisted that the messages be erased in front of her eyes.

Finally, the relational aspect of an e-mail message is the way in which communicators attempt to humanize interaction. The relational aspect addresses the relationship between the communicators. The relational aspect is often revealed in greetings, e.g., "hey buddy"; "hi magnet man." Some of these are personalized; others are not, such as when communicators have a standard sign-off or quote at the end of their message (e.g., "Seize the day"). Relational messages build common ground (e.g., "What did you think of that Bulls game?"). Very simple statements can go a long way toward humanizing electronic interaction (e.g., "It's late and I am eating dinner now").

Some communicators never deal with the relational aspect; they focus on content and procedure, and supply enough affective markers to have their messages understood. About one week into their exchange, Christy made a comment to the Japanese manager in her e-mail that she and her husband recently had a baby. This elicited a disclosure on the part of the Japanese manager about his newborn son, and they had an exchange about parenting.

When There's Trouble in the Airwaves

Despite the best of intentions, communications often go awry and negotiators get off on the wrong foot. Most commonly, the following happens:

- **Misunderstood messages:** Messages can be misunderstood and misinterpreted in electronic exchanges more readily than in face-to-face encounters.

- Delays can be frustrating in electronic communication. It can take four times as long for a three-person group to make a decision in a real-time computer conference as in a face-to-face conference, and take as much as 10 times as long in a four-person group that lacks time restrictions.
- **Sinister attribution error,** or "he's up to no good." In the absence of contextual cues, like vocal information and facial expressions, people are more uncertain about others' behavior. Heightened uncertainty leads to paranoia and sinister attribution errors (Kramer, 1995).

A Case Study of Electronic Mail Negotiations

In 1996, a study of electronic mail negotiations in an MBA course was undertaken (Thompson and Kurtzberg, 1997).[4] The following presents a brief summary of effective and detrimental strategies in electronic negotiations. Approximately 50 percent of the sample reached level 3, pareto-efficient outcomes. What was unique about their e-mail correspondence? Not surprisingly, this group used many of the integrative bargaining strategies presented in chapter 4:

- They made multiple offers of the same value within a single message.
- They invited suggestions from their opponent (this decreased hostility and encouraged mutual exploration).
- They shared information about their priorities.

So much for what went right. How did electronic negotiations go wrong?

- Offer avoidance: Negotiators who failed to attain level 2 and 3 outcomes did not make many clear offers (as judged by independent third parties). Rather, they wrote long paragraphs, often covering several screens, that contained sweeping, general statements. They discussed past issues and, in short, appeared to load the screen with a lot of irrelevant information.
- Accusations and labeling: Negotiators who did not reach optimal outcomes accused the other party of lying, being unfair, greedy, and malicious. Further, they labeled the other's behavior (e.g., "That is completely ridiculous," or "Your offer is absurd").
- Short fuse: Those who did not do well were much more likely to make "take it or leave it" offers that were not supported by a good BATNA (e.g., "It is late and this is my final offer; take it or leave it").

We do not suggest that negotiators should never criticize or challenge each other's views. Electronic discussion groups with a "planted" group member who criticized others produced more new ideas and achieved more than groups whose planted member was highly supportive. Groups with the critical group member did not like their group and incorrectly thought the group did poorly, whereas groups with the supportive member liked their group and incorrectly thought they did very well (Connolly, Jessup, and Valacich, 1990).

One examination of face-to-face versus computer-mediated negotiation revealed that computer-mediated negotiations were less accurate in judging the interests of the opponent, obtained lower outcomes, and distributed resources more unequally than face-to-face negotiators (Arunchalam and Dilla, 1995).

---

[4] There was no control group of face-to-face interaction; it is impossible to compare face-to-face with electronic interaction.

Technological changes in communication have forced the issue of culture to the forefront of management. Within the global village, the exchange of goods, services, and resources knows few boundaries. Our ability to skillfully deal with cultural issues will dictate our success or failure.

NEGOTIATIONS ACROSS CULTURES

A Japanese manager, Ken Kameda, and an American manager, Lee Coates, communicated via e-mail for a few weeks prior to setting a date and time at which the Japanese manager would visit the plant of the American manager. The American manager regarded the Japanese manager's e-mail messages as somewhat strange. Even after repeatedly signing off with his first name, the Japanese manager continued to address the American manager by his formal name. Lee was flattered and impressed that a manager from a major Japanese company wanted to visit his plant. He tried to make the visit worthwhile by setting up meetings with members of some of his project teams. On the day of arrival, Lee waited in his office for Ken. When he arrived, Mr. Kameda waited at the door, bowed, and presented his business card. Lee stood up, reached out for his hand, and said, "Nice to meet you, Ken!" and slapped Ken's back. Lee then said, "Well what do you want to see first?" Mr. Kameda smiled and said nothing. At the end of the day, Lee gave Ken a proposal to look over for his approval. Ken replied "yes" after receiving it. Lee phoned his supervisor to indicate that the proposal was accepted. Several weeks later, it became clear that the proposal had not been accepted. Ken's "yes" response was a common Japanese conversational marker that simply indicates that he was listening to what was being proposed—not that he agreed to it (Okamoto, 1993).

The interchange between Ken and Lee illustrates a cultural clash: Two people from different cultures who come together for the purpose of bettering their mutual interests step all over each other's toes and don't even know what went wrong. Lee made a number of minor errors (e.g., failing to understand the importance of exchanging cards). Sometimes, major errors can result from a cultural clash, as when nations go to war over a minor misunderstanding.

Negotiations across cultures are more and more commonplace and, in many cases, a requirement for effective management in multinational and international companies. Even domestic companies that are not multinational in their structure must face the challenge of internationalization. Most managers today cannot expect to negotiate with people of their own culture throughout their career. North Americans are a minority—about 7 percent of the world's population. To give a sense of this, if there were 100 people in the world, 55 would be Asians, 21 Europeans, 9 Africans, 8 South Americans, and 7 North Americans (Triandis, 1994).

There are two approaches to dealing with the issue of diversity and intercultural interaction. One approach is to stereotype the members of a particular culture and then memorize key attributes (e.g., "They eat with chopsticks," "They exchange business cards," "They go by surnames," etc.). We don't regard this approach to be beneficial. To see the triviality of the approach, imagine that a Japanese business manager wants to understand a North American manager. He goes to his bookstore and buys a book about negotiation with Americans. How many of the following apply? Americans:

- prefer either pizza or steak.
- live in the suburbs.
- drink microbrews and specialty coffees.

- have a spouse who works.
- love sports (to watch them more than play them).
- love cars (particularly sport utility vehicles).
- ski in the winter.
- like to spend an evening watching a movie in a theater and eating dinner out.
- send their kids to summer camp.
- value independence more than anything.
- want to "have fun."
- would never dream of living with their parents.

The above list is a set of stereotypes. Most North Americans find this list to be annoyingly restrictive and not very descriptive of their lifestyle. Obviously, the Japanese manager needs to understand a lot more about North American culture than the stereotypes in this list.

A more useful approach is to avoid the temptation to use stereotypes and develop a framework for thinking about culture. There are several advantages to the latter approach. First, there is a great deal of diversity among people in a culture. A cultural framework is more sensitive to variation within groups. Second, U.S. culture today is quite different than it was even 10 years ago. We need a dynamic framework that allows us to learn how cultures change and grow. A cultural framework allows us to better structure interaction if we understand where the dissimilarities are. Thus, in this chapter, we do not provide a quickie guide to dealing with Japanese, East Asian, and Italian people. We provide a means by which to examine our own culturally based attitudes and behaviors and those of others.

Culture: A Definition

Culture itself is invisible, but its influence on our lives is enormous (Matsumoto, 1996). Many people conceive of culture strictly in terms of geography. However, culture does not only pertain to nations and countries. Companies and organizations have cultures that may not be understood or appreciated by outsiders or new recruits. In this sense, it is critical to examine the fit between job recruits and organizations (Chatman, Caldwell, and O'Reilly, 1995). The importance of person–job fit is documented in a case study of managers who were given person–job fit inventories while they were enrolled in an MBA program; those measures predicted job performance and retention as much as 5 to 6 years later (Chatman, Caldwell, and O'Reilly, 1995).

To broaden our thinking about culture, all of the following can be conceived of as containing cultural differences:

- families
- social groups and departments in an organization
- organizations
- industries
- states
- regions
- countries
- societies (e.g., foragers, horticultural, pastoral, agrarian, industrial, service, information)
- continents

Thus, nations, occupational groups, social classes, genders, races, tribes, corporations, clubs, and social movements may become the bases of specific subcultures. When thinking about culture and diversity, avoid the temptation to think of it as a single dimension (e.g., country of origin); culture is a complex whole, and it is best to use many criteria to discriminate one culture from another.

A simple way of thinking about culture and behavior is to consider the following framework (Triandis, 1994):

$$\text{ecology} \rightarrow \text{culture} \rightarrow \text{socialization} \rightarrow \text{personality} \rightarrow \text{behavior}$$

Ecology is the physical and geographical environment which contains particular resources (e.g., lakes, farmland, animals for hunting, oil, mountains, etc.). These resources make it possible for certain behaviors to lead to rewards; behaviors that are rewarded become automatic and the customs of culture. These factors create particular ways of looking at the social environment. Subjective culture includes how events are categorized and named (e.g., language), norms, roles, and values. In short, culture is the human-made part of the environment (Herskovits, 1955). When attitudes and norms are shared, they are part of culture. When they are held by an individual, they are part of his or her personality. "**Culture** is a set of human-made objective and subjective elements that in the past have increased the probability of survival and resulted in satisfaction for the participants in an ecological niche, and thus became shared among those who could communicate with each other because they had a common language and they lived in the same time and place" (Triandis, 1994, p. 22).

Vive la Différence

In the old Gershwin song, two people face a cultural clash: "You say pota*toe* and I say pota*ta*; you say tomat*oe* and I say tomat*a*," etc. Cultural differences are not simply a matter of "you say it this way and I do it this way." Rather, there are *degrees* of difference. The cultural differences between some groups are not as large (e.g., North Americans and Canadians) as are others (e.g., North Americans and South Africans). Anthropologists consider the following cultural regions as most distinct from each other (Burton, Moore, Whiting, and Romney, 1992):

- Europe and regions where people are heavily influenced by Europe, such as North America and the Mediterranean (e.g., North Africa and Israel)
- Africa south of the Sahara
- East Asia (Japan, China) and South Asia (e.g., India)
- Pacific Islands, including Australian aboriginal
- North American Indians
- South American Indians

Culture: A Framework

You have been placed on special assignment by your diversified products company to explore possibilities for a joint venture with a firm in Thailand. Your supervisor has told you that if you are successful, you will be put on more assignments. Your company clearly has global initiatives. You have one week to prepare for the cultural aspect of your first meeting with officials in Thailand (you have already prepared the business aspects of your meeting).

What is the most important information you can collect to help you better avoid cultural clash? The following is a checklist of where to be sensitive for possible differences in culture (Triandis, 1994):

- *Language.* Languages have "families." Some languages are more similar to one another than other languages. How comfortable are you with the language? Do you have a translator?

- *Family structure and sex roles.* Suppose that you learn upon meeting your Thai counterpart that he has three wives. Should you be surprised or not? Family structure ranges from polygamous (husband has many wives) and polyandrous (wife has many husbands) to monogamous (one spouse) and from extended (e.g., all resources are shared by all the brothers and their families) to nuclear (father, mother, children) (Todd, 1983). What should you expect in terms of familial structure?

- *Organizational character.* Lammers and Hickson (1979) suggest the existence of three different types of national character in organizations: the **Latin type,** the **Anglo-Saxon type,** and the **Third World type.** The Latin type is characterized as a classic bureaucracy, with centralized power and decision making and hierarchical levels. The Anglo-Saxon type is more or less the opposite, with less centralization, more diffusion of power and decision making and less hierarchy in the bureaucracy. The Third World type is characterized by greater centralization of decision making, less formalization of values, and a more paternalistic or traditional family orientation.

- *Religion.* There are many different varieties of religions even within the Christian, Jewish, Muslim, Hindu, Buddhist, Shinto, and animist categories. Further, some countries are more religious than are others (e.g., two-thirds of United States; six-sevenths of India; one-fifth of Japan).

- *Level of affluence.* There are huge differences in wealth and wealth distribution in countries. Gross national product per capita is used to assess wealth. The range can be enormous (e.g., $150 for Bangladesh to $23,000 for Sweden). What does this mean in terms of remuneration and worker incentives?

- *Values.* Fundamental values differ in important ways. The following is a list of key values/attitudes/behaviors worth assessing before your trip:

  1. Personal greetings and address: How should you address the other person?
  2. Self-disclosure: What is appropriate to reveal about yourself?
  3. Social visits: Is it polite to inquire about one's personal life or to engage in nonbusiness, family activities?
  4. Swearing
  5. Showing emotions such as happiness, anger, sadness, anxiety and stress
  6. Public affection: Is it appropriate to show positive regard for others?
  7. Touching: What parts of the body are public? Are handshakes acceptable?
  8. Joking: Is humor appreciated?
  9. Appearance and dress: Formal or informal?
  10. Conversational turn-taking: Who goes first? For how long? When do you ask questions?
  11. Discussing finances: When is it appropriate to discuss figures and money?
  12. Meeting structuring and scheduling: Who sets the agenda?
  13. Sharing news and information: How should good and bad news be communicated?
  14. Eye contact: Is it rude to look someone directly in the eye?

15. Organization norms: Do employees work on weekends, etc.?

16. Time: Is the culture punctual or is time not kept by the clock?

Collectivism–Individualism

We have made the point that cultures can differ in many dramatic ways. However, a key way in which many cultures differ is in terms of individualism and collectivism (Triandis, 1994). Individualistic cultures value the individual; his or her independence, autonomy, pursuit of happiness, and personal welfare are paramount. In contrast, collectivists cultures are rooted in social groups; individuals are viewed as members of groups. There are two kinds of collectivism: one emphasizes interdependence and "oneness" (**horizontal collectivism**); the other emphasizes the group and might be called **vertical collectivism** (Triandis, 1994).

People in individualistic cultures give priority to their personal goals, even when these goals conflict with those of their family, work group, or country. In contrast, people in collectivist cultures give priority to in-group goals. People of collectivist cultures view their work groups and organizations as a fundamental part of themselves. People in individualistic cultures, however, more easily separate themselves from their jobs. Collectivists tend to be concerned about the results of their actions on members of their in-group, share resources with in-group members, feel interdependent with in-group members, and feel involved in the lives of in-group members (Hui and Triandis, 1986; Billings, 1989). Not surprisingly, collectivist cultures are much more concerned with the maintenance of harmony in interpersonal relationships with the in-group than are individualistic cultures. For example, collectivists would rather negotiate than go to court (Leung, 1988). Individualists want to save their own face; collectivists are concerned with others' outcomes as well.

What cultures are collectivist? Hofstede (1980) analyzed the responses that IBM employees gave to a values questionnaire. The respondents were diverse in nationality, occupation within IBM, age, and sex. Figure 14–2 presents a grid of where different countries fall in terms of individualism and power distance. Power distance reflects the tendency to see a large distance between those in the upper part of a social structure and those in the lower part of that structure.

It is clear from Figure 14–2 that individualism and power distance are highly correlated: Countries high in collectivism are also high in power distance. The most collectivist high-power countries are Venezuela, several other Latin American countries, the Philippines, and Yugoslavia. The most individualistic, low-power distance countries were English-speaking Scandinavia, Austria, and Israel.

When East Meets West

Japan and the United States are major business partners (Graham and Sano, 1984). Successful negotiations between eastern cultures and the United States have major implications for the economies of both countries. Yet, stories like those of Ken Kameda and Lee Coates abound. In fact, intracultural negotiations (American–American, Japanese–Japanese) are more integrative than intercultural negotiations (American–Japanese) (Brett and Okumura, 1997). In intercultural (but not intracultural) negotiations, there is less understanding of the priorities of the other party. Negotiators within different cultures use different strategies: Japanese negotiators use heuristic trial and error combined with power when negotiating with a Japanese person. In contrast, U.S. negotiators engage in information exchange about preferences (Adair, Okumura, and Brett, 1997).

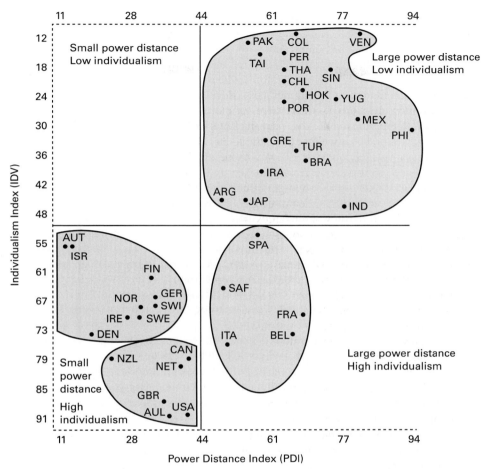

FIGURE 14–2. Position of Countries on Power Distance and Individualism

Source: Hofstede, G. (1980). *Culture's consequences: International differences in work-related values.*
Beverly Hills: Sage. 223. Reprinted by permission of Sage Publications, Inc.

In one study, U.S. and Hong Kong students negotiated with someone whom they believed to be a friend or a stranger from their own culture. As expected based upon their collectivist orientation, the Hong Kong students changed their behavior more when interacting with a friend than did the U.S. students (Chan et al., 1994).

Asian, Black, and Hispanic individuals have a more collectivist–cooperative orientation to a dilemma task than do Anglo individuals. Ethnically diverse groups composed of Asians, Blacks, Hispanics, and Anglos are more cooperative than all-Anglo groups (Cox, Lobel, and McLeod, 1991). In a comparison of Japanese and U.S. students, American students displayed higher levels of trust and cooperated more in the absence of a sanctioning system than did Japanese students (Yamagishi, 1988). In chapter 9, we examined social loafing in groups. In a study of social loafing among management trainees in the United States and the People's Republic of China, American students loafed (individual performance declined) in a group setting, but Chinese students did not (Earley, 1989). In fact, among Japanese participants, the opposite pattern occurred: **social striving**—a group enhances individual performance! (Shirakashi, 1985; Yamaguchi, Okamoto, and Oka, 1985.)

Collectivism also has implications for the concept of ownership and volume of goods (Carnevale, 1995). In chapter 6, we analyzed the endowment effect, wherein people value a good more once it is in their possession (coffee mug example). Whereas individualist cultures show an endowment effect, members of collectivist cultures do not—rather, they show a **group endowment effect**—they value a good more in contexts where they believe others can share it (Carnevale and Radhakrishnan, 1994, experiment 2).

Dealing with Clashes

Succeeding in international business requires that people gain international competence as well as business competence (Matsumoto, 1996). You've done your homework, researched your negotiation opponent's culture, and have a good idea of what to expect during the meeting and which customs are important. You've also uncovered an unsettling fact: In your client's culture, women are regarded as property and second-class citizens. They are not supposed to be opinionated or hold jobs with decision-making importance. Imagine that you are a man and your key business associate is a woman, trained at an Ivy League university, well-versed in cultural issues and your client's strategic situation. For you both to sit at the bargaining table would be an insult to your client. Your supervisor is pressing you to open the door to this client's company. What do you do?

This is an unenviable situation. It's difficult to imagine leaving our colleague behind; you need her skills and, moreover, you don't want to break up your partnership. Yet, bringing her involves an inevitable culture clash. Further, shutting the door on this client shuts the door on the entire country. You have thoughts about enlightening your client, but realistically wonder whether a five-minute lesson from you can overcome centuries of discrimination sewn in the fabric of a country.

There is no best answer to this dilemma. However, the manager that identifies this situation early on is in a better situation to positively address it than is the manager who naïvely steps off the plane with the issue unresolved.

Before reading further, think about what courses of action you might take. Berry (1980) described four ways for two cultures to relate to each other (see Figure 14–3). The first issue is whether the individual (or group) finds it valuable to maintain their distinct cultural identity and characteristics. The second issue is whether the individual (or group) desires to maintain relationships with other (cultural) groups.

- **Integration** is a type of acculturation whereby each group maintains its own culture and also maintains contact with the other culture. Thus, you bring your client to the meetings, and clearly uphold your firm's egalitarian attitudes, yet also make it clear that you have a strong desire to build relationships with the other group.

- **Assimilation** occurs when a group or person does not maintain its culture but does maintain contact with the other culture. You leave your associate at home and try to follow the mores of the other party's culture.

- **Separation** occurs when a group or individual maintains its culture but does not maintain contact with the other culture. You bring your associate to the meetings and remain oblivious to the other group's culture, or, you tell your supervisor you don't want this assignment.

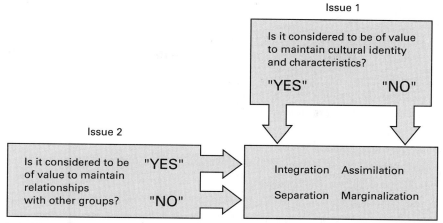

FIGURE 14–3. Acculturation Framework

Source: Berry, J. W. (1980). Acculturation as varieties of adaptation. In *Acculturation: Theory, models, and some new findings.* A. Padilla (ed.). Boulder, CO: Westview. Reprinted with permission.

- **Marginalization** occurs when neither maintenance of the group's own culture nor contact with the other culture is attempted. You leave your associate at home and do not attempt to understand the cultural values of the other firm. Marginalization is the most unfavorable condition (Berry, Poortinga, Segall, and Dasen, 1992).

PREDICTORS OF SUCCESS ABROAD

Your pharmaceutical company wants to expand their international base. You are charged with the task of selecting 26 managers to participate in a special global initiatives assignment in various countries. You know that failure rates as high as 70 percent can be avoided (Copeland and Griggs, 1985). These costs include not only the lost salary of an executive, the cost of transporting the family, and the cost of setting up an office abroad, but also include damage to your organization, lost sales, on-the-job mistakes, and loss of goodwill. Unfortunately, ready-made personality measures are not good predictors of success abroad. The following have some value in predicting success (Triandis, 1994; Martin, 1989):

- Conceptual complexity: People who are conceptually complex (think in terms of shades of gray, rather than black and white) show less social distance to different others (Gardiner, 1972).
- People who use broad categories adjust to new environments better than do narrow categorizers (Detweiler, 1980).
- empathy
- sociability
- critical acceptance of stereotypes
- openness to different points of view

- interest in host culture
- task orientation
- cultural flexibility (the ability to substitute activities in the host culture for own culture valued activities)
- social orientation (the ability to establish new intercultural relationships)
- willingness to communicate (e.g., use the host language without fear of making mistakes)
- patience (suspend judgment)
- intercultural sensitivity
- tolerance for differences among people
- sense of humor
- skills in collaborative conflict resolution

CONCLUSION

In this chapter, we have dealt with three of the most challenging aspects that face negotiators. In many instances, a negotiator is required to deal with all of these issues at one time, such as when a person is negotiating with someone of a different culture via e-mail about the apportionment of a natural resource. As a general principle, greater experience in each of these domains predicts greater negotiation success. However, as we learned in chapter 13, for experience to be effective, the negotiator must seek feedback and develop an accurate mental model of the situation.

TAKE-AWAYS

- In complex conflicts, people disagree about how scarce resources should be divided as well as what values are appropriate to hold and preserve.
- People make value tradeoffs every day, but they don't realize it.
- Electronic negotiations (as opposed to face-to-face negotiations) tend to equalize power differences and lead to greater contentiousness.
- Negotiators who make their electronic messages concise and clear, use emotion, talk about procedures, and refer to the relationship are more likely to be successful than those who don't make clear proposals, label others' behavior, and make take-it-or-leave-it offers.
- Avoid stereotyping cultures as a way of dealing with diversity; instead, assess the following information: language, family structure, religion, affluence, and values.
- Individualists differ dramatically from collectivist cultures in terms of face saving, preference for negotiation, and endowment effects.

Glossary

accuracy In terms of judgment, the degree of conformity to a standard; absence of error.

acquiescence bias The response set representing a tendency to agree with attitude statements regardless of their content.

active misrepresentation A strategy in which a negotiator deliberately misleads his or her opponent.

actor–observer effect The tendency to attribute our own behavior mainly to situational causes but the behavior of others mainly to dispositional causes.

actors People involved in an exchange relationship.

adaptive rationality The strategy of adapting one's behavior upon experiential learning.

additive task A group task in which performance depends on the sum of each individual's effort.

affect The whole range of a person's preferences, evaluations, moods, and emotions.

affiliation bias Bias that occurs when people evaluate a person's actions on the basis of their group affiliations rather than on the merits of the behavior itself.

agent An intermediary who represents the interests of a principal, but may not have interests that are compatible with those of the principal.

alternatives The choices available to negotiators for each issue to be resolved.

analogical reasoning The process by which a problem solver maps the solution for one problem into a solution for another problem.

anchoring and adjustment The tendency for people to make insufficient adjustments from a reference point when making judgments.

Anglo-Saxon type A national characteristic of an organization which is opposite the Latin type, with less centralization, more diffusion of power and decision making, and less hierarchy in the bureaucracy.

approach–approach conflict A type of intrapersonal conflict in which we are attracted to two (or more) options but may choose only one.

approach–avoidance conflict A type of intrapersonal conflict in which we consider a single option that has both attractive and unpleasant aspects.

arbitration A settlement process in dispute resolution in which principals present their case or final offers to a third party who has power to impose a solution.

aspirational deprivation Discrepancies that occur when people's capabilities remain constant but their expectations increase.

assimilation A situation that occurs when a group or person does not maintain its own culture but does maintain contact with another culture.

asymmetric descriptive–prescriptive approach A strategy which assumes that the focal negotiator is rational but may face a negotiator who is not. Therefore, certain prescriptions may be altered when encountering someone who is not assumed to behave rationally in that situation.

automatic processing Thoughts that are not under our control.

avoidance–avoidance conflict A type of intrapersonal conflict in which we must choose among two (or more) undesirable options.

backward induction A mechanism for making rational decisions in a multistage game in which a person reasons backward from the last stage of the game.

bargaining surplus, also surplus The amount of overlap between parties' reservation points.

bargaining zone The region between parties' reservation points in which a final settlement should be obtained.

BATNA (Best Alternative to a Negotiated Agreement)

betweenness axiom An axiom which states that if *x* is preferred to *y*, then *x* must be preferred to any probability mixture of *x* and *y*, which in turn must be preferred to *y*.

biased punctuation of conflict The tendency for people to interpret interactions with their adversaries in self-serving and other-derogating terms.

bipolar negotiator A negotiator who fluctuates between good moods to instigate creative thinking, and occasional anger to communicate resolve.

blaming-the-victim attributions Attributions that enable observers to deal with the perceived inequities in others' lives and maintain the belief that the world is just.

blind justice See equality rule.

boulwarism A bargaining style named for Boulware, former CEO of General Electric, in which one's first offer is one's final offer.

brainstorming A technique used to stimulate creativity in groups in which the goal is to increase the quality and quantity of group ideas by encouraging free exchange and by removing criticism.

bridging A type of integrative solution in which a new option is created that satisfies both parties' vital interests.

causal relationship An empirical relationship in which changes in A are predicted to produce subsequent changes in B.

certainty effect A principle which states that people overweight guaranteed outcomes relative to outcomes that are merely probable.

chunk, chunking Grouping together information at higher levels of abstraction.

circular logrolling In group negotiation, tradeoffs that require each group member to offer another member a concession on one issue, while receiving a concession from yet another group member on a different issue.

closure, need for A desire to have immediate answers and resolutions to situations.

closure property A property which states that if *x* and *y* are available alternatives, then so are all the gambles that can be formed with *x* and *y* as outcomes.

coalition A subgroup of two or more individuals who join together in using their resources to affect the outcome of a decision in a mixed-motive situation.

coalitional integrity The tendency for actors to remain loyal to a coalition, even when they can obtain more resources outside of that coalition.

coercive power Power that derives from a person's ability to influence the behavior of another person by punishing or threatening with punishment.

cognitive control How consistent a person is in employing his or her own judgment policy, regardless of how accurate the policy is.

cognitive feedback Information about relations in the environment rather than outcomes.

cognitive tuning The process by which an actor take the attitudes of his or her audience into account when delivering a message.

collateral relationships People and parties to whom the principal is accountable.

collective fences Exist when the short-term aversive consequences of an act deter us from performing the act and when the act would produce long-term positive benefits to ourselves and to others if performed.

collective traps See resource conservation dilemmas.

commitment An obligation or pledge to do something.

common-bond group Groups composed of members who are attracted to particular members in the group.

common-identity group A group composed of members who are attracted to the group for what it represents.

common information bias The tendency of members of a group to share and discuss only information that is common to all members, as opposed to unique information.

communal relationships Relationships in which parties do not keep track of benefits received and costs incurred but, rather, respond to each other's needs.

communication In negotiation, all of the interaction that occurs between parties.

communication networks The arrangement (or pattern) of communication channels among the members of a group.

comparison with similar others Comparison that occurs when people choose someone of like background, skills, and ability with whom to compare.

complex conflict A situation in which people are in disagreement concerning their ideologies and scarce resources are at stake.

compound gamble Gambles in which the outcomes themselves are gambles rather than pure outcomes.

compromise A midpoint agreement between two arbitrary values or stated positions.

concave utility function Situation in which a person's utility for money decreases marginally; additional monetary gains bring smaller increases in satisfaction.

conceptual loss A threat to the productivity of a group which occurs when group interaction hinders the ability of group members to think.

condorcet paradox A result in a group which demonstrates that the winners of majority rule elections change as a function of the order in which alternatives are voted upon.

confirmation error A tendency for people to seek support for their beliefs that may lead them to overlook or discount relevant information that is not supportive.

confirmatory feedback A tendency of people to elicit feedback from others that supports their beliefs and when asked, to offer information that is believed to be consistent with what a perceiver believes.

conflict The perception of differences of interests among interdependent people.

conflicts of interest Conflicts that concern people's preferences regarding the allocation of scarce resources.

conjunctive tasks Tasks in which performance depends on how well the least talented member of a team performs.

consensus conflict Conflict that occurs when one person's opinions, ideas, or beliefs are incompatible with those of another.

consistency principle The fundamental need to appear to be consistent in our beliefs, feelings, and behaviors, not only to others, but also to ourselves.

consistency tests Questions designed to check whether a person is lying; inconsistencies will emerge when a person is lying.

consortium A united subset of a larger group or collective.

constituent The party whom the principal represents.

contagion The tendency for people to "catch" the emotions and behaviors of other people.

contextual rationality The extent to which choice behavior is affected by the demands on the attention of the decision maker, thereby rendering rationality to be based upon arbitrary features of a situation.

contextualized learning A deep thought process in which a person generalizes an idea to another problem in the same context.

contingency contracts Agreements wherein negotiators make bets based upon their differences in beliefs, forecasts, risk profiles, and interests.

continuity axiom In utility theory, states that for any set of outcomes, a decision maker should always prefer a gamble between the best and worst outcome to a sure intermediate outcome if the odds of the best outcome are good enough.

contractual risk A situation in which settlement outcomes are determined with uncertainty at the time of settlement.

control group In an experiment, a group of persons who are not given treatment.

cooperation A social process in which achievement of a goal by each group member facilitates goal achievement by other group members.

cooperative bargaining situation A situation in which parties make mutual decisions that are binding.

coordination loss A threat to the productivity of a group which occurs when group members do not optimally organize their efforts.

correspondent inference phenomenon The tendency of perceivers to overattribute the cause of a person's behavior to his or her disposition and underestimate the causal influence of situational factors.

cost-cutting A type of integrative agreement in which one party gets what he or she wants, and the other party's costs are reduced or eliminated.

counterfactual thinking The act of thinking about how things might have turned out differently.

creativity The ability to form new concepts using existing knowledge.

creeping determinism A phenomenon in which, once we know the outcome of an event, we perceive the outcome to be an inevitable consequence of the factors leading up to it.

crossover point The point at which subjective weights are exactly identical to objective probability.

crude law of social relations A view that the characteristic processes and effects elicited by a given type of social relationship tend also to elicit that type of social relationship.

culture A shared set of enduring meanings, values, and beliefs that characterize rational, ethnic, or other groups and orient behavior.

data-based processing Information processing that is determined by features of the stimulus situation, rather than by pre-existing beliefs; bottom-up processing.

deadlock An end to negotiations wherein parties do not reach a settlement.

decision making Either choosing among alternative prospects or evaluating the value of a given prospect.

decremental deprivation Discrepancies that occur when expectations are constant but capabilities to meet them decrease.

defection The act of maximizing one's own interests at the expense of another person or group.

defensive attributions See blaming-the-victim attributions.

degree of concessions Extent to which one party has conceded from an initial stated position.

demonstrable tasks Tasks which have an obvious, correct answer.

descriptive model A model that states how people actually behave, in contrast to a prescriptive model.

dictator games Situations in which player 1 makes an offer to player 2 concerning a proposed division of some scarce resource and player 2 does not have the option to reject.

differential retrieval An attempt to retrieve specific instances when making judgments.

diffusion of responsibility In a group, the tendency for each individual to feel less responsible and less likely to act than if he or she were alone.

diminishing marginal utility principle The tendency for increasing units of a resource (e.g., money) to result in decreasing levels of satisfaction.

direct effect A feedback mechanism in which outcomes are used to inform subsequent judgments and actions.

discrete transactions Transactions that are of limited time duration.

discretionary tasks Tasks that permit some members of groups to combine their individual contributions in any way that they wish.

disjunctive tasks Tasks in which performance depends on how well the most talented member of a team performs.

distributive justice The fair allocation of resources to a circle of recipients.

distributive negotiation Refers to how negotiators divide the resources to be allocated.

dominance principle A principle which states that one alternative dominates another if it is just as good on all the pertinent aspect dimensions and better on at least one.

double auction A situation in which one player owns a good and the other player is a potential buyer. Both parties name a price at the same time; if a positive overlap exists, trade occurs, otherwise not.

downward social comparison Situations in which people compare themselves to someone or a group who is less fortunate, able, accomplished, or lower in status.

dyadic conflict Conflict between two persons.

ecological validity The extent to which an observed cue, such as grade point average, is related to an unobservable criterion of interest, such as academic achievement.

ecology A physical and geographical environment which contains particular resources.

egocentric judgment The tendency for people to assume greater responsibility for joint activities than is actually warranted.

egoistic deprivation A feeling of inequality produced by interpersonal comparisons.

emblems Gestures with specific meanings within specific cultures; e.g., cultural signs such as "OK" with the hand, or shrugging to indicate one doesn't care.

emotion A complex assortment of affects, beyond merely good feelings and bad, that may vary terms of arousal and pleasantness.

emotional contagion A process whereby the emotions experienced by one person are transmitted to those of another.

emotional expressivity The extent to which a person expresses feeling states that are easily observed.

emotional feedback A process in which our facial, vocal, and postural behaviors provide information about our emotions.

emotional labor The work that a person does to regulate the nature, intensity, and frequency of his or her emotional expression.

emotional tuning When an actor tailors a communication to the emotional state and disposition of the audience.

encoding An information process by which stimulus items are translated into an internal representation.

environment The circumstances or conditions by which one is surrounded.

episodic memory Memory of specific events and concrete experiences.

equality rule A principle which prescribes equal shares for all.

equilibrium outcome An outcome in which no player can unilaterally (single-handedly) improve his or her outcome by making a different choice.

equilibrium principle A principle which states that people choose the behavior that maximizes their interest; behavior is stable in the sense that they will not want to move away from a course of action because it will reduce their utility.

equity rule A principle which prescribes that distribution of resources should be proportional to a person's contribution.

escalation of commitment A situation in which decision makers fail to adapt their reference point and continue to make risky decisions, which often prove unprofitable.

evaluations In person perception, simple positive and negative reactions to others, such as attraction, liking, prejudice, and so on.

event schemas Schemas that represent stereotypical or routine sequences of events, such as going to a restaurant or to a football game.

exchange relationships Relationships in which parties keep track of benefits received and costs incurred.

expand the pie A type of integrative solution in which a way is found to augment a scarce resource.

expected utility The amount of satisfaction of the potential outcomes of a prospect, each weighted by its probability.

expected value principle A principle which states that the expected value of a prospect is the sum of the objective values of the outcomes multiplied by the probability of their occurrence.

experienced negotiator A person who has undergone several trials of natural experience but no formal training.

experienced utility Our actual experience of the pleasure we derive from something, as opposed to anticipated utility.

expert A person who has years of experience in a domain.

expert power Power that derives from a person's knowledge, skills, and abilities.

explicit bargaining A bargaining situation in which people are able to communicate with one another.

extrinsic motivation Motivation that originates from outside a person (such as external rewards).

false conflict A situation in which conflict does not exist between people, but they erroneously perceive the presence of conflict.

false consensus The belief that others are more similar to ourselves in attitudes and behaviors than is actually the case.

false uniqueness The tendency to view ourselves as different (in a positive direction) from others, which is often incorrect.

fate control A situation in which each person in an interdependent realationship has control over the outcome of the others in the group.

field In terms of creativity, a set of social institutions that selects from the variations produced by individual members those that are worth preserving.

fixed-pie perception The belief that the other party's interests are directly and completely opposed to one's own.

focal negotiator The party of interest in a negotiation situation.

focal points Arbitrary points such as salient numbers, figures, or values that appear to be valid but may have no basis in fact.

foot-in-the-door technique A technique in which a person is asked to agree to a small favor and later is confronted with a larger request. People who accede to the small favor first are likely to agree to the larger favor later.

forked-tail impression A tendency to see people as having other undesirable characteristics in completely unrelated domains once we have identified one negative trait.

functional fixedness A tendency to represent objects as serving conventional problem-solving funtions and thus failing to see that they also serve novel functions.

fundamental attribution error Error that occurs when people attribute the behavior of others to underlying dispositions and discount the role of situational factors.

game rationality The extent to which organizations and other social institutions consist of individuals acting in relation to each other to pursue individual objectives by means of individual calculations of self-interest.

generalized learning The ability to apply an idea or behavior to different contexts.

graduated reduction in tension relations (GRIT) Unilateral conciliatory actions designed to de-escalate a conflict.

Gresham law of conflict Conflict in which harmful and dangerous elements drive out those elements that would keep conflict within bounds.

group-based fraternal deprivation Deprivation produced by intergroup comparisons.

group efficacy The collective perception held by members of a group that their efforts, decisions, and products are superior, valued, and worthwhile.

group endowment effect The tendency for a group to more highly value something that is in their possession than they would value it if it was not in their possession.

group goals Objectives that group members consensually agree upon or impose.

group potency A collective belief held by members of a group that their efforts, decisions, and products are superior, valued, and worthwhile.

group schemas Frameworks that contain our beliefs about social groups, also known as stereotypes.

group structure A pattern of relationships among positions held in a group.

group superiority effect In team negotiation, the tendency for groups to outperform individuals under certain conditions.

halo effect The assumption that if people possess one socially desirable characteristic, then they also possess other attractive traits.

heartfelt interests Convictions which derive from social and moral values that are independent of self interest.

heuristics Rules or principles that allow individuals to make judgments rapidly and with reduced effort; mental shortcuts.

hidden table The negotiations that take place behind the scene between a principal and his or her constituents.

hindsight bias A pervasive tendency for people to be remarkably adept at inferring a process once the outcome is known but unable to predict outcomes when the processes and precipitating events are unknown.

horizontal collectivism A type of culture emphasizing the interdependence and "oneness" of social groups.

identity goals Goals that arise from people's desire to understand themselves.

ideological conflict Occurs when two or more people disagree about a state of the world, fact, opinion, but do not have to allocate scarce resources.

illustrators Nonverbal gestures that people make when they are communicting that do not contain specific meaning (as do emblems), but enhance communication (such as talking with one's hands).

impasse An end to negotiations wherein parties do not reach a settlement.

impossibility theorem A theorem which states that the derivation of group preference from individual preference is indeterminate if certain conditions prevail.

impression management Techniques designed to create a favorable opinion of oneself in others.

independence of irrelevant alternatives An axiom which states that the best outcome in a feasible set of outcomes will also be the best outcome in any smaller subset of feasible outcomes that still contains that outcome.

indeterminacy The inability to predict negotiation outcomes.

indirect effect A feedback mechanism based on a person's interpretation or evaluation of the outcomes of a negotiation, which may be biased.

individual rationality In negotiation, the principle which states that individuals should not agree to a utility payoff less desirable than their reservation point.

inefficient outcomes Negotiation outcomes in which parties either fail to reach an agreement, in the case of a positive bargaining zone, or reach an agreement for which there exists another agreement in which at least one party's utility would increase, without reducing the utility of the other parties.

inference The mental act of assuming something beyond what is presented by the date available.

influence The method or strategy by which people exercise or use their power.

information-conserving tasks In groups, a task that allows each individual member's contribution to be clearly identified.

information dilemma A situation in which information exchange is necessary for the discovery and creation of integrative agreements, but may place the negotiator at a disadvantage in terms of relative gain.

information pooling In group interaction, the strategy of collecting information from all members in a systematic fashion.

information-processing approach An approach which assumes that cognitive activity may be analyzed conceptually in terms of a series of stages during which abstract information is transformed or recoded by particular components or mechanisms.

information-reducing tasks In groups, a task that combines individual members' inputs in such a manner that it is not possible to determine who did what.

informational conflict A situation in which people are in disagreement about ideologies or the facts of a situation but do not have to apportion scarce resources.

informational influence In groups, social persuasion exerted by providing a target person with information necessary to consent to a decision.

in-group bias Positive evaluations of one's own group relative to an out-group.

input An investment in a relationship which usually entails costs.

insightful learning The ability to develop a new insight based upon existing concepts.

integration In terms of cultural relations, a type of acculturation whereby each group maintains its own culture while also maintaining contact with another culture.

integrative agreement A negotiated outcome that is efficient, such that all potential resources are utilized by parties.

integrative negotiation A process by which negotiators seek to expand the amount of available resources.

integrative potential Availability of a mutually beneficial solution to a conflict.

interaction gains In group interaction, the tendency for performance to be enhanced.

interaction losses In group interaction, the usually unforeseen factors that detract from potential performance.

interest-driven value A situation in which a person's own concerns or self-interests drive or dictate their values.

interests The underlying needs that a negotiator tries to fulfill.

intergroup conflict Conflict that occurs between members of different groups representing personally relevant social, cultural, or political categories.

intergroup negotiations Negotiations in which parties identify with their organization and treat the other party in terms of his or her membership in other organizations.

intermediary A person who serves as agent or intervenes between two or more principals in a negotiation.

internal consistency The degree to which a theory, data, beliefs, or argument does not contradict itself.

interpersonal conflict Conflict that occurs between persons.

intragroup Analysis which examines the internal dynamics of groups or teams.

intrapersonal conflict Conflict that occurs within one person.

intrinsic motivation Motivation derived from a person's internal drives; e.g., an enjoyment of doing worthwhile activities, taking on challenges, and learning.

intuitive lawyer A negotiation role in which one wants to make the best case for a particular, preselected conclusion.

intuitive scientist A negotiation role in which one wants to find the correct or optimal conclusion, independent of one's personal interests.

irrationality Behavior which is inconsistent and unpredictable.

issue mix The union of both parties' issue sets.

issues The resources to be allocated or the considerations to be resolved in negotiation.

joint rationality The principle that two negotiators should not agree to a settlement outcome if another outcome exists that is pareto-superior.

judgment policy In decision making, the method by which a person evaluates and combines cues (information) to arrive at a judgment.

knowledge goals Goals in which individuals are dependent on others for information.

labeling To describe with a fixed identification or description.

latent conflict Conflict that exists but is not perceived.

Latin type A national characteristic of organizations: a classic bureaucracy, with centralized power and decision making and hierarchical levels.

law of large numbers A principle which states that the mean return will get closer and closer to its expected value the more times a gamble is repeated.

learning The process of acquiring new skills and knowledge.

legitimate power Power that derives from a person's authorization to tell another what to do.

lexicographic decision rule A decision rule in which alternatives are first compared with respect to the most important attribute to determine which is most attractive. The decision maker compares the alternatives on one attribute at a time rather than examining each alternative separately as a whole.

limited information Information such as name, appearance, workplace, and age that we use to form immediate impressions of others.

limited rationality The extent to which people simplify a decision problem because of the difficulties of anticipating or considering all alternatives and all information.

logrolling A type of integrative strategy of trading off interests where each party concedes on issues of low priority to the self and of high priority to the other party.

long-term memory The repository of our more permanent knowledge and skills, such as beliefs about physical relationships in the environment, properties of objects, people, ourselves, organizations, and motor and perceptual skills.

lose–lose agreements Agreements in which negotiators settle for outcomes that both prefer less than some other readily available outcome.

loyalists People who prefer to split resources equally, except in antagonistic relationships.

marginalization A situation that occurs when neither maintenance of a group's own culture nor contact with another culture is attempted.

maxim of pleasantness The act of communicating a message to an audience in such a way that it will be favorably received.

maxim of regulation Attempts by speakers to tailor their messages so as to control the audience's emotional reaction.

maxim of relevance Attempts by speakers to communicate information most pertinent to their audience.

maximizing utility The act of choosing so as to increase the satisfaction received from consuming commodities.

mediation A form of outside intervention in which a third party aids disputants in reaching a voluntary agreement but has no power to impose a settlement.

mental accounting A concept wherein decision makers have mental budgets for various items.

mental models The ways in which people understand social and physical systems.

mere exposure effect A phenomenon in which repeated exposure to an image, item, or idea leads people to like it more, even if they are not aware of having been exposed to it.

mimicry A process wherein people copy the facial expressions, voice tone, posture, and movement of others.

minimax strategy A negotiation strategy in which the objective is to minimize the worst possible consequences.

misunderstood messages Messages which are wrongly interpreted by another party, usually in a manner that is worse than was intended.

mixed-motive negotiation The tension between cooperation and competition in negotiation: negotiators want to cooperate with the other party to reach mutual agreement but must compete to maximize their share of the joint gains.

mode of communication; communication mode The medium by which negotiators interact.

monolithic party A member of a group that acts as a single unit; i.e., there is no divergence within the group.

mood A low-intensity, diffuse, and relatively enduring affective state.

motivation loss A situation that occurs when members of a group do not try as hard as they could when working together as when working alone.

multiattribute utility technique (MAUT) A method of analyzing decision situations, involving four main tasks: (1) identifying the alternatives; (2) identifying dimensions or attributes of the alternatives; (3) evaluating the utility associated with each dimension; and (4) weighting or prioritizing each dimension in terms of importance.

multilithic group A negotiation situation in which the members of a group may have different values and beliefs but must ultimately act in concert as a decision-making unit.

multiparty conflict Conflict among three or more persons.

multiple offers A strategy that involves a negotiator simultaneously presenting the other party with two or more proposals of equal value.

multiple trials A situation in which parties do not make a single choice but instead make a choice, receive feedback about the other player's choice, experience the outcome, and make another choice.

naïve person A person who has not received formal training in an area or domain.

naïve realism A principle in which people expect others to hold views of the world similar to their own.

Nash solution Postulates that the agreement point of a negotiation will satisfy the following five axioms: uniqueness, pareto-optimality, symmetry, independence of equivalent utility representations, and independence of irrelevant alternatives.

nature view A strategy in which negotiators' preferences are the "givens" in a negotiation; to reach integrative agreements, negotiators must discover the potential that underlies their preferences.

needs-based rule A rule which states that benefits people receive should be proportional to their needs; also called welfare-based allocation.

negative bargaining zone A negotiation situation in which there is no positive overlap between parties' reservation points.

negativity effect In impression formation, an effect that occurs when negative information carries more weight in our impressions of others than does positive information.

negotiation A decision-making process by which two or more people agree on how to allocate scarce resources.

negotiation dance The process of making offers and counteroffers.

negotiation outcome The product or endpoint of a bargaining situation.

negotiation process The events and interactions that occur between parties before the outcome.

negotiation schemas Cognitive structures that contain our knowledge and expectations regarding bargaining situations.

negotiator's dilemma A situation in which revealing information about your interests may maximize joint gain but put you at a strategic disadvantage.

negotiator's surplus The positive difference between the settlement outcome and the negotiator's reservation point.

nominal groups A group composed by pooling the outputs of randomly chosen individuals who have worked alone.

noncooperative bargaining situation A bargaining situation in which parties make independent choices and any attempt to coordinate behavior is not binding.

nonrational behavior Behavior that does not conform to prescriptions of economics models, but that may nevertheless be consistent and predictable.

nonspecific compensation A type of integrative bargaining in which one party receives his or her most desirable alternative, and the other party is repaid in some unrelated coin.

norms Behavioral rules imposed and adhered to by members of a group; a felt obligation, behavior, or attitude approved and expected by a group.

norm of commitment The tendency for people to feel psychologically committed to follow through with their word.

novice A person who is currently receiving training or has received training and is becoming an expert in an area or domain.

nurture view A strategy in which negotiators construct and develop integrative potential through their evolving and changing preferences.

opponent The party with whom we negotiate; however, that party's interests are not necessarily opposed to ours.

organizational autocrat A person who imposes decisions on others by virtue of having complete decision control.

organizational puppet A person who is elected to serve the interests of the larger constituency and negotiates on behalf of these constituents.

outcome feedback Knowledge of the results of a decision.

outcomes In negotiation, the results or consequences of mutual decision making.

output Something that a person receives from a relationship.

overconfidence effect Unwarranted levels of confidence in people's judgment of their abilities and the occurrence of positive events and underestimates of the likelihood of negative events.

parallel concepts In social judgment theory, the assumption that human and environmental systems should be described in symmetrical terms.

pareto-efficient frontier The set of outcomes corresponding to the entire set of agreements that leaves no portion of the total amount of resources unallocated.

pareto-optimal frontier A situation in which no other feasible agreement exists that would improve one party's outcome while simultaneously not hurting the other party's outcome.

particularism The extent to which the value of a resource depends on who is providing it.

partner A party whose interests are highly coordinated with one's own.

party A participant in conflict. Parties can be individuals, groups, organizations, communities, or nations.

passive misrepresentation A strategy in which a negotiator does not convey his or her true preferences and allows the other party to arrive at an erroneous conclusion.

pattern of concessions In negotiation, the sequence of consecutive concessions made by parties.

person schemas Cognitive structures that people form to mentally represent other people.

personal identity The unique or idiosyncratic aspects of oneself.

pivotal power The ability to change a losing coalition into a winning coalition.

polyad A group of three or more individuals, each representing their own interests, who attempt to resolve perceived differences of interest; see multiparty conflict.

positional bargaining A strategy wherein a negotiator makes a claim for a given position and is inflexible with regard to achieving that position.

positions The stated "wants" a negotiator has for a particular issue.

positive bargaining zone An area in a negotiation in which the parties' reservation points overlap.

posterior rationality Reasoning that emphasizes the discovery of intentions by interpreting action rather than as a result of a prior position.

postsettlement settlement A strategy in which negotiators reach a binding settlement, but agree to explore other options with the goal of finding another that both prefer more than the current one; if one is not found, the current settlement is imposed.

potential productivity The ability of a group to perform depends upon three factors: task demands, resources available to the group, and the group process.

power The basis of a person's influence over another in an interdependent context.

power law of practice The phenomenon that states that the benefits of practice are most dramatic early on; although the benefit of further practice rapidly diminishes additional practice always helps.

predicted utility Projections about what we like and don't like.

preference reversals Inconsistencies in choice that are produced when subtle wording differences lead people to make different judgments.

preferences Choices made based on an individual's priorities in a negotiation situation.

premature concessions Making concessions on issues before they are even requested.

preparation The important work of planning for a negotiation which takes place before the negotiator is seated at the bargaining table.

preparation–response In problem solving, the time that is used in preparing to solve an analogy and making a response.

prescriptive model A model that specifies how people ought to behave to be considered rational, in contrast to a descriptive model.

primacy effect The tendency to assign greater weight to information that is presented initially rather than to later evidence, even if the evidence is equally objectively valuable.

primary table The most basic, fundamental form of negotiation, involving two people facing one another at the bargaining table.

priming An enhancement of the processing of a stimulus as a function of prior exposure.

principals The key players in a negotiation.

prisoner's dilemma A mixed-motive game in which the payoffs for joint competition and joint cooperation fall between the payoffs for the combination of cooperation by one participant (who loses the most) and competition by the other party (who gains the most).

probability The chance that a given outcome will occur.

procedural justice The evaluation of social experiences in terms of the form of social interaction; the extent to which procedures and social processes are just and fair.

procedure invariance A fundamental axiom of expected utility theory which requires that strategically equivalent methods of elicitation should yield the same preference order.

process feedback Feedback given to a decision maker that provides information about relations in the environment in addition to outcomes.

process rationality Rationality which emphasizes the extent to which decisions find their sense in attributes of the decision process rather than in attributes of decision outcomes.

production blocking The tendency for the potential contributions of people in groups to be blocked because others are talking.

progressive deprivation Discrepancies that occur when expectations and capabilities both increase but expectations increase at a faster rate than capabilities.

pseudosacred The strategy of claiming that issues are sacred, or heartfelt, when they are not.

psychological entrapment A situation in which decision makers fail to adapt their reference point and continue to make risky decisions, which often prove unprofitable.

psychological reactance The tendency of people to do the opposite of what someone is trying to get them to do in an attempt to assert their freedom.

public goods dilemmas Situations in which individuals have the choice to contribute resources to a common pool or community. Contributing helps the group, but is costly to the individual; if all individuals fail to contribute, the public good cannot exist.

pure conflict Negotiation situations in which parties' interests are directly opposed in a fixed-sum fashion.

pure coordination Negotiation situations in which parties' interests are perfectly compatible.

ratio concept A resource distribution situation in which participants are allocated outcomes proportional to their inputs.

rational behavior Behavior that maximizes a person's utility or the satisfaction derived from a particular outcome or choice.

reactive devaluation The tendency for people to devalue an option previously considered to be more attractive, merely as a consequence of it being offered by the other side.

reciprocal tradeoffs A tradeoff fashioned between two parties where each gives up one thing in exchange for making gains on another issue.

reciprocity principle A situation in which we feel obligated to return in kind what others have offered or given to us.

reducibility axiom States that if two risky alternatives include identical and equally probable outcomes among their possible consequences, then the utility of these outcomes should be ignored in choosing between these two options.

reference point A focal amount of the pertinent outcome at which smaller amounts are considered losses and larger amounts gains.

referent power Power that derives from a person's respect and admiration for another.

regressiveness principle A principle in which extreme values of some quantity do not deviate very much from the average value of that quantity.

regulation of collective material resources Rules that include guidelines for use of public funds, public property, and natural resources.

regulation of personal material resource transactions Rules that support the maintenance of equitable exchange, contracts, and norms of reciprocity in negotiation.

regulation of personal status resource transactions Rules that support the social order by specifying how people of equal and unequal status should interact.

relational exchanges Trades and interactions that occur when parties anticipate a shared future together.

relationship The degree of commitment and satisfaction existing between interdependent individuals or groups.

relationship market Situation in which the objective is to find the best match in a market of several persons.

relative deprivation How people evaluate outcomes in comparison to those they expect, have received in the past, or see others receive.

representation Proposals that attempt to explain how different types of information are encoded and processed.

reputation Recognition of some characteristic or ability as judged by other people.

reservation point The point at which a negotiator is indifferent between reaching a settlement and walking away from the bargaining table.

resource assessment The identification of the bargaining alternatives for each issue.

resource conservation dilemma A situation in which individuals take or harvest resources from a common pool when no external monitors are available; the maintenance of the pool depends upon individuals exercising restraint in their harvesting.

resources Anything that has value or utility; in a group, the relevant abilities, skills, and tools possessed by people attempting to perform a task.

retributive justice The distribution of "bads" or the allocation of punishments.

revealed preferences Preferences that are not observable but must be inferred from people's choices and willful behavior.

reward power Power that derives from a person's ability to influence the behavior of another person by providing or withholding rewards.

risk attitude A person's preferences concerning outcomes that are gambles or sure things of equal expected value.

risk averse Preference for a sure thing rather than a gamble.

risk indifferent See risk neutral.

risk neutral An indifference between a gamble and a sure outcome of equal expected value.

risk seeking Preference for a gamble of equal expected value to a sure thing.

riskless choice Choice under certainty; i.e., when outcomes are fully known.

roles The expected behaviors of the occupant of a given position in a group by other group members.

role schemas Schemas that contain our beliefs about persons who occupy particular roles or positions, such as bill collectors, insurance adjusters, chief executive officers, used car salesmen, attorneys, and middle-level managers.

ruthless competitors People who prefer to have more resources than the other party, regardless of relationship.

sacred issues Issues which are deemed by the decision maker as those that cannot be compromised, traded, or even questioned.

saints People who prefer to split resources equally no matter whether their relationship with another party is positive, neutral, or negative.

satisfaction Utility associated with an object or circumstance; in relationships, satisfaction is a function of a person's comparison of his or her real-life circumstances to what he or she expects that he or she should have.

satisficing A tradeoff in decision making that results from doing just enough to make a reasonable solution.

scarce resource competition Competition that exists when people perceive one another as desiring the same limited resources.

scarcity principle A principle which states that we find those things which appear to be rare, hard to get, or in high demand to be most appealing.

schemas Cognitive structures which consist of our knowledge, beliefs, and expectations pertaining to some stimulus domain, containing both factual, objective information and subjective impressions.

scripts Cognitive structures which consist of our knowledge, beliefs, and expectations concerning a stereotyped temporal event.

second table The relationship that parties share with their constituents; see hidden table.

secular issues Issues which are deemed by the decision maker as those that can be compromised, traded, and associated with a monetary outcome.

selected rationality Rationality that emphasizes the process of selection among individuals or organizations through survival or growth; rules of behavior achieve the status of rationality by virtue of the survival and growth of social institutions in which such rules are followed.

selective attention, encoding and storage The tendency for the human information-processing system to focus on only a biased subset of what can be attended to at any one time.

self-enhancement The desire to maintain or enhance a positive view of oneself.

self-evaluation The act of assessing one's strengths and weaknesses in comparison to others.

self-fulfilling prophecy A situation that occurs when the beliefs held by a perceiver elicit behavior from a target person in a manner that confirms the perceiver's expectations.

self-improvement A situation in which people compare themselves with others who can serve as models of success.

self-schema The mental representation we have of ourselves, which includes information about our appearance, personality, behavior, roles, feelings, and self-concept.

self-serving bias The tendency to process information and draw inferences in a fashion that serves one's own interests; e.g., attributing positive outcomes to internal causes (one's own traits) but negative outcomes or events to external causes (e.g., chance or task difficulty).

self-verify The tendency we have to want others to have the same impression of us that we have of ourselves.

semantic memory Memory which comprises the meaning of concepts; our "mental dictionary."

separation A situation that occurs when a group or individual maintains its own culture but does not maintain contact with another culture.

short-term memory A proposed intermediate memory system in which information resides on its journey from sensory memory to long-term memory; the part of our central processor that holds the symbols currently in the focus of our attention and conscious processing, which is limited to about 5–9 things.

similarity–attraction effect The tendency for people who are similar to each other to like one another on the basis of very little or even trivial information.

sinister attribution error The tendency to ascribe ill will and evil motives to others when we try to make sense of their behavior.

situational attribution The act of ascribing external forces as the cause of behavior.

social context The relationship between parties and the emotions at the bargaining table.

social desirability The tendency for people to want to be favorably evaluated by others.

social dilemma A situation that results when people engage in behaviors that seem perfectly rational on an individual basis but lead to collective disaster.

social facilitation The effect that the mere presence of others has upon the behavior of individuals; the presence of others facilitates behavior if the task is well-learned, but debilitates behavior if the task is not well-learned.

social identity An individual's self-definition of who he or she is. This identity includes personal attributes (one's self-concept) as well as membership in various groups.

social loafing A form of motivation loss in which people in a group fail to contribute as much or work as hard as they would if they worked independently.

social proof principle A situation in which we look to the behavior of others to determine what is desirable, appropriate, and correct.

social status The evaluation of each position by the members of the group, in terms of prestige, importance, and value to the group.

social striving The opposite of social loafing; a situation in which members of a group work harder in a group than they would if working alone.

social utility Concern for the outcomes of others.

stalemate An end to negotiations wherein parties do not reach a settlement.

status quo bias A tendency in decision making and negotiation to prefer current circumstances over proposed ones.

status system The presence of a hierarchy of prestigious positions in a group.

sticky slope A situation created when the party who makes a concession is assured that further ground is not also imperiled.

St. Petersburg paradox The observed reluctance to play a game of chance, despite its infinite expected value.

strategic conceptualization A cognitive framework that allows an individual to understand and apply integrative strategies to different negotiation situations.

strategic creativity A situation in which negotiators create more resources for the purpose of maximizing their own gain in situations where it appears that they have completely opposing interests.

strategic misrepresentation A situation in which a negotiator misrepresents his or her true preferences so as to gain advantage over the other party.

subcertainty In prospect theory, the observation that people's subjective weightings for mutually exclusive and exhaustive events do not sum to 1.

subgame perfect equilibrium The rational strategy which states that a best move in a given trial of a game should also be the best move in a multiple-trial game.

subjective status A person's evaluation of how his or her own outcomes compare with those attained by other members of a group.

subordinate A party who is under the authority of a principal.

substitutability axiom An axiom which states that gambles that have outcomes about which people are indifferent are interchangeable.

superficial learning The ability to parrot back an idea or behavior that a person has observed or enacted.

superior A party who has authority over a principal.

superrationality Our need to believe that (1) others are rational and (2) that others believe us to be rational.

sure thing principle A principle which states that if alternative *x* is preferred to *y*, in the condition that some event, *a*, occurs, and if *x* is also preferred to *y*, in the condition that some event, *a*, does not occur, then *x* should be preferred to *y*, even when it is not known whether *a* will occur or not.

taboo tradeoff A proposal to exchange sacred values for secular ones.

tacit bargaining A bargaining situation in which people are unable to communicate but coordinate through their independent actions.

target negotiator The opponent in a negotiation situation.

target point A negotiator's most preferred or ideal settlement; aspiration point.

task demands In a group context, the requirements imposed upon the group by the task itself and the rules governing task performance.

team A group of people who are interdependent and working toward a common goal.

team effect In negotiation, the tendency for parties represented by a bargaining team to reach more integrative settlements.

temporal Schemas which are organized in terms of sequences of events.

theory-based processing Information processing which is guided by our expectations, pre-existing views, and beliefs; top-down processing.

Third World type A national characteristic of organizations marked by centralized decision making, informal values, and a paternalistic or traditional family orientation.

thought-induced affect A phenomenon in which merely thinking about something or someone can polarize our feelings toward that object or person.

tit-for-tat strategy A strategy which always cooperates on the first trial, and on subsequent trials it does whatever its opponent did on the previous trial.

tradeoff Giving up one thing in return for another.

transaction market Market in which the objective is to complete as many profitable transactions as possible.

transactive emotion Systems which develop within dyads and groups for perceiving, signaling, feeling, and expressing emotion.

transactive memory A shared system within a group for the encoding, processing, storage, and retrieval of information.

transitivity property A property which states that if we prefer *x* to *y* and *y* to *z*, then we should prefer *x* to *z*.

triangle hypothesis A theory in which competitive people see the world to be more homogeneous than is really the case, and thus act competitively with everyone, thereby inducing cooperative people to behave competitively.

uniqueness axiom An axiom which states that there is a unique solution to each bargaining situation or game.

unpacking Division of large, all-encompassing issues into smaller, more manageable ones.

upward comparison The tendency of people to compare themselves to someone who is better off, more accomplished, or higher in status.

utilitarian goals Goals which result in tangible outcomes.

utility The satisfaction a person derives from any experience or commodity.

utility function The quantification of a person's preferences with respect to certain objects.

value-driven interests A model in which a person's interests reflect his or her underlying values.

veridical conflict Conflict that actually exists between people and they perceive it as such.

vertical collectivism A type of culture emphasizing the group rather than the individual.

volunteer dilemma A situation in which at least one person in a group must sacrifice his or her own interests to better the group.

weak ties Relations between people in a network who are not close.

winner's curse A situation in which a negotiator makes an offer that is immediately accepted by the opponent, thus signalling the fact that the negotiator offered too much.

working memory A storage receptacle in the human information processing system that maintains information about local context, which is neither the subject of our immediate attention nor present in the recesses of long-term memory.

References

Abelson, R. (1976). Script processing in attitude formation and decision making. In *Cognition and social behavior.* J. S. Carroll and J. W. Payne, eds. Hillsdale, NJ: Erlbaum: 33–46.

Abelson, R. and A. Levi (1985). Decision making and decision theory. In *The handbook of social psychology.* 3rd ed. G. Lindzey and E. Aronson, eds. New York: Random House: **1:** 231–310.

Adair, W., T. Okumura, and J. Brett (1997). Culturally linked schema for negotiations: How U.S. and Japanese intra-cultural dyads maximize joint gain. Unpublished manuscript, Northwestern University.

Adams, S. (1965). Inequity in social exchange. In *Advances in experimental social psychology.* L. Berkowitz, ed. New York: Academic Press: **2.**

Adamson, R. E. and D. W. Taylor (1954). Functional fixedness as related to elapsed time and situation. *Journal of Experimental Psychology* **47:** 122–216.

Akerlof, G. (1970). The market for lemons: Quality uncertainty and the market mechanism. *Quarterly Journal of Economics* **84:** 488–500.

Alicke, M. D. (1990). Incapacitating conditions and alteration of blame. *Journal of Social Behavior and Personality* **5:** 651–664.

Allison, S. T. and D. M. Messick (1990). Social decision heuristics in the use of shared resources. *Journal of Behavioral Decision Making* **3**(3): 195–204.

Allred, K., J. S. Mallozzi, F. Matsui, and C. P. Raia (1996). Anger and compassion in negotiation. Working paper.

Ancona, D. G., R. A. Friedman, and D. M. Kolb (1991). The group and what happens on the way to "yes." *Negotiation Journal* **2:** 155–173.

Argyle, M. and M. Henderson (1984). The rules of relationships. In *Understanding personal relationships: An interdisciplinary approach.* S. Duck and D. Perlman, eds. Beverly Hills, CA: Sage.

Arndt, J. (1979). Toward a concept of domesticated markets. *Journal of Marketing* **43**(Fall): 69–75.

Aronson, E. (1992). The return of the repressed: Dissonance theory makes a comeback. *Psychological Inquiry* **3:** 303–311.

Aronson, E. and D. Bridgeman (1979). Jigsaw groups and the desegregated classroom: In pursuit of common goals. *Personality and Social Psychology Bulletin* **5:** 438–446.

Arrow, K. J. (1963). *Social choice and individual values.* New Haven, CT: Yale University Press.

Arunchalam, V. and W. Dilla (1995). Judgment accuracy and outcomes in negotiation: A causal modeling analysis of decision-aiding effects. *Organizational Behavior and Human Decision Processes* **61**(3): 289–304.

Asch, S. (1946). Forming impressions of personality. *Journal of Abnormal and Social Psychology* **41:** 258–290.

Aubert, V. (1963). Competition and dissensus: Two types of conflict and conflict resolution. *Conflict Resolution* **7**: 26–42.

Austin, W. (1980). Friendship and fairness: Effects of type of relationship and task performance on choice of distribution rules. *Personality and Social Psychology Bulletin* **6**: 402–408.

Averill, J. R. (1980). On the paucity of positive emotions. In *Advances in the study of communication and affect,* Vol. 6: Assessment and modification of emotional behavior. K. Blankstein, P. Pliner, and J. Polivy, eds. New York, Plenum: 7–45.

Babcock, L., G. Loewenstein, S. Issacharoff, and C. Camerer (1995). Biased judgments of fairness in bargaining. *The American Economic Review* **85**(5): 1337–1343.

Babcock, L., L. Thompson, M. Pilluta, and K. Murnighan (1997). The information dilemma in negotiations: Effects of experience, incentives and integrative potential. Pittsburgh, PA: Carnegie-Mellon University (unpublished manuscript).

Back, K. W. (1951). Influence through social communication. *Journal of Abnormal Social Psychology* **46**: 9–23.

Bales, R. F. (1958). Task roles and social roles in problem–solving groups. *Readings in social psychology.* E. E. Maccoby, T. M. Newcomb, and E. I. Hartley. New York: Holt, Rinehart, and Winston.

Balke, W. M., K. R. Hammond, and G. D. Meyer (1973). An alternate approach to labor–management relations. *Administrative Science Quarterly* **18**: 311–327.

Ball, S. B., M. H. Bazerman, and J. S. Carroll (1991). An evaluation of learning in the bilateral winner's curse. *Organizational Behavior and Human Decision Processes* **48**: 1–22.

Balzer, W., M. Doherty, and R. O'Connor (1989). Effects of cognitive feedback on performance. *Psychological Bulletin* **106**: 410–433.

Bargh, J. A., W. J. Lombardi, and E. T. Higgins (1988). Automaticity of chronically accessible constructs in person–situation effects on person perception: It's just a matter of time. *Journal of Personality and Social Psychology* **55**(4): 599–605.

Barker, C. and R. Lemle (1987). Informal helping in partner and stranger dyads. *Journal of Marriage and the Family* **49**: 541–547.

Baron, J. (1988). Decision analysis and utility measurement. *Thinking and deciding.* Boston: Cambridge University Press: 330–351.

Baron, R. A. (1990). Environmentally induced positive affect: Its impact on self-efficacy, task performance, negotiation, and conflict. *Journal of Applied Social Psychology* **20**(5): 368–384.

Bar-Tal, D. and N. Geva (1986). A cognitive basis of international conflicts. In *Psychology of Intergroup Relations.* S. Worchel and W. G. Austin, eds. Chicago: Nelson Hall: 118–133.

Baumeister, R. and L. Newman (1994). Self-regulation of cognitive inference and decision processes. *Personality and Social Psychology Bulletin* **20**: 3–19.

Bazerman, M. H. (1993). Fairness, social comparison, and irrationality. In *Social psychology in organizations.* K. Murnighan, ed. New York: Prentice Hall: 184–203.

Bazerman, M. H. and J. S. Carroll (1987). Negotiator cognition. *Research in Organizational Behavior* **9**: 247–288.

Bazerman, M. H., G. Loewenstein, and S. White (1992). Reversals of preference in allocating decisions: Judging an alternative versus choosing among alternatives. *Administrative Science Quarterly 37:* 220–240.

Bazerman, M. H., T. Magliozzi, and M. A. Neale (1985). Integrative bargaining in a competitive market. *Organizational Behavior and Human Decision Processes* **35**(3): 294–313.

Bazerman, M. H., E. Mannix, and L. Thompson (1988). Groups as mixed-motive negotiations. In *Advances in group processes: Theory and research.* E. J. Lawler and B. Markovsky, eds. Greenwich, CT: JAI Press: **5.**

Bazerman, M. H. and M. A. Neale (1982). Improving negotiation effectiveness under final offer arbitration: The role of selection and training. *Journal of Applied Psychology* **67**(5): 543–548.

Bazerman, M. H. and M. A. Neale (1983). Heuristics in negotiation: Limitations to effective dispute resolution. In *Negotiating in Organizations.* M. H. Bazerman and R. J. Lewicki, eds. Beverly Hills: Sage: 51–67.

Bazerman, M. H. and M. Neale (1992). *Negotiating rationally.* New York: Free Press.

Bazerman, M. H., M. A. Neale, K. Valley, E. Zajac, and P. Kim (1992). The effect of agents and mediators on negotiation outcomes. *Organizational Behavior and Human Decision Processes* **53**: 55–73.

Bazerman, M. H., L. E. Russ, and E. Yakura (1987). Post-settlement settlements in dyadic negotiations: The need for renegotiation in complex environments. *Negotiation Journal* **3**: 283–297.

Beach, L. R. and R. Lipshitz (1993). Why classical decision theory is an inappropriate standard for evaluating and aiding most human decision making. In *Decision making in action: Models and methods.* G. A. Klein, J. Orasanu, R. Calderwood, and C. E. Zsambok, eds. Norwood, NJ: Ablex: 21–35.

Beckman, L. (1970). Effects of students' performance on teachers' and observers' attributions of causality. *Journal of Educational Psychology* **61**: 76–82.

Ben-Yoav, O. and D. G. Pruitt (1984). Resistance to yielding and the expectation of cooperative future interaction in negotiation. *Journal of Experimental Social Psychology* **20**: 323–353.

Ben-Yoav, O. and D. G. Pruitt (1984). Accountability to constituents: A two-edged sword. *Organization Behavior and Human Processes* **34**: 282–295.

Berger, J., H. Fisek, R. Z. Norman, and D. G. Wagner (1983). The formation of reward expectations in status situations. In *Equity theory: Psychological and sociological perspectives.* D. Messick and K. S. Cook, ed. New York: Praeger.

Berkowitz, L. (1972). Social norms, feelings and other factors affecting helping behavior and altruism. In *Advances in experimental social psychology.* L. Berkowitz, ed. New York: Academic Press: **6:** 63–108.

Bernieri, F. J., J. M. Davis, C. R. Knee, and R. Rosenthal (1991). Interactional synchrony and the social affordance of rapport: A validation study. Unpublished manuscript, Oregon State University, Corvallis.

Bernouilli, D. (L. Sommer, trans.) (1954). Exposition of a new theory on the measurement of risk. (Original work published in 1738.) *Econometrica* **22**: 23–36.

Berry, J. W. (1980). Acculturation as varieties of adaptation. In *Acculturation: Theory, models, and some new findings.* A. Padilla, ed. Boulder, CO: Westview.

Berry, J. W., Y. H. Poortinga, M. H. Segall, and P. R. Dasen (1992). *Cross-cultural psychology: Research and applications.* New York: Cambridge University Press.

Bettenhausen, K. and K. Murnighan (1985). The emergence of norms in competitive decision-making groups. *Administrative Science Quarterly* 30: 350–372.

Billings, D. K. (1989). Individualism and group orientation. In *Heterogeneity in cross-cultural psychology.* D. M. Keats, D. Munroe, and L. Mann, eds. Lisse, The Netherlands: Swets and Zeitlinger: 22–103.

Blau, P. M. (1964). *Exchange and power in social life.* New York: Wiley.

Bottom, W. P. (1996). Negotiating risks: Sources of uncertainty and the impact of reference points on concession-making and settlements. Unpublished manuscript, Washington University.

Bottom, W. P., C. L. Eavey, and G. J. Miller (1996). Getting to the core: Coalitional integrity as a constraint on the power of agenda setters. *Journal of Conflict Resolution* **40**(2): 298–319.

Bottom, W. P., K. Gibson, S. Daniels, and J. K. Murnighan (1996). Rebuilding relationships: Defection, repentance, forgiveness and reconciliation. Working paper, Washington University.

Bottom, W. P. and P. W. Paese (1996). False consensus, stereotypic cues, and the perception of integrative potential in negotiation. Unpublished manuscript, Washington University.

Bottom, W. P. and A. Studt (1993). Framing effects and the distributive aspect of integrative bargaining. *Organizational Behavior and Human Decision Processes* **56**(3): 459–474.

Bower, G. (1977). *Human memory.* New York: Academic Press.

Bransford, J. D. and M. K. Johnson (1972). Contextual prerequisites for understanding: Some investigations of comprehension and recall. *Journal of Verbal Learning and Verbal Behavior* **11:** 717–726.

Brehm, J. W. (1966). *A theory of psychological reactance.* Morristown, NJ: General Learning Press.

Brett, J. M. and T. Okumura (1997). Inter- and intra-cultural negotiations: U.S. and Japanese negotiations. Unpublished manuscript, Northwestern University.

Brewer, M. (1979). In-group bias in the minimal intergroup situation: A cognitive–motivational analysis. *Psychological Bulletin* **86:** 307–324.

Brockner, J. and J. Z. Rubin (1985). *Entrapment in escalating conflicts.* New York: Springer-Verlag.

Brown, B. (1968). The effects of need to maintain face on interpersonal bargaining. *Journal of Experimental Social Psychology* **4:** 107–122.

Bruner, J. S., J. J. Goodnow, and G. A. Austin (1956). *A study of thinking.* New York: Wiley.

Brunswick, E. (1952). *The conceptual framework of psychology.* Chicago: University of Chicago Press.

Burton, M. L., C. C. Moore, J. W. Whiting, and A. K. Romney (1992). World cultural regions. Paper presented at the Society for Cross-Cultural Research Conference, Santa Fe, New Mexico, February.

Camerer, C. and G. Loewenstein (1993). In *Psychological perspectives on justice.* B. A. Mellers and J. Baron, eds. Boston: Cambridge University Press: 155–181.

Cappella, J. N. and M. T. Palmer (1990). Attitude similarity, relational history and attraction: The mediating effects of kinesia and vocal behavior. *Communication Monographs* **57:** 161–183.

Carnevale, P. J. (1995). Property, culture, and negotiation. In *Negotiation as a social process: New trends in theory and research.* R. M. Kramer and D. M. Messick, eds. Thousand Oaks, CA: Sage: 309–323.

Carnevale, P. J. and A. Isen (1986). The influence of positive affect and visual access on the discovery of integrative solutions in bilateral negotiations. *Organizational Behavior and Human Decision Processes* **37:** 1–13.

Carnevale, P. J., K. M. O'Connor, and C. McCusker (1993). Time pressure in negotiation and mediation. *Time pressure and stress in human judgment and decision making.* O. Svenson and A. J. Maule, eds. New York: Plenum Press: **335:** 117–127.

Carnevale, P. J. and D. G. Pruitt (1992). Negotiation and mediation. *Annual Review of Psychology* **43:** 531–582.

Carnevale, P. J., D. G. Pruitt, and S. Britton (1979). Looking tough: The negotiator under constituent surveillance. *Personality and Social Psychology Bulletin* **5:** 118–121.

Carnevale, P. J., D. Pruitt, and S. Seilheimmer (1981). Looking and competing: Accountability and visual access in integrative bargaining. *Journal of Personality and Social Psychology* **40:** 111–120.

Carnevale, P. J. and S. Radhakrishnan (1994). Group endowment and the theory of collectivism. Unpublished manuscript, Department of Psychology, University of Illinois at Urbana–Champaign.

Cartwright, D. and A. Zander (1968). *Group dynamics.* New York: Harper & Row.

Chaiken, S. (1980). Heuristic versus systematic information processing and the use of source versus messsage cues in persuasion. *Journal of Personality and Social Psychology* **39**(5): 752–766.

Chaiken, S., V. Liberman, and E. Eagley (1989). Heuristic and systematic information processing within and beyond the persuasion context. In *Unintended thought.* J. S. Vleman and J. A. Bargh, eds. New York: Guilford Press: 212–252.

Chan, D. K. S., H. C. Triandis, P. J. Carnevale, A. Tam, and M. H. Bond (1994). Comparing negotiation across cultures: Effects of collectivism, relationship between negotiators, and concession pattern on negotiation behavior. Unpublished manuscript, Department of Psychology, University of Illinois at Urbana–Champaign.

Chapman, L. J. and J. P. Chapman (1967). Genesis of popular but erroneous diagnostic observations. *Journal of Abnormal Psychology* **72:** 193–204.

Chatman, J. A., D. F. Caldwell, and C. O'Reilly (1995). Managerial personality fit and early career success: A profile comparison approach. Unpublished manuscript, University of California at Berkeley.

Chechile, R. (1984). Logical foundations for a fair and rational method of voting. In *Group decision making.* W. Swapp, ed. Beverly Hills: Sage.

Chelius, J. R. and J. B. Dworkin (1980). The economic analysis of final-offer arbitration as a conflict resolution device. *Journal of Conflict Resolution* **24:** 293–310.

Chicago Tribune, November 14, 1995.

Cialdini, R. B. (1993). *Influence: Science and practice.* New York: HarperCollins.

Clark, M. S. (1984). Record keeping in two types of relationships. *Journal of Personality and Social Psychology* **47:** 549–577.

Clark, M. and J. Mills (1979). Interpersonal attraction in exchange and communal relationships. *Journal of Personality and Social Psychology* **37:** 12–24.

Clynes, M. (1980). The communication of emotion: Theory of sentics. In *Emotion: Theory, research, and experience,* Vol. 1. Theories of emotion. R. Plutchik and H. Kellerman, eds. New York: Academic Press: 271–304.

Cohen, L. J. (1981). Can human irrationality be experimentally demonstrated? *Behavioral and Brain Science* **4:** 317–331.

Cohen, M. D. and J. G. March (1974). *Leadership and ambiguity: The American college president.* New York: McGraw Hill.

Coleman, J. (1961). *Papers on non-market decision-making.* New York: Vantage Press.

Conlon, D. E. (1993). Some tests of the self-interest and group-value models of procedural justice: Evidence from an organizational appeal procedure. *Academy of Management Journal* **36**(5): 1109–1124.

Connolly, T., L. M. Jessup, and J. S. Valacich (1989). Effects of anonymity and evaluative tone on idea generation in computer-mediated groups. *Management Science* **36:** 689–703.

Connolly, T., L. M. Jessup, and J. S. Valacich (1990). Idea generation using GDSS: Effects of anonymity and evaluative tone. *Management Science* **36**(6): 689–703.

Coombs, C. and G. S. Avrunin (1988). *The structure of conflict.* Hillsdale, NJ: Erlbaum.

Coombs, C. H., R. M. Dawes, and A. Tversky (1970). *Mathematical psychology: An elementary introduction.* Englewood Cliffs, NJ: Prentice Hall.

Copeland, L. and L. Griggs (1985). *Going international.* New York: Random House.

Cox, T. H., S. A. Lobel, and P. L. McLeod (1991). Effects of ethnic group cultural differences on cooperative and competitive behavior in a group task. *Academy of Management Journal* **34**(4): 827–847.

Crosby, F. (1976). A model of egoistical relative deprivation. *Psychological Review* **83:** 85–113.

Crosby, F. (1982). *Relative deprivation and working women.* New York: Oxford University Press.

Crosby, F. (1984). Relative deprivation in organizational settings. *Research in Organizational Behavior* **6:** 51–93.

Csikszentmihalyi, M. (1988). Society, culture and person: A systems view of creativity. In *The nature of productivity: Contemporary psychological perspectives.* R. Sternberg, ed. New York: Cambridge University Press.

Cyert, R. M. and J. G. March (1963). *A behavioral theory of the firm.* Englewood Cliffs, NJ: Prentice Hall.

Darley, J. M., J. H. Fleming, J. L. Hilton, and W. B. Swann (1988). Dispelling negative expectancies: The impact of interaction goals and target characteristics on the expectancy confirmation process. *Journal of Experimental Social Psychology* **24:** 19–36.

Darley, J. M. and B. Latane (1968). When will people help in a crisis? *Psychology Today* **2**(7): 1968.

Davis, J. (1959). A formal interpretation of the theory of relative deprivation. *American Sociological Review* **27:** 5–19.

Davis, J. A. (1962). Toward a theory of revolution. *American Sociological Review* **27: 5–19.**

Davis, J. (1969). *Group performance.* Reading, MA: Addison-Wesley.

Davis, J. (1982). Social interaction as a combinatorial process in group decision. In Group decision making. H. Branstatter, J. Davis, and G. Stocker-Kreichgauer, eds. London, Academic Press.

Dawes, R. (1980). Social dilemmas. *Annual Review of Psychology* **31:** 169–193.

Dayton, T., F. T. Durso, and J. D. Shepard (1990). A measure of the knowledge reorganization underlying insight. In *Pathfinder associative networks: Studies in knowledge organization.* R. W. Schraneveldt, ed. Norwood, NJ: Ablex.

de Dreu, C. K. W., P. J. D. Carnevale, B. J. K. Emans, and E. van de Vliert (1992). Effects of gain–loss frames in negotiation: Loss aversion, mismatching, and frame adoption. *Organizational Behavior and Human Decision Processes* **60**(1): 90–107.

DeGroot, A. D. (1965). *Thought and choice in chess.* The Hague: Mouton.

DePaulo, B. (1992). Noverbal behavior and self presentation. *Psychological Bulletin* **111**(2): 203–243.

Deprét, E. F. and S. T. Fiske (1993). Social cognition and power: Some cognitive consequences of social structure as a source of control deprivation. In *Control, motivation and social cognition*. G. Weary, F. Gleicher, and K. Marsh, eds. New York: Springer-Verlag: 176–202.

Detweiler, R. (1980). The categorization of the actions of people from another culture: A conceptual analysis and behavioral outcome. *International Journal of Intercultural Relations* **4:** 275–293.

Deutsch, M. (1953). The effects of cooperation and competition upon group processes. In *Group dynamics*. D. Cartwright and A. Zander, eds. Evanston, IL: Row, Peterson: 319–353.

Deutsch, M. (1973). *The resolution of conflict.* New Haven, CT: Yale University Press.

Deutsch, M. (1985). *Distributive justice: A social–psychological perspective.* New Haven, CT: Yale University Press.

Deutsch, M. and H. B. Gerard (1955). A study of normative and informational social influence upon individual judgment. *Journal of Abnormal and Social Psychology* **51:** 629–636.

Devine, P. (1989). Stereotypes and prejudice: Their automatic and controlled components. *Journal of Personality and Social Psychology* **56:** 5–18.

Devine, P. G., C. Sedikides, and R. W. Furhman (1989). Goals in social information processing: A case of anticipated interaction. *Journal of Personality and Social Psychology* **56:** 680–690.

Diehl, M. and W. Stroebe (1987). Productivity loss in brainstorming groups: Toward the solution of a riddle. *Journal of Personality and Social Psychology* **61:** 392–403.

Diekmann, K. A., S. M. Samuels, L. Ross, and M. H. Bazerman (1997). Self-interest and fairness in problems of resource allocation. *Journal of Personality and Social Psychology,* in press.

Diekmann, K., A. Tenbrunsel, and M. H. Bazerman (1998). Escalation and negotiation: Two central themes in the work of Jeffrey Z. Rubin. In *Essays in memory of Jeffrey Z. Rubin.* D. Kolb and M. Aaron, eds. Cambridge, MA: Program on Negotiation.

Dimberg, U. (1982). Facial reactions to facial expressions. *Psychophysiology* **19:** 643–647.

Dion, K., E. Berscheid, and E. Walster (1972). What is beautiful is good. *Journal of Personality and Social Psychology* **24**(3): 285–290.

Doise, W. (1978). *Groups and individuals: Explanations in social psychology.* Cambridge: Cambridge University Press.

Dornbusch, S. M., A. H. Hastorf, S. A. Richardson, R. E. Muzzy, and R. S. Vreeland (1965). The perceiver and perceived: Their relative influence on categories of interpersonal perception. *Journal of Personality and Social Psychology* **1:** 434–440.

Drolet, A. L. and M. W. Morris (1995). Communication media and interpersonal trust in conflicts: The role of rapport and synchrony of nonverbal behavior. Unpublished manuscript, Stanford University.

Druckman, D. and K. Zechmeister (1973). Conflict of interest and value dissensus: Propositions on the sociology of conflict. *Human Relations* **26:** 449–466.

Dunbar, K. (1995). How scientists really reason: Scientific reasoning in real-world laboratories. In *The nature of insight.* R. J. Sternberg and J. E. Davidson, eds. Cambridge, MA: MIT Press: 365–395.

Duncker, K. (1945). On problem solving. *Psychological Monographs* **58:** 270.

Dunning, D., J. Meyerowitz, and A. Holzberg (1989). Ambiguity and self-evaluation: The role of idiosyncratic trait definitions in self-serving assessments of ability. *Journal of Personality and Social Psychology* **57:** 1082–1090.

Dwyer, F. R., P. H. Schurr and Oh, S. (1987). Developing buyer–seller relationships. *Journal of Marketing* **51**(April): 11–27.

Earley, P. C. (1989). Social loafing and collectivism: A comparison of the United States and the People's Republic of China. *Administrative Science Quarterly* **34**: 565–581.

Edwards, W. (1961). Behavioral decision theory. *Annual Review of Psychology* **12**: 473–498.

Einhorn, H. and R. Hogarth (1978). Confidence in judgment: Persistence in the illusion of validity. *Psychological Review* **85**: 395–416.

Eisenberg, N., R. A. Fabes, P. A. Miller, J. Fultz, R. Shell, R. M. Mathy and R. R. Reno (1989). Relation of sympathy and personal distress to prosocial behavior: A multimethod study. *Journal of Personality and Social Psychology* **57**: 55–66.

Ekman, P. (1972). Universals and cultural differences in facial expressions of emotion. In *Nebraska Symposium on Motivation.* J. K. Cole, eds. Lincoln, NE: University of Nebraska Press: **19**: 207–283.

Ekman, P. (1984). The nature and function of the expression of emotion. In *Approaches to emotion.* K. Scherer and P. Ekman, eds. Hillsdale, NJ: Erlbaum.

Ekman, P., W. V. Friesen and K. Scherer (1976). Body movements and voice pitch in deceptive interaction. *Semiotica* **16:** 23–27.

Ekman, P., B. Roper, and J. C. Hager (1980). Deliberate facial movement. *Child Development* **51:** 886–891.

Ekman, P., E. R. Sorenson, and W. V. Friesen (1969). Pan-cultural elements in facial displays of emotions. *Science* 164.

Ellemers, N. and W. Van Rijswijk (1996). Identity needs versus social opportunities: The use of group level and individual level identity management strategies as a function of relative group size, status, and in-group identification. Unpublished manuscript, Free University, The Netherlands.

Ellemers, N., W. Van Rijswijk, M. Roefs and C. Simons (1997). Bias in intergroup perceptions: Balancing group identity with social reality. *Personality and Social Psychology Bulletin* **23**(2): 186–198.

Ellsworth, P. C. and C. A. Smith (1988). From appraisal to emotion: Differences among unpleasant feelings. *Motivation and emotion* **12:** 271–302.

Elster, J. (1995). Strategic uses of argument. *Barriers to conflict resolution.* K. Arrow, R. H. Mnookin, L. Ross, A. Tversky, and R. Wilson, eds. New York: Norton: 236–257.

Englebart, D. (1989). Bootstrapping organizations into the 21st century. Paper presented at a seminar at the Software Engineering Institute, Pittsburgh, November.

Englis, B. G., K. B. Vaughan, and J. T. Lanzetta (1981). Conditioning of counter-empathic emotional responses. *Journal of Experimental Social Psychology* **18:** 375–391.

Erber, R. and S. T. Fiske (1984). Outcome dependency and attention to inconsistent information. *Journal of Personality and Social Psychology* **47:** 709–726.

Ericsson, K. A. and J. Smith, eds. (1991). *Toward a general theory of expertise: Prospects and limits.* New York: Cambridge University Press.

Ericsson, K. A. and H. A. Simon (1980). Verbal reports as data. *Psychological Review* **87:** 215–251.

Espeland, W. (1994). Legally mediated identity: The national environmental policy act and the bureaucratic construction of interests. *Law and Society Review* **28**(5): 1149–1179.

Evans, C. R. and K. L. Dion (1991). Group cohesion and performance: A meta-analysis. *Small Group Research* **22:** 175–186.

Eveland, J. D. and T. K. Bikson (1988). Work group structures and computer support: A field experiment. *Transactions on Office Information Systems* **6**(4): 354–379.

Farber, H. S. (1981). Splitting the difference in interest arbitration. *Industrial and Labor Relations Review* **35:** 70–77.

Farber, H. S. and M. H. Bazerman (1986). The general basis of arbitrator behavior: An empirical analysis of conventional and final offer arbitration. *Econometrica* **54:** 1503–1528.

Farber, H. S. and M. H. Bazerman (1989). Divergent expectations as a cause of disagreement in bargaining: Evidence from a comparison of arbitration schemes. *Quarterly Journal of Economics* **104:** 99–120.

Farrell, J. and R. Gibbons (1989). Cheap talk can matter in bargaining. *Journal of Economic Theory* **48:** 221–237.

Feingold, A. (1992). Good-looking people are not what we think. *Psychological Bulletin* **111:** 304–341.

Feller, W. (1968). *An introduction to probability theory and its applications.* Vol. 1 (3rd ed.). New York: Wiley.

Festinger, L. (1950). Informal social communication. *Psychological Review* **57:** 271–282.

Festinger, L. (1957). *A theory of cognitive dissonance.* Evanston, IL: Row, Peterson.

Fischer, K. W., P. R. Shaver, and P. Carnochan (1990). How emotions develop and how they organize development. *Cognition and Emotion* **4:** 81–127.

Fischhoff, B. (1975). Hindsight does not equal foresight: The effect of outcome knowledge on judgment under uncertainty. *Journal of Experimental Psychology: Human Perception and Performance* **1:** 288–299.

Fisher, R., W. Ury, and B. Patton (1991). *Getting to yes.* 2nd ed. New York: Penguin.

Fiske, S. T. and E. Deprét (1996). Control, interdependence and power: Understanding social cognition in its social context. In *European review of social psychology.* W. Stroebe and M. Hewstone, eds. **17:** 31–37.

Fiske, S. T. and S. L. Neuberg (1990). A continuum of impression formation, from category-based to individuating processes: Influences of information and motivation on attention and interpretation. In *Advances in experimental social psychology.* M. P. Zanna, ed. New York: Academic Press: **23:** 1–74.

Fiske, S. T. and S. E. Taylor (1991). *Social cognition.* New York: McGraw Hill.

Foa, U. and E. Foa (1975). *Resource theory of social exchange.* Morristown, NJ: General Learning Press.

Forgas, J. P. and S. J. Moylan (1996). On feeling good and getting your way: Mood effects on expected and actual negotiation strategies and outcomes. Unpublished manuscript, University of New South Wales.

Forsythe, R., J. Horowitz, N. E. Savin, and M. Sefton (1994). Fairness in simple bargaining experiments. *Games and Economic Behavior* **6:** 347–369.

Fox, C. R. and A. Tversky (in press). A belief-based model of decision under certainty. *Management Science.*

Frank, R. H. (1988). *Passions within reason: The strategic role of the emotions.* New York: Norton.

Freedman, J. L. and S. C. Fraser (1966). Compliance without pressure: The foot-in-the-door technique. *Journal of Personality and Social Psychology* **4:** 195–203.

French, J. and B. Raven (1959). The bases of social power. In *Studies in social power.* D. Cartwright, ed. Ann Arbor: University of Michigan Press.

Friedman, R. (1992). The culture of mediation: Private understandings in the context of public conflict. In *Hidden conflict: Uncovering behind-the-scenes disputes.* D. Kolb and J. Bartunek, eds. Beverly Hills: Sage: 143–164.

Froman, L. A. and M. D. Cohen (1970). Compromise and logroll: Comparing the efficiency of two bargaining processes. *Behavioral Science* **30:** 180–183.

Fry, W. R., I. Firestone, and Williams (1983). Negotiation process and outcome of stranger dyads and dating couples: Do lovers lose? *Basic and Applied Social Psychology* **4:** 1–16.

Fulton, L., L. Thompson, and R. Gonzalez (1997). Analogical reasoning in negotiation. Working paper, Northwestern University.

Gallois, C. (1994). Group membership, social rules and power: A social-psychological perspective on emotional communication. *Journal of Pragmatics* **22:** 301–324.

Gamson, W. (1964). Experimental studies in coalition formation. *Advances in experimental social psychology.* L. Berkowitz, ed. New York: Academic Press: **1.**

Gardiner, G. S. (1972). *Agression.* Morristown, NJ: General Learning Corp.

Gentner, D. and D. R. Gentner (1983). Flowing waters or teeming crowds: Mental models of electricity. In *Mental models.* D. Gentner and A. Stevens, eds. Hillsdale, NY: Erlbaum.

George, J. M. (1990). Personality, afffect, and behavior in groups. *Journal of Applied Psychology* **75**(2): 107–116.

Gibson, K., L. Thompson and M. H. Bazerman (1994). Biases and rationality in the mediation process. In *Application of heuristics and biases to social issues.* L. Heath, F. Bryant, J. Edwards, et al. New York: Plenum: **3.**

Gick, M. L. and K. J. Holyoak (1980). Analogical problem solving. *Cognitive Psychology* **12:** 306–355.

Gick, M. L. and K. J. Holyoak (1983). Scema induction and analogical transfer. *Cognitive Psychology* **15:** 1–38.

Gigone, D. and R. Hastie (1993). The common knowledge effect: Information sharing and group judgment. *Journal of Personality and Social Psychology* **65:** 959–974.

Gilbert, D. T. and P. S. Malone (1995). The correspondence bias. *Psychological Bulletin* **95:** 21–38.

Gilovich, T. (1981). Seeing the past in the present: The effect of associations to familiar events on judgments and decisions. *Journal of Personality and Social Psychology* **40**(5): 797–808.

Gilovich, T. and V. H. Medvec (1994). The temporal pattern to the experience of regret. *Journal of Personality and Social Psychology* **67**(3): 357–365.

Goffman, E. (1959). *The presentation of self in everyday life.* Garden City, NY: Doubleday.

Goffman, E. (1967). *Interaction rituals: Essays on face to face interaction.* Garden City, NY: Anchor.

Goldberg, L. R. (1968). Simple models or simple processes? Some research on clinical judgments. *American Psychologist* **23:** 483–496.

Gottman, J. M. (1979). *Marital interaction: Experimental investigations.* New York: Academic Press.

Gouldner, A. W. (1960). The norm of reciprocity: A preliminary statement. *American Sociological Review* **25:** 161–179.

Graham, J. L. and Y. Sano (1984). *Smart bargaining: Doing business with the Japanese.* Cambridge, MA: Ballinger.

Granovetter, M. (1973). The strength of weak ties. *American Journal of Sociology* **78:** 1360–1379.

Greenberg, J. (1988). Equity and workplace status: A field experiment. *Journal of Applied Psychology* **73:** 606–613.

Greenberg, J. (1990). Employee theft as a reaction to underpayment inequity: The hidden cost of pay cuts. *Journal of Applied Psychology* **75:** 561–568.

Greenhalgh, L. and D. I. Chapman (1995). Joint decision-making: The inseparability of relationships and negotiation. In *Negotiation as a social process.* R. M. Kramer and D. M. Messick, eds.. Thousand Oaks, CA: Sage: 166–185.

Grether, D. and C. R. Plott (1979). Economic theory of choice and the preference reversal phenomenon. *American Economics Review* **69:** 623–638.

Grice, H. P. (1975). Logic and conversation. In *Syntax and semantics 3: Speech acts.* P. Cole and J. L. Morgan, eds. New York: Academic Press: 95–113.

Griffin, E. and G. G. Sparks (1990). Friends forever: A longitudinal exploration of intimacy in same-sex friends and platonic pairs. *Journal of Social and Personal Relations* **7:** 29–46.

Gruenfeld, D. H, E. A. Mannix, K. Williams, and M. A. Neale (1996). Group composition and decision making: How member familiarity and information distribution affect process and performance. *Organizational Behavior and Human Decision Processes* **67**(1): 1–15.

Guilford, J. P. (1959). *Personality.* New York: McGraw Hill.

Guilford, J. P. (1967). The nature of human intelligence. *Intelligence* **1:** 274–280.

Gurr, T. R. (1970). *Why men rebel.* Princeton: Princeton University Press.

Guzzo, R. A., P. R. Yost, J. J. Campbell, and G. P. Shea (1993). Potency in groups: Articulating a construct. *British Journal of Social Psychology* **32:** 87–106.

Hackman, R. (1996). Presentation on group behavior, J. L. Kellogg Graduate School of Management.

Hall, J. A. (1984). *Nonverbal sex differences: Communication accuracy and expressive style.* Baltimore: Johns Hopkins University Press.

Halpern, J. (1992). The effect of friendship on bargaining: Experimental studies of personal business transactions. Conference presentation, Academy of Management, Las Vegas.

Hamilton, D. (1981). Organizational processes in impression formation. In *Social cognition: The Ontario Symposium.* E. T. Higgins, C. P. Herman, and M. P. Zanna, eds. Hillsdale, NJ: Erlbaum: **1:** 135–160.

Hamilton, D. L. and R. K. Gifford (1976). Illusory correlation in interpersonal perception: A cognitive basis of sterotypic judgments. *Journal of Experimental Social Psychology* **12:** 392–407.

Hammond, K. R., J. Rohrbaugh, J. Mumpower, and Adelman, L. (1977). Social judgment theory: Applications in policy formation. In *Human judgment and decision processes in applied settings.* M. F. Kaplan and S. Schwartz, eds. New York: Academic Press.

Hammond, K. R., T. Stewart, B. Brehmer, and D. Steinmann (1975). Social judgment theory. In *Human judgment and decision processes.* M. Kaplan and S. Schwartz, eds. New York: Academic Press: 271–312.

Hammond, K. R., D. A. Summers, and D. H. Deane (1973). Negative effects of outcome feedback in multiple-cue probability learning. *Organizational Behavior and Human Performance* **9**: 30–34.

Hardin, C. and E. T. Higgins (1995). Shared reality: How social verification makes the subjective objective. In *Handbook of motivation and cognition: Foundations of social behavior.* R. M. Sorrentino and E. T. Higgins, eds. New York: Guilford: **3.**

Hardin, G. (1968). The tragedy of the commons. *Science* **162**: 1243–1248.

Harris, R. J. and M. Joyce (1980). What's fair? It depends on how you ask the question. *Journal of Personality and Social Psychology* **38**: 165–170.

Harsanyi, J. C. (1990). Bargaining. In *The new palgrave: A dictionary of economics.* J. Eatwell, M. Milgate, and P. Newman, eds. New York: Norton: 54–67.

Harsanyi, J. C. and R. Selten (1972). A generalized Nash solution for two-person bargaining games with incomplete information. *Management Science* **18**(5): January (Part 2).

Hastie, R. (1986). Experimental evidence on group accuracy. In *Decision research.* B. Grofman and G. Owen, eds. Greenwich, CT: JAI Press: **2.**

Hastorf, A. and H. Cantril (1954). They saw a game: A case study. *Journal of Abnormal and Social Psychology* **49**: 129–134.

Hatfield, E., J. T. Cacioppo, and R. L. Rapson (1992). Primitive emotional contagion. *Review of personality and social psychology.* Vol. 14: Emotion and social behavior. M. S. Clark, ed. Newbury Park, CA: Sage: 151–177.

Hatfield, E., J. T. Cacioppo, and R. L. Rapson (1994). *Emotional contagion.* Paris: Cambridge University Press.

Hays, J. R. (1981). *The complete problem solver.* Philadelphia: Franklin Institute Press.

Heath, C. (1995). Escalation and *de*-escalation of commitment in response to sunk costs: The role of budgeting in mental accounting. *Organizational Behavior and Human Decision Processes* **62**(1): 38–54.

Heath, J. (1996). The social psychology of agency relationships: Biased inferences about how others are motivated. Unpublished manuscript, University of Chicago.

Heider, F. (1958). *The psychology of interpersonal relations.* New York: Wiley.

Herskovits, M. J. (1955). *Cultural anthropology.* New York: Knopf.

Hesse, M. (1966). *Models and analogies in science.* Notre Dame, IN: Notre Dame University Press.

Higgins, E. T., W. S. Rholes, and C. R. Jones (1977). Category accessibility and impression formation. *Journal of Experimental Social Psychology* **13**(2): 141–154.

Higgins, T. (1992). Achieving "shared reality" in the communication game: A social action that creates meaning. *Journal of Language and Social Psychology* **11**: 107–131.

Hill, G. W. (1982). Group versus individual performance: Are N+1 heads better than one? *Psychological Bulletin* **91**: 517–539.

Hilty, J. and P. J. Carnevale (1993). Black-hat/white-hat strategy in bilateral negotiation. *Organizational Behavior and Human Decision Processes* **55**(3): 444–469.

Hoffman, A. J. and J. R. Ehrenfeld (1995). Reconstructing corporate environmentalism, or, What are we really talking about here? Paper presented at the 4th Conference of the Greening of Industry Network, Toronto, November.

Hofstadter, D. (1983). Metamathematical themes. *Scientific American* **248**: 14–28.

Hofstede, G. (1980). *Culture's consequences: International differences in work-related values.* Beverly Hills: Sage.

Hogan, R. and N. P. Emler (1981). Retributive justice. In *The justice motive in social behavior.* M. J. Lerner and S. C. Lerner, eds. New York: Academic Press.

Hogarth, R. M. (1987). *Judgement and choice.* New York: Wiley.

Hogg, M. and D. Abrams (1988). *Social identifications.* New York: Routledge.

Holsti, O. R. (1989). Crisis decision making. In *Behavior, society and nuclear war.* P. E. Tetlock, J. L. Husbands, R. Jervis, P. C. Stern and C. Tilly, eds. New York: Oxford University Press: **1:** 8–84.

Homans, G. C. (1961). *Social behavior: Its elementary forms.* New York: Harcourt, Brace, Jovanovich.

Hook, J. G. and T. D. Cook (1979). Equity theory and the cognitive ability of children. *Psychological Bulletin* **86:** 429–445.

Howes, M. J., J. E. Hokanson, and D. A. Loewenstein (1985). Induction of depressive affect after prolonged exposure to a mildly depressed individual. *Journal of Personality and Social Psychology* **49:** 1110–1113.

Hsee, C. K., E. Hatfield, and C. Chemtob (1991). Assessment of the emotional states of others: Conscious judgments versus emotional contagion. *Journal of Social and Clinical Psychology* **11:** 119–128.

Huber, V. and M. Neale (1986). Effects of cognitive heuristics and goals on negotiator performance and subsequent goal setting. *Organizational Behavior and Human Decision Processes* **40:** 342–365.

Huber, V. and M. Neale (1987). Effects of self- and competitor goals on performance in an interdependent bargaining task. *Journal of Applied Psychology* **72:** 197–203.

Hui, C. H. and H. C. Triandis (1986). Individualism–collectivism: A study of cross-cultural researchers. *Journal of Cultural Psychology* **17:** 225–248.

Ikle, F. and N. Leites (1962). Political negotiation as a process of modifying utilities. *Journal of Conflict Resolution* **6:** 19–28.

Isen, A. M. and R. A. Baron (1991). Affect and organizational behavior. In *Research in organizational behavior.* B. M. Staw and L. L. Cummings, eds. Greenwich, CT: JAI Press. **15:** 1–53.

Isen, A. M., K. A. Daubman, and G. P. Nowicki (1987). Positive affect facilitates creative problem solving. *Journal of Personality and Social Psychology* **52:** 1122–1131.

Jacobs, R. C. and D. T. Campbell (1961). The perpetuation of an arbitrary tradition through several generations of a laboratory microculture. *Journal of Abnormal and Social Psychology* **62:** 649–658.

James, W. (1890/1984). Emotions. *Psychology: Briefer course.* Cambridge, MA: Harvard University Press: 324–338.

Janis, E. (1972). *Victims of groupthink.* Boston: Houghton Mifflin.

Janis, I. L. and L. Mann (1977). *Decision making: A psychological analysis of conflict, choice, and commitment.* New York: Free Press.

Jensen, M. C. and W. H. Meckling (1976). Theory of the firm: Managerial behavior, agency costs, and ownership structure. *Journal of Financial Economics* **3:** 305–360.

Johansen, R. (1988). *Groupware: Computer support for business teams.* New York: Free Press.

Johnson-Laird, P. N. (1983). *Mental models.* Cambridge, MA: Harvard University Press.

Jones, E. E. and H. B. Gerard (1967). *Foundations of social psychology.* New York: Wiley.

Jones, E. E. and R. Nisbett (1972). The actor and the observer: Divergent perceptions of the causes of behavior. In *Attribution: Perceiving the causes of behavior.* E. Jones, D. Kanouse, H. Kelley, et al., eds. Morristown, NJ: General Learning Press: 79–94.

Jones, E. E., L. Rock, K. G. Shaver, G. R. Goethals, and L. M. Ward (1968). Pattern of performance and ability attribution: An unexpected primacy effect. *Journal of Personality and Social Psychology* **10:** 317–340.

Jourard, S. M. (1959). Self-disclosure and other cathexis. *Journal of Abnormal and Social Psychology* **59:** 428–431.

Kahn, R. L. and R. M. Kramer (1990). *Untying the knot: De-escalatory processes in international conflict.* San Francisco, CA: Jossey-Bass.

Kahneman, D., B. L. Fredrickson, C. A. Schreiber, and D. A. Redelmeier (1993). When more pain is preferred to less: Adding a better end. *Psychological Science* **4**(6): 401–405.

Kahneman, D., J. L. Knetsch, and R. H. Thaler (1990). Experimental tests of the endowment effect and the Coase theorem. *Journal of Political Economy* **98**(6): 1325–1348.

Kahneman, D. and D. Miller (1986). Norm theory: Comparing reality to its alternatives. *Psychological Review* **93:** 136–153.

Kahneman, D., P. Slovic, and A. Tversky (1982). Judgment under uncertainty: Heuristics and biases. Cambridge: Cambridge University Press.

Kahneman, D. and A. Tversky (1979). Prospect theory: An analysis of decision under risk. *Econometrica* **47:** 263–291.

Kahneman, D. and A. Tversky (1982). On the study of statistical intuitions. *Cognition* **11**(2): 123–141.

Kaplan, S. and R. Kaplan (1982). *Cognition and environment: Functioning in an uncertain world.* New York: Praeger.

Karambayya, R. and J. M. Brett (1989). Managers handling disputes: Third-party roles and perceptions of fairness. *Academy of Management Journal* **32:** 687–704.

Keenan, J. and R. B. Wilson (1993). Bargaining with private information. *Journal of Economic Literature* **31**(1): 45–104.

Keeney, R. (1992). *Value-focused thinking.* Cambridge, MA: Harvard University Press.

Keeney, R. L. and H. Raiffa (1976). *Decisions with multiple objectives: Preferences and value tradeoffs.* New York: Wiley.

Keisler, S. and L. Sproull (1992). Group decision making and communication technology. *Organizational Behavior and Human Decision Processes* **52:** 96–123.

Kelley, H. H. (1972). Attribution in social interaction. In *Attribution: Perceiving the causes of behavior.* E. E. Jones, D. E. Kanouse, H. H. Kelley, et al., eds. Morristown, NJ: General Learning Press: 1–26.

Kelley, H. (1979). *Personal relationships.* Hillsdale, NJ: Erlbaum.

Kelley, H. and A. J. Stahelski (1970). Social interaction basis of cooperators' and competitors' beliefs about others. *Journal of Personality and Social Psychology* **16**(1): 66–91.

Kelley, H. and J. Thibaut (1969). Group problem solving. In *Handbook of social psychology.* G. Lindzey and E. Aronson, eds. Reading, MA: Addison-Wesley: 1–101.

Kelley, H. and J. Thibaut (1978). *Interpersonal relations: A theory of interdependence.* New York: Wiley.

Keltner, D. (1994). Emotion, nonverbal behavior, and social conflict. Paper presented to the Harvard Project on Negotiation.

Keltner, D. (1995). Signs of appeasement: Evidence for the distinct displays of embarrassment, amusement, and shame. *Journal of Personality and Social Psychology* **68**: 441–454.

Keltner, D. and B. Busswell (1994). The antecedents of embarrassment, shame, and guilt: Constants and individual differences in emotion antecedents. Under review.

Keltner, D., P. C. Ellsworth, and K. Edwards (1993). Beyond simple pessimism: Effects of sadness and anger on social perception. *Journal of Personality and Social Psychology* **64**(5): 740–752.

Klar, Y., D. Bar-Tal, and A. W. Kruglanski (1988). Conflict as a cognitive schema: Toward a social cognitive analysis of conflict and conflict termination. In *The social psychology of intergroup conflict.* W. Stroebe, A. Kruglanski, D. Bar-Tal, and M. Hewstone, eds. Berlin: Springer-Verlag.

Klayman, J. and Y. W. Ha (1987). Confirmation, disconfirmation, and information in hypothesis testing. *Psychological Review* **94**: 211–228.

Klimoski, R. and S. Mohammed (1994). Team mental model: Construct or metaphor? *Journal of Management* **20**(2): 403–437.

Knox, R. E. and J. A. Inkster (1968). Postdecision dissonance at post time. *Journal of Personality and Social Psychology* **8**: 319–323.

Koestler, A. (1964). *The act of creation.* New York: MacMillan.

Kolb, D. (1983). *The mediators.* Cambridge, MA: M.I.T. Press.

Kollock, P. (1994). The emergence of exchange structures: An experimental study of uncertainty, commitment and trust. *American Journal of Sociology* **100**(2): 313–345.

Komorita, S. and C. Parks (1994). *Social dilemmas.* Madison, WI: Brown & Benchmark.

Komorita, S. S. and C. D. Parks (1995). Interpersonal relations: Mixed-motive interaction. *Annual Review of Psychology* **46**: 183–207.

Kramer, R. (1990). The effects of resource scarcity on group conflict and cooperation. In *Advances in group processes.* E. Lawler and B. Markovsky. Hillsdale, NJ: JAI Press.

Kramer, R. (1991). The more the merrier? Social psychological aspects of multiparty negotiations in organizations. In *Research on negotiation in organizations: Handbook of negotiation research.* M. H. Bazerman, R. J. Lewicki, and B. H. Sheppard, eds. Greenwich, CT: JAI Press: **3**: 307–332.

Kramer, R. (1995). Dubious battle: Heightened accountability, dysphoric cognition, and self-defeating bargaining behavior. In *Negotiation as a social process.* R. Kramer and D. Messick, eds. Thousand Oaks, CA: Sage: 95–120.

Kramer, R. and M. Brewer (1984). Effects of group identity on resource use in a simulated commons dilemma. *Journal of Personality and Social Psychology* **46**: 1044–1057.

Kramer, R. and M. Brewer (1986). Social group identity and the emergence of cooperation in resource conservation dilemmas. In *Experimental studies of social dilemmas.* H. Wilke, C. Rutte, and D. Messick, eds. Frankfurt, Peter Lang.

Kramer, R., P. Pommerenke, and E. Newton (1993). The social context of negotiation: Effects of social identity and accountability on negotiator judgment and decision making. *Journal of Conflict Resolution* **37**: 633–654.

Kreps, D. M., P. Milgrom, J. Roberts, and R. Wilson (1982). Rational cooperation in the finitely repeated prisoner's dilemma. *Journal of Economic Theory* **27**: 245–252.

Kruglanski, A. (1989). *Lay-epistemics and human knowledge: Cognitive and motivational bases.* New York: Plenum.

Kruglanski, A. (1990). Lay-epistemic theory in social-cognitive psychology. *Psychological Inquiry* **1**: 181–197.

Kruglanski, A. W., N. Peri, and D. Zakai (1991). Interactive effects of need for closure and initial confidence on social information seeking. *Social Cognition* **9**: 127–148.

Kunda, Z. (1990). The case for motivated reasoning. *Psychological Bulletin* **108**: 480–498.

Lamm, H. and E. Kayser (1978). An analysis of negoitation concerning the allocation of jointly produced profit or loss: The roles of justice norms, politenss, profit maximization, and tactics. *International Journal of Group Tensions* **8**: 64–80.

Lammers, C. J. and D. J. Hickson, eds. (1979). *Organizations alike and unlike: International and interinstitutional studies in the sociology of organizations.* London: Routledge & Kegan Paul.

Landy, D. and H. Sigall (1974). Beauty is talent: Task evaluation as a function of the performer's physical attractiveness. *Journal of Personality and Social Psychology* **29**(3): 299–304.

Langer, E. (1975). The illusion of control. *Journal of Personality and Social Psychology* **32**: 311–328.

Langer, E. J. (1989). Minding matters: The consequences of mindlessness–mindfulness. In *Advances in experimental social psychology.* L. Berkowitz, ed. San Diego, CA: Academic Press: **22**: 137–174.

Langer, E. J., A. Blank, and B. Chanowitz (1978). The mindlessness of ostensibly thoughtful action: The role of "placebic" information in interpersonal attraction. *Journal of Personality and Social Psychology* **36**: 635–642.

Larson, J. R., C. Christensen, A. S. Abbott and T. M. Franz (1996). Diagnosing groups: Charting the flow of information in medical decision-making teams. *Journal of Personality and Social Psychology* **71**(2): 315–330.

Latane, B. (1981). The psychology of social impact. *American Psychologist* **36**: 343–356.

Laughlin, P. R. (1980). Social combination processes of cooperative problem-solving groups on verbal interactive tasks. In *Progress in Social Psychology.* M. Fishbein, ed. Hillsdale, NJ: Erlbaum: **1**.

Lax, D. A. and J. K. Sebenius (1986). *The manager as negotiator.* New York: Free Press.

Lazarus, R. S. (1991). Cognition and motivation in emotion. *American Psychologist* **46**: 352–367.

Leavitt, H. (1951). Some effects of certain communication patterns on group performance. *Journal of Abnormal and Social Psychology* **46**: 38–50.

Lee, W. (1971). *Decision theory and human behavior.* New York: Wiley.

Lerner, M. (1977). The justice motive in social behavior: Some hypotheses as to its origins and forms. *Journal of Personality* **45**: 1–52.

Lerner, M. (1980). *The belief in a just world: The fundamental delusion.* New York: Plenum.

Leung, K. (1988). Some determinants of conflict avoidance. *Journal of Cross-cultural Psychology* **19**: 125–136.

Leventhal, H. (1976). The distribution of rewards and resources in groups and organizations. In *Advances in experimental social psychology.* L. Berkowitz and E. Walster, eds. New York: Academic Press: **9**: 92–133.

Leventhal, H. (1979). Effects of external conflict on resource allocation and fairness within groups and organizations. In *The social psychology of intergroup relations.* W. Austin and S. Worchel. Monterey, CA: Brooks–Cole.

Leventhal, H. (1980). What should be done with equity theory? New approaches to the study of fairness in social exchange. In *Social exchange: Advances in theory and research.* K. Gergen, M. Greenberg, and R. Willis, eds. New York: Plenum Press: 27–55.

Levine, J. M. and R. L. Moreland (1987). Social comparison and outcome evaluation in group contexts. In *Social comparison, social justice, and relative deprivation: Theoretical, empirical, and policy perspectives.* J. C. Masters and W. P. Smith, eds. Hillsdale, NJ: Erlbaum.

Levine, J. and R. L. Moreland (1994). Group socialization: Theory and research. In *The European review of social psychology.* I. W. Stroebe and M. Hewstone, eds. Chichester, England: Wiley: **5:** 305–336.

Levine, J. and L. Thompson (1996). Conflict in groups. In *Social psychology: Handbook of basic principles.* E. T. Higgins and A. Kruglanski, eds. New York: Guilford: 745–776.

Lewin, K. (1935). *A dynamic theory of personality.* New York: McGraw Hill.

Lichtenstein, S. and P. Slovic (1971). Reversals of preference between bids and choices in gambling decisions. *Journal of Experimental Psychology* **89**(1): 46–55.

Liebrand, W. B. G., D. M. Messick, and H. Wilke, eds. (1992). *Social dilemmas: Theoretical issues and research findings.* Oxford, England: Pergamon Press.

Lim, T. S. and J. W. Bowers (1991). Facework: Solidarity, approbation and tact. *Human Communication Research* **17**(3): 415–450.

Lind, E. A., L. Kray, and L. Thompson (1996). Adversity in organizations: Reactions to injustice. Paper presented at the Psychology of Adversity Conference, Amherst, MA.

Lind, E. A. and T. R. Tyler (1988). *The social psychology of procedural justice.* New York: Plenum.

Lindskold, S. (1978). Trust development, the GRIT proposal, and the effects of concilliatory acts on conflict and cooperation. *Psychological Bulletin* **85:** 772–793.

Linville, P. W., G. W. Fischer, and P. Salovey (1989). Perceived distributions of the characteristics of in-group and out-group members: Empirical evidence and a computer simulation. *Journal of Personality and Social Psychology* **57:** 165–188.

Loewenstein, G. F., L. Thompson, and M. H. Bazerman (1989). Social utility and decision making in interpersonal contexts. *Journal of Personality and Social Psychology* **57**(3): 426–441.

Lopes, L. L. (1994). Psychology and economics: Perspectives on risk, cooperation, and the marketplace. *Annual Review of Psychology* **45:** 197–227.

Lord, C. G., M. R. Lepper, and L. Ross (1979). Biased assimilation and attitude polarization: The effects of prior theories on subsequently considered evidence. *Journal of Personality and Social Psychology* **37:** 2098–2109.

MacCrimmon, K. and D. Messick (1976). Framework of social motives. *Behavioral Science* **21:** 86–100.

Mackie, D. M. and G. R. Goethals (1987). Individual and group goals. In *Group processes.* C. Hendrick, ed. Newbury Park, CA: Sage: 144–166.

Macneil, I. R. (1978). Contracts: Adjustment of long-term economic relations under classical, neoclassical and relational contract law. *Northwestern University Law Review* **72:** 854–902.

Macneil, I. R. (1980). *The new social contract: An inquiry into modern contractual relations.* New Haven, CT: Yale University Press.

Maier, N. R. F. (1931). Reasoning in humans: II. The solution of a problem and its appearance in consciousness. *Journal of Comparative Psychology* **12**: 181–194.

Manktelow, K. I. and D. E. Over (1993). Introduction: The study of rationality. In *Rationality: Psychological and philosophical perspectives*. K. Manktelow and D. E. Over, eds. London: Routledge: 1–5.

Mannix, E. (1993). Organizations as resource dilemmas: The effects of power balance on coalition formation in small groups. *Organizational Behavior and Human Decision Processes* **55**: 1–22.

Mannix, E. and G. Loewenstein (1993). Managerial time horizons and inter-firm mobility: An experimental investigation. *Organizational Behavior and Human Decision Processes* **56**: 266–284.

Mannix, E. A., L. L. Thompson, and M. H. Bazerman (1989). Negotiation in small groups. *Journal of Applied Psychology* **74**(3): 508–517.

Mannix, E. A., C. H. Tinsley, and M. H. Bazerman (1995). Negotiating over time: Impediments to integrative solutions. *Organizational Behavior and Human Decision Processes* **62**(3): 241–251.

March, J. G. (1973). Model bias in social action. *Review of Educational Research* **42**: 413–429.

March, J. (1988). Bounded rationality, ambiguity and the engineering of choice. In *Decision making: Prescriptive normative and prescriptive interactions*. D. E. Bell, H. Raiffa, and A. Tversky, eds. New York: Cambridge University Press: 33–57.

March, J. G. and H. A. Simon (1958). *Organizations*. New York: Wiley.

Marcus, H. M. and R. Zajonc (1986). The cognitive perspective in social psychology. *Handbook of social psychology*. 3rd ed. G. Lindzey and E. Aronson, eds. New York: Random House: **1**: 137–230.

Markus, H. (1977). Self-schemata and processing information about the self. *Journal of Personality and Social Psychology* **42**: 38–50.

Marlowe, D., K. Gergen, and A. Doob (1966). Opponents' personality, expectation of social interaction and interpersonal bargaining. *Journal of Personality and Social Psychology* **3**: 206–213.

Martin, J. N. (1989). Intercultural communication competence. *International Journal of Intercultural Relations* **13**: 227–428.

Matsumoto, D. (1996). *Culture and psychology*. Pacific Grove, CA: Brooks–Cole.

May, K. (1982). A set of independent, necessary and sufficient conditions for simple majority decisions. In *Rational man and irrational society*. B. Barry and R. Hardin, eds. Beverly Hills: Sage.

Mayer, R. E. (1983). *Thinking, problem solving and cognition*. New York: Freeman.

McAlister, L., M. H. Bazerman, and P. Fader (1986). Power and goal setting in channel negotiations. *Journal of Marketing Research* **23**: 238–263.

McClelland, G. and J. Rohrbaugh (1978). Who accepts the pareto axiom? The role of utility and equity in arbitration decisions. *Behavioral Science* **23**: 446–456.

McClintock, C. G. and E. van Avermaet (1982). Social values and rules of fairness: A theoretic perspective. In *Cooperaiton and helping behavior*. V. J. Derleya and J. Grezlak, eds. New York: Academic Press: 43–71.

McClintock, C., D. Messick, D. Kuhlman and F. Campos (1973). Motivational bases of choice in three-choice decomposed games. *Journal of Experimental Social Psychology* **9**: 572–590.

McFarland, C. and D. T. Miller (1990). Judgments of self–other similarity: Just like other people, only more so. *Personality and Social Psychology Bulletin* **6:** 475–484.

McGrath, J. E. (1984). *Groups: Interaction and performance.* Englewood Cliffs, NJ: Prentice Hall.

McGrath, J. E. and A. B. Hollingshead (1994). *Groups interacting with technology.* Thousand Oaks, CA: Sage.

McGuire, T., S. Keisler, and J. Siegel (1987). Group and computer-mediated discussion effects in risk decision-making. *Journal of Personality and Social Psychology* **52**(5): 917–930.

McKelvey, R. D. and P. C. Ordeshook (1980). Vote trading: An experimental study. *Public Choice* **35:** 151–184.

Medvec, V. H., S. F. Madey, and T. Gilovich (1995). When less is more: Counterfactual thinking and satisfaction among Olympic medalists. *Journal of Personality and Social Psychology* **69**(4): 603–610.

Mehrabian, A. (1971). *Silent messages.* Belmont, CA: Wadsworth.

Menasco, M. B. and D. J. Curry (1989). Utility and choice: An empirical study of wife/husband decision making. *Journal of Consumer Research* **16:** 87–97.

Messick, D. M. (1991). Social dilemmas, shared resources, and social justice. In *Social justice in human relations.* M. Steensma and R. Vermunt, eds. New York: Plenum Press: **2:** 49–69.

Messick, D. M. (1993). Equality as a decision heuristic. *Psychological perspectives on justice.* B. A. Mellers and J. Baron, eds. New York: Cambridge University Press: 11–31.

Messick, D. and M. Brewer (1983). Solving social dilemmas: A review. *Review of personality and social psychology.* L. Wheeler and P. Shaver, eds. Beverly Hills: Sage: **4:** 11–44.

Messick, D. and C. McClintock (1968). Motivational bases of choice in experimental games. *Journal of Experimental Social Psychology* **4:** 1–25.

Messick, D. M. and C. G. Rutte (1992). The provision of public goods by experts: The Groningen study. In *Social dilemmas: Theoretical issues and research findings.* W. B. G. Liebrand, D. M. Messick, and H. A. M. Wilke. Oxford, England: Pergamon Press: 101–109.

Messick, D. M. and K. P. Sentis (1979). Fairness and preference. *Journal of Experimental Social Psychology* **15**(4): 418–434.

Messick, D. M. and K. Sentis (1983). Fairness, preference and fairness biases. *Equity theory: Psychological and sociological perspectives.* D. Messick and K. Cook, eds. New York: Praeger.

Messick, D. and K. Sentis (1985). Estimating social and nonsocial utility functions from ordinal data. European Journal of Social Psychology **57:** 389–399.

Michaels, S. W., J. M. Blommel, R. M. Brocato, R. A. Linkons, and J. S. Rowe (1982). Social facilitation in a natural setting. *Replications in Social Psychology* **2:** 21–24.

Mikula, G. (1980). On the role of justice in allocation decisions. In *Justice and social interaction.* G. Mikula, ed. New York: Springer-Verlag.

Milgram, S. (1963). Behavioral study of obedience. *Journal of Abnormal and Social Psychology* **67:** 371–378.

Milgram, S. (1974). *Obedience to authority.* New York: Harper.

Millar, M. G. and A. Tesser (1986). Thought-induced attitude change: The effects of schema structure and commitment. *Journal of Personality and Social Psychology* **51:** 259–269.

Miller, C. T. and D. M. Felicio (1990). Person-positivity bias: Are individuals liked better than groups? *Journal of Experimental Social Psychology* **26:** 408–420.

Miller, D. T. and N. Vidmar (1981). The social psychology of punishment reactions. In *The justice motive in social behavior.* M. J. Lerner and S. C. Lerner, eds. New York: Academic Press.

Miller, G. A. (1956). The magical number seven plus or minus two: Some limits on our capacity for processing information. *Psychological Review* **63:** 81–97.

Miller, N. E. (1944). Experimental studies of conflict. In *Personality and the behavior disorders.* J. M. Hunt, ed. New York: Ronald Press. **1:** 431–465.

Miller, R. S. (1992). The nature and severity of self-reported embarrassing circumstances. *Personality and Social Psychology Bulletin* **18:** 190–198.

Miller, R. S. and M. R. Leary (1992). Social sources and interactive functions of embarrassment. In *Emotion and social behavior.* M. Clark, ed. New York: Sage.

Mitchell, T. and L. Thompson (1994). A theory of temporal adjustments of the evaluation of events: Rosy prospection and rosy retrospection. In *Advances in managerial cognition and organizational information processing.* C. Stubbart, J. Porac, and J. Meindl, eds. Greenwich, CT: JAI Press: **5.**

Mitchell, T. R., L. Thompson, E. Peterson, and R. Cronk (in press). Temporal adjustments in the evaluation of events: The "rosy view." *Journal of Experimental Social Psychology.*

Moreland, R. L. and J. M. Levine (1982). Socialization in small groups. Temporal changes in individual–group relation. In *Advances in Experimental Social Psychology.* Vol. 15. L. Berkowitz, ed. New York: Academic Press: 137–192.

Moreland, R. L. and J. M. Levine (1988). Group dynamics over time: Development and socialization in small groups. In *The social psychology of time: New perspectives.* J. E. McGrath, ed. Newbury Park, CA: Sage: 151–181.

Morris, J. A. and D. C. Feldman (1996). The dimensions, antecedents and consequences of emotional labor. *Academy of Management Review* **21**(4): 986–1010.

Morris, M. W., R. E. Nisbett, and K. Peng (1994). Causal attribution across domains and cultures. In *Causal cognition.* G. Lewis, D. Premack, and D. Sperber, eds. New York: Oxford University Press.

Morris, M. W., D. S. Sim, and Girrotto (1995). Time of decision, ethical obligation, and causal illusion: Temporal cues and social heuristics in the prisoner's dilemma. *Negotiation as a social process.* R. Kramer and D. Messick, eds. Thousand Oaks, CA: Sage: 209–239.

Morris, M. W. and S. K. Su (1995). The hostile mediator phenomenon: When each side perceives the mediator to be partial to the other. Unpublished manuscript, Stanford University Graduate School of Business.

Murnighan, K. (1978). Models of coalition behavior: Game theoretic, social psychological, and political perspectives. *Psychological Bulletin* **85:** 1130–1153.

Murnighan, J. K. (1992). *Bargaining games.* New York: William Morrow.

Murnighan, J. K., T. R. King, and F. Schoumaker (1990). The dynamics of cooperation in asymmetric dilemmas. In *Advances in group processes.* E. Lawler, B. Markovsky, C. Ridgeway, and H. Walker, eds. Greenwich, CT: JAI Press: **7:** 179–202.

Murray, N., H. Sujan, E. R. Hirt, and M. Sujan (1990). The influence of mood on categorization: A cognitive flexibility interpretation. *Journal of Personality and Social Psychology* **59**(3): 411–425.

Myerson, R. B. and M. Satterthwaite (1989). Efficient mechanisms or bilateral trading. *Journal of Economic Theory* **29**(2): 265–281.

Nash, J. (1950). The bargaining problem. *Econometrica* **18:** 155–162.

Nash, J. (1953). Two-person cooperative games. *Econometrica* **21:** 128–140.

National Public Radio, Morning Edition, November 3, 1995.

Neale, M. A. and M. H. Bazerman (1983). The role of perspective taking ability in negotiating under different forms of arbitration. *Industrial and Labor Relations Review* **36:** 378–388.

Neale, M. A. and M. H. Bazerman (1991). *Cognition and rationality in negotiation.* New York: Free Press.

Neale, M. A., V. L. Huber, and G. Northcraft (1987). The framing of negotiations: Contextual versus task frames. *Organizational Behavior and Human Decision Processes* **39**(2): 228–241.

Neale, M. and G. Northcraft (1986). Experts, amateurs, and refrigerators: Comparing expert and amateur negotiators in a novel task. *Organizational Behavior and Human Decision Processes* **38:** 305–317.

Neale, M. A., G. B. Northcraft, and P. C. Earley (1990). The joint effects of goal setting and expertise on negotiator performance. Northwestern University.

Nelson, J. and F. Aboud (1985). The resolution of social conflict between friends. *Child Development* **56:** 1009–1017.

Neuberg, S. (1989). The goal of forming accurate impressions during social interactions: Attenuating the impact of negative expectancies. *Journal of Personality and Social Psychology* **56:** 374–386.

Newell, A. (1990). *Unified theories of cognition.* Cambridge, MA: Harvard University Press.

Newell, A. and P. S. Rosenbloom (1981). Mechanisms of skill acquisition and the law of practice. J. R. Anderson, ed. Hillsdale, NJ: Erlbaum.

Newell, A. and H. A. Simon (1972). *Human problem solving.* Englewood Cliffs, NJ: Prentice Hall.

Nisbett, R. E. and L. Ross (1980). *Human inference: Strategies and shortcomings of social judgment.* Englewood Cliffs, NJ: Prentice Hall.

Northcraft, G. B. and M. A. Neale (1987). Experts, amateurs, and real estate: An anchoring-and-adjustment perspective on property pricing decisions. *Organizational Behavior and Human Decision Processes* **39**(1): 84–97.

Northcraft, G. B. and M. A. Neale (1991). Dyadic negotiation. In *Research on negotiation in organizations: Handbook of negotiation research.* M. H. Bazerman, R. J. Lewicki, and B. H. Sheppard, eds. Greenwich, CT: JAI Press: **3.**

Northcraft, G. B. and M. A. Neale (1993). Negotiating successful research collaboration. In *Social psychology in organizations: Advances in theory and research.* J. K. Murnighan, ed. Englewood Cliffs, NJ: Prentice Hall.

O'Connor, K. M. (1994). Negotiation teams: The impact of accountability and representation structure on negotiator cognition and performance. International Association of Conflict Management, Eugene, OR.

O'Connor, K. M. (1997). Groups and solos in context: The effects of accountability on team negotiation. Unpublished manuscript, J. L. Kellogg Graduate School of Management, Northwestern University.

O'Connor, K. M. and A. A. Adams (1996). Thinking about negotiation: An investigation of negotiators' scripts. Unpublished manuscript, Northwestern University.

O'Connor, K. M. and P. J. Carnevale (in press). A nasty but effective negotiation strategy: Misrepresentation of a common-value issue. *Personality and Social Psychology Bulletin.*

Ohbuchi, K., N. Kameda, and M. Agarie (1989). Apology as aggression control: Its role in mediating appraisal of and response to harm. *Journal of Personality and Social Psychology* **56:** 219–227.

Ohman, A., U. Dimberg, and F. Esteves (1989). Preattentive activation of aversive emotions. In *Aversion, avoidance and anxiety: Perspectives on aversively motivated behavior.* T. Archer and L. G. Nilsson, eds. Hillsdale, NJ: Erlbaum.

Okamoto, K. (1993). *Nihonjin no YES wa Naxe No Ka? (Why is a Japanese yes a no?).* Tokyo: PHP Research Laboratory.

Olson, J. M., N. J. Roese, J. Meen, and D. J. Robertson (1995). The preconditions and consequences of relative deprivation: Two field studies. *Journal of Applied Social Psychology* **25**(11): 944–964.

O'Quin, K. and J. Aronoff (1981). Humor as a technique of social influence. *Social Psychology Quarterly* **44**(4): 349–357.

Ordeshook, P. (1986). *Game theory and political theory: An introduction.* Cambridge: Cambridge University Press.

Osborn, A. F. (1957). *Applied imagination.* New York: Scribner.

Osgood, C. E. (1962). *An alternative to war or surrender.* Urbana: University of Illinois Press.

Osgood, C. E. (1980). GRIT: A strategy for survival in mankind's nuclear age. Paper presented at the Pugwash Conference on New Directions in Disarmament, Racine, Wisconsin.

Osgood, C. E., G. J. Suci, and P. H. Tannenbaum (1957). *The measurement of meaning.* Urbana: University of Illinois Press.

Oskamp, S. (1965). Attitudes toward U.S. and Russian actions: A double standard. *Psychological Reports* **16:** 43–46.

Oskamp, S. and D. Perlman (1965). Factors affecting cooperation in a prisoner's dilemma game. *Journal of Conflict Resolution* **9:** 359–374.

Oskamp, S. and D. Perlman (1966). Effects of friendship and disliking on cooperation in a mixed-motive game. *Journal of Conflict Resolution* **10:** 221–226.

Pacelle, M. (1995). Real estate: Japan's U.S. property deals: A poor report card. *The Wall Street Journal:* June 9, B1.

Pacelle, M. and S. Lipin (1995). Japanese owner seeks court protection for Manhattan's Rockefeller Center. *The Wall Street Journal:* May 12, A3.

Palmer, L. G. and L. Thompson (1995). Negotiation in triads: Communication constraints and tradeoff structure. *Journal of Experimental Psychology: Applied* **2**: 83–94.

Parkinson, B. (1995). *Ideas and realities of emotion.* London: Routledge.

Peterson, E. and L. Thompson (1997). Negotiation teamwork: The impact of information distribution and accountability on performance depends on the relationship among team members. Unpublished manuscript, George Washington University.

Philip, G. and E. S. Young (1987). Man-machine interaction by voice: Developments in speech technology. Part I: The state-of-the-art. *Journal of Information Science* **13:** 3–14.

Pinkley, R. (1993). The impact of knowledge regarding alternatives to settlement in dyadic negotiation: Whose knowledge counts? Southern Methodist University.

Pinkley, R., M. Neale, and R. Bennett (in press). The impact of alternatives to settlement in dyadic negotiation. *Organizational Behavior and Human Decision Processes.*

Pinkley, R. L. and G. B. Northcraft (1994). Conflict frames of reference: Implications for dispute processes and outcomes. *Academy of Management Journal* **37**(1): 193–205.

Plott, C. (1976). Axiomatic social choice theory: An overview and interpretation. *American Journal of Political Science* **20**: 511–596.

Plott, C. and M. Levine (1978). A model of agenda influence on committee decisions. *American Economic Review* **68**: 146–160.

Popkin, S. (1981). Public choice and rural development—free riders, lemons, and institutional design. In *Public choice and rural development.* C. Russel and N. Nicholson, ed. Washington, DC: Resources for the Future: 43–80.

Prentice, D. A., D. T. Miller, and J. R. Lightdale (1994). Asymmetries in attachments to groups and to their members: Distinguishing between common-identity and common-bond groups. *Personality and Social Psychology Bulletin* **20**: 484–493.

Pretty, G. H. and C. Seligman (1984). Affect and the overjustification effect. *Journal of Personality and Social Psychology* **46**: 1241–1253.

Pruitt, D. G. and P. J. Carnevale (1993). *Negotiation in social conflict.* Pacific Grove, CA: Brooks–Cole.

Pruitt, D. and J. Rubin (1986). *Social conflict: Escalation, stalemate, and settlement.* New York: Random House.

Raiffa, H. (1982). *The art and science of negotiation.* Cambridge, MA: Belknap.

Rand, K. A. and P. J. Carnevale (1994). The benefits of team support in bilateral negotiations. Unpublished manuscript, University of Illinois.

Rapoport, A. (1960). *Fights, games, and debates.* Ann Arbor: University of Michigan Press.

Rawls, J. (1971). *A theory of justice.* Cambridge, MA: Harvard University Press.

Reibstein, L. and N. Joseph (1988). Mimic your way to the top. *Newsweek* **August 8:** 50.

Robinson, R. J. and D. Keltner (1996). Much ado about nothing? Revisionists and traditionalists choose an introductory English syllabus. *Psychological Science* **7**(1): 18–24.

Robinson, R., D. Keltner, A. Ward and L. Ross (1994). Actual versus assumed differences in construal: "Naïve realism" in intergroup perception and conflict. *Journal of Personality and Social Psychology* **68**: 404–417.

Romano, S. T. and J. E. Bordieri (1989). Physical attractiveness stereotypes and students' perceptions of college professors. *Psychological Reports* **64**: 1099–1102.

Rosenthal, R. and B. M. DePaulo (1979). Sex differences in accommodation in nonverbal communication. *Skill in non-verbal communication: Individual differences.* R. Rosenthal, ed. Cambridge, MA: Oelgeschlager, Gunn & Hain: 68–103.

Rosenthal, R. and L. Jacobson (1968). *Pygmalion in the classroom: Teacher expectation and student intellectual development.* New York: Holt, Rinehart & Winston.

Ross, L. (1977). The intuitive psychologist and his shortcomings: Distortions in the attribution process. In *Advances in Experimental Social Psychology.* L. Berkowitz, ed. Orlando, FL: Academic Press: **10**: 173–220.

Ross, L., D. Greene, and R. House (1977). The false consensus phenomenon: An attributional bias in self perception and social perception processes. *Journal of Experimental Social Psychology* **13**: 279–301.

Ross, L. and M. R. Lepper (1980). The perseverance of beliefs: Empirical and normative considerations. In *New directions for methodology of behavioral science: Fallible judgment in behavioral research.* R. A. Shweder, ed. San Francisco: Jossey-Bass.

Ross, L. and R. Nisbett (1991). *The person and the situation.* New York: McGraw Hill.

Ross, L. and S. M. Samuels (1993). The predictive power of personal reputation vs. labels and construal in the prisoner's dilemma game. Stanford University.

Ross, L. and C. Stillinger (1991). Barriers to conflict resolution. *Negotiation Journal* **8:** 389–404.

Ross, L. and A. Ward (1994). Psychological barriers to dispute resolution. In *Advances in Experimental Social Psychology.* M. Zanna, ed. **27.**

Ross, L. and A. Ward (in press). Naïve realism: Implications for social conflict and misunderstanding. In *Values and knowledge.* T. Brown, E. Reed, and E. Turiel, eds. Hillsdale, NJ: Erlbaum.

Ross, M. and F. Sicoly (1979). Egocentric biases in availability attribution. *Journal of Personality and Social Psychology* **8:** 322–336.

Rossi, P. H., E. Waite, C. E. Bose, and R. E. Berk (1974). The seriousness of crimes: Normative structure and individual differences. *American Sociological Review* **39:** 224–237.

Roth, A. E. (1993). Bargaining experiments. In *Handbook of Experimental Economics.* J. Kagel and A. E. Roth, eds. Princeton: Princeton University Press.

Rothbart, M. and W. Hallmark (1988). In-group and out-group differences in the perceived efficacy of coercion and concilliation in resolving social conflict. *Journal of Personality and Social Psychology* **55:** 248–257.

Rouse, W. and N. Morris (1986). On looking into the black box: Prospects and limits in the search for mental models. *Psychological Bulletin* **100:** 359–363.

Rozin, P., J. Haidt, and C. R. McCauley (1992). Disgust. In *Handbook of emotions.* M. Lewis and J. Haviland, eds. New York, Guilford: 575–594.

Rubin, J. Z. and B. Brown (1975). *The social psychology of bargaining and negotiations.* New York: Academic Press.

Rubin, J. Z., D. G. Pruitt, and S. H. Kim (1994). *Social conflict: Escalation, stalemate and settlement.* New York: McGraw Hill.

Rubin, J. Z. and F. E. A. Sander (1988). When should we use agents? Direct vs. representative negotiation. *Negotiation Journal* **October:** 395–401.

Runciman, W. C. (1966). *Relative deprivation and social justice.* Berkeley: University of California Press.

Rusbult, C. (1983). A longitudinal test of the investment model: The development (and deterioration of) satisfaction and commitment in heterosexual involvement. *Journal of Personality and Social Psychology* **45:** 101–117.

Ruscher, J. B. and S. T. Fiske (1990). Interpersonal competition can cause an individuating impression formation. *Journal of Personality and Social Psychology* **58:** 832–842.

Russell, J. A. (1978). Evidence of convergent validity on the dimensions of affect. *Journal of Personality and Social Psychology* **36:** 1152–1168.

Russell, J. A. (1983). Pancultural aspects of the human conceptual organization of emotions. *Journal of Personality and Social Psychology* **45:** 1281–1288.

Sally, D. F. (in press). Conversation and cooperation in social dilemmas: Experimental evidence from 1958 to 1992. *Rationality and Society.*

Samuelson, W. F. and M. H. Bazerman (1985). Negotiating under the winner's curse. In *Research in Experimental Economics.* V. Smith, ed. New York: JAI Press: **3.**

Saunders, D. G. and P. B. Size (1986). Attitudes about woman abuse among police officers, victims, and victim advocates. *Journal of Interpersonal Violence* **1:** 1986.

Savage, L. J. (1954). *The foundations of statistics.* New York: Wiley.

Schachter, S. (1951). Deviation, rejection, and communication. *Journal of Abnormal and Social Psychology* **46:** 190–207.

Schachter, S. and J. Singer (1962). Cognitive, social, and physiological determinants of emotional state. *Psychological Review* **69:** 379–399.

Schelling, T. (1960). *The strategy of conflict.* Cambridge, MA: Harvard University Press.

Scherer, K. (1982). Methods of research on vocal communication: Paradigms and parameters. In *Handbook of methods in nonverbal behavior research.* K. R. Scherer and P. Ekman, eds. New York: Cambridge University Press: 136–198.

Schlenker, B. R. (1980). *Impression management: The self-concept, social identity and interpersonal relations.* Belmont, CA: Brooks–Cole.

Schlenker, B. R., M. F. Weigold, and J. R. Hallam (1990). Self-serving attributions in social context: Effects of self-esteem and social pressure. *Journal of Personality and Social Psychology* **58:** 855–863.

Schmitt, D. and G. Marwell (1972). Withdrawal and reward reallocation in response to inequity. *Journal of Experimental Social Psychology* **8:** 207–221.

Schoeninger, D. and W. Wood (1969). Comparison of married and ad hoc mixed-sex dyads negotiating the division of a reward. *Journal of Experimental Social Psychology* **5:** 483–499.

Schuur, P. (1987). Effects of gain and loss decision frames on risky purchase negotiations. *Journal of Applied Psychology* **72:** 351–358.

Schwartz, N. (1990). Feelings as information. In *Handbook of innovation and cognition.* R. Sorrentino and E. T. Higgins, eds. New York: Guilford: **2:** 527–561.

Schwinger, T. (1980). Just allocations of goods: Decisions among three principles. In *Justice and social interaction: Experimental and theoretical contributions from psychological research.* G. Mikula, ed. New York: Springer-Verlag.

Sears, D. O. (1983). The person positivity bias. *Journal of Personality and Social Psychology* **44:** 233–250.

Selten, R. (1975). Re-examination of the perfectness concept for equilibrium points in extensive games. *International Journal of Game Theory* **4:** 25–55.

Sessa, V. J. (1996). Using perspective taking to manage conflict and affect in teams. *Journal of Applied Behavioral Science* **32**(1): 101–115.

Shafir, E. (1994). Uncertainty and the difficulty of thinking through disjunctions. *Cognition* **50:** 403–430.

Shafir, E., I. Simonson, and A. Tversky (1993). Reason-based choice. Special issue: Reasoning and decision making. *Cognition* **49**(1–2): 11–36.

Shafir, E. and A. Tversky (1992). Thinking through uncertainty: Nonconsequential reasoning and choice. *Cognitive Psychology* **24**(4): 449–474.

Shah, P. P. and K. A. Jehn (1993). Do friends perform better than acquaintances: The interaction of friendship, conflict, and task. *Group Decision and Negotiation* **2:** 149–166.

Shapley, L. S. (1977). The St. Petersburg Paradox: A con game? *Journal of Economic Theory* **14:** 353–409.

Shaver, P., J. Schwartz, D. Kirson, and C. O'Connor (1987). Emotion knowledge: Further exploration of a prototype approach. *Journal of Personality and Social Psychology* **52:** 1061–1086.

Shaw, M. E. (1932). A comparison of individuals and small groups in the rational solution of complex problems. *American Journal of Psychology* **44:** 491–504.

Shaw, M. (1981). *Group dynamics: The psychology of small group behavior.* New York: McGraw Hill.

Sheppard, B. H. (1984). Third-party intervention: A procedural framework. *Research in organizational behavior.* B. M. Staw and L. L. Cummings, eds. Greenwich, CT: JAI Press: **6.**

Sheppard, J. A., J. A. Ouellette, and J. K. Fernandez (1996). Abandoning unrealistic optimism: Performance estimates and the temporal proximity of self-relevant feedback. *Journal of Personality and Social Psychology* **70**(4): 844–855.

Sherif (1936). *The psychology of social norms.* New York: Harper & Row.

Sherif, M., O. J. Harvey, B. J. White, W. R. Hood, and C. W. Sherif (1961). *Intergroup conflict and cooperation: The Robber's Cave experiment.* Norman, OK: University of Oklahoma Press.

Shirakashi, S. (1985). Social loafing of Japanese students. *Hiroshima Forum for Psychology* **10:** 35–40.

Sholtz, R., A. Fleisher, and A. Bentpup (1982). Aspiration forming and predictions based on aspiration levels compared between professional and nonprofessional bargainers. In *Aspiration levels in bargaining and economic decision making.* R. Tietz, ed. Berlin: Springer-Verlag: 104–121.

Siamwalla, A. (1978). Farmers and middlemen: Aspects of agricultural marketing in Thailand. *Economic Bulletin for Asia and the Pacific* **June:** 38–50.

Siegel, S. and L. E. Fouraker (1960). *Bargaining and group decision making.* New York: McGraw Hill.

Simon, H. (1955). A behavioral model of rational choice. *Quarterly Journal of Economics* **69:** 99–118.

Simonson, I. (1989). Choice based on reasons: The case of attraction and compromise effects. *Journal of Consumer Research* **16:** 158–174.

Slovic, P. (1962). Convergent validation of risk-taking measures. *Journal of Abnormal and Social Psychology* **65:** 68–71.

Slovic, P. (1964). Assessment of risk-taking behavior. *Psychological Bulletin* **61:** 220–233.

Slovic, P. and S. Lichtenstein (1983). Preference reversals: A broader perspective. *American Economic Review* **73:** 596–605.

Smith, C. A. and P. C. Ellsworth (1985). Patterns of cognitive appraisal in emotion. *Journal of Personality and Social Psychology* **48:** 813–838.

Smith, K. K. and S. D. Crandell (1984). Exploring collective emotion. *American Behavioral Scientist* **27**(6): 813–828.

Sniezek, J. A. and R. A. Henry (1989). Accuracy and confidence in group judgment. *Organizational Behavior and Human Decision Processes* **43:** 1–28.

Snyder, M. (1984). When belief creates reality. In *Advances in experimental social psychology.* L. Berkowitz, ed. New York: Academic Press: **18:** 248–306.

Snyder, M., E. D. Tanke, and E. Berscheid (1977). Social perception and interpersonal behavior: On the self-fulfilling nature of social stereotypes. *Journal of Personality and Social Psychology* **35:** 656–666.

Solomon, R. C. (1990). A passion for justice. Reading, MA: Addison Wesley.

Sondak, H. and M. H. Bazerman (1989). Matching and negotiation processes in quasi-markets. *Organizational Behavior and Human Decision Processes* **44**(2): 261–280.

Sondak, H. and M. Moore (1994). Relationship frames and cooperation. *Group Decision and Negotiation* **2:** 103–118.

Sondak, H., M. Neale, and R. Pinkley (1995). The negotiated allocation of benefits and burdens: The impact of outcome valence, contribution and relationship. *Organizational Behavior and Human Decision Processes* **64**(3): 249–260.

Sproull, L. and S. Keisler (1991). *Connections: New ways of working in the networked organization.* Cambridge, MA: MIT Press.

Stasser, G. (1992). Pooling of unshared information during group discussion. In *Group processes and productivity.* S. Worchel, W. Wood, and J. A. Simpson, eds. Newbury Park, CA: Sage: 48–67.

Stasser, G. and D. Stewart (1992). Discovery of hidden profiles by decision-making groups: Solving a problem versus making a judgment. *Journal of Personality and Social Psychology* **63:** 426–434.

Staw, B. M. and J. Ross (1987). Behavior in escalation situations: Antecedents, prototypes, and solutions. *Research in Organizational Behavior* **9:** 39–78.

Steele, G. L. (1983). *The hacker's dictionary.* New York: Harper & Row.

Steil, J. M. and D. G. Makowski (1989). Equity, equality, and need: A study of the patterns and outcomes associated with their use in intimate relationships. *Social Justice Research* **3:** 121–137.

Steiner, I. (1972). *Group process and productivity.* New York: Academic Press.

Stephan, W. and C. W. Stephan (1985). Intergroup anxiety. *Journal of Social Issues* **41:** 157–175.

Sternberg, R. J. (1977). *Intelligence, information processing and analogical reasoning.* Hillsdale, NJ: Erlbaum.

Sternberg, R. J. (1988). A three-facet model of creativity. In *The nature of creativity.* R. J. Sternberg, ed. New York: Cambridge University Press: 125–147.

Storms, M. (1973). Videotape and the attribution process: Reversing actors' and observers' points of view. *Journal of Personality and Social Psychology* **27:** 165–175.

Stouffer, S. A., E. A. Suchman, L. C. DeVinney, S. A. Star, and R. M. Williams, Jr. (1949). *The American soldier: Adjustment during army life.* Princeton: Princeton University Press.

Stroebe, W., A. W. Kruglanski, D. Bar-Tal and M. Hewstone, eds. (1988). *The social psychology of intergroup conflict.* Berlin: Springer-Verlag.

Swann, W. B. and R. J. Ely (1984). A battle of wills: Self-verification versus behavioral confirmation. *Journal of Personality and Social Psychology* **46:** 1287–1302.

Swann, W. B., B. W. Pelham, and D. C. Roberts (1987). Causal chunking: Memory and inference in ongoing interaction. *Journal of Personality and Social Psychology* **53**(5): 858–865.

Tajfel, H. (1968). Second thoughts about cross-cultural research and international. *International Journal of Psychology* **3**(3): 213–219.

Tajfel, H. (1970). Experiments in intergroup discrimination. *Scientific American* **223:** 96–102.

Tajfel, H. (1979). The exit of social mobility and the voice of social change: Notes on the social psychology of intergroup relations. *Przeglad Psychologiczny* **22**(1): 17–38.

Tajfel, H. and J. C. Turner (1979). An integrative theory of intergroup conflict. In *The social psychology of intergroup relations.* W. Austin and S. Worchel, eds. Monterey, CA: Brooks–Cole: 33–47.

Tajfel, H. and J. C. Turner (1981). The social identity theory of intergroup behavior. In *Psychology of intergroup relations.* S. Worchel and W. G. Austin, eds. Chicago: Nelson-Hall: 7–24.

Tajfel, H. and J. Turner (1986). The social identity theory of intergroup behavior. In *Psychology of intergroup relations.* S. Worchel and W. Austin, eds. Chicago: Nelson-Hall: 7–24.

Tangney, J. P. (1992). Situational determinants of shame and guilt in young adulthood. *Personality and Social Psychology Bulletin* **18**: 199–206.

Tapscott, D. (1996). *The digital economy: Promise and peril in the age of networked intelligence.* New York: McGraw Hill.

Taylor, M. C. (1982). Improved conditions, rising expectations and dissatisfaction: A test of the past/present relative deprivation hypothesis. *Social Psychology Quarterly* **45**: 24–33.

Taylor, S. E. and J. Brown (1988). Illusion and well-being: A social–psychological perspective. *Psychological Bulletin* **103**: 193–210.

Taylor, S. E. and J. Crocker (1981). Schematic bases of social information processing. In *Social cognition: The Ontario Symposium.* E. T. Higgins, C. P. Herman, and M. P. Zanna, eds. Hillsdale, NJ: Erlbaum: **1**: 89–134.

Taylor, S. E. and M. Lobel (1989). Social comparision activity under threat: Downward evaluation and upward contacts. *Psychological Bulletin* **96**: 569–575.

Tesser, A. (1978). Self-generated attitude change. In *Advances in experimental social psychology.* L. Berkowitz, ed. New York: Academic Press: **11**: 288–338.

Tesser, A. (1988). Toward a self-evaluation maintenance model of social behavior. In *Advances in experimental social psychology.* L. Berkowitz, ed. Orlando, FL: Academic Press. **21**: 181–227.

Tetlock, P. (1985). Accountability: A social check on the fundamental attribution error. *Social Psychology Quarterly* **48**: 227–236.

Tetlock, P. (1992). The impact of accountability on judgment and choice: Toward a social contingency model. *Advances in Experimental Social Psychology* **25**: 331–376.

Tetlock, P. E., R. Peterson, and J. Lerner (1996). Revising the value pluralism model: Incorporating social content and context postulates. In *The psychology of values: The Ontario symposium.* C. Seligman, J. Olson, and M. Zanna, eds. Mahwah, NJ: **8.**

Thaler, R. (1985). Mental accounting and consumer choice. *Marketing Science* **3**: 199–214.

Thibaut, J. and H. Kelley (1959). *The social psychology of groups.* New York: Wiley.

Thibaut, J. and L. Walker (1975). *Procedural justice: A psychological analysis.* Hillsdale, NJ: Erlbaum.

Thibaut, J. and L. Walker (1978). A theory of procedure. *California Law Review* **60**: 541–566.

Thompson, L. (1990a). An examination of naïve and experienced negotiators. *Journal of Personality and Social Psychology* **59**(1): 82–90.

Thompson, L. (1990b). The influence of experience on negotiation performance. *Journal of Experimental Social Psychology* **26**(6): 528–544.

Thompson, L. (1991). Information exchange in negotiation. *Journal of Experimental Social Psychology* **27**(2): 161–179.

Thompson, L. (1993). The impact of negotiation on intergroup relations. *Journal of Experimental Social Psychology* **29**(4): 304–325.

Thompson, L. (1995a). The impact of minimum goals and aspirations on judgments of success in negotiations. *Group Decision Making and Negotiation* **4**: 513–524.

Thompson, L. (1995b). "They saw a negotiation": Partisanship and involvement. *Journal of Personality and Social Psychology* **68**(5): 839–853.

Thompson, L. and T. DeHarpport (1994). Social judgment, feedback, and interpersonal learning in negotiation. *Organizational Behavior and Human Decision Processes* **58**(3): 327–345.

Thompson, L. and T. DeHarpport (1998). Relationships, good incompatibility, and communal orientation in negotiations. *Basic and Applied Social Psychology.*

Thompson, L. and C. Fox (in press). Negotiation within and between groups in organizations: Levels of analysis. In *Groups at work: Advances in theory and research.* M. Turner, ed. Hillsdale, NJ: Erlbaum.

Thompson, L. and R. Gonzalez (1997). Environmental disputes: Competition for scarce resources and clashing of values. In *Environment, ethics, and behavior.* M. Bazerman, D. Messick, A. Tenbrunsel, and K. Wade-Benzoni, eds. San Francisco: New Lexington Press: 75–104.

Thompson, L. and R. Hastie (1990). Social perception in negotiation. *Organizational Behavior and Human Decision Processes* **47**(1): 98–123.

Thompson, L. and D. Hrebec (1996). Lose–lose agreements in interdependent decision making. *Psychological Bulletin* **120**(3): 396–409.

Thompson, L., L. Kray, and A. Lind (1994). The bright and dark side of social identity. Paper presented at the Society of Experimental Social Psychologists Conference, Lake Tahoe, NV.

Thompson, L. and T. Kurtzberg (1997). Information technology and the negotiator. Working paper, Northwestern University.

Thompson, L. and G. Loewenstein (1992). Egocentric interpretations of fairness and negotiation. *Organizational Behavior and Human Decision Processes* **51**: 176–197.

Thompson, L., E. Mannix, and M. H. Bazerman (1988). Group negotiation: Effects of decision rule, agenda, and aspiration. *Journal of Personality and Social Psychology* **54**: 86–95.

Thompson, L., J. Nadler, and P. Kim (in press). Some like it hot: The case for the emotional negotiator. In *Shared cognition in organizations: The management of knowledge.* L. Thompson, J. Levine, and D. Messick, eds. Erlbaum.

Thompson, L., E. Peterson, and S. Brodt (1996). Team negotiation: An examination of integrative and distributive bargaining. *Journal of Personality and Social Psychology* **70**(1): 66–78.

Thompson, L., E. Peterson, and L. Kray (1995). Social context in negotiation: An information processing perspective. In *Negotiation as a social process.* R. Kramer and D. Messick, eds. Beverly Hills: Sage.

Thompson, L., K. L. Valley, and R. Kramer (1995). The bittersweet feeling of success: An examination of social perception in negotiation. *Journal of Experimental Social Psychology* **31**(6): 467–492.

Thornton, B. (1992). Repression and its mediating influence on the defensive attribution of responsibility. *Journal of Research in Personality* **26**: 44–57.

Tickle-Degner, L. and R. Rosenthal (1990). The nature of rapport and its nonverbal correlates. *Psychological Bulletin* **1**(4): 285–293.

Todd, E. (1983). *La troisième planète.* Paris: Editions du Seuil.

Tornow, W. W. and P. R. Pinto (1976). The development of a managerial job taxonomy: A system for describing, classifying, and evaluating executive positions. *Journal of Applied Psychology* **61**: 410–418.

Triandis, H. C. (1994). *Culture and social behavior.* New York: McGraw Hill: 29–54.

Triplett, N. (1988). The dynamogenic factors in pacemaking and competition. *Journal of Psychology* **9**: 507–533.

Turner, J. (1982). Toward a cognitive redefinition of the group. In *Social identity and intergroup relations.* H. Tajfel, ed. Cambridge: Cambridge University Press.

Tversky, A. and C. R. Fox (1995). Weighing risk and uncertainty. *Psychological Review* **102**(2): 269–283.

Tversky, A. and D. Kahneman (1974). Judgment under uncertainty: Heuristics and biases. *Science* **185**: 1124–1131.

Tversky, A. and D. Kahneman (1992). Advances in prospect theory: Cumulative representation of uncertainty. *Journal of Risk and Uncertainty* **5**: 297–323.

Tversky, A., S. Sattath, and P. Slovic (1988). Contingent weighting in judgment and choice. *Psychological Review* **95**(3): 371–384.

Tversky, A. and E. Shafir (1992). Choice under conflict: The dynamics of deferred decision. *Psychological Science* **3**(6): 358–361.

Tversky, A. and E. Shafir (1992). The disjunction effect in choice under uncertainty. *Psychological Science* **3**(5): 305–309.

Tyler, T. R. and P. Degoey (1995). Collective restraint in social dilemmas: Procedural justice and social identification effects on support for authorities. *Journal of Personality and Social Psychology* **69**(3): 482–497.

Tyler, T., P. Degoey, and H. Smith (1996). Understanding why the justice of group procedures matters: A test of the psychological dynamics of the group-value model. *Journal of Personality and Social Psychology* **70**(5): 913–930.

Tyler, T. and A. Lind (1992). A relational model of authority in groups. *Advances in Experimental Social Psychology* **25**: 115–191.

Tyler, T. R. and H. J. Smith (1995). Social justice and social movements. In *Handbook of social psychology.* D. Gilbert, S. T. Fiske, and G. Lindzey, eds. New York: McGraw Hill: **1.**

Valley, K., J. Moag, and M. H. Bazerman (1997). Avoiding the curse: Relationships and communication in dyadic bargaining.

Valley, K. and M. A. Neale (1993). Intimacy and integrativeness: The role of relationships in negotiations. Working paper, Cornell University, Ithaca, NY.

Valley, K., M. Neale, and E. Mannix (1995). Friends, lovers, colleagues, strangers: The effects of relationship on the process and outcome of dyadic negotiations. In *Research on negotiation in organizations: Handbook of negotiation research.* R. J. Bies, R. J. Lewicki, and B. H. Sheppard, eds. Greenwich, CT: JAI Press: **5**: 65–93.

Valley, K., L. Thompson, R. Gibbons, and M. H. Bazerman (1997). Is talk really cheap? Outperforming equilibrium models of communication in bargaining games. Unpublished manuscript, Harvard University.

Valley, K. L., S. B. White, M. A. Neale, and M. H. Bazerman (1992). Agents as information brokers: The effects of information disclosure on negotiated outcomes. Special Issue: Decision processes in negotiation. *Organizational Behavior and Human Decision Processes* **51**(2): 220–236.

Vallone, R. P., L. Ross, and M. Lepper (1985). The hostile media phenomenon: Biased perception and perceptions of media bias in coverage of the "Beirut Massacre." *Journal of Personality and Social Psychology* **49**: 577–585.

van Avermaet, E. (1974). Equity: A theoretical and experimental analysis. University of California, Santa Barbara.

Van Boven, L. and L. Thompson (1996). A look into the mind of the negotiator. Paper presented at the Academy of Management meetings, Cincinnati, Ohio.

Vaughan, K. B. and J. T. Lanzetta (1980). Vicarious instigation and conditioning of facial expressive and autonomic responses to a model's expressive display of pain. *Journal of Personality and Social Psychology* **38**: 909–923.

von Neumann, J. and O. Morgenstern (1947). *Theory of games and economic behavior.* Princeton, NJ: Princeton University Press.

Walker, I. and T. F. Pettigrew (1984). Relative deprivation theory: An overview and conceptual critique. *British Journal of Social Psychology* **23**: 301–310.

Walster, E., E. Berscheid, and G. W. Walster (1973). New directions in equity research. *Journal of Personality and Social Psychology* **25**: 151–176.

Walster, E., G. W. Walster, and E. Berscheid (1978). *Equity: Theory and research.* Boston: Allyn & Bacon.

Walton, R. E. and R. B. McKersie (1965). *A behavioral theory of labor relations.* New York: McGraw Hill.

Watson, D. and A. Tellegen (1985). Toward a consensual structure of mood. *Psychological Bulletin* **98**: 219–235.

Wegner, D. (1986). Transactive memory: A contemporary analysis of the group mind. In *Theories of group behavior.* B. Mullen and G. Goethals, eds. New York: Springer-Verlag: 185–208.

Wegner, D. (1989). *White bears and other unwanted thoughts.* New York: Viking/Penguin.

Wegner, D. M. (1994). Ironic processes of mental control. *Psychological Review* **101**: 34–52.

Weick, K. E. (1969). *The social psychology of organizing.* Reading, MA: Addison-Wesley.

Weldon, E. and L. Mustari (1988). Felt dispensibility in groups of coactors: The effects of shared responsibility and explicit autonomy on cognitive effort. *Organizational Behavior and Human Decision Processes* **41**: 330–351.

Wheeler, L. and J. Nezlek (1977). Sex differences in social participation. *Journal of Personality and Social Psychology* **35**: 742–754.

White, S. B. and M. A. Neale (1994). The role of negotiator aspirations and settlement expectancies on bargaining outcomes. *Organizational Behavior and Human Decision Processes* **57**: 91–108.

Whorf, B. L. (1956). Science and linguistics. In *Language, thought, and reality. Selected writings of Benjamin Whorf.* J. B. Carroll, ed. New York: Wiley.

Williams, K. (1994). Social ostracism. Paper presented at the meeting of the Society of Experimental Social Psychologists, Lake Tahoe, NY, October.

Wills, T. A. (1981). Downward comparison principles in social psychology. *Psychological Bulletin* **90**: 245–271.

Wilson, T. and D. S. Dunn (1986). Effects of introspection on attitude-behavior consistency: Analyzing reasons versus focusing on feelings. *Journal of Experimental Social Psychology* **22:** 249–263.

Woodroofe, M. (1975). *Probability with applications.* New York, McGraw Hill.

Worchel, S. and W. G. Austin, eds. (1986). *Psychology of intergroup* relations. Chicago: Nelson-Hall.

Worringham, C. J. and D. M. Messick (1983). Social facilitation of running: An unobtrusive study. *Journal of Social Psychology* **121:** 23–29.

Worthy, M., A. L. Gary, and G. M. Kahn (1969). Self-disclosure as an exchange process. *Journal of Personality and Social Psychology* **13:** 59–63.

Yamagishi, T. (1988). The provision of a sanctioning system in the United States and Japan. *Social Psychology Quarterly* **51**(3): 265–271.

Yamaguchi, S., K. Okamoto and T. Oka (1985). Effects of coactors' presence: Social loafing and social facilitation. *Japanese Psychological Research* **27:** 215–222.

Yates, J. F. (1990). *Judgment and decision making.* Englewood Cliffs, NJ: Prentice Hall.

Zajonc, R. B. (1960). The process of cognitive tuning in communications. *Journal of Abnormal and Social Psychology* **61:** 159–167.

Zajonc, R. (1968). Attitudinal effects of mere exposure. *Journal of Personality and Social Psychology* **9**(monograph supplement No. 2, Part 2).

Ziemba, S. (1995). *Chicago Tribune,* November 10.

Subject Index

Author Index